ON
BORROWED
TIME

ON
BORROWED
TIME

How the Growth in
Entitlement Spending
Threatens America's Future

Peter G. Peterson
and
Neil Howe

ICS PRESS

ICS

Institute for Contemporary Studies
San Francisco, California

Inquiries, book orders, and catalogue requests should be addressed
to ICS Press, Institute for Contemporary Studies, 243 Kearny
Street, San Francisco, California, 94108.
(415) 981-5353.

The analyses, conclusions, and opinions expressed in ICS Press
publications are those of the authors and not necessarily those of
the Institute for Contemporary Studies, or of the Institute's
officers, directors, or others associated with, or funding, its work.

Distributed to the trade by Kampmann & Co., New York.

Library of Congress Cataloging-in-Publication Data

Peterson, Peter G.
    On borrowed time/Peter G. Peterson and Neil Howe.
        p.   cm.
    Includes index.
    ISBN 1-558-15003-X : $24.95
    1. Entitlement spending—United States. 2. Budget deficits—
United States. 3. United States—Economic policy—1981–
4. Economic forecasting—United States. I. Howe, Neil. II. Title.
HJ2052.P48 1988
353.0084—dc19   88-23798
                                                        CIP

Peter G. Peterson dedicates this book to the memory of his father, George, for the tireless labors he shouldered on behalf of his children.

Neil Howe dedicates this book to his wife, Simona, whose assiduous attention to the future is an inspiration to all who know her.

Contents

Part Three: From Complacency to Reform

Conclusion

Foreword

It is surprising that the term "entitlements" is not better known, for it represents the largest and fastest-growing portion of our federal budget. Attempts to reduce the nation's huge budget deficit at the recent "budget summit" proved futile largely because entitlements are regarded as sacrosanct by our lawmakers.

We believe this is due primarily to a lack of knowledge about the functions these programs actually perform and the people they benefit. This book is a step toward educating policymakers, the public, and their elected representatives that there can be no resolution of the budget-deficit issue unless our entitlements system is reformed.

On Borrowed Time follows two pathbreaking Institute publications, *The Crisis in Social Security,* edited by Michael J. Boskin and published in 1977, and *The World Crisis in Social Security,* edited by Jean-Jacques Rosa and published in 1982. As the authors of the present volume write, the entitlements issue is certain to be with us for a long time to come. This book outlines the dilemmas we face today and prudently predicts the problems of tomorrow. The choices we make will play a great role in determining the economic and political future of our nation.

Robert B. Hawkins, Jr.
President, Institute for
Contemporary Studies

San Francisco
August 1988

Acknowledgments

Peter G. Peterson wishes most of all to thank his children—John, Jim, David and his wife Paige, Holly, and Michael—for they are the reason he has undertaken this effort. They have all, to be sure, found his denunciations of budget deficits utterly eye-glazing. His twenty-nine-year-old son, David, has made this point with well-aimed humor. ("Dad," he said excitedly one day, "Alexandra has just spoken her first word." "Wonderful, David—I hope for your sake it was 'Daddy.'" "No," he said with a twinkle, "it was 'deficits.'") He offers this book in the hope that it might someday capture his children's interest—until then it will simply speak up for their future. He also thanks his wife, Joan Ganz Cooney, cofounder, chairman, and CEO of The Children's Television Workshop and mother of Big Bird. In part, she deserves a special acknowledgment for the many lost weekends this book represents. Mostly, she deserves it because her work touches the lives of children everywhere.

Neil Howe wishes to thank Richard Jackson, who has so successfully managed the transition from historian to policy analyst. This book benefits greatly from both his dedication to research and his passion for style. He thanks Paul Hewitt for his wise counsel on thematic strategy; Phillip Longman for his abundant insights; Bill Strauss for his imagination and ever-lively wit; Fabio Sampoli for his early help in research; and his wife, Simona, for her assistance and support on a project that sometimes seemed never-ending. He also wishes to thank so many analysts—too numerous to name—at the Social Security Administration's Office of the Actuary, at the Health

Care Financing Administration, at the Congressional Research Service, at the Bureau of Labor Statistics, and on congressional staffs.

Both authors wish to thank Jim Sebenius, who helped in shaping these arguments from the early days of the authors' collaboration. His familiarity with public policy as well as his incisive questions have made this a better book. For their invaluable advice and comments, the authors also wish to thank A. Haeworth Robertson and the Retirement Policy Institute; Carol Cox and the Committee for a Responsible Federal Budget; James Capra, Senior Vice President at Shearson, Lehman, Hutton, Inc.; Michael Boskin, Professor of Economics at Stanford University; Neilson S. Buchanan, President of El Camino Hospital, Mountain View, California; Senator Dave Durenberger and Congressman Jim Jones, Chairman and President (respectively) of Americans for Generational Equity; Governor Dick Lamm, Director of the Center for Public Policy and Contemporary Issues at the University of Denver; J. Alexander McMahon, Professor of Health Administration at Duke University Medical Center; David A. Stockman; Congressman Hastings Keith, Chairman of the National Committee on Public Employee Pension Systems; Frank Pena; Veronica Buckley; and Patricia Zagari.

Introduction

Peter G. Peterson

I N THE SUMMER OF 1986, within a few short weeks, I experienced three of life's thresholds: the death of my father, a remarkable role model whose generosity to his children and community remains an inspiration; the birth of my first grandchild, Alexandra; and the celebration—if in a rather melancholy way—of my own sixtieth birthday. Taken together, these three events focused my thoughts on questions that had been worrying me for years: What kind of opportunities will my generation bestow on all the Alexandras of her generation? How do these opportunities compare with those bestowed on Americans of my generation when I was young? What responsibilities do we bear as parents, citizens, voters, and public servants for America's future?

I liked none of the answers. I felt a sense of unease—indeed, guilt. In Dietrich Bonhoeffer's words, "The ultimate test of a moral society is what kind of world it leaves to its children." I did not feel very moral. In the language of the Apaches, I am told, the word for grandfather and grandchild is the same—symbolizing the link and the lock between generations. Is my generation to be the one that breaks this historic link? That question lent a special urgency to my concern for our collective destiny.

My sixtieth birthday, coming as it did alongside these rites of passage, concentrated my mind on the horizon of my own life and

1

prompted me to consider how I could do as much for Alexandra and her peers as my father had done for me and mine. In my public life, I had for quite some time spoken and written on how our pervasive consumption ethos was threatening our national prospects. But now it hit home personally. It was clear to me that my generation was not behaving as a responsible steward of our national resources, that the endowment we were leaving was not equal to the one we had received, and that, in short, we were not fulfilling the implicit promise embodied in the American Dream. In those transcendent weeks in the summer of 1986, the abstraction that many have called the "generational contract" suddenly acquired new life and meaning.

When I speak with others my age, I find that a growing number of them share my concern about the pervasive evidence that we are no longer passing on what was given to us. The evidence speaks of budget and trade deficits, of foreign indebtedness, of declining living standards among young families, and of rising poverty rates among children. It calls our attention to crumbling public infrastructure, to antiquated plant and equipment, to lost competitiveness in international markets, and to an undereducated generation of young Americans. In the words of the 1983 report of our National Commission on Excellence in Education, "for the first time in history, the education skills of one generation will not surpass, will not equal, will not even approach, those of their parents." Other evidence calls attention to an unprecedented drop in the real incomes of young workers; as a result, fewer young Americans are now able to share in a touchstone of the American dream—owning their own home—than were young Americans of my generation. In the tersely worded observation of Senator Moynihan, "The United States has now become the first society in history in which a person is more likely to be worse off if young rather than old."

The roots of this fall from grace go back several decades, but most of us sense, at least instinctively, that the slide has been accelerated during the 1980s. Consider, for instance, that in the space of three short years, what had been the world's largest creditor nation has become the world's largest debtor nation, and that a country that once prided itself on thrift and investment now shoulders an official national debt of $2.4 trillion—an enormous public liability with no corresponding public asset, only the memory of helter-skelter consumption promises kept to all of us who are older, and who, it seems, are "entitled" to more than we earn as a nation. This figure is so huge that each 1 percent rise in interest rates adds another $1 billion or so to the total every two weeks. Yet in 1987 we enjoyed our highest rate of consumption since the end of World War II, even as we sunk to our lowest rate of savings. Already some $1 trillion worth of our financial assets are in foreign hands; already the stability of our economy has grown dependent on the confidence—whims, really—of central banks and private investors abroad.

Like Damocles, we feast, while the power of foreign capital hangs uneasily over our heads, just as that proverbial sword hung over his— by a single thread. Damocles was at least aware of the precariousness of his predicament. Sadly, we are not. We apparently hope either that our children will someday do our saving for us or that the sword will not fall until we have blissfully passed from the scene.

As we go through another election season, I find to my dismay that far from girding ourselves to address the problems that jeopardize our national future, we continue to embrace dangerous myths and false optimism. Though the candidates this year are different, the campaign is being conducted like most others. There are speeches and press conferences, baby kissings and photo opportunities, charges and countercharges. Following the established script, there is also a welter of "if-elected" promises, some of them airy "reinvest-in-America" and "competitiveness" proposals, others further promises of subsidized consumption directed at the plethora of special interest groups that have become the hallmark of contemporary American politics.

How these promises will be redeemed, and at what cost to succeeding generations, is, as in most political campaigns, rarely if ever specified. To listen to the candidates, both of them good and decent men, one might conclude that the future will, multitrillion-dollar mortgage and all, simply take care of itself. It cannot. As our population ages, as health-care costs soar, as domestic and foreign debts accumulate, and as we continue our woefully inadequate record of investment in physical and human capital, things, indeed, can easily get worse. Unless, of course, we decide to take our destiny into our own hands once again.

This is a book about that destiny, the economic policies that are shaping it, and the troubles that lie in store for us. It is a book about politics and ignorance and apathy and greed and special interest—and how all have conspired to rob not just our treasury, but our young.

It is a book about the emerging American conviction that resources are limitless and that tomorrow will take care of itself. It is a book about our public compulsion to spend more than we earn, to consume more than we produce, and to pass the hidden check on to those too innocent to understand what is at stake. It is a book about possible generational conflict, the prospering of the old and the powerful at the expense of the young and the weak.

It is, at its core, a book about what we have come to call "entitlements," a beneficent-sounding word that, more than any other, points to the causes of our current predicament.

Finally and necessarily, it is a book that grows out of my own experiences: as a businessman, as a government official and cabinet officer, as an investment banker, and as a father and grandfather who looks uncomfortably at the world his progeny will inherit.

George Petropoulos and the American Dream

Like so many Americans of my generation, my basic values and expectations were forged by the experience of growing up in an immigrant family of modest means during the Great Depression and World War II. I've never forgotten that I am a son of Greek immigrants. My father and mother both arrived in America when they were only in their teens. They came from a remote farm village and had nothing more than a grade school education. They were understandably fearful, yet full of hope and confidence. After all, this was not only a country of irrepressible optimism—a land of limitless frontiers and resources—but it was also a country whose future was entirely unmortgaged and whose optimism had not yet publicly reversed the causal order between work and reward.

So, like many others, my father, George Petropoulos, headed west. He took menial work wherever an immigrant speaking a foreign tongue could find it. One of his first jobs was with the Union Pacific Railroad. There the newly christened George "Peterson" (Petropoulos means "son of Peter"; the change came about because the foreman could not pronounce the family surname) worked long hours as a dishwasher in the sweltering heat of a caboose kitchen. He suffered more hardships than I can easily imagine. He saved much of what little he earned; he rarely borrowed, and when he did it was as little as possible and only to build a better future.

Bit by painstaking bit his savings mounted up, and eventually he was able to open his own restaurant—the Central Cafe in Kearney, Nebraska, an establishment that was distinguished not for its cuisine,

4

but for the fact that for over twenty-five years it stayed open twenty-four hours a day, seven days a week, 365 days a year. During those hours, days, and years, my father and mother worked and saved—even during the years of the Great Depression—fully confident that their sons would "do better" and lead a "better life" than they had. To them, and to millions like them, this was the essence of the American Dream. And for all the hardships they suffered, it did not let them down, nor did it let their children down.

By most standards, I have enjoyed a rewarding career. In a word, I have felt blessed—and the ultimate source of that blessing is the faith that my parents had in themselves, in the future, and in the wonders that hard work, thrift, and investment could accomplish for their children. Theirs was a deeply rooted set of values. As a first-generation immigrant, my father knew that the opportunities and privileges he enjoyed came with corollary responsibilities. He never asked what kind of education he could afford for my brother John and me (as if it were one consumption claim among many); he instead asked what was the best education money could buy (as if it were an investment, which took priority over any consumption claim).

In this respect, my father was not atypical of his generation. When I was a boy in Kearney, it seemed as though the focus of the community was its children. Children were not necessarily the center of attention, and they were certainly not indulged by their parents or other adults. But they were central to the community's purpose. Parents worked, saved, and invested so that their children could work more productively (no one could possibly work any harder), enjoy a rising standard of living, and in their own turn continue to save and invest for the next generation. This was the thrift ethic at its best. I was indeed fortunate to be born into such a family, in such a community, at such a time.

Today, the ethic that kept the Central Cafe open all those days and nights is breaking down. If not as individuals and families, as a nation we seem to have lost our willingness to save and sacrifice so that our children can enjoy better lives. Collectively, we seem bent on living for the moment, on indulging today's pleasures at the expense of future prosperity. Our public policy debates center on the next quarter or the next year; economic projections "all the way" to 1992 pass for farsightedness. For an individual or a family, such myopia would be irresponsible: no household expects to provide for a child's college education or plan for a parent's retirement with only a two-year time horizon. Yet for a nation, we seem to think that it is perfectly consistent with statesmanship.

We confuse the ups and downs of the business cycle with long-term economic trends. And as daily headlines flit from high interest rates to inflation, and then to recession or recovery or deficits, we make no concerted effort to look at where all of us have been and where all of us are headed. We turn away from the most obvious signposts along the road we are traveling—burgeoning debt, flagging productivity, deficient education, and disadvantaged children. If we paid attention, we might recognize that they are all symptoms of a kind of disease, a contagion that began many years ago and that, if allowed to run its course, may eventually put an end to the American Dream. In the words of a recent French visitor to America, a contemporary Tocqueville, "America is a country trying to forget its future."

Mr. Peterson Goes to Washington

My own realization that something was dangerously awry—not just with our economy, but with the stewardship function of our government—began in 1971, when President Nixon invited me to Washington to serve as his Assistant for International Economic Affairs. Not coincidentally, the origins of this book also date back to that year. Having run Bell and Howell, a manufacturer of photographic equipment, I had become increasingly absorbed in the problems posed by foreign competition, and like most of my colleagues in the "real world," I realized that for the first time in the postwar era American industry faced difficult challenges in world markets. The wind was no longer at our backs.

On arriving in Washington, I naively expected that I would be greeted by in-depth analyses of our worsening global posture and by serious and coherent proposals on how we might improve it. Instead, I quickly discovered that almost no one was really looking at—let alone seeking solutions to—the root causes of what later came to be known as our "competitiveness" problem.

One reason for this myopia is the way each federal bureaucracy stakes out its own turf and fiercely protects its interests. Simply to take the pulse of the global economy, for instance, I had to place my fingers separately on half a dozen different departments and agencies, and even then, there was not much interest in the questions I was raising. Henry Kissinger, for one, chided me for being overly preoccupied with "minor commercial affairs" (to Henry, all commercial affairs in those days were minor ones), while senior officials in the State Department didn't seem to think there were any serious economic problems at all. The Justice Department's antitrust division took somewhat the same view, arguing that foreign competition was not a significant issue. Most of our economists were meanwhile debating the merits of wage and price controls. In contrast, at the departments of Commerce and Labor, the problem was not complacency, but hysteria. Obsessed with "unfair" trade practices overseas and unsettled by the permanent shift in the United States from a manufacturing to a service economy, the folks at Commerce and Labor apparently could think of nothing better to do than talk about "protecting" our manufacturing industries by means of tariffs, quotas, and subsidies.

By default, the task of looking at the overall problem somehow fell to me. With the enthusiasm of an amateur (and the naivete of a non-economist), I set about gathering pertinent information from every conceivable source, public and private, and then presented it in the form of simple charts and tables as a color slide show: "The U.S. in a Changing World Economy." The first audience for what became known as the "Peterson Slide Show" was the Council on International Economic Policy, chaired by Richard Nixon. But in the months that followed, I inflicted it on any number of unsuspecting groups of legislators, businessmen, labor leaders, or journalists that I could convince to sit still for an hour or so.

Indeed, this book began as an effort to update these slides as a favor to Senator Howard Baker. He felt that international economic issues should play a key role in his 1980 campaign for the Republican presidential nomination. Howard soon went on to other pursuits; I just kept on running and updating the slide show, but this time with a new colleague at my side, Neil Howe. Neil was then, as now, a gifted analyst with wide-ranging expertise in both history and economics. Currently a senior fellow at the Retirement Policy Institute, he is the coauthor of this book.

The story that emerged from the original 1971 slide show (and which still can be read clearly in a few of the reworked charts and tables included in this book) is one of deep and self-inflicted wounds. To be sure, there were "unfair" trade practices then, as now. But the overall message was that our economic problems were neither made in Japan nor smuggled here in OPEC's oil barrels. Nor were they caused primarily by the misguided policies of any domestic group of conspirators on either the left or the right. Rather, it turned out that it was the American people of all political persuasions who, by choosing to acquiesce in a massive public diversion of resources to objectives other than the nation's future prosperity, had clouded their own and their children's economic prospects.

Upon leaving the White House staff in early 1972, I became Secretary of Commerce and Chairman of the Productivity Commission. I soon learned firsthand the extent to which America's political forum had been taken over by monomaniacs and narrowly focused constituencies. My first order of business was neither competitiveness nor productivity, but soothing a much more powerful constituency not known for its preoccupation with either of those subjects—the *porpoise* constituency. I suddenly found myself, all appointments canceled, racing to San Diego so I could feed fish to Flipper. I could never have envisioned that the following scene had become an integral part of the Commerce Secretary's job definition: as the television cameras whirred, there I was, the nation's "chief commercial officer," patting Flipper, our nation's number-one porpoise, while announcing a research program on a new tuna-fishing net designed to keep porpoises from getting entangled.

In our search for scapegoats, we need not have looked further than the mirror.

The Sins of the Fathers. . .

The centerpiece of my original slide show—which my wife, an inveterate punster, now calls "The American Slide"—was a series of pointed comparisons I drew between Japan and the United States. Today, even more than in 1971, this contrast provides the most striking illustration of how we have systematically turned away from the future.

Japan is a country with virtually no natural resources. Her people understand that they can escape scarcity only through calculated effort—effort consciously aimed at squeezing out waste and limiting consumption in favor of efficiency, hard work, and investment. Reinforced by the devastation of World War II, these cultural attitudes have produced a political economy of unique realism, one in which all the participants appreciate that prosperity is self-created.

Put more crudely, the Japanese do not behave as though the world owes them a living; they assume—correctly—that the world could not care less. Nor do the Japanese meet economic adversity by looking for scapegoats. Instead, whenever trouble arrives (for instance, when world oil prices soar) the Japanese react by coolly recalculating the requirements for sustained prosperity. They adjust, stoically suffering rapid changes in industrial and consumption patterns. And, as they adjust, they redouble their efforts to improve quality and increase productivity. Japan is an object lesson in a political economy that respects the connection between today's allocation of resources (the "inputs" of prosperity) and tomorrow's profile of employment, wages, and consumption (the "outputs" of prosperity).

Consider these figures. Over the past decade and a half, Japan's investment rate in new business plant and equipment—a net 8.1 percent of GNP—has been triple the rate in the United States (and yet Americans ask why our industries aren't competitive). It has invested ten times more in public "infrastructure" as a share of GNP (yet Americans wonder why we have sagging bridges, crumbling highways, bursting water mains, and antiquated and unreliable mass-transit systems). Japan currently invests 36 percent more in civilian research and development as a share of its GNP, exclusive of R&D for space and defense. And it has consistently invested far more in educating its young people, including three times more than the United States in early science and math education. As a consequence, Japan is currently turning out, on a per capita basis, more than twice as many engineers as we do, and Japanese youth surpass American youth according to virtually every measure of educational attainment.

There are, in short, no mystical political or cultural qualities unique to the Japanese national character that explain their economic "miracle." Japan's phenomenal productivity gains, conquest of world markets, and rapidly rising standards of living are primarily explained by hard economic facts: extraordinarily high levels of savings and investment, both public and private; the enlightened response of business and labor to the abundance of capital; and the ongoing accumulation of material and intellectual endowments for the benefit of posterity. In sum, there is a broad consensus in Japan that the future matters. Perhaps the real question we should be asking is how we have lost this consensus, and whether there are any hidden political or cultural traits in the American national character—or, better yet, any collective public decisions we have made—that are leading us to do so little for our own posterity.

The figures on those slides made it clear that, unlike the Japanese, we were not investing in our future. But they also made it clear that our economy was—and is—oriented toward current consumption to a degree unequaled by any other industrial country. Just how have we managed to consume our "limitless" resources? The answer lies at the heart of what this book is about. We have managed it through the creation of public entitlements: a system of "free" benefits designed (especially at the federal level) not to alleviate poverty, unemployment, or any other social ill, but rather to subsidize the consumption standards of mature Americans at all income levels.

Between 1965 and 1987, federal disbursements through entitlement programs have grown from about 5 to 11 percent of GNP. As we will see, these figures do not include parallel growth in state and local entitlements; nor do they reflect the large and regressive benefits handed out through consumption-oriented tax breaks, let alone the massive unfunded benefit liabilities we are passing down to our children. Yet consider that this increase alone amounts to 6 percent of GNP, a slice of our national product nearly equivalent to our entire defense budget. It is *twice* our net domestic investment in U.S. businesses, *four times* greater than the R&D development budgets of all U.S. corporations, and *twelve times* greater than our net national investment in public infrastructure.

Relative to the size of our entire economy, of course, 5 or 10 percent of GNP may not seem inordinately large. But the relevant comparison is not with our entire GNP. Instead, it is with that small margin—that 5 or 10 percent—that is not consumed, but saved and invested, and that therefore constitutes a society's lifeline to the future. It goes without saying that all societies devote the great majority of their national product to current consumption. Where societies differ, however, is in their collective ability to widen or narrow the unconsumed endowment that they pass on to their descendants.

That is why entitlements are so important. So long as we insist on increasing our public consumption without a political consensus to cut our private consumption, we effectively guarantee that we will shrink our endowment. Such a choice enriches the present at the expense of the future. It benefits today's parents and grandparents at the expense of today's children and grandchildren. And if other societies (such as Japan) continue to make a very different choice of saving and investing vastly more, it condemns us to steadily declining stature in the world of the twenty-first century.

A central theme in this book is that the American concept of "entitlement" is inherently prejudicial against the young. The prejudice is severe enough in the way we treat children *as children*: our federal budget currently allocates eleven times more benefit dollars per capita to Americans over age sixty-five than it does to children under age eighteen. Yet the prejudice is even more grievous in the way we treat children *as future adults*. We are now passing them the bill for some $10 trillion in unfunded federal benefit liabilities* above and beyond our official national debt, and we are now quietly expecting them to pay as much as one-third to one-half of their paychecks before the middle of the next century to finance our own public retirement and health-care programs.

The only way our numerically small cadre of children can escape such a trap, of course, is to achieve phenomenal growth in their future (per-worker) productivity. Many visionaries are counting on precisely this—a supercharged, high-tech economy in the twenty-first century that will effortlessly propel our children over all resource limitations. Yet behind the unprecedented optimism of our rhetoric lies the unprecedented emptiness of our behavior: not just record-low savings rates—which deny our children the bricks and mortar with which they can build their future—but a systematic pattern of familial, educational, and budgetary neglect that is throwing into jeopardy their minds and bodies, their job skills and work habits. Let us fix our attention on the composite statistics of the typical high-school class in the year 2000. In each classroom of twenty children, eight will have lived with only one parent, five will be living in poverty, eight will belong to a racial minority (of whom many will also be "underclass" members of the first two groups), three will have physical or mental handicaps, and seven will drop out before completing their senior year.† No one knows how many of these children will someday be active (or "competitive," if you will) contributors to our computerized, cornucopian "information economy." But if it is more than just a few at the top of the class, clearly it will be despite, not due to, our current efforts. We are failing our children.

*Our unfunded benefit liabilities are equivalent to what we would have to set aside today to pay for the amount by which future benefit payments to current program participants (all current workers and retirees) are projected to exceed *both* the future tax contributions by these same individuals *and* the accumulated balances in our current benefit trust funds. We will return to this concept.

†These estimates come from an unpublished 1988 study of the Children's Television Workshop.

Cooking the Books

Three epigrams spring to mind. The first was coined by Herbert Hoover, a predecessor of mine as Secretary of Commerce. "Blessed are the young," he once said, "for they shall inherit the national debt." The second is from Tocqueville: "The American republic will endure until the politicians find they can bribe the people with their own money." And their children's money, he might have added. The third, most cynical of all, is attributed to a German philosopher: "It is the duty of the old to lie to the young."

We are indeed lying to the young—as well as to ourselves. The reason, perhaps, is that many of us feel a discomfort about how we are shortchanging the future, and therefore we make every effort to conceal it from ourselves, as well as from our children.

To begin with, we have refused to assess realistically the probable future costs of diverting resources toward today's consumption. Not long ago, it did not seem to matter much. After all, resources were limitless, or so people like John Kenneth Galbraith and Vance Packard were then telling us. The real issues were not so much economic as political; they had to do not so much with creating wealth as distributing it.

Thus great oaks are forever springing up from supposedly tiny acorns. This was the case, for instance, with the 20 percent Social Security benefit hike and simultaneous implementation of a 100 percent cost-of-living indexing formula that sailed through Congress back in 1972. As a member of the White House staff when this tiny acorn was planted, I had an opportunity to observe firsthand how presidential candidates (and, in particular, Wilbur Mills in his vain quest for the Democratic nomination) vied with each other in trying to put together the most generous benefit package. There were a few feverish days of promises outbidding promises—all to the pleasure of current constituents and all seemingly without a thought to the eventual burden on tomorrow's taxpayers.

In addition, when programs or promises become awkwardly expensive, we "cook the books," shifting them "off-budget" in order to conceal the true extent of the liabilities we are passing on to our children. In 1975 I got a close-up glimpse of this political number-twisting practice when President Ford appointed me Chairman of the Quadrennial Commission on Executive, Congressional and Judicial Pay. One of the commission's tasks was to determine the "comparability" of compensation between the public and private sectors. But there was, I soon discovered, a basic problem. In corporate America, comparability takes into account all costs, including such fringe benefits as vacations, sick pay, holidays, health benefits, and, of course, pensions. But for federal employees, comparability is only supposed to deal with pay; pensions and other fringes are "another matter."

Moreover, corporations are by law required not only to fund pensions, but to include these costs on their annual profit and loss statements. Government, however, keeps massive, unfunded pension liabilities "off-the-books," where their real costs are hidden from public view. Despite our presidential charter, we on the Commission experienced great difficulty in obtaining even the crudest estimates of these liabilities, and when one was finally turned over to us, it turned out to be grossly understated. As we will see, if all federal retirement benefits were funded as private pensions are by law, U.S. budget outlays and deficits would have been about $150 billion larger, each year, over the last decade and a half.

But if our reverse endowments are being neglected in embarrassed silence or papered over with unrealistic projections and accounting tricks, no such reticence stops us from talking about what we will receive as opposed to what we will give. It appears that everyone today, rich or poor, is entitled to something—from the elderly, who are "entitled" to more tax-free Social Security benefits than they have earned and more health care than they need; to veterans, who are, among numerous other things, "entitled" to free health care whether or not their disabilities are service-related; to farmers and ranchers, who, in good times or bad, are "entitled" to income transfer payments, subsidized electric power, cheap water, and free grazing rights; to public service employees, some of whom are "entitled" in retirement to more income than they ever earned in government service; and—yes, you guessed it—to Peter G. Peterson, whose simple citizenship "entitles" him to a panoply of tax-free government benefits upon his retirement, regardless of his financial need and regardless of whether he has paid for them.

Economic Amateurism and the Vending-Machine Ethic

Given the success with which Americans have traditionally prepared for tomorrow privately, as families and as businesses, it is fair to ask why our federal government is proving so unsuccessful as a steward of our national future—in short, why it is failing to institute a coherent set of policies designed to sustain economic growth. Here the contrast with certain other governments can be especially striking.

I remember well, for example, listening to former West German Chancellor Willy Brandt as he described how, as a child, he had to pack his family's lifetime savings of deutschmarks into bags and take them to the local orphanage. There they were used to start a fire so the children could be kept warm. "You Americans simply have never experienced the hell that can take place in a country if it doesn't get inflation under control," Brandt said. "It is what brought us Adolf Hitler. It's what transformed, in a hideous way, our entire values and society." Out of that common misery, though, the Germans eventually forged a common consensus, an agreement between labor and management to accept certain fundamental economic principles: the necessity of significant productivity increases and the capital investment to make those increases possible; wage increases directly tied to increases in worker output; orderly, moderate increases in the money supply; and, finally, the imperative of global competitiveness.

In contrast, our modern federal government was in large part created to protect the citizenry *against* the excesses of the powerful and successful private enterprises responsible for economic progress. And as the relative size of our federal government steadily grew since the 1920s, not even the Great Depression shook our popular belief that such a division of labor was fitting. Economic progress should remain the exclusive sphere of private actors; moderating, humanizing, and consuming such progress should be the primary concern of the public sector.

Today, of course, the institutions, programs, and policies of the federal government have grown to vast proportions and exercise a profound—even preponderant—influence on the ability of the private sector to go about its business of creating wealth and then setting aside a share of that wealth for posterity. Yet, tragically, Washington has never developed a tradition guaranteeing that its policies are conducive to sustainable growth. Allow me to single out three unfortunate symptoms of our singular course of political development: a long-standing fiscal infatuation with a crude version of Keynesian theory, the general aversion to economic worldliness on the part of our political leaders, and the triumph of interest-group politics.

As for the theorizing of Lord Keynes, the fault lies not so much with that much-maligned English economist as with his latter-day American interpreters, who seized single-mindedly on his assertion that the private economy tended inexorably toward "excessive savings." That

Introduction

may have been a problem for the world in which Keynes was writing during the 1930s—and for an America that suffered from a variety of policy-induced maladies, such as tariff mania and monetary contraction, no less than from a catastrophic implosion of business and household demand. Yet it has hardly been a major problem over most of the postwar era, when our savings rate has consistently lagged far behind those of most faster-growing nations. And it cannot possibly have been a problem at all over the past decade, years in which our national savings rate has proved insufficient to meet even our nation's most minimal public and private investment needs.

Nonetheless, our policymakers have long persisted in seeking to stimulate consumption (until recently, for instance, consumer loan interest was fully tax-deductible), even while imposing extra burdens on those who save (taxing interest on savings as "unearned income," for example). Abroad, the incentives are just the reverse. Most foreign leaders, whatever their party stripe, understand instinctively that increased savings and investment are the key to future prosperity. Only in Washington have politicians institutionalized the virtue of consumption. According to textbook Keynesian theory, of course, the federal government was only supposed to stimulate demand during cyclical downturns. This was the so-called balance wheel function of deficit spending. But who today even remembers that this same theory prescribed *budget surpluses* during periods of economic boom? Long after the theory itself has grown irrelevant, the consumption-oriented constituencies served by deficit spending still manage to roll on without it.

Washington's economic amateurism has often been remarked on. One notable, though hardly unique, example was Wilbur Mills, who controlled the tax system for many years and who regularly boasted that he had never been to Europe. Compare him with someone like former West German chancellor Helmut Schmidt, an accomplished economist, who made it a practice to know what major export orders German companies were seeking, so that, if the occasion arose, he could lend a hand with a personal sales pitch. Although this is not a practice I necessarily recommend to U.S. Cabinet officers, much less to our chief of state, it is emblematic of a great difference in perspective. Abroad, leaders naturally take a vital daily interest in their countries' global economic performance; here, it is just as legitimate to express an open contempt for how well—or indeed, whether—we are earning our way in the world.

Finally, it is worth pointing out that when government becomes single-mindedly obsessed by consuming, as opposed to saving, it inevitably encourages a fragmentation of the common bonds of citizenship and the rise of special interest constituencies, each one an entrepreneur for its own private advancement. (This loosening of common bonds and virtual scorn for cooperative productive enterprise is mirrored in the fact that some 90 percent of all civil suits filed anywhere in the world are filed in America!) By the late 1960s or early 1970s, most Americans were beginning to assume that Washington had become a giant vending machine and that the sole purpose of political action was to elbow one's way to the front of the line. Who stocks the vending machine and how we can ensure that it will not run out of goods were, then as now, questions that no longer generated any particular passion.

Inevitably, people and programs not so adept at pushing to the front of the line were given short shrift. Thus a program like farm price supports, which had a huge lobbying constituency, routinely sailed through Congress, while Medicaid, which benefited only the under-represented poor, faced far stormier weather. In similar fashion, civil service pensioners had little trouble winning the allegiance of powerful protectors (and from time to time gained wonderful benefit expansions), while more vulnerable constituencies, such as unwed mothers relying on Aid to Families with Dependent Children, found themselves under nearly constant assault.

In the end, what we wound up with was a kind of "government by grievance." Each nonpoverty entitlement program acquired and nurtured a public constituency, which, with the aid of its corresponding bureaucratic and congressional constituency (not to mention the battalions of special interest lawyers), protected and assured its continual expansion. As time went on, the entire fiscal system acquired a strong bias favoring budget deficits and the current consumption of national resources. What was lost in the process was that old-fashioned consensus that government—like individuals and families—should live within its means.

Free Lunch for the Middle Class

By the end of the 1970s—with the economy reeling from double-digit inflation and interest rates—I was ready for a radical political change, and so, obviously, was the American public. In voting for Ronald

Reagan, I was casting my ballot, or so I thought, for a policy of increased savings, enhanced investment, and renewed productivity. But when I read the new President's first budget, I became both puzzled and depressed.

I had expected to see economic incentives for savings and investment. Instead, I found that the budget would result in massive *dissaving* generated by unprecedented budget deficits. The more I read on, the more it was apparent that the first Reagan budget was not about economics at all; it was about psychology and hope. Moreover, the assumptions on which it was based seemed the product of almost pathologically wishful thinking. In one fell swoop, the new administration was promising the biggest tax cuts in history, the biggest defense increases in history, and, most astonishing of all, a Republican reaffirmation of the biggest domestic spending programs—especially middle-class entitlements. All this and a balanced budget, too. The old Wall Street aphorism seemed to sum it up best: "If it sounds too good to be true, it probably is."

To be fair, not all of Reagan's economic agenda was badly aimed. Staying the course while double-digit inflation was tamed—the one instance when the administration (or more precisely, Paul Volcker's Federal Reserve Board) tested our threshold of pain—is a feat for which the President deserves credit; as he does also for courageously taking on the Air Traffic Controllers Union, an action that moderated the wage binge of the 1970s. And he was surely correct in advocating cuts in marginal tax rates. We know now that a maximum tax rate of 50 percent not only encourages budding entrepreneurs, but actually generates *more* revenue from the wealthy than does a maximum tax rate of 70 percent. In the same spirit, the President should be applauded for cutting back excessive regulation, and for sweeping from the nation's agenda such unsound policies as national planning, wage-and-price controls, and large-scale jobs programs.

As for the basic allocation of our economy's resources, however, Reaganomics has either opted for or acquiesced in some of the worst future-averting choices America has ever made. The full implications of the misguided policies and political spinelessness of the 1980s may not be known for years. One result, unfortunately, is already clear: all the rhetoric about Reaganomics providing "a safety net for the truly needy" has turned out to be just that—rhetoric. The 1981 budget, for instance, cut means-tested programs targeted at the poor *three times* as much as the much larger, non-means-tested programs that benefit

17

everyone. Rather than being a safety net (except for the politicians, who could avoid making tough choices), the Reagan budget was a well-padded hammock for those of us in the middle and upper classes.

Against the background of widening budget deficits and the impending bankruptcy of the Social Security system, I set about studying the whole issue in earnest. Eventually, my findings were distilled in an article for the *New York Times Magazine* entitled "No More Free Lunch for the Middle Class."* The article detailed the ruinous cost and wasteful targeting of these programs; it also helped to introduce the terms "means-tested" and "non-means-tested" to the nonspecialist public (terms we shall frequently return to in this book). Encouraged by the storm of (mostly favorable) reaction that greeted its appearance, I decided that year to delve still deeper into that granddaddy of all middle-class entitlements, Social Security.

In the course of my research, which later served as the basis for a series of in-depth articles in the *New York Review of Books*,† I discovered that Social Security was neither the "insurance" program nor the "poverty" program that its backers claimed. Far from simply "getting back" the payments they had made into the system through the years, *current* beneficiaries were actually receiving many times what they had contributed, although *future* beneficiaries will be quite lucky just to break even. As for the alleviation of poverty, which allegedly constitutes a primary goal of the program, I found that there was overwhelming evidence that the entire system is in fact regressive over the lives of beneficiaries—in other words, that the unearned benefits enjoyed by wealthy recipients are far greater than the unearned benefits enjoyed by poor recipients. And speaking of the poor, I also discovered that the Social Security system discriminates most of all against low-income minorities, since they tend to start work earlier (and therefore contribute payroll taxes for more years), and die younger (and thereby collect fewer years of retirement benefits).

Yet most important of all, the effort alerted me to some of the great social and demographic forces that must—even in the best of circumstances—cause our entitlements burden to grow much larger early in the next century. Much of this growth will come from health-care benefits. Already, Medicare devotes nearly one-third of its giant $80-

*"No More Free Lunch for the Middle Class" by Peter G. Peterson, *New York Times Magazine* (January 12, 1982).

†"Social Security: The Coming Crash" and "A Plan for Salvation" by Peter G. Peterson, *New York Review of Books* (December 2 and 16, 1982).

billion budget to Americans in their last year of life. (I've wondered at times if our preoccupation with postponing death is still another manifestation of our no-limits mentality, one that cannot even accept the *ultimate* limit—death.) And this figure, awesome though it may be, is just for openers. With costly, high-technology, death-postponing techniques sprouting daily from the laboratories, our federal budget could easily be spending $300 billion on health care for the elderly by the turn of the century, roughly 110 times today's total federal investment in Head Start, in prenatal care, in child immunization, and in vocational education—all of which constitute rare but genuine examples of how we might "reinvest" in U.S. "competitiveness." We are left with a perversely ironic statistic: our country is the industrial world's leader at the back end of life, with the greatest longevity at age eighty, but the laggard at the beginning of life, with the industrial world's highest rate of infant mortality.

The Bipartisan Budget Appeal Meets the Gray Lobby

My examination of Social Security—and my growing alarm about what lay ahead—led me in 1982 to join with five former secretaries of the Treasury (W. Michael Blumenthal, John B. Connally, C. Douglas Dillon, Henry H. Fowler, and William E. Simon) in organizing what came to be known as the Bipartisan Budget Appeal. Composed of more than 500 distinguished Americans from both political parties, the Budget Appeal took out newspaper ads, cajoled Congress, sponsored press conferences and forums, and beat on administration doors, all to one purpose: to announce, loudly and clearly, that the economy was in long-term trouble, and that the trouble would get markedly worse unless we moved quickly to control our entitlement programs.

The results of our efforts, I must confess, were mixed. While privately we received considerable encouragement from leaders both in Congress and the administration, publicly almost no one was prepared to endorse our recommendations: a one-year freeze on 100 percent cost-of-living adjustments (COLAs) for non-means-tested entitlements, and a structural reform of Medicare and federal retirement programs, including Social Security. Repeatedly we were told that what we sought was "absolutely necessary" but "not yet politically possible." Reform of Social Security was surely "inevitable," but any overt undertaking was still "unmentionable."

Just what we were up against politically was brought home to me when I visited the office of Texas Congressman Kent Hance. We had a long and good and sobering talk, the Congressman and I, mostly about my personal *bête noire*, COLA indexing for programs like Social Security and federal pensions. I was reviewing with Congressman Hance a curious asymmetry: our 1981 indexation of the tax system reduced revenues, yet our refusal to modify automatic indexation of entitlement benefits prevented us from achieving a commensurate reduction in spending. As our discussion was winding to a close, Congressman Hance turned to his aide and asked her to bring in any communications from constituents who opposed even the most trivial modification of COLA indexing. "You mean all of them?" the aide gasped, and proceeded to bring in a huge stack of letters and telegrams. The Congressman then said, "I wonder if you could now bring in to Mr. Peterson the letters and wires and other communications that favor the kind of indexing reform he is proposing." "But Congressman," the aide exclaimed, "We don't ever get any letters like that."

Indeed, congressmen don't, and the reason they don't is that the forces pushing for benefit expansions, at the cost of today's taxpayers and future generations alike, are both huge and well organized. Actual and potential federal retirees, to cite but one example, make up the core population of the Washington area and wield "insider" influence on Capitol Hill. The elderly have even more clout. For one thing, they are far more likely to work in political primaries than younger citizens; for another, they also vote in far greater numbers. Moreover, their ranks are growing and they are superbly organized—as witnessed by the avalanche of protest mail that regularly greets even the most modest entitlements reform proposal.

When an issue concerns the elderly, the halls of Congress fill up with lobbyists from the AARP (American Association of Retired Persons), SOS (Save Our Security), NCSC (National Council of Senior Citizens), NRTA (National Retired Teachers Association), the Gray Panthers, the Postal Workers Union, and the retired military officers associations—not to mention another thirty-five or forty pressure groups that claim a combined membership of 100 million.

They also have an impressive command of politically seductive, if misleading, rhetoric. In pushing their agenda, they almost never use words like "cost" and "taxes." Instead, they prefer terms like "earned," "fair," and "comparable." In the same fashion, their pronouncements on Social Security are peppered with phrases like "trust accounts" and "getting your money back." And it is not accidental that the blanket prohibition against federal funding for lobbies has but one huge and glaring exception: subsidies for national, state, and local senior advocacy groups (who receive, as "approved contractors," most of the $1.1 billion in federal funds doled out yearly through the Older Americans Act of 1965).

The power the entitlements lobby and its allies possess was vividly brought home to me at the time of the November 1987 budget summit following the stock-market panic. During the early stages of the summit, which was called to thrash out a compromise that would at least begin to scale down the size of the annual deficit, the latest advertisement of the Bipartisan Budget Appeal was posted prominently in the conferees' working chambers and referred to frequently as the "bipartisan solution to the problem." But as their deliberations were winding to a close, the *Washington Post* reported that the budget summiteers received a videocassette from Congressman Claude Pepper, that indefatigable champion of the elderly, in which the Congressman warned of a roll-call vote that would identify anyone in Congress supporting entitlements reform—and intimated how they would be punished by millions of "gray lobby" voters come the 1988 elections. When the tape was over, the Budget Appeal's advertisement was taken down. "Thereafter," one of the participants reported, "it was back to politics as usual."

Just to afford ourselves some perspective, consider for a moment how Japan handles such questions. Several years ago, the Japanese government brought to light official projections that revealed that the cost of its major public retirement system would rise to unaffordable heights early in the next century. After some serious discussion, the government passed and enacted a major reform of the system in 1986 that will reduce average future benefit levels by roughly 20 percent twenty years from now. There was hardly a murmur of protest. After all, as the Ministry of Health and Welfare explained, the need was self-evident:

> The basis of the public pension system is social solidarity. Therefore, with a view to the impending aging of society in the twenty-first century, and in order to ensure stability over the long term, it is essential to ensure equity and to create a system in which people can have confidence. Consideration also has been given to the balance between the level of pension received by the elderly generation and the living

To the Congress, the Administration, and the American People:

Time for Decisive Action: A Bipartisan Budget Plan

We have joined together to urge our fellow Americans and this Nation's leaders to rise above politics as usual, to set aside differences — of party, region, ideology, and even immediate self-interest — in order to resolve our worsening economic problems before it is too late. Though Presidents and Congresses going back many years must share in the blame, we have no interest in finger-pointing: our mutual interest now lies in contributing to the solution.

The recent upheavals on Wall Street dramatize our unbalanced and increasingly risky economy. Although we believe in the underlying strength of the economy, we have for too long consumed more than we have produced, forcing a dangerous dependence on massive foreign borrowing. Our budget and trade deficits raise the risks of a huge interest rate increase and rising inflation, an economic slow-down with growing unemployment, a resurgence of the Third World debt crisis, a global trade pull-back, or even a deep worldwide recession. Our concern is not just where the stock market is today, but where our economy, our standard of living, and our world standing will be tomorrow.

Together — we, the American people, and our leaders — can set in motion basic changes to cure this condition. That is the way to prevent a stock market collapse from spreading to the broader economy. Fiscal reform is the indispensable key to solving our immediate problem, to reducing both long- and short-term interest rates, and to laying the foundations for healthy and sustainable economic growth. Congress and the Administration must:

1. Cut federal budget deficits so that the markets believe the long-term problem is really being solved.

■ The deficit reductions must be significant, at least $30-40 billion in the first year.

■ The cuts must be credible, multi-year, and increasing so that the budget can move toward balance by 1992.

■ One-shot measures must be avoided; cuts must be permanent and grow over time.

■ The plan must be based on extremely prudent economic projections.

2. Put everything on the table — except programs for the poor.

■ Spending cuts of all kinds should be top priority.

■ Defense spending must be restrained to levels consistent with our essential national security needs.

■ Cuts must be made in non-defense programs, especially all the other entitle-ment, transfer, and subsidy programs that are not means-tested. In particular, reductions should come from the bene-fits received by upper income groups in excess of their accumulated contribu-tions. COLA modifications should also be part of any long-term budget reform.

■ Only when larger spending cuts are assured should revenue increases be considered, and any such revenues should be raised in ways that discourage consumption and encourage savings and investment.

■ The burdens of deficit reduction should be shared fairly among all of us who can afford them.

3. Rapidly adopt a credible deficit reduction plan to give the President a stronger hand in negotiations for more global economic cooperation.

■ Get our economic allies to stimulate domestic demand and boost their imports.

■ Work out coordinated interest rate reductions with Europe and Japan.

■ Renew our collective commitment to fight protectionism.

■ Stimulate a flow of capital to Third World countries to help them grow and to service their debts by exporting to more open markets in the developed world; in turn, this will permit Third World countries to become significant export markets for goods and services from developed countries.

■ Work toward increased military and economic burden-sharing by our allies.

We recognize that the bold political action now needed is impossible unless the people allow it — indeed, unless they demand it. For us, for our children, and for our grandchildren, we must work together, as Americans, to rescue our economy...and our country.

We pledge a national, bipartisan effort to help persuade the American people to let their leaders know that they are ready to support the immediate adoption of a program like that outlined above.

Send this message to tell your Washington, D.C. representatives that you support the Bipartisan Budget Plan.

To:

I support immediate adoption of measures along the lines of the Bipartisan Budget Plan, including credible, multi-year deficit reductions, of at least $30-40 billion in the first year. Other than programs for the poor, everything should be on the table, including COLAs for the non-means-tested entitlement programs. Only after larger spending cuts are assured should revenue increases be considered — but only in ways that discourage consump-tion and encourage savings and investment. I also support negotiations for more effec-tive global economic cooperation and burden sharing.

Sincerely,

NAME

ADDRESS

standards and liabilities of the working generation supporting the
system (equity between the generations).*

What could be more straightforward? Yet what could be less imaginable in our own country, given the state of our political system? Perhaps it is worth mentioning that Japan has no "gray lobby." One reason is that most elderly Japanese men are still employed at least part time and two-thirds of all Japanese elderly live under the same roof as their children and their grandchildren. Quite simply, there doesn't seem much point in generational lobbying. Yet another, more fundamental reason is that when a society's attention is fixed on its future, it does not treat consumption promises to its oldest members as its highest public priority. To the Japanese, it seems self-evident from a societal perspective that most spending on the young constitutes *investment* in the long-term future, whereas most spending on the elderly is inherently *consumption*.

Saul Steinberg's View from Washington

Before most audiences, I have found that any discussion of entitlements reform leads very directly to earnest questions about the political obstacles and incentives facing our national leaders—the ones who, after all, will have to make some of the biggest and riskiest choices. Any answer to such questions must try to offer some overall impression of the political forces brought to bear on the daily life of the typical member of Congress or agency director. It is not enough to say the obvious: that these leaders are tossed about in a sea of media stories, voter surveys, lobbyist visits, constituent complaints, speech invitations, and partisan attacks and praise, not to mention the occasional shady temptation. The real questions are: Who speaks the loudest? Who offers the surest rewards? Who can make or break a political career? Where do politicians run when they want to play it safe?

My attempts at answering such questions started me wondering what the resulting portrait would look like if painted as a political map of America—a map portraying the country as seen through the eyes of a typical national politician. One is reminded of the famous Saul Steinberg painting of how a New Yorker sees the world. In that picture, as many will recall, the Manhattan skyscrapers dominate the foreground.

---

*Statement released by Japan's Ministry of Health and Welfare in 1985, as cited by Samuel H. Preston and Shigemi Kono in "Trends and Well-Being Among Children and the Elderly in Japan" (1987, unpublished).

Off in the distance a bit is the Hudson River, and far beyond that are some tiny bumps that are the Rocky Mountains. Farther still is a pond-like body of water—the Pacific Ocean—and really far in the distance are little promontories with names like China and Japan. The point, of course, is that New Yorkers tend to see their own city as all-important and everything else as a distant and dreamlike backdrop.

One could find similar distortions in Washington's political perspective on America. I would guess that in the foreground of the map we would see as giants, almost colossal in size, the powerful organizations aimed at protecting entitlements for today's retired and elderly Americans. The young workers who foot the bill for those entitlements would appear diminutive and lemminglike.

The map would also show a political forum full of monomaniacs, practiced at shouting their favorite slogans, indifferent to anyone or anything else, and convinced that government is a giant vending machine and that the sole purpose of political action is to get to the front of the line. How the vending machine is stocked is an issue that generates no political fervor and that, accordingly, is neglected. On the other hand, the big issues on the map would be the special interest road signs directing the distribution of pleasure—Social Security, federal pensions, military pensions, farm subsidies, weapons contracts, and so forth.

On this political map, the future would lie in the distant background. There we would find most children. There too we would find the general interests of most families. Those who would benefit from improvement in general economic conditions constitute a majority. But they are an ineffective majority, a vast silent majority far outstripped in passion and organization by those who want something particular from government. The general interest has on its side only economic logic. That makes (or has made) for a very uneven political contest. As a governor of a major state once put it to me, "There is no constituency for fiscal responsibility."

In any event, such a political map would, I fear, portray all too clearly the view of the typical legislator. There is obviously some truth in the conventional pronouncement that to advocate significant reform of non-means-tested entitlements in general, and of Social Security in particular, is to commit political suicide. So let us not be naive. The restructuring of entitlements will be protracted, intense, and demanding. To a large extent, it will be a struggle waged with facts

24

and words—hence this book. But it will also be a struggle waged with images—hence the need for a more positive vision.

It is to be hoped, as we contemplate this Steinberg-like drawing, that we will conclude that America's political landscape must be reshaped. A one-time glimpse does not, after all, represent a permanent reality. The only thing we must truly fear is the self-defeating conviction that redrawing this map is "politically impossible." In part, I cannot accept this because I for one have too much faith in the good sense of the American people. A public that is informed about the true stakes in the entitlements debate will be able, I believe, to break from past patterns and place on the map a new force to be reckoned with. And in part, I do not accept the conventional wisdom because the consequences of believing it are, quite simply, too appalling. If politics does render Social Security and the entitlements problem unsolvable, then there is a significant danger that our old politics will consign us to an all-too-bleak economic future, as well as foster a potentially ugly social conflict between the generations—a rebellion by tax-crushed young workers against the entire notion of supporting the elderly at a decent level of income.

The Errors of the Right and the Left

As we learned during the recent budget summit, bringing about fundamental reform is no mean trick. The interests fighting change are well entrenched, and so, unfortunately, is wrongheaded economic thinking. Being a Republican (and a pretty conservative one, at that), I have been increasingly distressed with the ideologues of the so-called New Right. By and large, they disparage attacks on deficit spending on the theory that "supply-side" economics, along with such trendy palliatives as tax cuts, easy money, and a return to the gold standard, will "let us grow our way out of our problems." Theirs is the politics of pleasure and consumption—with the notable exception of programs for the poor, where they have sanctioned real cuts. Exactly why today's conservatives seem indifferent to the dangers inherent in vast government spending only when it is shrouded in metaphors of contract and entitlement is a little hard to fathom. Their apparent tolerance for social spending not directed to the poor is especially disturbing when juxtaposed with their intolerance for social programs like Food Stamps or Aid to Families with Dependent Children that do direct their benefits to the needy. In some cases, it may be hard to escape the inference that the cause is lack of compassion, rather than skepticism about government and faith in the free market. Or perhaps these conservatives don't look at the numbers any more closely than the liberals.

To listen to their spokesmen, such as New York Congressman Jack Kemp, they apparently believe that virtually everything is affordable. As Kemp himself put it: "Today the neoconservative is on the offensive. It's no longer austerity and pain and sacrifice. Today it is growth and hope and opportunity." Those are fine words, but they deftly sidestep a troubling problem: What happens to such an ideology when some measure of sacrifice is a prerequisite to any measure of success? Like their counterparts on the left, neoconservatives promise cures that are fast and painless, and therefore politically potent. And, to give them their due, these "fiscal radicals"—as I like to call them— have been riding high in the Republican Party. Such is their clout that anyone with the temerity to suggest that budgetary responsibility is in order, not to mention the possibility of a tax increase, is automatically written off as a hopeless pessimist. Inevitably, though, there will be a staggering bill to pay, and when it comes due, there is a very real chance that the "happy-time Republicans," Ronald Reagan chief among them, will be consigned to the obloquy of Herbert Hoover.

But if New Right conservatives are tragically misguided, so too are traditional liberals, who assume that any critique of domestic spending is merely camouflage for an attack on America's long-standing commitment to progressive social goals. This reaction is ill-conceived on two counts. First, it ignores the reality that much domestic spending does not serve progressive goals at all, but rather is a form of subsidy— welfare, really—lavished on "entitled" interest groups, regardless of those groups' legitimate needs. Second, it consistently overlooks the crucial relationship between economic growth and society's willingness to devote resources to the achievement of social goals. It is no accident that this country's liberal agenda was developed during the boom years of the 1960s. By the same token, it should come as no surprise that societies with stagnating standards of living are as a rule harsh, intolerant, and socially regressive.

Just how vulnerable poverty programs are in times of economic stress has been dramatically highlighted by the events of the last few years. From 1981 to 1986, means-tested programs have, on a percentage basis, been cut about twice as much as non-means-tested entitlements. Faced with this development, many advocates for the poor

26

wind up backing universal entitlement programs. However exorbitant their cost, so the argument runs, they do incidentally benefit the needy, and it is these programs alone that can hope to survive politically. In effect, they are opting for the politics of bribery. Thus, while the liberals may well be right to fear for their transcendent social goals, they are wrong to cling to social spending in its current form—and especially to universal entitlement programs—in the hope of protecting those goals. In so doing, they are racing down a road toward an economic chaos that, in the end, will jeopardize the prosperity on which all progressive social goals depend.

Toward a New Politics

So where do we stand late in 1988 as we approach the presidential election? If the formulations of both the New Right and the traditional liberals are mistaken, what is the answer? Indeed, is there an answer, given the power of the entitlements lobby and the natural instinct of politicians to bend before it? Despite the obstacles—and only a fool would underestimate them—I believe that there is an answer. It lies in the formation of a new political consensus that is, at once, conservative in its approach to economic issues and compassionate in its approach to social problems, tough-minded on foreign policy but not mesmerized by each new proposal for a costly weapons system. This new politics must forge a coalition for investment that is willing to trade present consumption for future prosperity; it must be a bi-partisan grouping prepared to endure some pain today in order to avoid future economic calamity. We must, in short, succeed in renewing the endowment ethic and rekindling the ideal of generational stewardship.

But if all of this is to happen, we must have some clear idea of where we are heading and what the tangible benefits will be. After all, effective coalitions cannot be built solely on ideals and abstractions. As Abraham Lincoln once noted: "Few can be induced to labor exclusively for posterity, and none will do it enthusiastically. Posterity has done nothing for us; and, theorize on it as we may, practically we shall do very little for it unless we are made to think we are, at the same time, doing something for ourselves."

In this respect, I am reminded of a visit I made several years ago to a successful medical doctor, Dr. Herbert Spiegel, who specializes in weight control. He explained why eager eaters like myself will not or cannot stay on a diet: most people cannot sustain any program that is based on a *negative* vision, or a notion of denial, unless their very lives are at stake. The doctor then asked: What did I want to weigh? How important was it to me? Why was it important to me? If for reasons of health, precisely what was the "better health" that I would enjoy? If for reasons of appearance, did I have a positive vision of what I wanted to look like?

After some thought, I set a positive goal of 175 pounds—a seemingly impossible target given my then current weight of 215 pounds! Dr. Spiegel then asked me to stand in front of an ingenious mirror that changes the visual proportions of the body without the grotesque distortion typical of amusement-park mirrors. He dialed in 175 pounds. There I stood, a much leaner and, if I do say so, more physically appealing Pete Peterson. He asked that I study this more positive vision, try to lock it in my mind, and retrieve it frequently as a concrete image of my own positive goal. In the months thereafter, I lost thirty pounds.

Are there similar positive images we can focus on as a nation? Consider this one. It so happens that the real net rate of return on additions to our stock of plant and equipment runs at about 11 percent a year. Translated from economic jargon, what this means is that by foregoing a dollar's consumption today, the nation can have two dollars in consumption in just six or seven years. Or, to put it in economy-wide terms, if we take the steps necessary to make the 1990s the "Decade of Investment," the turn of the century could become a new era of real prosperity and influence for the United States—one that will bring with it a more competitive economy, better education, more secure jobs, rising real incomes, and the ability to "stand tall" in the world without at the same time borrowing on bended knee. It would signify a more satisfying life for ourselves and the generations that follow—in other words, a rekindling of the American Dream.

Will we be willing to take the necessary steps? Given the distemper in our political economy, it may require getting the hell scared out of us before we act: another Black Monday, or a fantastic rise in interest rates or unemployment, or some other domestic or international crisis that finally convinces us that our course is leading to disaster.

As things stand now, we have many politicians who are adept at giving speeches about capital formation, education, technological innovation, competitiveness, and balanced budgets, but few who are willing to do anything effective about it. Politicians and their constituents alike have become experts at avoiding the really tough questions: What are we willing to give up to get back our "competitiveness"—in other words, to *fund* a program of "reinvestment" in America? *Who* among us will be called on to make sacrifices? *Whose* resources will be dedicated to building up the nation's future productive capacity? The answer, of course, is every one of us who is able to contribute. In all fairness, we cannot continue to soak the poor as a matter of public policy, and as for soaking the rich, as some voices recommend, we have yet to find a policy device for achieving this purpose that does not also create massive incentives against private savings and investment.

I can imagine few ethical goals more universal than fairness to our children and grandchildren and fairness to the poor. If the children and the poor deserve better treatment, then the rest of us have a responsibility to find the resources to honor that commitment.

The New President: An Agenda

The nation missed a great opportunity in 1981. It is imperative that we do not miss another. The new president faces unprecedented dangers and historic opportunities. He also has very little time. If the stylized deception about the budget deficit and our dangerous dependence on foreign capital continue, we will risk any number of unhappy outcomes: from crash landings to hard landings to a British "stop and go" to stagflation. If the new president wants to avoid becoming Herbert Hoover redux (and if he remembers FDR's first 100 days), he should boldly seize this opportunity and tackle the "twin towers" of the budget and trade deficits with a twin summit strategy: a domestic summit followed by an international summit, distinguished not by the quality of the photos but by the concrete results.

The budget agenda for the domestic summit must include structural reform of entitlements. (Other important elements in the reform package, as suggested in the Bipartisan Budget Appeal advertisement that ran in November 1987, would be moderating defense growth and implementing consumption-based taxes.) To revive long-term prosperity, however, the burdens of entitlements reform must be grounded in reality and fairly shared. If they are not, we will at best arrive at a new stalemate; more likely still, we will also generate social discord and intergenerational conflict.

In looking where to cut, in deciding whose ox is to be gored, the obvious domestic targets are the fattest ones, the programs that account for the largest share of government spending and tax subsidies. These are the non-means-tested entitlements like Social Security, Medicare, and federal pensions. The vast majority of these benefits flow to the middle and upper classes; if any should bear the sacrifice it should be they. I am not suggesting that these programs be abandoned; to do so is not only politically impossible but morally unconscionable given the plight of those citizens now huddled in the basement of our economy. I am rather suggesting that we follow the prescription of former Office of Management and Budget Director David Stockman. The correct way to scale back entitlement spending, as Stockman said in a now-famous *Atlantic Monthly* interview, is to attack the weakest claims, not the weakest claimants.

In other words, we must move from age-based to need-based programs, applying sensible and humane indices of genuine need to our decisions about federal benefit spending, rather than guaranteeing that programs will run out of control by deeming benefits universal "rights" or "sacred contracts" or "entitlements." This will involve not only a substantial restructuring of entitlement programs themselves, but also a substantial modification of the way we think about them. And if the political opponents of reform are to be overcome, it will also be necessary to foster a renewed understanding of the most basic obligations of citizenship. In our policy debates, we all too often define ourselves and our interests largely in terms of the entitlement programs from which we stand to benefit. To build a coalition for investment, we must redefine ourselves as common stewards of the nation's future—in short, as citizens with a common stake in tomorrow.

I believe that early in 1989, the American public, yearning for greatness once again and nervously optimistic, may be ready to face up to reality. I hope that the new president will remember that his largest window of opportunity, his greatest degree of freedom, and his highest level of credibility are in the *early months* of his new term. I further hope that the new president will realize that tying our national fortunes to the whims of foreign lenders for another four years would be self-destructive. Finally, I believe he will be able to persuade his congressional colleagues of the wisdom of bearing the fiscal pain early (especially while unemployment is down and economic demand is strong) and enjoying the political gains later—in time for the next election.

Setting America back on the road toward the right future must start with putting ourselves on a durable and credible path toward budget balance, but this is certainly not the end of the process. An overall *global bargain* will be required in which our foreign partners make equally demanding contributions. Beyond boosting domestic demand and increasing imports, these will include stimulating major capital flows to Third World countries (here Japan and the wealthier newly industrialized countries such as Taiwan and South Korea must take the lead); shouldering a greater share of our mutual military burdens (this task will fall to our NATO allies); and fighting protectionism. Above all, as Fred Bergsten of the Institute for International Economics has stressed, the industrial democracies must reaffirm their commitment to working their way out of today's massive global imbalances through *cooperation* and *growth,* not through the 1930s approach of transoceanic bashing and trade-led recessions.

After the consensus among key domestic players in early 1989, the new president's next step should be to convene an immediate international summit. There, armed with proof that the United States is finally prepared to do its part, he will be able to bargain effectively with our trading partners. Their willingness, in turn, to bear part of the readjustment burden should make the domestic "deal" easier.

What would all this do to fuel America's investment revival that we so glibly talk about? A great deal. The more uncertain the long-term future and the higher the long-term real (inflation-adjusted) interest rate, the greater the inclination to stand back and just clip coupons. These real interest rates are at historic levels—4 to 6 percent rather than the historical 1 to 2 percent. Some of the brightest financial traders tell me that an effective and comprehensive global bargain would give our optionless Federal Reserve Board more running room, reassure our stock and bond markets, and, indeed, lower these economically crucial interest rates by perhaps 2 percent or even more. Lower long-term interest rates, of course, stimulate the housing industry and encourage business investment, but they also have other pain-averting effects: a 2 percent interest-rate decline would reduce the federal deficit by over $40 billion and would make the Third World debt bomb much less likely to explode.

But let us be clear. The chances for a decline in long-term interest rates depend on the absolute, certain belief of the financial markets that we are determined to carry out a sustained program of long-term reform. It may seem paradoxical, but we will not enjoy the short-term benefits unless we are prepared to endure the long-term costs.

The new president—instead of becoming another Herbert Hoover, as some who decided not to run assumed was inevitable—could well be the Franklin Delano Roosevelt of the 1990s. It may be one of those fortunate moments when good politics and good economics meet, when what is the right thing to do for the long term is also the right thing to do for the short term.

A Passion For Education—and Fundamentals

America has been sliding now for a generation, and it will take at least a decade to climb back. I have little patience, therefore, with "solutions" bred of impatience—be they a return to the gold standard, cutting taxes, or setting the money supply on a path of generous, automatic growth. Nor do I have much faith in systematic government intervention as a spur to prosperity. Perhaps there exists a major "industrial" policy adopted over the last twenty years that actually accomplished its grandiose purposes without baleful side effects. If so, however, the story is a well-guarded secret. Neither quick macro-fixes nor market manipulation will solve our problem.

Instead, I am a believer in fundamentals, and none is more bedrock than education. Americans are today prolonging their lives through self-taught habits of eating and exercise that ultimately derive from the much-wider diffusion of basic facts about health over the last twenty years. If we can learn as a nation to smoke less, limber up more, and avoid saturated fats, I cannot believe that the economic habit of investing in our collective future in vital areas like science and math education is beyond our ken.

It is through ignorance that we have lost control of our economic destiny. The shortsighted decisions of the last twenty years would not, I think, have been made had their likely consequences been well advertised and widely appreciated. The American people are not by nature foolish, and our political system, for all its flaws, need not have set us on a road toward national impoverishment. But for economic logic to prevail, the electorate must have full access to the economic facts—which is why this book is crammed full of them. However we go at the problem—whether through self-education, through lobbying, or simply through insisting on straight answers from our leaders—there is a role for all of us, experts and nonexperts, politicians and voters. In the last analysis, the federal government is our government. It not only leads and directs, it follows and represents. As Herbert Stein so wonderfully put it, it is we "who will have to make the world safe for politicians to do the right thing."

We are good indeed at doing the right thing when we have to fight a common enemy in a war. But now the common enemy seems to be within ourselves: the mindset that allows so many of us to regard the highest duty of government as dispensing short-term benefits to "entitled" interest groups. The danger is that defeat will creep up on us so gradually that we will hardly notice—that we will leave the blinders on until it is too late.

As a purely substantive matter, there is no call for pessimism. We have the economic capacity to put our financial system on a sound footing. We have the scientific base and the traditions of enterprise required to boost the rate of technological progress. Our material and intellectual resources are fully adequate for us to increase investment substantially without subjecting any group of Americans to severe austerity. What we have lacked, at least until now, is a genuine long-term consensus—which ultimately must be a moral consensus—that those resources must be harnessed for the common good. This book, the authors hope, provides some beginnings of one.

Whether we act on this, or any blueprint for fundamental change, depends entirely on us. If we fail to create a sense of urgency and to develop a balance of compassion and realism, the consequences will be grave, not only for ourselves, but for our children. We will become a much poorer country than we might have been, and a much less generous country than we ought to be. We will become more divided, less outward looking. In the end, we, as a people, will not be as good. These are fates we must not accept. The authors hope the reader will join us in that conviction.

July 11, 1988
New York City

33

I

Posterity in Danger

1

The Imperiled
American Dream

"The principle of spending money to be paid by posterity, under the name of [deficit] funding, is but swindling
futurity on a large scale."

— Thomas Jefferson,
as quoted by Henry Adams

I N THE WAKE of the stock-market panic in October 1987,
leaders from Congress and the Reagan administration loosed a
chorus of dismay over the size of the federal budget deficit. Since
many Americans had feared for years that our deficits were threatening our long-term future, there was no need for any of us to act as
though we were stumbling across the problem for the first time. But
with the stock market on everyone's mind, our leaders could not avoid
expressing new shock over ongoing revelations of our national prof-
ligacy—more red ink, graver projections, and still-larger liabilities
handed down to our children.

So once again we moved through our periodic ritual of atonement.
Once again a profoundly troubling milestone is reached, a clarion call
to action is sounded, political gridlock sets in, and eventually the
meaning of the event recedes from public awareness. As a consequence of the panic on Wall Street, the ritual was replayed with more
than the usual fanfare: press conferences, camera floodlights, television spots, and fist pounding in congressional committees—all re-
minding us of our predicament.

Newsclip interviews with bond dealers at the World Trade Center reminded us that current levels of direct and indirect federal borrowing, which devour nearly one-half of all funds raised from all U.S. lenders, represent a chokehold on investment and force us to hawk our IOUs abroad. Directors of foreign central banks reminded us that the United States cannot go on indefinitely borrowing over $150 billion per year, net, from foreign creditors. (That is about two-thirds of our net domestic investment in business and housing, or about 1 percent of our national worth, sold yearly to foreigners with the agreement that we can rent it back.) Think-tank academics, scribbling on op-ed pages, gave us a lesson in simple economics: it is absurd to delude ourselves with "competitiveness" mottos so long as we choose to consume over 97 percent of our national income—while the equivalent consumption rate is less than 90 percent in Europe and less than 85 percent in Japan.

There was much else to tell, but not, perhaps, enough time to tell it all. We might have listened to mayors and governors talk about how, despite all the public borrowing, we cannot maintain our streets, buses, sewers, and airports. Similarly, we might have asked college teachers why incoming freshmen today are not as well schooled as they themselves were; or plant foremen why our most capital-intensive manufactures are losing out to Asian competitors; or foreign service officers why the smallest foreign aid bill has now become a "budget" issue; or scrambling entrepreneurs why they have trouble finding investors willing to fund the development of new production technologies.

Most of all, we might have asked both our national leaders and ourselves why the widening flood of public debt seems to spare hardly a rivulet on behalf of America's most disadvantaged minority: young parents and their children. Compared with older households, they have the highest rate of poverty, the least access to health care, and the lowest per capita incomes. Indeed, over the last two decades, younger Americans as a group (under age thirty-five) have been experiencing a continuous and unprecedented decline in real income. Yet they alone constitute the human resources on whom we must rely not only to service our exploding federal and foreign debts (on the order of $100,000 per working adult by the year 2000), but also to care for the exploding numbers of us who will retire in the decades thereafter. They also just happen to represent the furthest living reach of posterity, the only means by which we can hope to safeguard our national destiny.

The problem the Crash of '87 brought once again to the attention of our national leaders was, in short, our blunt failure to provide for our economic future.

To their credit, Congress and the administration set out with passionate pronouncements of resolute action. They organized a budget summit and worked furiously through the last week of October and well into November to negotiate a "grand compromise" on the federal deficit. Newspaper headlines hinted at a great breakthrough on entitlement benefits, defense, and taxes. Television interview shows and newspaper op-ed pages staged debates on comprehensive spending freezes, new approaches to Medicare physician payments, and permanent changes in benefit cost-of-living adjustments (COLAs). During the second week of November, there was growing optimism that the negotiators might agree on subtracting two percentage points from all nonpoverty COLAs over the next five years. This single reform, affecting the largest and most persistently growing sector of the federal budget, would save an estimated $27 billion annually by fiscal year 1992.

The optimism died, however, when the able House majority leader Thomas Foley, chairman of the talks, was unable to get key leaders in either the administration or Congress to make the first move. On one side, the administration felt hemmed in by prior promises not to touch Social Security or taxes. On the other, congressional forces advocating COLA reform (known in the Senate as the "COLA caucus") were neutralized by the forces of their opponents (the "unCOLAs"). Over the weekend of November 14–15, several key negotiators announced that they were opposed to any COLA reform. The clincher came on Monday, when Congressman Claude Pepper implied that he would rally senior and retiree groups against any change in Social Security COLAs. "There will be political fallout if this is pursued," he warned. But of course if the Social Security lobby wouldn't budge, neither would the civil service or military retirees. Rather than face even greater cuts alone, their lobbies vowed to fight to the death rather than have their benefits touched. In rapid succession there soon followed similar protests by farmers, veterans, homebuilders, doctors, hospitals, and colleges.

Seeing few openings through the thicket of beneficiary lobbies, the weary negotiators turned to the defense budget. Here they fought another pitched battle among themselves, all over a couple of billion dollars, and came out with about the same meager savings as they did in benefits (the savings in both benefits and defense totaled about $24 billion over two years in a $1.1 trillion budget). Another $26 billion was picked up in additional tax revenue. After that, the "grand compromise" wore down to nickel-and-dime skirmishes over a very narrow field of action.

With the negotiators claiming that the economic future of our country was hanging in the balance, the public might have expected decisive action. If so, it was disappointed. The final compromise, revealed after many delays on November 22 (one month and three days after Black Monday), showed that as the echo of the crash faded, Washington had failed once again to move beyond gesture. With little comment and more than a few apologies ("We'd be doing exactly what we are doing today if the Dow was at 3,000 and everybody was celebrating on Wall Street," lamented Congressman Foley), Congress passed the compromise only days before Christmas. The Reagan administration, receiving a ramshackle 2,000-page budget resolution just a few hours before all federal operations were due to be shut down for lack of funds, signed it with hardly enough time to leaf through all its pages.

Even at face value, the overall projected savings for fiscal year 1988 was unimpressive. At $30.5 billion, it represented only 17 percent of the projected deficit and 3 percent of total projected spending. But even this figure was puffed up by every manner of accounting foolery: $5 billion, for instance, saved through "asset sales" (as if a family could save money by selling its furniture); another $2 billion saved by refinancing loans by the Rural Electrification Agency (a peculiar accounting transaction in which the U.S. Treasury was credited when selling the loans but not debited when buying them back—at lower interest rates); and $3 billion more in fanciful interest savings, in improved IRS collections, and in outlay and revenue timing changes. Altogether, the "real" deficit cuts amounted to less than $23 billion. And even these savings represented not a single strategic decision on either national defense or entitlement benefits (in fact, more than half of the benefit changes include "sunset" provisions; they will, in other words, expire after fiscal year 1989).*

The final embarrassment was not to come until February 1988, when the Congressional Budget Office (CBO) laconically reported

---

*Two-year sunset provisions will apply to fully 70 percent of the savings from Medicare, our fastest-growing benefit program. Permanent or "structural" benefit savings amount to only $3 billion in fiscal year 1990.

that new budget projections, based on a slower-growth economic scenario, showed a baseline 1990 deficit that was $20 billion higher than it was last November. At one stroke, nearly all the real savings of the "grand compromise" had suddenly evaporated. Now, as before, we look forward to endless years of federal mortgages on our nation's future: deficits in the $130 to $170 billion range by the early 1990s— *if* we have no recession and *if* we keep consuming all of the growing surpluses our large generation of younger workers is supposed to be accumulating in its retirement trust funds. Assuming a recession, we are looking at deficits of at least $250 billion; and leaving aside the reserves earmarked on behalf of our younger workers, the numbers grow by another $100 billion.

But the shock of October 1987 is now behind us. Although the stock-market panic excited alarm at first, ultimately it failed to make us change course, like so many earlier warning signals along the road we have been traveling: the beginning of our productivity stagnation (1974), our first postwar manufacturing trade deficit (1978), our first federal deficit over $100 billion (1982), and our entry into the roster of international debtors (1985). Eventually, a rhetorical "consensus" is all that is left behind, an empty shell signifying the stewardship of our nation's future. Once again, it is time to get on with business as usual: to sidestep tough choices, to talk about magic solutions ranging from the gold standard to tariff retaliation, and to banish the candidates who dare to ask where we will find resources while embracing those who discuss at length where they will spend them.

Without the slightest idea how we can afford the consumption claims we have already made on our future, America's present and soon-to-be elected representatives have returned to more pleasurable pastimes—such as designing unprecedented expansions of Medicare benefits, finding offices for our new Veterans Department, and debating the virtues of bigger Social Security checks to our so-called Notch Retirees. And while families and financial markets struggle to peer thirty years into the future, federal budget projections "all the way" to 1992 pass for farsighted statesmanship in our nation's capital.

The moral of this tale, and the message of this book, is simple. Sooner or later—sooner, we hope—Americans will have to confront the pervasive consumption ethos that is shaping our national life and endangering our future. We are no longer enjoying the sort of productivity performance that allows us to "bank on growth"; nor are we raising sufficiently large families to "bank on kids"—and even if we were, we are doing precious little to invest in their ability to provide for us.

But didn't the Reagan Revolution steer us in a new direction and vanquish our problems? The answer, to a great degree, is no. Instead, the great victory of the Reagan Revolution belongs to our myth of invincibility and our refusal to admit unpleasant choices, a victory that has created a dangerously skewed perception of current economic reality. During the 1980s, far from reversing the most disturbing trends of the 1970s, we have actually accelerated them by devoting an ever-shrinking share of national resources to productive investment. At the same time, we have managed to enjoy a consumption bacchanalia fueled by deficit spending and financed by capital inflows from abroad and cuts in investment at home. Far from renewing our savings habits or bolstering the "supply side" of our economy, the 1980s have turned out to be the most consumption-biased "demand-side" decade experienced by any major industrial country during the postwar era.

To be sure, our consumption ethos is not a problem confined to our federal government alone. It shapes our private decisions as individuals as well as our collective decisions as voters. In our personal and family lives, this ethos is reflected in our net private savings rate, which was already one of the lowest among industrial countries during the 1970s and which has fallen still lower during the 1980s. In 1987 our personal savings rate (at 3.8 percent of disposable income) was the lowest in forty years. But it is in our public lives, especially in the electoral judgments we pass on federal policy, that our consumption ethos has come to play an unprecedented role in allocating resources away from the future and toward the present.

Every economist from Adam Smith to Karl Marx has recognized the link between savings and investment on the one hand and productivity growth and future standards of living on the other. Similarly, every previous generation of Americans has implicitly understood that some significant portion of potential consumption must be deferred in order to create an endowment for the future. The point is painfully obvious, yet needs to be stressed: in both our public and private economic choices we are already shaping the world posterity will inherit in ways that few of us would argue are desirable.

The Problem of Entitlements

In the broadest sense, this book is about the long-term consequences of our consumption ethos. More specifically, its subject is federal entitlements—benefits paid automatically to "entitled" recipients by virtue of quasi-contracts between the government and its citizens. Entitlements reflect the "public" or "voter" side of our consumption ethos in its purest form. Almost by definition, they are designed to be consumed—rather than saved or invested—by those who receive them. This book will explain the role of entitlements in subsidizing private consumption and creating our structural budget deficits, and will explore the ways in which they threaten to undermine our hopes for posterity. In this and later chapters, we will describe how the major nonpoverty entitlement programs such as Social Security and Medicare, and the deficits and unfunded liabilities to which they have given rise, have brought about an unprecedented transfer of resources between generations—from the young to the old. In 1965 federal spending on disability and retirement programs plus interest on the federal debt together amounted to about *three-quarters* of what we spent on national defense; today, despite the much-discussed (and unsustainable) arms build-up during the Reagan years, it amounts to over *double* what we spend on national defense.

We will also learn that our entitlement programs were developed by New Deal and Great Society policymakers whose future-oriented social goals were formulated in an entirely different environment than the one prevailing today. Because the economic, demographic, and cultural assumptions underlying these public benefit programs have been betrayed by subsequent experience, they are failing in today's world to fulfill their most basic policy objectives, such as protecting the vulnerable and alleviating poverty, with which they are closely associated in popular U.S. mythology. Moreover, we will demonstrate that federal entitlement programs, as they are currently structured, will in future decades grow so large relative to our economy that they will be patently unsustainable no matter how they are financed.

Why is a reconsideration of our federal entitlement programs so very important? The *economic* reasons are straightforward: the large share of our Gross National Product that entitlements consume prevents us from investing in our most vital present and future public goals. They are a direct cause of our federal deficits, and thus "crowd out" investment in private capital markets. At the same time, they "crowd out" future-oriented and progressive programs from our government's public spending agenda. And their unfunded liabilities may even be one indirect cause of our woefully low private-sector savings rate, since to the extent that "entitled" individuals feel wealthier because they are counting on future benefits, they are inclined to consume a greater proportion of their personal income.

But there is a *moral* dimension to the entitlements problem as well. The purpose of the vast majority of federal benefit spending is not the elimination of poverty or the achievement of any other coherent public purpose. In 1986 only 15 percent of all federal entitlement benefits was targeted at the poor. The rest (about $396 billion in fiscal year 1986) went to those groups least likely to be poor. Above all, it went to older Americans—a group enjoying a higher per capita income than younger households and the lowest poverty rate of any age-group (less than 3 percent) when the calculation includes total benefit income.

In the next chapter, we will return to the popular myth that entitlement spending is directed to the needy. For the moment, let us emphasize that, far from harming the poor, reform of our vast middle- and upper-class entitlement programs is the prerequisite not only to achieving adequate levels of national savings and investment, but also to finding the resources to create a more adequate system of social welfare than we can now afford. In the 1980s, cuts in federal benefit programs have been almost entirely limited to that small fraction of entitlement spending explicitly targeted at Americans in poverty (chiefly Medicaid, Food Stamps, and Aid to Families with Dependent Children). The much larger nonpoverty entitlements that are the main subject of this book have, on the other hand, been left virtually untouched. It is time we question a public policy that taxes poor workers to provide subsidies to entitled beneficiaries regardless of their actual need, that favors the rich over the poor, and that rewards the present at the expense of the future.

Finally—even if we could sustain its near-term economic cost and overlook its moral ambiguities—our current system of entitlements *must eventually exact an insupportable price from savings and living standards in the next century.* Quite simply, there is no "muddling through." Between 1965 and 1986, federal spending on entitlements has grown from 5.3 percent to 11.1 percent of GNP. For the foreseeable future, the cost will continue to grow. By the year 2025—

as the last members of the Baby Boom generation enter retirement—the aging of our population, exploding health-care costs, and automatic cost-of-living indexing formulas may well drive that share up to about 20 percent of GNP, a sum nearly equal to the entire federal budget today. Meanwhile, outlays for Social Security and "Part A" of Medicare may alone consume 30 percent of each worker's taxable payroll (more than double today's share).

Sooner or later, such a massive and growing diversion of the nation's resources from younger workers toward consumption by older, "entitled" Americans will make the challenge of adequate savings insurmountable and the burden of inequity intolerable. Without reform, therefore, our current system of entitlements will hobble our productivity performance, act as a growing drag on living standards, foster generational strife, and, in time, diminish the leadership of the United States in world affairs.

Our Structural Deficit Economy

The full implications of our entitlements problem cannot be understood without reviewing what has happened to our economy in recent decades. In this section, we clarify the connection between budget deficits on the one hand and declining domestic investment and mounting foreign indebtedness on the other. Subsequently, we consider the historical reasons why we allowed our entitlements system to keep growing long after such growth became unaffordable; we refute the recent "supply-side" claim that strong economic growth in the 1980s will allow us to afford any likely level of entitlement spending; and finally, we examine more closely the growing role of entitlements in determining the overall composition of federal spending.

Over the course of the last generation, the United States has acquired a structural deficit economy, meaning that at no stage of the business cycle can we generate the amount of savings necessary for minimally adequate investment. Fifteen years ago when we began to move in this direction, we made do by investing a bit less. In the 1980s, we reached the point at which we simply could not function without savings imported from abroad. In 1986 the federal deficit consumed 92 percent of all net private-sector savings. As a result, nearly three-quarters of our net investment that year in housing and in business plant and equipment would not have occurred without dollars saved by foreigners.

To say that our growing addiction to federal borrowing lies near the root of our problem is not, of course, to say that all public borrowing is bad. To borrow is to defer the pain of bearing the cost for something—a choice which often makes sense. If we borrow to invest, for instance, we reasonably defer a cost so that it coincides with the expected benefits (college for a student; a harbor for a city). Or if we borrow to meet some catastrophe, we reasonably defer a cost in order to spread unusual pain over time and make it bearable (illness for a family; war for a nation).

Our current borrowing, however, meets neither criterion and offers us neither excuse. As for investment, the last couple of decades has seen not more, but *less* federal investment. Net real investment in public infrastructure—roads, bridges, mass transit, and other public works—has dropped by 75 percent since the late 1960s.* During the Reagan years in particular, investment in our environment and in human capital has also plummeted; from 1979 to 1986, real spending on natural resources has been cut by 24 percent, nondefense R&D by 25 percent, and aid to schools by 14 percent. And as for deferring unusual pain, what pain could we have possibly endured during a two-decade span in which federal entitlements (which almost exclusively represent consumption) grew by nearly 6 percentage points of GNP? Such growth is alone greater than the net sum we currently invest in all business plant and equipment, plus all civilian R&D, plus all public infrastructure.

Consider: thus far in the 1980s, our federal government has borrowed more (in inflation-adjusted dollars) than it did during the entire 1940s decade, a period in which our country fought a global war for national survival and purchased the infrastructure that raised us out of the worst economic depression in our history. All in all, the debt we inherit from the 1940s is a burden that today's young taxpayers can readily accept. But how will tomorrow's young taxpayers view the debt we are incurring during the 1980s? What memorable asset are we leaving behind? Alternatively, what great pain are we deferring—other than the pain of paying our own way?

---

*After a long series of recent studies that all came to the same conclusion—that the United States must soon invest much more in infrastructure just to maintain and replace what we have—it is worth noting the newly released report of the National Council on Public Works Improvement (of its five members, three were appointed by the Reagan administration). Citing "enormous problems that imperil future economic growth," the report issued an urgent call for increasing U.S. public works budgets by $45 billion *annually* by the year 2000.

The legacy of the 1980s, therefore, consists of mountainous liabilities, and little more, handed down to future decades. By the 1990s, servicing our domestic and international debts will threaten to consume a crippling share of our national resources. With federal budget deficits averaging 4.1 percent of GNP from 1980 to 1986, net interest payments on our national debt have already doubled as a share of total federal spending over the past half-dozen years—and are now equivalent to 80 percent of the federal government's total outlays for nondefense discretionary programs. And with foreign debt currently accumulating at an annual rate of 3.5 percent of GNP, even if the United States were to reverse the upward trend in its foreign borrowing next year and return to a current-account balance by the mid-1990s, our debt service payments would by then still be equivalent, as a share of exports, to those of many developing nations and on a par with Germany's reparations burden after World War I.

If Americans were great private savers, this massive public dissaving unmatched by public investment might have been affordable. In other words, the federal government might have been able to finance current levels of consumption through deficit spending without relying on a river of foreign capital to make up the domestic shortfall. But given our dearth of private savings, the "crowding out" effects of federal budgetary policy were inevitable. Over the same period in which we acquiesced in the crumbling of our public infrastructure, net private domestic investment has slipped from a feeble average of 6.9 percent of GNP in the 1970s to 4.7 percent of GNP in the 1980s, the weakest effort in our postwar history.* Meanwhile, productivity growth—always the ultimate determinant of living standards—dropped from an average of 0.8 percent yearly during the economically disastrous 1970s to 0.6 percent yearly during the "boom" of the 1980s.† In terms of international comparisons, these measures are even more revealing. In the 1980s, the U.S. investment rate has been the second-lowest in the industrialized world (just above Britain's); the U.S. productivity growth rate has been the absolute lowest.

In the wake of the stock-market panic, we have seen Wall Street and Capitol Hill turn their attention sporadically toward the dangers

---

*"Net" savings or investment means net of depreciation (see Notes).

†Productivity here and in Table 1-1 is real net national product per full-time equivalent worker (see Notes).

FIGURE 1-1   **Net Savings and Investment as a
Percent of GNP, 1965–87**

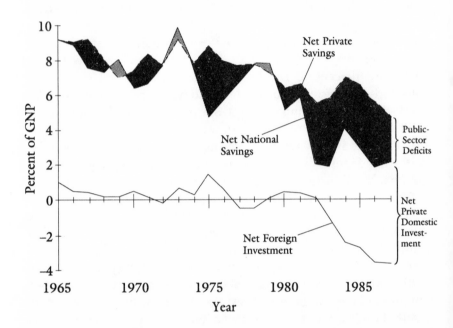

Source: BEA (Commerce)

posed by our twin deficits (budget and trade)—though the failure to
arrive at a political consensus on entitlements reform has thus far
prevented substantive progress toward a solution of our indebtedness
problem. In order to frame a workable solution, it is essential to realize
that we are indeed talking about different aspects of the same problem.
Policymakers abroad agree almost unanimously that our twin deficits
are closely linked. Only here at home do a significant number of
opinion leaders insist that the two deficits are separate issues, and that
they may not even be problems at all.

Perhaps the easiest way to appreciate the connection between our
budget and foreign trade deficits is to examine the historical data on
net U.S. savings and investment rates presented in Figure 1-1. The predictions of supply-side prophets notwithstanding, net private savings
in the United States has continued to decline in recent years (from 8.1

percent of GNP in the 1970s to 5.8 percent of GNP in the 1980s). Moreover, because the United States has been running huge budget deficits, net national savings (which equals net private savings minus public-sector dissavings) has dropped even more sharply (from 7.1 percent of GNP in the 1970s to 3.1 percent of GNP in the 1980s). Given our anemic net private savings rate, enormous inflows of foreign capital have thus proved inevitable. Without these funds it would have been impossible for the United States to finance its budget deficits while maintaining even minimally adequate levels of net domestic investment. The toll of our budget deficits is thus twofold: their financing both "crowds out" productive private-sector investment and "pulls in" foreign credit.

In terms of our balance of payments, capital inflows simply represent the flip side of our trade deficit. As long as we cannot function without dollars saved abroad, exchange rates will fluctuate or interest rates will go up until we can attract those dollars back as loans. And the only means for foreigners to obtain the dollars they lend us is to sell us more than they buy from us. Viewed in another way, America runs a trade deficit because it buys more than it produces (which is yet another manifestation of our pervasive consumption ethos). Dollars that flow abroad to purchase imports always flow back; the only question is whether they will buy our goods and services or our IOUs. During the 1980s, we have decided that our biggest export would be IOUs.

The magnitude of our current payments imbalance is unprecedented. Back in the early 1970s, the industrial world still accepted the basics of the Bretton Woods agreement: fixed exchange rates and relatively little mobility of capital between nations. But the problem with fixed exchange rates (or so thought a growing number of experts at the time) is that they did not allow us the "freedom" to determine our own macroeconomic fate. So we closed the gold window in 1971 and shook ourselves entirely loose from fixed currency parities by 1975. By the late 1970s and early 1980s, as the dollar heaved up and down in ever-larger waves, the global financial community accommodated our proud creation, the "float," by greatly liberalizing the flow of capital across borders. The result is that every nation—especially the United States, as owner of the world's reserve currency—now has much greater latitude to borrow as it pleases abroad, with few restrictions other than the specter of national bankruptcy in the mind of the creditor. Fifteen years ago, a U.S. current-account deficit (in other words, a capital inflow) of 3.5 percent of GNP would have created a national emergency. In 1987 it created, well, nothing really. It was a number you could read about toward the end of the business news section.

In time, as we have pointed out elsewhere, America must change its course.* Since our indebtedness cannot grow indefinitely as a share of our GNP—at some point foreign creditors will regard us as a growing credit risk that must be compensated for by prohibitively high interest rates—our current-account deficit must in the end decline substantially. In fact, sometime over the course of the next decade it is almost inevitable that the United States will be constrained to become a net exporter of goods and services in order to service its foreign debt. To say that the United States will have to correct its current-account imbalance is equivalent to saying that we will have to make an enormous shift from consumption to savings—a painful process that will likely repeal the huge increase in real per-worker disposable income that we have enjoyed in the 1980s.

But if the shift itself is inevitable, how it will happen is still an open question. If we continue our present course and simply hope we will somehow emerge unscathed, we will at best trade excessive borrowing abroad for even lower levels of investment here at home—with paralyzing consequences for our long-term economic growth. Then again, a very late but sudden shift could throw the world economy into serious stagflation, either by generating (or merely threatening) a series of trade-led recessions in other industrial countries or by precipitating a series of debt defaults among the less-developed countries (starting with those most dependent upon our consumption of their exports).† Such a "crash" could also—though this is by no means inevitable—result in a major U.S. depression and a bleak future in which we would have to pay off our debts through indefinite impoverishment. These scenarios underscore the need for close coordination of international policy during the difficult transition period that lies ahead. They should also persuade us to make fundamental and lasting changes in the direction of our domestic economic policies, away from consumption and toward savings, as soon as possible.

One clear way of illustrating our overconsumption problem is to

---

*In "The Morning After," *The Atlantic Monthly* (October 1987).

†The less-developed economies today are sustained almost singlehandedly by American consumption; in 1986, 63 percent of their manufactured exports came to the United States.

TABLE 1-1   **Average Real Yearly Increases in Net National Product per U.S. Worker, in 1986 Dollars**

	1950s (1949–59)	1960s (1959–69)	1970s (1969–79)	1980s (1979–86)
Total Net National Product	+$576	+$552	+$256	+$218
Less				
Net Private Domestic Investment	+82	+52	+32	−124
Net Foreign Investment	−15	+12	−3	−200
Equals				
Total Resources Available for Consumption	+$509	+$488	+$227	+$541
Of which:				
Personal Consumption	+307	+314	+254	+375
(Privately Funded)	+226	+208	+105	+215
(Publicly Funded)	+81	+208	+105	+215
(Publicly Funded)	+81	+106	+149	+160
Government Purchases[1]	+202	+174	−27	+166
Additional Per-Worker Consumption as Percent of Additional Per-Worker Product	88%	88%	89%	248%

[1]Including defense, which from an *economic* perspective must be considered "consumption."
Source: BEA (Commerce) and authors' calculations (see Notes)

compare increases in real net national product per worker—a fundamental measure of our economic productivity—with increases in real consumption per worker. As Table 1-1 shows, between 1979 and 1986 real per-worker product increased by only $218 yearly, or by 79 percent of the annual rate in the 1970s and a mere 28 percent of the rate in the 1950s and 1960s. At the same time, however, real per-worker consumption climbed by fully $541 yearly. What happened during the 1980s therefore has no precedent. Here we see a large, absolute decline in investment—both at home (by $124 yearly per worker) and abroad (by $200 yearly per worker). The result is a totally disproportionate increase in the resources available for consumption. In every other decade (see Figure 1-2 and the last line of Table 1-1), we consumed slightly less than 90 percent of our increase in production; since the beginning of the 1980s, we have consumed 248 percent of it, and the extra 148 percent has been reflected in shrinking per-worker net assets abroad and a smaller net investment in plant and equipment at home. This is how we managed to create a make-believe

51

FIGURE 1-2   **Average Annual Change in Real Production and Consumption per U.S. Worker, in 1986 Dollars**

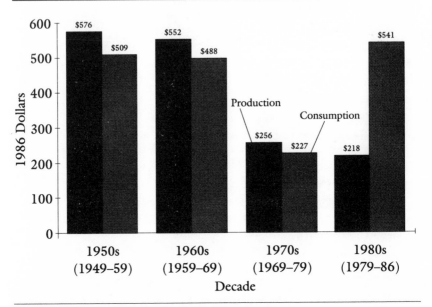

Source: BEA (Commerce) and authors' calculations (see Notes)

1960s all over again, a decade of "feeling good" and "having it all," without the bother of actually producing it.

Reagan was right in his debates with Carter: the 1970s *were* tough in comparison with the 1960s. He was also right in observing that lower productivity growth and higher public benefit spending during the 1970s "squeezed out" defense spending and privately earned consumption.What looks quite significant in retrospect, however, is that at least the squeezing did in fact take place. Few Americans watching those debates ever imagined that we would simply ignore the law that limits consumption to production. During the 1980s, with smaller yearly increases in production per employed American, we have managed huge leaps forward in every type of consumption: in privately earned consumption, in "600-ship navy" consumption (defense spending is included in Table 1-1 as "government purchases"), and in publicly funded consumption. This last type of consumption is also known as "entitlements"; it is, significantly, the only type that has been rising ever faster during each of the last four decades.

Deficit spending has of course been the primary catalyst for this consumption binge, both by allowing private households greater after-tax purchasing power and by allowing the government to ignore the limits imposed by its own tax revenue. (Of the 1980s increase in total per-worker consumption, well over half is attributable to defense and entitlements.) Government policy seems to have replaced the reviled "tax and spend" motto of the 1970s with a new motto, "borrow and spend." Behind the pleasurable observation that real U.S. consumption per worker has risen by $3,800 between 1979 and 1986—and this is the real cause of much of the 1980s optimism—lies the unpleasant reality that only $1,500 of this extra annual consumption has been paid for by growth in what each of us produces; the other $2,300 has been funded by cuts in domestic investment and a widening river of foreign debt. It is impossible to continue consuming indefinitely in this manner. The longer we remain on our current economic course, the bleaker the prospects for posterity will become.

Future Generations and the American Dream

Ever since the Enlightenment, Western societies have judged themselves according to their success in advancing the general level of civilization from generation to generation. With the rise of the middle class and the coming of the Industrial Revolution, this uniquely Western notion of progress became inextricably linked to the expectation that the level of material culture—or "standard of living," to use the economic term—would rise steadily over time. More than any other Western country, America was a creation of the Enlightenment and the Industrial Revolution—and its middle-class ethos, loosely embodied in the American Dream, has always been rooted in the belief that each succeeding generation will be better off than the previous one. Over the course of American history, this expectation has repeatedly been fulfilled by rising living standards that have approximately doubled every other generation.

We did especially well, of course, in the two decades or so following World War II. The war had left the economies of our competitors devastated, while the United States emerged from it with its productive capacity unscathed. To the United States fell the task of reconstruction. We easily funded the Marshall Plan, dominated the free world's industries, and assumed the mantle of world leadership as the "arsenal of democracy." Our successes abroad were closely linked to the rapid expansion of our domestic economy. During the 1950s and

1960s, real take-home pay increased at a yearly rate of 2.5 percent, while our productivity growth rate averaged 2.3 percent. In the span of twenty years, real GNP doubled and real per capita GNP rose by 50 percent. By the mid-1960s, the expectation that seemingly effortless economic growth would continue indefinitely had become an unspoken article of national faith.

Then we faltered.

Although it is the failed policies of the 1980s that have finally pushed our economy up against the fundamental equation linking long-term economic outputs with long-term economic inputs, we all recall that the prospects for the American Dream were already grim when Ronald Reagan assumed office in 1981. After all, it was during the course of the 1970s—not the 1980s—that the engine that had been driving U.S. economic growth since World War II first stalled. Between 1969 and 1979, real net national product per fully employed person rose at an annual rate of 0.8 percent, compared with a rate of 1.9 percent in the 1960s and 2.5 percent in the 1950s. By 1973 average real weekly earnings had reached their postwar peak; through the rest of the 1970s the trend was downward. The assumption on which the American Dream was based, that standards of living would increase dramatically with each passing generation, had been shattered.

What went wrong? Perhaps the word "hubris" sums it up best. During the course of those boom years, Americans gradually came to assume that any combination of national objectives could be achieved without straining our economy—that our resources were limitless and future prosperity assured. Without raising taxes or otherwise moderating the rapid growth in private household consumption, we believed we could still afford to fight a major war in Asia, rebuild our cities, cure age-old diseases, fly to the moon, and—most fatefully in terms of cost—reallocate wealth through public benefits to achieve a bewildering variety of national objectives. Some of these objectives represented expansions of old goals, such as the further protection of the elderly through the addition of Medicare to the original Social Security system; others represented entirely new goals, such as the alleviation of poverty through the establishment of Medicaid and Food Stamps. Between 1962 and 1972, we tripled real spending on federal entitlements without making any compensating cuts in real defense outlays. But over the same period, because our economy was still growing rapidly, total federal spending only climbed from 19.2 percent to 20.0 percent of GNP.

54

In retrospect, it seems amazing that we accomplished so much. The spirit of that era of limitless expectations is best embodied in the slogans of the times: John F. Kennedy's "Pay any price" and Lyndon B. Johnson's "Guns and butter."

During the 1970s, however, the cumulative effects of this publicly engineered reallocation of national resources—exacerbated by our consumption-biased tax code and a series of unexpected external shocks (the energy crisis, double-digit inflation, and an overall slide in world economic growth)—inevitably slowed the engine that had been driving our economy. After the early 1970s, although our GNP continued to grow briskly due to a huge expansion in the work force, growth in productivity slowed to a standstill and workers experienced an utter stagnation in real wage growth. At the same time, federal entitlement spending, placed on automatic pilot, increased from under 7.0 percent of GNP in 1970 to 9.5 percent of GNP in 1979; as a share of federal budget outlays, it grew from 34 percent to 46 percent. By the close of the 1970s, it was clear to many Americans that—wittingly or not—we had acquiesced in the creation of a political economy that devoted too little of its energy to producing wealth, while lavishing too much attention on devising creative means for its consumption.

Ronald Reagan's landslide election in 1980—it hardly needs to be pointed out—was largely the result of widespread discontent with U.S. economic performance in the 1970s. After a decade of shattered expectations, most Americans seemed ready to endorse a program of national renewal. The radical centerpiece of this program was of course the 1981 supply-side tax cut, whose stimulative effects were supposed to boost savings and investment, promote rapid economic growth, and at the same time generate increased federal revenues. We were promised a high-savings, high-productivity, highly competitive economy, with balanced budgets and trade surpluses. Instead we were given a consumption boom financed by foreign borrowing and cuts in private investment, with debt-financed hikes in public spending and huge balance-of-payments deficits. In the finest tradition of Euripidean irony, measures meant to save us have in the end worked to afflict us. They fueled, rather than dampened, our underlying urge to overconsume.

Ultimately, such a course must lead from purely economic or "smokestack" pathologies—with symptoms such as our inadequate investment in plant, equipment, infrastructure, and R&D—to social

FIGURE 1–3   **Average Annual Change in Real Median Family Income by Age of Householder, 1955–86**

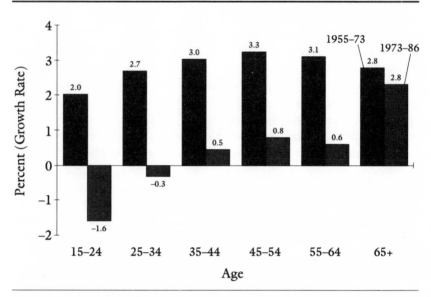

Self-reported, pretax cash income.

Source: Current Population Reports (Series P-60, Census)

or "flesh and blood" pathologies whose symptoms show up in the manifest hardships we are passing on to our children. Quite simply, a society that turns away from its economic future is very likely a society that treats its younger members worse than its older members. One reason is that treating younger members well is what looking toward the future is all about—youth being any society's most important investment. Perhaps another reason is that stagnating living standards naturally prompt older members to try to defend their economic expectations by protecting their own income growth and letting the burden fall on those who come after. Unfortunately, this can only be a one-shot solution. It sets up the next generation for a vicious circle of declining opportunities: poorer young families, which means fewer and less productive children, which darkens still further the prospects of all succeeding generations.

We may already be entering such a dark cycle. It is sobering, for instance, to consider the evidence in Figure 1-3, which reveals how the dramatic slowdown in the growth of living standards since the early

1970s has masked a vast disparity in the trends for different age-groups. The elderly, at one extreme, have hardly been affected—thanks in large part to an extraordinary growth in federal entitlement income; this income now makes up nearly 60 percent of all federal benefits, or an average of $12,000 per elderly household. Their real median family income has risen by more than a third since 1973. Working-age adults, in turn, have done less well, with the real family incomes of older adults (aged forty-five to sixty-four) just keeping up with inflation and the family incomes of younger workers (especially under thirty-five) falling far behind it.

The media obsession with affluent "yuppies" notwithstanding, younger workers have experienced substantial deterioration of their economic well-being during the 1970s and 1980s.* Much of this deterioration is not measurable by standard "take-home" pay measures, since it involves cuts in vital noncash health-insurance and pension-plan benefits—due to practices that implicitly discriminate against the young, such as "two-tier" job classifications and the rising use of "temps" and contracted help.† But even a direct comparison of take-home earnings for workers at different ages shows that the overall trend has been unmistakably negative. Twenty years ago the median full-time wage of a young man under age twenty-five was 74 percent of the median for working men aged twenty-five and over; today it is 51 percent and dropping. A similar decline has occurred for young working women (see Figure 1-4).

One dramatic symptom of the downward economic mobility of younger families has been the sharp decline in their rate of home ownership. During the 1980s alone, for instance, the share of all householders aged 36 to 40 who own their own home has declined from 71 to 64 percent; of householders aged 31 to 35, from 63 to 53 percent; of householders aged 26 to 30, from 43 to 36 percent.‡

*The fabled "yuppie" world of BMWs and Bermuda vacations does exist, but one must look carefully at the Census data to find it. Of the 76.1 million persons aged 20 through 39 who worked in 1986, 37.6 million (or 49 percent) had total pretax incomes of less than $12,500; only 2.2 million (less than 3 percent) had total pretax incomes of $50,000 or more.

†Virtually unknown before the 1980s, explicit two-tier contracts (which pay new workers less than current workers for the same job) now comprise an estimated 15 to 20 percent of all wage settlements with nonmanufacturing firms. In certain sectors, the figure is much higher (70 percent in the airline industry, for example). Meanwhile, it is generally agreed that a rising (though unknown) share of all young workers are "temping" full time—that is, working on a piece-work cash basis without benefits.

‡Reliable data by age before 1980 do not exist. It is believed that home-ownership rates for young families peaked sometime in the mid-1970s.

FIGURE 1-4   Median Weekly Earnings of Full-Time
              Workers Aged 18 to 24 as a Percent of
              Median for All Older Workers

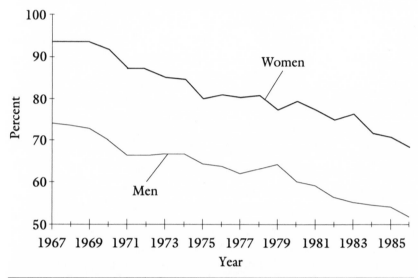

Data for month of May used for 1967–78; annual data for 1979–85; third quarter for 1986.
Source: Weekly Earnings of Wage and Salary Workers (BLS, Labor)

(Meanwhile, the home-ownership rate for all elderly households has continued to *rise* slightly, from 73 to 75 percent.) Young families looking for homes today are constrained not only by lower real incomes, but by much higher real interest rates (reflecting our new age of capital scarcity). For the typical couple at age thirty, the after-tax cost of financing a typical starter home amounted to about 30 percent of income in 1987—up from 20 percent in the 1960s and under 15 percent in the late 1940s. Unlike the days of Levittown, when most home sales were to first-home buyers, the vast majority of home purchases today involve older couples buying and selling their second, third, or fourth residence.

Another far more painful symptom has been the resurgence in poverty among young families, which has in turn caused an unprecedented rise in the poverty rates for children. Again, as we can see in Figure 1-5, the trends for our youngest and oldest Americans are headed in opposite directions. The official poverty rate for children, which reached a low in the early 1970s, is now back about where it was in the mid-1960s before our "war on poverty" got started.

FIGURE 1-5   **Official U.S. Poverty Rates for the
Elderly (Aged 65 and Over) and Children
(Under Age 18), 1959–86**

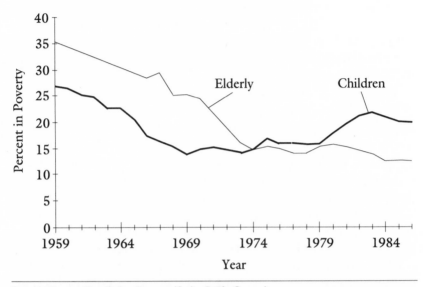

Source: Current Population Reports (Series P-60, Census)

Meanwhile, the official poverty rate for the elderly has continued to decline almost without interruption. In 1974 it dropped beneath the rate for children for the first time since "poverty" had been measured (and undoubtedly for the first time in our nation's history). Today, an American under age eighteen is 60 percent more likely to be poor than an American over age sixty-five.*

Since the trends depicted in Figures 1-3 and 1-4 reflect income before taxes, it is worth noting that the disparity between working-age and retirement-age households would be larger still if the Census Bureau measured income after taxes. Needless to say, the great rise in tax rates for most households over the past two decades has fallen disproportionately on wage-earning families. This is especially true for Social Security payroll taxes, which represent a direct income transfer from young to old. In the late 1950s, very few wage earners regarded them as a significant burden. By the late 1970s, however, *half* of all

---

*As we will see in Chapter 2, these "official" poverty rates considerably understate the actual difference between the young and old.

covered workers were paying more in Federal Insurance Contributions Act taxes (employer and employee contributions combined) than in federal income taxes. And in 1988, with the enactment of another FICA rate hike, the Brookings Institution calculates that this share has now risen to *three-quarters* of all covered workers.* Being a regressive, flat-rate tax, FICA hits the lower-income (and younger) workers hardest. Thus, among parents under age thirty-five, it is estimated that *at least nine out of ten* now pay more in FICA taxes than in federal income taxes.

What is truly ominous about this decline in real incomes for younger families is that it has occurred despite a massive shift of married women from the household economy to the market economy—a shift young families view increasingly as a necessity rather than an option. Since the mid-1960s, the share of all married women with children who are in the labor force has grown from one-fifth to nearly two-thirds (see Figure 1-6).

Not surprisingly, the same period has seen a visible weakening in every type of security and nurturing—economic, familial, and emotional—once considered necessary for a child's development. When we talk about children today, we therefore refer to a laundry list of pathologies as diverse as the hardships they suffer: not just overburdened teachers and rising poverty rates, but problems of suicide, drugs, "latchkey" kids, abuse, teenage pregnancy, absent fathers, emotional depression, inadequate discipline, and inner-city welfare dependency. This is especially true when we talk about minority children, who will constitute between 30 and 40 percent of all new entrants into the labor force by early in the twenty-first century. Today, more than 40 percent of black and Hispanic children are in poverty; 60 percent of black children live in broken homes; and last year 75 percent of all black infants were born to unwed mothers (of these, half were to teenagers). We all like to talk about building a competitive economy, but few of us like to talk about how we can build one with an uncompetitive work force—one in which one-third of all teenagers entering are deemed "functionally illiterate."†

---

*In *Federal Tax Policy* (5th ed.) by Joseph A. Pechman (Brookings Institution, 1987). In 1988, it is estimated that the FICA payroll tax will exceed the federal income tax for working single persons with incomes beneath $28,555; for working married couples with incomes beneath $47,013; and for working married couples with two children with incomes beneath $50,913. In 1990, when the FICA tax is scheduled for another hike, the share will jump even higher.

†See *Children in Need: Investment Strategies for the Educationally Disadvantaged* (Committee for Economic Development, 1987).

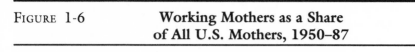

FIGURE 1-6   **Working Mothers as a Share of All U.S. Mothers, 1950–87**

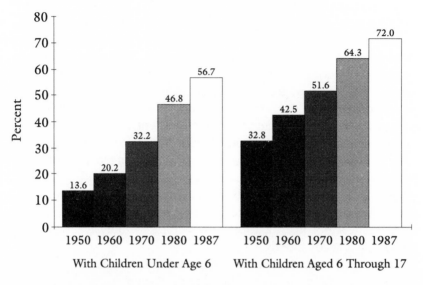

Including married, divorced, and separated mothers; not including never-married mothers.
Source: Current Population Surveys (BLS, Labor)

The shift of adult parents from the home economy to the market economy may therefore represent just one more way of passing liabilities down the generational chain. The advantages of this shift are already evident in our income statistics. The disadvantages have yet to be witnessed, but may include not only the diminished productivity of our children, but perhaps as well the need to create further unfunded public entitlements (such as day care or long-term care) to fill the vacuum left behind.

If so, we are witnessing how adults of all ages find ways to protect their economic expectations. Retirees can pass the burden on to workers, older workers can pass it on to younger workers, and young parents can ultimately join the rest of us in passing it on to children. Opinion surveys indicate, as we might expect, that no one *personally* likes what is happening. The elderly are mortified to think they may be a burden on their adult children, and parents agonize over how they can do better for their kids. But what we feel personally and how we feel compelled to act collectively do not always match. The vast

61

majority of Baby Boomers, for instance, confide to pollsters that having a parent at home is "better" for children,* but only one out of every five Baby-Boom families with kids has a stay-at-home parent.

To be sure, no one can fairly blame all social or economic afflictions affecting individual age-groups on federal policy. We can, however, be realistic in assessing how current trends may be worsened by further intergenerational income transfers, engineered largely through entitlement spending and financed by domestic disinvestment and international dissaving. By the year 2000, it is quite possible that America will be constrained to produce and sell $1.30 worth of exports for every $1.00 we import just to meet our debt service payments to foreign creditors. It is also possible that we may be constrained to raise $1.30 in federal tax revenue for every $1.00 of federal money we spend—excluding interest—just to meet our debt service payments to affluent (and older) Treasury bondholders. If so, the economic welfare of young families will decline even further—with unfortunate consequences not just for tomorrow's children, but, eventually, for tomorrow's needy elderly.

In the final analysis, much of the blame for our current debacle lies not in some mysterious economic ailment. Rather, it lies in the failure of our political institutions to cope with the difficult trade-offs between the long-term health of the U.S. economy and the consumption-oriented benefits owed current entitled constituencies. As the bleakness of the long-term U.S. economic outlook became increasingly apparent during the 1970s, the logical course would have been to designate the 1980s a decade in which we would allocate fewer resources toward consumption and increase the share of our national product to be invested in productive physical and human capital. To give the Reagan administration its due, such an outcome was at least the intent of the supply-side revolution. Unfortunately, when it became obvious that the supply-side experiment had failed, a shameful lack of fiscal and political resolve in both the White House and Congress, coupled with unrealistic expectations, allowed us to continue blindly on a course toward the wrong future.

Whatever Happened to "Morning in America"?

Despite the obvious imbalances in our economy—as well as the less apparent symptoms of underlying stagnation—the prevailing national

---

*See, for instance, the recent poll of Baby Boomers in *Rolling Stone* (March 22 and April 19, 1988).

mood throughout the 1980s has been one of renewed optimism about the future. After all, the American economic landscape seems to be bursting with new jobs, new businesses, and a dynamic entrepreneurial spirit. The double-digit inflation of the 1970s has been decisively tamed; and, once the severe recession of 1982 was weathered, corporate profits have climbed, the unemployment rate has declined, and interest rates have moderated. Americans are enjoying the benefits of a steep rise in real consumption per household, and at least until Black Monday, investors were basking in Dow-Jones euphoria. To the casual observer, it might seem as if the economic "malaise" that plagued the United States throughout the 1970s has been cured.

As we have seen, little could be further from the truth.

Perhaps the most frequent defense of our recent economic performance is that the U.S. economy in the present decade has grown "as fast as" or "faster than" the collective economy of the rest of the industrial world. So far as it goes, this assertion is correct. From 1979 through 1986, our real GNP grew at an annual rate of 2.1 percent—about the same yearly growth rate as that of the collective GNP of all other industrial nations. In the United States, however, most of the growth (70 percent) was due to increases in the number of workers, while in the other countries most of the growth (85 percent) was due to increases in output per worker.* Our way of augmenting production, in other words, is by adding more working bodies (what classical economists used to call the "dismal" Asian model). It does not raise our standard of living. Only augmenting production per worker does that, and the European and Japanese economies remain far more successful in this respect than our own.

Is it wrong to take pride in being the "world's greatest job machine"?† Not entirely. To the extent that our achievement has been

---

*This is equivalent to saying, as we pointed out earlier, that productivity growth in the other industrial countries has exceeded our own during the 1980s. At the beginning of the decade, according to the Bureau of Labor Statistics, GNP per worker in the other "Big Seven" countries (Japan, Canada, West Germany, France, Italy, and Britain) averaged 71 percent of the U.S. level; by 1986 it had climbed to 76 percent (see Notes).

†Even here our performance in the 1980s cannot match that of the 1970s. The number of full-time equivalent jobs (as defined by the Bureau of Economic Analysis, Commerce Department) climbed, on average, by 1.7 million yearly from 1969 to 1979; it climbed by 2.0 million yearly from 1973 to 1979—an especially bad period for productivity growth. From 1979 through 1986, on the other hand, the number has climbed by 1.3 million yearly. The numerical impact of the Baby Boom and more working women is already subsiding.

due to lower unemployment rates than those abroad, we can thank the flexibility of our relatively open and unregulated labor markets. (This is a welcome reversal from the early 1970s: high structural unemployment is now *their* problem, not ours.) Yet we also must understand that the dominant reason for our job record is not our superiority in finding jobs for all of those seeking them, but rather the huge net growth in the number of Americans looking for work. This, in turn, has been due to two facts: the demographic fact that we gave birth some thirty years ago to by far the world's largest baby boom (hardly an economic achievement), and the social fact that an ever-larger share of women are entering the labor force (a trend that, to the extent it is compelled by marital separation or financial necessity, might well be viewed with concern). In any event, neither fact can work in our favor much longer. The youngest members of the Baby Boom will be fully employed by the early 1990s at the latest—at which point a "baby bust" generation will throw our job demographics into reverse. And the share of women seeking work obviously cannot rise forever.

Indeed, what is most disturbing is what did *not* happen during our great recent job boom. The employment of the largest and best-educated generation in the history of the industrial nations should have caused U.S. GNP to rise far faster than GNP in any other country—as it should also have pushed up our savings rate, since presumably this new generation of workers would want to allocate some share of extra production to provide for their children and their own retirement (as the Baby Boom becomes the Senior Boom). We are still one of the youngest industrial societies and should be taking advantage of this "Indian summer" to prepare for the inevitable aging of the U.S. population. Instead, we have barely managed to keep pace with the GNPs of our competitors, and our savings rate has declined. This is not success, but rather a large-scale failure.

How have these foreign economies managed to engineer their higher rates of productivity growth? The most apparent factor has been much higher investment levels. The comparison shown in Figure 1-7 needs little elaboration. We can see that the United States has always had a relatively low rate of savings and investment, even in the 1950s and 1960s (when we still believed that other countries were catching up to us through "postwar reconstruction"). What has changed in the 1970s and 1980s is that savings and investment rates have declined proportionately throughout the industrial world. Abroad, this decline has been accompanied by a somewhat slower

FIGURE 1-7 **Net National Savings and Investment as a Percent of GNP, Average Annual Rate per Period, 1960–79 and 1980–87**

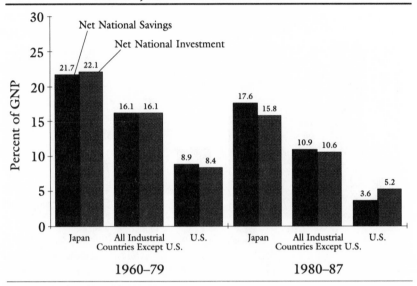

Including both public and private sectors.

Source: National Accounts (OECD, Paris)

productivity growth. In the United States, it has been accompanied by a near halt in productivity growth, and ultimately—in the 1980s—by the need for foreign credit to fill a wide and growing gap between how much we save and how much we invest.

Although the United States remains the poorest investor in both the private and public sectors, Figure 1-8 shows that our latter performance has been especially abysmal. As a share of GNP, Japan invests ten times more than the United States in public infrastructure; the other "Big Seven" nations invest between four and six times as much. The United States is the only industrial country in which the per-worker net stock of public works has actually been declining over the past decade. Americans should not wonder why our public buildings, roads, bridges, harbors, and waterways look increasingly decrepit compared with public facilities abroad, nor why new breakthroughs in infrastructure technology, from magnetically powered trains to undersea tunnels, never seem to make it to this country. We do not have them because we have chosen not to pay for them. Abroad there

FIGURE 1-8   **Net Public-Sector Investment as a Percent of GNP, Average Annual Rate, 1971–84**

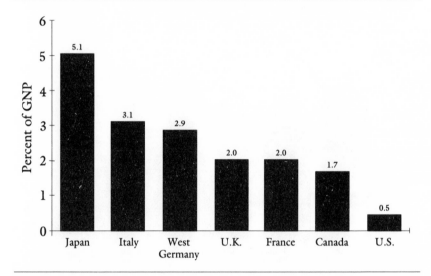

Not including state-owned businesses.
Source: National Accounts (OECD, Paris)

is a working political consensus that—whatever else might happen economically from year to year—investment in every form is a fundamental prerequisite to growth in the standard of living over the long haul. In America, we do not have such a consensus.

The comparison between Japan and the United States, respectively the savings leader and the savings laggard of the industrial world, is both dramatic and instructive (see Figure 1-9). From the 1960s to the 1980s, to be sure, Japan's total net investment rate (for both the private and public sectors) has fallen from about 23 to 16 percent of GNP. The latter figure, however, is still more than three times larger than the equivalent figure for the United States during the 1980s (5.2 percent of GNP). Japanese net investment in 1986 (at that year's exchange rates) amounted to $285 billion, while U.S. net investment amounted to only $240 billion. It is a spectacle that ought to shock Americans: a population half the size of our own, living on a group of islands the size of California, is adding more each year to their stock of factories, bridges, and laboratories—in absolute terms—than we are to ours. And Japan still has savings left over, about $75 billion in

FIGURE 1-9   **Net National Savings and Investment as a Percent of GNP, U.S. and Japan, 1960–87**

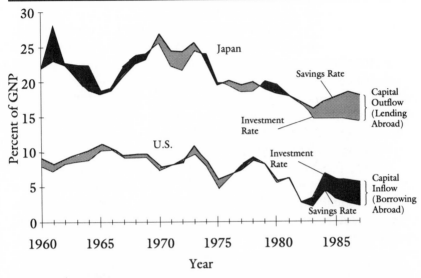

Including both public and private sectors.
Source: National Accounts (OECD, Paris)

1986, to lend to thriftless foreigners. (About $50 billion of that sum was lent to us.) Between the two countries, therefore, the 1986 disparity in net savings ($360 billion in Japan versus only $105 billion in the United States, a 7-to-1 per capita difference) was even more lopsided.

Another misguided defense of the U.S. economic record during the 1980s is the argument that our heavy foreign borrowing is actually a sign of economic strength. Alan Reynolds, the supply-side guru, has compared our huge current-account deficit today to Japan's big trade deficits in the 1950s, claiming that what the two situations clearly have in common is buoyant growth expectations.*

The argument is half right. Japan was a capital importer during the 1950s, since it was a rapidly growing economy and was literally reconstructing itself after a war that had largely wiped out its industrial base. It borrowed abroad to finance a higher investment level than would have been possible by relying on its already hefty savings rate

*"Growing Away from Large Deficits" by Alan Reynolds, *The Wall Street Journal* (March 5, 1987).

alone. Such capital inflows made sense because they rapidly paid for themselves in increased economic output. From 1950 to 1960, the Japanese economy grew at an average real rate of nearly 10.0 percent a year; real net output per worker grew at the extraordinary rate of 6.6 percent a year. The parallel between the United States and Japan, however, is hard to fathom. Here in the United States, over the course of the 1980s, the growth rate in real output per worker (at 0.6 percent a year) has been less than *one-tenth* of what the Japanese were experiencing thirty years ago. Japanese productivity in the 1950s, in other words, grew more in eleven months than ours now grows over ten years. One reason for such an astounding difference is that the Japanese were borrowing to invest, while we are borrowing to consume.

To find a proper parallel for our current situation, we should look neither to Japan in the 1950s, nor to America in the 1870s (when we became a capital importer in order to finance our huge investment in railroads and heavy industry), but rather to those rare historical occasions when an economy's large size, its world-class currency, and its open capital markets have allowed it to borrow immense sums primarily for the purpose of consumption and without regard to productive return. The illustrations of lumbering, deficit-hobbled, low-growth economies that come most easily to mind are Spain in the late sixteenth century, France in the 1780s, and Britain in the 1920s.

In the case of Imperial Spain, history records that the Hapsburg throne borrowed such sums from foreigners that shipments of gold from the New World were entirely signed over to northern European bankers years before they actually arrived at Seville. In the case of America today, we have our industrial and financial assets to sign over. An estimated 6 percent of the total net worth of the United States is now owned by foreigners—a level growing at more than one percentage point per year. Ten percent of the federal debt is now in the hands of foreign creditors, and by 1990 one out of every ten U.S. manufacturing workers will report to a foreign employer. We find today that a growing number of familiar domestic trademarks and landmarks belong to owners abroad—from RCA television sets and CBS Records to Firestone and Carnation, from Brooks Brothers and Bloomingdale's to United Press International and J. Walter Thompson, from New York's Exxon building to the choicest real estate in Waikiki. Japan now owns the world's ten largest banks, five of the ten largest commercial banks in California, and significant shares of the largest and fastest-growing investment banks in New York.

Americans are understandably confused and troubled by these trends. One recent poll indicates that three-quarters of the American public is in favor of legal barriers "to limit the extent of foreign investment in American business and real estate."* But the effect of such laws would be like treating a fever with an ice bath: they would attack the symptoms, not the illness itself. Foreign capital flows to the United States because the real (inflation-adjusted) return on U.S. assets is higher here than abroad; our return is higher because our economy is starved for investment; and we lack investment because we do not save enough. Without foreign capital, we would face even higher real interest rates and we would have to make do with even less investment.† To work for a foreign-owned factory may be unpopular in the abstract. But to have no factory at all to work for is hardly preferable to the workers in question.

In the end, all economic and political policies must be judged by their ability to secure a better future. No matter what objective measure we choose as a yardstick, there is cause for grave concern that recent U.S. public policy has failed in this respect. We have already seen that savings, investment, and productivity growth rates have all continued to decline during the 1980s. And we have also noted that poverty rates among children are now the highest for any age-group and that the living standards of young families have been falling for nearly two decades. There is no denying, of course, the genuine accomplishments of the Reagan Revolution: taming inflation, renewing the popularity of markets and entrepreneurial risk, and eliminating the worst vices of regulation. But as far as the basic allocation of our economic resources is concerned, the trends of the 1980s do not bode well for posterity.

Entitlements and Our National Balance Sheet

Exactly how do entitlements fit into this picture? Until fifteen years ago, most federal spending was discretionary and unindexed to inflation, and federal tax policy still functioned under the very strong presumption that federal dollars spent should be paid for out of

---

*Conducted by the Washington, D.C., firm of Smick-Medley & Associates in January 1988.

†A typical estimate made by Scott E. Pardee, vice chairman of Yamaichi International (and former senior Federal Reserve Board official) is that—without Japanese purchases of U.S. Treasury debt during 1987—the interest rates on all long-term U.S. securities would have been at least one-quarter of one percent higher.

TABLE 1-2   **Federal Outlays by General Function as a Percent of GNP, Fiscal Years 1965–86**

	1965	1979	Change 1965–79	1986	Change 1979–86
Total Outlays	17.56%	20.52%	+2.96%	23.63%	+3.11%
Entitlements	5.29	9.50	+4.21	11.13	+1.63
Defense	7.51	4.74	−2.77	6.53	+1.78
Nondefense Discretionary minus Offset[1]	3.49	4.54	+1.06	2.73	−1.81
Net Interest	1.28	1.74	+0.46	3.25	+1.51
Memo: Entitlements plus Interest	6.57%	11.24%	+4.67%	14.37%	+3.13%
Total Income	17.34%	18.89%	+1.55%	18.35%	−0.53%
Balance	(0.22%)	(1.63%)	−1.41%	(5.27%)	−3.64%

[1]Offset refers to "offsetting receipts"—special types of income (such as civil service payroll contributions and royalties for oil-drilling rights) that the federal budget counts as negative outlays rather than revenue.

Source: CBO and OMB

revenue. This was as true for Social Security and the newly created Medicare and Medicaid programs as it was for the defense budget. Large deficits, therefore, were difficult to achieve, because so many easy corrective options were available, both in spending and in taxing. The spending rule was first eliminated in the early 1970s by our decision to transform most nonpoverty benefit programs into untouchable and inflation-proof entitlements. The taxing rule was then eliminated during the early 1980s by the incantations of supply-side economists. Our deficit has thus become no one's responsibility. It is still subject to "projection" but no longer to control.

Table 1-2 illustrates the effects of these developments by tabulating budget outlays according to general function as a percentage of GNP. From fiscal year 1979 to 1986, federal revenue fell from 18.9 percent to 18.3 percent of GNP, while federal outlays rose from 20.6 percent to 23.6 percent of GNP. The big growth areas over the past seven years have been defense, entitlement benefits, and interest on our national debt; all other spending has been cut back dramatically.

Over the longer term, however, it is entitlements alone that dominate the picture. Since 1965 they have grown from 5.3 percent to 11.1 percent of GNP; all other spending excluding the cost of interest (which simply represents the permanent cost of cumulative deficits) has actually declined from 11.0 to 9.3 percent of GNP. Even per-GNP defense spending—now shrinking rapidly—rose only half as much from 1979 to its peak in 1986 as it declined from 1969 to 1979.

Our budget cutting efforts during the 1980s have failed because we have not contained entitlement spending—the one category of federal spending that had already risen to unprecedented heights in the previous decade. Even where the 1980s budget ax has fallen hard, the major victims have been those rare programs whose purpose is investment in physical or human capital rather than publicly funded consumption.

This last point is worth emphasizing, for it explains the unique vulnerability of that small area of the federal budget labeled "discretionary nondefense spending." That is the old type of spending in which Congress—unconstrained by entitlement indexing formulas or prior-year weapons contracts—votes on bills each year, presumably for the best interest of our national future. Unfortunately, since the future has no lobby, the administration and Congress have found this the perfect place to demonstrate their budget-cutting zeal, even while allowing all other types of spending to keep rising. It is this budget category, of course, that accounts for spending on public infrastructure and human capital, including research, education, job skills, and remedial social services. At the same time, it should hardly come as a surprise to learn that the explosive growth in entitlement spending during the 1980s is entirely attributable to our huge nonpoverty benefit programs; the small portion of all entitlements that constitute our true "social safety net" has hardly experienced any growth as a share of GNP since 1979 (and has actually shrunk as a share of the federal budget).

Far from forcing a "revolution" in the role of federal government, public policy during the 1980s has instead turned the federal budget into an ever-larger consumption machine. In the mid-1960s, checks mailed out automatically (to bondholders, health insurers, retirees, and state and local benefit administrators) accounted for about 58 percent of all federal nondefense spending. By 1979 their share stood at 68 percent; in 1988 it has grown to nearly 80 percent. The United

States has now reached the point where even if we eliminated *all* discretionary nondefense spending—say we shut down the national parks, closed the National Institutes of Health, abolished the FBI, and fired all civilian federal workers and replaced them with a giant check-writing machine—the federal budget would *still* be running a deficit.

Over the past generation, federal entitlement benefits have grown about twice as fast as our economy. The obstacles to effective entitlements reform are formidable, since policymakers are held captive by special interest groups, and politicians and constituents alike cling to a series of dangerous myths about the supposed social goals and benefits of these programs—myths we will discuss in Chapter 2. As for the power that entitled constituencies can exercise over politicians, we need only cite one suggestive example: the American Association of Retired Persons (AARP).

With its 28 million members and more than 5,000 state and local chapters, AARP is not just the most important force in the "gray lobby," it is unquestionably the nation's largest and most powerful interest group. Its voluntary membership, which includes one in every four registered U.S. voters, is larger than that of any other organization in America aside from the Catholic Church; it is *twice* the size of the AFL-CIO; and it is growing by several thousand members daily. With an operating budget of $200 million, AARP is also the largest single business entity in the Washington, D.C., metropolitan area; its annual cash flow (now about $5 billion) would put it near the top of the Fortune 500 if it were a public corporation. AARP's mail-order drug business is the nation's largest; its health-insurance programs, driver education courses, and tax advisory services are among the nation's largest; and its magazine (*Modern Maturity*) now has a circulation second only to *TV Guide*. When AARP speaks—and it speaks loud and clear on the question of entitlements—you can bet that Congress listens.

Yet despite the political obstacles, reform is more crucial now than ever. It is not just that our system of federal entitlements places a dangerous burden on today's resources; or that it fails to fulfill the legitimate goals that most of us assume a social welfare system should be designed to address. As it is currently structured, our system of federal entitlements is ill-prepared to confront the challenges of the next century—an aging population, a shrinking work force, rapidly escalating health-care costs, and a slowing economy. The first three of these trends may be moderated, but their direction cannot be altered.

As for preventing the fourth—a slowing economy—that is the whole purpose of entitlements reform. Indeed, that is why our consumption ethos, together with the whole range of cultural expectations reflected by it, will have to change.

Over the course of the last several generations, Americans have decided to socialize much of the cost of growing old, but very little of the cost of raising children. As our population ages and we all become ever more dependent on the economic contributions of young families, it will become self-defeating for public policy to continue to regard the young only as convenient sources for revenue; public policy must instead begin to regard them as vital targets for investment. This will inevitably mean reassessing the role of families in providing care for both young and old dependents, and creating a social and economic environment in which it once more becomes attractive for tomorrow's parents to raise and educate new generations of Americans. It will also require the development of more positive attitudes toward aging, and more opportunities for the elderly to think of themselves not exclusively as dependents, retiring at ever-earlier ages, but also as productive contributors.

The penalty for failure to restructure our entitlement programs will almost certainly be stagnating standards of living and intergenerational strife. With the cost of our current system of federal entitlements projected to reach about 22 percent of GNP by the year 2025—and the total federal budget an impossible 57 percent of GNP—it is inevitable that change will come. The only question is whether we will be forced to live through a crisis from which we all emerge poorer than we might have been, or whether we will be able to shift our national priorities gradually, so that necessary adjustments can be made without economic and social upheaval.

The thesis of this book is straightforward. In order to ensure future prosperity—and a more equitable distribution of society's resources both between and within generations—we must implement policy measures that encourage much higher levels of national savings. The additional savings must be sufficient not only to substitute for the savings we are now importing from abroad, but also to finance higher levels of investment at home. This will necessarily involve controlling federal outlays—and entitlement programs hold the key to the federal budget. But the challenge we face is not just economic, it is also cultural and ultimately moral. We need to find the courage to forge a new social welfare system that transcends the special interests of "entitled" constituencies. Only in this fashion will we be able to meet the legitimate needs of the poor and vulnerable in our society. And only in this fashion can we create an economic climate in which all generations, both present and future, can continue to participate in the American Dream.

In the three chapters constituting Part Three of this book, we will take a close look at the history and current condition of our major federal entitlement programs: Social Security cash benefits, civil service and military retirement, and Medicare along with other health-care benefits. At the end of each chapter, we will suggest a set of structural reforms for these programs that can limit their future growth to a level our economy can afford in the next century. Let us make clear at the outset that haphazard cost-cutting is not what we have in mind. Any successful approach to entitlements reform, we believe, must be carefully grounded on six general principles.

First, the reforms must be based on *prudent assumptions* about our nation's economic and demographic future. As we will see, the unrealistic, even Panglossian assumptions we have used in the past are a major reason we now face unenviable choices.

Second, the reforms must keep in mind our paramount national objective: *raising our collective level of savings.* While we are reducing benefit costs, in other words, we must also make sure we are thereby reducing deficits and unfunded benefit liabilities in the public sector, and encouraging genuine forms of savings (such as IRAs, company pension plans, and long-term health-care insurance) as substitutes in the private sector. In Chapter 10, we will spell out our long-term goal: to allocate to savings at least one-tenth of what we currently allocate to consumption.

Third, the reforms must be *equitable between generations.* Throwing the burden of cost-cutting entirely onto tomorrow's elderly or today's young working families is not only patently unfair, but also will undermine both the ability and willingness of future generations to support the system.

Fourth, the reforms must be *fair to the poor.* Reform should not make anyone near the poverty line worse off, nor should it proceed on the mistaken premise that budgetary savings and the alleviation of poverty are direct trade-offs. Quite to the contrary, successful reform should allow us to offer more comprehensive support to the poor.

Fifth, the reforms must be *gradual.* "Shock therapy" may occasionally make for good politics, but it nearly always makes for bad economics. Sudden income changes tend to inflict the maximum hardship (what we want to avoid), while allowing no time for behavioral changes in household spending, savings, and retirement habits (what we want to encourage). Gradualism, however, is only possible if we act now; each year that we do nothing makes it less feasible.

Finally, the reforms must recognize that programs such as Social Security and Medicare have become defining links between citizen and state in America. Reforms must, therefore, try to allow *institutional continuity* in our basic entitlement programs and avoid the impulse to "scrap" everything and start over again. Like gradualism, continuity implies that we act now. The economic and political turmoil that is likely to accompany discontinuous reform is, in fact, precisely what we want to avoid.

Even the best-designed reforms will necessarily entail some pain. Is it really necessary to make such a sacrifice today in the interests of a future that will always remain uncertain? The answer is simple: the price of our current overconsumption and undersaving must be a slower rate of economic growth, and the cumulative impact of even small differences in yearly growth rates should not be underestimated. They do indeed steer the destinies of nations. Britain's economic decline took seventy-five years of productivity growth rates that were half a percentage point lower than those of its industrial competitors. America's corresponding gap is more than three times as large, and its relative decline is thus proceeding far more swiftly.

Consider the year 2020, when those who are now infants will be in the prime of their working lives. If productivity growth proceeds at its 1980s rate (and does not decline still further), the average worker in 2020 will be producing $44,300 worth of real goods and services, only about 23 percent more than his or her parents are each producing today ($35,900). Given the likelihood that per-worker consumption will have to decline through most of the rest of this century in order to service our foreign debts, by 2020 the living standard of the typical worker will have risen by substantially less than 20 percent above its 1986 level. America's standard of living, for the first time in its history, will have hardly budged for a span of nearly forty years. The 1980s will be remembered, with bitterness, as a turning point in America's fortunes—a period when we took the British route to second-class economic status.

If, however, U.S. productivity now started growing again at the 2.2 percent average rate that prevailed during the 1950s and 1960s, our sons and daughters in 2020 would each be producing $75,200 worth of real goods and services—some 110 percent more than their parents are each producing today. Consumption standards would rise by nearly as much, since we would have been able to close our foreign borrowing gap and recoup our foreign liabilities by sometime in the early 1990s. In this case our grandchildren would look back on us as relative paupers, and by 2020 Americans would be enjoying buoyant prosperity and widening social opportunities in a nation that would still be a leading force in the world's economic and political affairs.

Is there really any doubt which future we should choose?

2

The Myths of Entitlements

> "Between craft and credulity, the voice of reason is stifled."
>
> — *Edmund Burke*

A N ENORMOUS STREAM of entitlement payments now flows from the U.S. Treasury at the rate of $50 million per hour. It is a stream that dominates the federal budget. Yet the truth about where it goes and what it does often contradicts widespread assumptions that Americans hold about the proper role of government in allocating resources. Entitlements are not just a problem because Social Security and Medicare—the two largest programs—will inevitably become unaffordable during the course of the next century. Fiscal considerations aside, our entire entitlements system is marked by fundamental inequities in its benefit provisions and a lack of clear consensus about the economic and social goals it should be designed to accomplish.

What then are entitlements? The term *entitlements* usually refers to those benefits—whether in cash or in kind—that the federal government automatically pays to qualified individuals. As a rule, entitlement programs ostensibly contain some strong social welfare dimension, though in the case of Social Security and Medicare this is obscured by the insurance metaphors commonly used to describe payroll taxes and payroll taxes and benefits. As defined by the House and Senate Budget Committees, entitlements consist of any federal outlay that either requires no annual appropriation by Congress or must be appropriated by Congress according to the terms of some underlying statute or program legislation. Thus, as long as a given law remains in force, an "entitled" beneficiary can sue the government for failure to pay benefits. If the underlying statute or legislation were to be amended or abolished, however, program participants—as the Supreme Court decided in the case of Social Security in 1960—would have no legally enforceable right to receive their benefits.

In many respects, this legal definition used by Congress conforms well to the general public-policy usage of the term. Social Security and Medicare are legal entitlements, since they are constituted as autonomous trust funds that possess the authority to pay benefits without an annual appropriation by Congress. Many other individual benefit programs—including Medicaid, Supplemental Security Income (SSI), Aid to Families with Dependent Children (AFDC), and most Veterans Administration benefits—are also considered entitlements by Congress. Although these latter programs are not constituted as autonomous trust funds, Congress is legally bound to appropriate the money required to pay any benefits due in accordance with the terms of the underlying program legislation. Unfortunately, there are many areas in which the legal definition of entitlements fails to reflect its public-policy meaning. Congress, for example, categorizes interest paid to federal debt-holders as an entitlement (it is both mandatory and disbursed from a special trust fund), whereas from an economic or policy viewpoint it should be considered as payment for a service, rather than a benefit.

Federal entitlement spending is sometimes equated with "uncontrollable outlays," a budget category computed by the Office of Management and Budget (OMB). These include all outlays that the federal government may spend during the current year without an explicit congressional decision. To be sure, "uncontrollable outlays" have long been expanding as a share of the budget (to 73 percent in 1986), and much of this is due to the growth in entitlement spending. "Uncontrollables," however, also include types of spending (such as prior-year obligations to pay up on defense contracts) that have no clear relation to entitlements as a public-policy concept.

Another possibility, favored by many economists, is to equate entitlements with "federal transfer payments to individuals," a dollar figure in the National Income and Product Accounts that is calculated by the Commerce Department. Again, this concept comes close to what we usually mean by entitlements: it includes all major cash benefits and most in-kind benefits. But the NIPA figure is not consistent with official budget totals. Moreover, it excludes all loans (such as those under the Guaranteed Student Loan program), all subsidies (such as low-income housing assistance), and all grants (even for the direct purpose of funding state-administered benefits such as Medicaid).

For the purposes of the discussion in this book, we have settled on a definition of federal entitlements that corresponds closely to an informal budget category, "Entitlements and Other Mandatory Spending," first used by the Congressional Budget Office in 1983. The CBO definition includes most legal entitlements, but excludes interest payments and other irrelevant "uncontrollables." It also includes many nonlegal entitlements that nonetheless constitute discrete benefits, are paid to individuals according to specific eligibility criteria, and are approved by Congress on a largely automatic basis (Food Stamps, for example). In no case does the CBO include the cost of administering the program. One of the advantages of adopting our (slightly modified) CBO definition is that many proposals for entitlements reform use this informal budget category as their principal framework for discussion.* Table 2-1 presents a detailed breakdown of entitlement outlays by major program in fiscal year 1986 according to this definition; Table 2-2 presents a summary breakdown of historical outlays for fiscal years 1965, 1979, and 1986.

At $466 billion, spending on entitlement programs in fiscal year 1986 accounted for 47.1 percent of the federal budget, compared with 27.6 percent for defense and 16.3 percent for nondefense discretionary spending. It is well known that entitlement outlays have increased enormously over the course of the past two decades. In fiscal year 1965—the year Medicare was introduced—total entitlement spending amounted to a mere $35.6 billion, or 30.1 percent of the federal budget. The rapid expansion in entitlement spending since the mid-1960s has thus proceeded at an annual rate of 13.0 percent in current dollars (or 6.5 percent in constant, inflation-adjusted dollars).

---

*We make only two significant departures from the CBO definition. First, we include veterans' health-care benefits as an entitlement (which they clearly are) and take them out of the CBO's discretionary spending category. Second, we exclude General Revenue Sharing with state and local governments; while legally an entitlement, it clearly does not constitute benefits to individuals (see Notes).

What is less well known is that not all of this growth occurred during the 1960s and 1970s. From fiscal year 1979 to fiscal year 1986, entitlement spending has continued to climb at an annual rate of 10.5 percent in current dollars (or 4.3 percent in constant dollars)—in other words, at a growth rate that is still faster than that of our economy as a whole. In fact, between 1979 and 1986, federal entitlement spending expanded from 9.5 percent to 11.1 percent of GNP—a jump that accounted for nearly half the total increase in budget outlays as a share of GNP over the same period of time.* (The rest of that increase was divided between renewed spending on national defense and rising interest payments on the federal debt.) The much-publicized cuts in "social spending" of the Reagan years— contrary to widespread popular belief—have not done much to slow the overall growth in federal entitlement benefits.

The history, present status, and future outlook of most of the important nonpoverty entitlement programs will be discussed at length in Part Three. At the risk of anticipating ourselves, however, we will offer the reader an overview of the subject before proceeding further. Tables 2-1 and 2-2 (as well as Figure 2-1) group all entitlement programs under two subheadings: "means-tested" programs and "non-means-tested" programs. Financial need is always one of the criteria for eligibility in means-tested programs, which, by and large, constitute our true "social safety net." In contrast, eligibility for benefits in non-means-tested programs—the so-called middle-class entitlements—never requires an overall income or assets test to determine financial need. The distinction between means-tested and non-means-tested is fundamental, and will be returned to on numerous occasions in the chapters that follow.

In fiscal year 1986, spending on means-tested benefits amounted to $70.3 billion, or 7.1 percent of the federal budget and 15.1 percent of all federal entitlements. With outlays of $25.0 billion, Medicaid was by far the largest of these programs. A federal-state matching program that pays for the health-care expenses of more than 20 million poor and near-poor Americans, Medicaid was established in 1965 and is the counterpart to Medicare, which is a non-means-tested health benefit

*Around this upward trend, entitlement spending as a share of GNP rises and falls with the business cycle. Thus, after rising swiftly to a peak during the severe recession year of 1983 (at 12.3 percent of GNP), entitlement spending relative to GNP has fallen over the course of the recovery. Even so, the spending level in 1987 (at 11.0 percent of GNP) is still higher than in any year before 1982. We chose to compare the years 1965, 1979, and 1986—each coming at a roughly comparable stage of cyclical recovery—precisely to avoid this fluctuation.

TABLE 2-1   Federal Entitlements by Type,
                                   Fiscal Year 1986

	Billions of Dollars	Percent of GNP	Percent of Budget	Percent of All Entitlements
TOTAL	$466.0	11.1%	47.1%	100.0%
Total Non-Means-Tested	$395.7	9.4%	40.0%	84.9%
Social Security	274.8	6.6	27.8	59.0
Old-Age, Survivors, & Disability				
(OASDI)	198.9	4.8	20.1	42.7
Medicare	75.9	1.8	7.7	16.3
Hospital Insurance (HI)	50.0	1.2	5.1	10.7
Suppl. Medical Insurance (SMI)	25.9	0.6	2.6	5.6
Other Retirement & Disability	69.4	1.7	7.0	14.9
Federal Civil Service	24.1	0.6	2.4	5.2
Military	17.6	0.4	1.8	3.8
Veterans	22.8	0.5	2.3	4.9
Other	4.9	0.1	0.5	1.1
Unemployment Compensation	17.8	0.4	1.8	3.8
Other Programs	33.7	0.8	3.4	7.2
Farm Price Supports	25.8	0.6	2.6	5.5
Social Services	4.0	0.1	0.4	0.9
Other	3.9	0.1	0.4	0.8
Total Means-Tested	$70.3	1.7%	7.1%	15.1%
Medicaid	25.0	0.6	2.5	5.4
Food Stamps	11.6	0.3	1.2	2.5
Supplemental Security Income	10.3	0.3	1.0	2.2
Aid to Families with Dependent Children	9.3	0.2	0.9	2.0
Veterans Pensions	3.9	0.1	0.4	0.8
Child Nutrition	3.8	0.1	0.4	0.8
Guaranteed Student Loans	3.4	0.1	0.3	0.7
Other	3.0	0.1	0.3	0.6
Memo: Total Health-Care Benefits	$110.8	2.6%	11.2%	23.8%

Source: CBO and OMB

program for the elderly and disabled. The great majority of Medicaid recipients qualify for assistance because they are enrolled in one of two means-tested cash benefit programs: Supplemental Security Income (SSI), whose beneficiaries are either elderly or disabled persons in poverty, or Aid to Families with Dependent Children (AFDC), which pays benefits to poor, single parents with dependent children. Taken together, SSI, AFDC, and Food Stamps—the three programs that perhaps best represent the paradigmatic public image of "welfare"—

TABLE 2-2 **Federal Entitlements by Type, Fiscal Years 1965, 1979, and 1986**

	Billions of Dollars			Percent of GNP		
Entitlements	**1965**	**1979**	**1986**	**1965**	**1979**	**1986**
TOTAL	$35.6	$233.0	$466.0	5.29%	9.50%	11.13%
Total Non-Means-Tested	$30.3	$193.5	$395.7	4.50%	7.89%	9.45%
Social Security	17.5	133.3	274.8	2.59	5.44	6.56
Old-Age, Survivors, & Disability						
(OASDI)	17.5	103.4	198.9	2.59	4.22	4.75
Medicare	0.0	29.9	75.9	0.00	1.22	1.81
Other Retirement & Disability	3.5	27.3	69.4	0.52	1.11	1.66
Unemployment Compensation	3.0	10.7	17.8	0.45	0.44	0.42
Other Non-Means-Tested	6.3	22.2	33.7	0.94	0.90	0.81
Total Means-Tested	$5.3	$39.5	$70.3	0.79%	1.61%	1.68%
Medicaid	0.3	12.4	25.0	0.04	0.51	0.60
Other Means-Tested	5.0	27.1	45.3	0.74	1.11	1.08
Memo: Total Health-Care Benefits	$1.6	$47.9	$110.8	0.23%	1.95%	2.64%

	Percent of Budget			Percent of All Entitlements		
Entitlements	**1965**	**1979**	**1986**	**1965**	**1979**	**1986**
TOTAL	30.1%	46.3%	47.1%	100.0%	100.0%	100.0%
Total Non-Means-Tested	25.6%	38.4%	40.0%	85.1%	83.0%	84.9%
Social Security	14.8	26.5	27.8	49.1	57.2	59.0
Old-Age, Survivors, & Disability						
(OASDI)	14.8	20.5	20.1	49.1	44.4	42.7
Medicare	0.0	5.9	7.7	0.0	12.8	16.3
Other Retirement & Disability	3.0	5.4	7.0	9.8	11.7	14.9
Unemployment Compensation	2.5	2.1	1.8	8.4	4.6	3.8
Other Non-Means-Tested	5.4	4.4	3.4	17.8	9.5	7.2
Total Means-Tested	4.5%	7.9%	7.1%	14.9%	17.0%	15.1%
Medicaid	0.3	2.5	2.5	0.8	5.3	5.4
Other Means-Tested	4.2	5.4	4.6	14.0	11.6	9.7
Memo: Total Health-Care Benefits	1.3%	9.5%	11.2%	4.4%	20.6%	23.8%

Source: CBO and OMB

FIGURE 2-1   **Federal Entitlements by Type as a Percent of GNP, Fiscal Years 1965, 1979, and 1986**

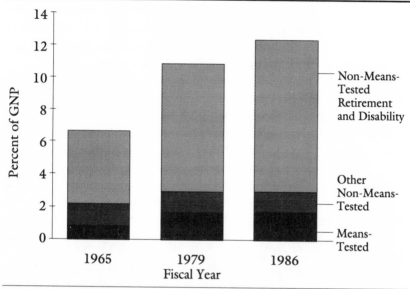

Source: CBO and OMB

accounted for $31.2 billion in federal benefit spending in fiscal year 1986. Of the remaining means-tested entitlement programs, at least two—veterans pensions and the Guaranteed Student Loan program —clearly have much less to do with the relief of poverty.

With the exception of Medicaid, which must be featured prominently in any discussion of the aging of the U.S. population or the ongoing explosion in health-care costs, means-tested entitlements will receive relatively little attention in this book. The reason is twofold: these programs comprise a negligible fraction of total federal spending, and, however ill-designed, they fulfill an unquestionably legitimate social function. To turn around a dictum often voiced by politicians over the past few years, when cutting the federal budget is on the agenda, "everything but antipoverty programs should be on the table."

The truth, however, is that it has been the vastly larger nonpoverty entitlement programs that we have largely decided to exempt from the budget cutting process. In fiscal year 1986, federal spending on non-means-tested benefits amounted to $395.7 billion, or 40.0 percent of the total budget and fully 84.9 percent of all entitlements. The decision to exempt middle- and upper-class entitlements from significant spending cuts has made it virtually impossible to eliminate our budget deficits by reducing federal outlays.

If we don't touch any entitlements, and further recognize that interest payments on the federal debt are mandatory, we have ruled 61 percent of the budget off-limits. That leaves nondefense discretionary spending and defense as the only areas remaining. Large savings in the former, the one area in which the budget cuts of the 1980s really did bite deep, are obviously out of the queston. In real dollars, nondefense discretionary spending is now smaller than in any year since 1974; as a share of GNP it is smaller than in any year since 1958. Cutting what is left would threaten activities that most Americans associate with the most basic functions of government (the Coast Guard, the national parks, the FBI, the foreign service, the Environmental Protection Agency, and the Federal Aviation Administration, to name a few). It would also threaten funding for basic research, infrastructure, and job training—investments we will need more of, not less of, in the years to come.

So at last we come to defense. At $273.4 billion in fiscal year 1986, defense spending accounted for 27.6 percent of federal outlays and 6.5 percent of GNP—percentage shares that, despite the Reagan defense buildup, are substantially below the level prevailing throughout the 1950s and 1960s (when we still had balanced, or nearly balanced, federal budgets). Nearly everyone agrees that we should try to save as much as possible by improving the efficiency of our military operations, by trimming waste and unnecessary duplication, and, of course, by eliminating fraud. Dramatic and permanent savings, however, are unlikely. To begin with, less than 40 percent (or about $105 billion) of the defense budget consists of procurement, testing, and R&D—the only areas in which substantial savings have been seriously proposed. And even here our options are limited, since most of the outlays planned in this category are for systems, weapons, and bases that are already in some stage of scheduled procurement.

We could, on the one hand, decide to delay or reduce these future purchases. But this would thrust us against the so-called spending bow wave: the massive inefficiencies and high unit costs that result from stretching out scheduled procurement and testing. We would end up paying far more tomorrow than what we save from not paying for it today (another form of borrowing disguised as "savings," since it doesn't show up on the budget books). We could, on the other hand, deem certain programs inessential, cut our losses, and cancel them right away. This is often a far better option. Unfortunately, it is one that our elected and appointed officials, hounded by constituency pressure for local jobs, find painfully difficult. It implies making irrevocable choices, ordering long-term priorities, and acknowledging that affordability has limits. These are, of course, the same difficulties that plague our approach to entitlements, and we should strive to overcome them in a balanced approach to budget restraint.

But even if Congress and the Pentagon do agree on a more sensible approach to military procurement (and to other large areas of the defense budget as well),* viable defense savings will not come close to curing our long-term deficit problem. The numbers involved are too small and our bipartisan consensus on what constitutes an effective and innovative defense program is too broad. It is instructive, for example, that during the 1987 budget summit the difference between the "bid" of the allegedly antidefense Democrats and the "ask" of the prodefense Republicans was only around $7 billion, a swing of about 2 percent of total defense outlays. Despite vocal Democratic criticism of certain high-ticket purchases by the Reagan administration—the Strategic Defense Initiative, the B-1 Bomber, two extra aircraft carriers, the Trident II refit program, and additional F-15s—the total cost at issue is surprisingly small. A complete cancellation of all of these items (leaving aside the strategic wisdom or political feasibility of such amputation) would save less than $15 billion yearly by the early 1990s.

What really narrows the options on defense is that its budget is already being subjected to deep cuts—both in real dollars and as a percent of GNP. From 1986 to 1988, real defense spending is expected to decline by $4 billion (in 1986 dollars), and by 1993 the CBO now assumes a further real decline of $3 billion.† All together, from 1986 to 1993, this amounts to a cut of more than one full percentage point of GNP—*a cut that has already been incorporated into current CBO deficit projections.* Just following through with what we have already scheduled may indeed prove daunting. No one yet

---

*Even within the defense budget, entitlements are a major problem. Military retirement (at $17.6 billion in 1987) is funded through an "offsetting receipt" transfer from the Pentagon to the rest of the budget; we will return to it in Chapter 8. And though we have *not* included military health care (at $11.1 billion) in our official tally of federal entitlements, its cost has been rising more rapidly than procurement in the 1980s; we will return to it in Chapters 5 and 9. Together, these two items account for more than 10 percent of our current defense budget—about what we spend on building and maintaining all of our strategic nuclear forces.

†It should be recognized, in fact, that defense outlays in fiscal year 1989 will be over $100 billion *less* than the original five-year Reagan administration projection in fiscal year 1984.

knows exactly how these savings are going to be made,* nor has anyone contemplated how the American public may react in the early 1990s if the new dip in defense spending coincides with an emergency abroad. Significantly, the defense-spending level now scheduled by the CBO for 1993 (5.3 percent of GNP) is precisely what we were spending in fiscal year 1981—when presidential candidates Jimmy Carter and Ronald Reagan both agreed that defense spending must rise swiftly in future years.

Unlike means-tested and nondefense discretionary spending, defense is an area that we should *want* to cut. Unfortunately, even with the Gorbachev-era promise of a wider field for arms negotiation, it may not be an area that we will be *able* to cut—at least not reliably, sufficiently, or permanently—given the current realities and long-term vicissitudes of world politics. Once again, we are forced back to where we started: nonpoverty entitlements. They comprise two-fifths of this year's federal budget, and without reform they will comprise an ever-larger share in the years to come.

Of all non-means-tested entitlement programs, Social Security is of course the largest and one of the oldest. All together (including Medicare), Social Security benefits amounted to $275 billion in fiscal year 1986, or 28 percent of federal outlays and 59 percent of all entitlement spending. The original cash-benefit program, Old-Age and Survivors Insurance, or OASI, was established in the late 1930s as part of the New Deal; Disability Insurance, or DI, is a later cash-benefit addition that dates from 1957. OASI pays benefits to covered workers after they retire, or to their survivors after they die. DI, the minor partner that accounts for only 10 percent of OASI and DI outlays combined, pays benefits to covered workers who become disabled. Both these components of Social Security are financed through payroll taxes levied on the covered work force (matched by equal employer "contributions"), and pay benefits out of specially earmarked trust funds. In 1986 about 122 million workers made "contributions" to the OASDI program, as it is properly called, and about 37.5 million persons received monthly benefit checks.

Medicare, the health-care component of Social Security, is one of the fastest growing of all the non-means-tested entitlements. The $75.9 billion spent by Medicare in fiscal year 1986 on reimbursements

---

*Senator Sam Nunn has estimated the "bow wave" generated by this cut—the excess cost of prescheduled purchases over projected outlays—at a fantastic $325 billion over the next five years.

for hospital and physician services accounted for half of all federal spending on health (including research). Eligibility for benefits under Medicare is generally the same as for Social Security cash benefits; in 1986, 28 million elderly persons and 3 million nonelderly disabled persons were covered by the program.

Medicare is actually composed of two distinct parts. The larger of the two is Hospital Insurance (HI)—also called Medicare "Part A"—which pays for inpatient hospital care and related services. Since the HI portion of Medicare is paid out from a separate HI trust fund supported by FICA payroll contributions, its tax base and method of financing, as well as its population of beneficiaries, are practically indistinguishable from those of OASDI.* The only difference is the type of benefit—reimbursements to hospitals rather than cash checks. Medicare "Part B" or Supplementary Medical Insurance (SMI), the smaller of Medicare's two parts, pays for physician and outpatient hospital services. SMI is not funded through payroll taxes; instead, it is funded through a combination of monthly premiums and general federal revenues (or deficits). But again, SMI serves virtually the same group of beneficiaries as OASDI or HI, and though membership is technically "voluntary," nearly everyone who is over age sixty-five or who receives DI benefits joins SMI in order to take advantage of the huge federal subsidy. As a rule, SMI premiums are automatically deducted from OASDI benefit checks.

Among the remaining non-means-tested entitlement programs, the federal Civil Service Retirement System (CSRS) and the military retirement system will receive the closest attention in this book. The CSRS was founded in 1920 as a staff retirement plan for federal workers; it currently covers 2.75 million federal civilian employees (including congressmen). The system is partially funded through a tax on covered workers' payrolls, but employee contributions amount to no more than 19 percent of total outlays; the remaining 81 percent of outlays is accounted for by matching contributions from the various federal employing agencies and by disbursements from general revenues. With total outlays of $24.1 billion in fiscal year 1986, the CSRS—which pays exceptionally generous benefits to some 2.0 million federal retirees and their survivors—is on a par with Medicaid in terms of its total cost.

*Nearly every covered worker is eligible for HI and SMI benefits at age sixty-five (whether he or she retires with OASI benefits earlier or later) or upon eligibility for DI benefits.

The federal military retirement system covers 2.2 million active-duty members of the armed forces as well as 1.1 million members of the Reserve Component. This entitlement program is designed to pay retirement, disability, and survivors benefits to career soldiers and their dependents; active-duty personnel who leave the military before completing twenty years of service receive no pension benefits. In fiscal year 1986, the military retirement system paid $17.6 billion in benefits to 1.5 million retirees and their survivors. This sum comes entirely out of general federal revenues, since historically (unlike the CSRS) military pensions have not made even a pretense of prefunding.

Taken together, CSRS and military retirement benefits amounted to $41.7 billion in 1986, or 8.9 percent of all federal entitlement spending. Of the other non-means-tested entitlement programs, only veterans benefits present sufficient long-term financing problems to receive more than passing attention in this book. Through the Veterans Administration (VA), the U.S. government provides a wide variety of benefits and services that compensate veterans for the presumed loss of earnings resulting from their service-related disabilities; they have, for instance, a non-means-tested cash compensation program and access to hospital and other health-care services that are in practice non-means-tested. Total non-means-tested VA benefits amounted to $22.8 billion in fiscal year 1986, or 4.9 percent of all entitlements. (VA pensions, the reader will note, is a means-tested program.) On the other hand, the agricultural price-support system (though it lacks a sound economic rationale) and unemployment compensation (the program with the soundest economic rationale) lie outside the long-term focus of this book.

Before examining the popular misconceptions surrounding entitlements, let us summarize some of the most important trends in federal benefit spending over the last few decades. After swift growth in the 1960s and 1970s, means-tested benefits have grown much more slowly than the rest of the entitlement budget during the 1980s. From fiscal year 1979 to fiscal year 1986, while other entitlement spending climbed at a real annual rate of 4.6 percent, means-tested benefits have grown at a rate of only 2.6 percent. Moreover, if growth in Medicaid is excluded, it turns out that federal spending on all other means-tested benefits has actually *declined* in real terms over the past seven years. In other words—health care aside—growth in entitlement expenditures during the 1980s has been entirely due to expansion of non-means-tested programs; with the exception of Medicaid, we spent less on our "social safety net" in 1986 than in 1980.

It is hardly surprising that Medicaid was the only means-tested entitlement program to experience significant growth during the 1980s. Overall federal outlays for health-care benefits have risen steadily as a share of all entitlement spending over the last two decades. In 1965, just before the introduction of Medicare, less than 0.9 percent (or $300 million) of federal entitlements outside the Veterans Administration were spent on health care. By 1970, however, outlays for Medicare and Medicaid had already climbed to 14.2 percent of all entitlements; and by fiscal year 1986, with combined outlays of $100.9 billion, Medicare and Medicaid together accounted for 21.7 percent of federal entitlement spending. Over the course of the past two decades, the creation and expansion of these two programs have pushed up federal health-care benefit outlays at a stunning *real* annual rate of 12.2 percent—nearly five times faster than the real growth rate of our economy.

In addition to noting the diminished role of means-tested programs and the increased importance of health-care benefits in shaping our entitlement budget, one further preliminary observation is in order. It is the elderly, of course, who receive the majority of federal benefit expenditures. Well over half—about 57 percent—of all federal benefits now go to the 12 percent of our population who are aged sixty-five and over. If we expand this calculation to include all retirement benefits to persons *under* age sixty-five, the figure would rise to 65 percent. The implications of this enormous disparity in benefit spending between generations raises issues of equity and long-term costs that will constitute major themes in this book. As the U.S. population ages and health-care costs continue to escalate, debate over entitlement spending will intensify. *Altogether, only one out of every five federal entitlement dollars go into any form of nonmedical aid to nonretired Americans*—including aid to the poor, the orphaned, the widowed, the disabled, and the unemployed, and including (even) *means-tested* aid to poor Americans who *are* retired or elderly. The rest all goes into a variety of non-means-tested pensions, into health-care benefits (with most of the latter allotted to those who receive the former), and into farm subsidies. If this policy debate is to be constructive, it is essential that the popular myths surrounding our system of nonpoverty entitlements be dispelled.

Myth One: "Entitlements Go Primarily to the Poor"

The ongoing growth in entitlement spending is often justified by the claim that such benefits serve as a protection against poverty. As such, entitlements would represent a national investment in the long-term social and economic benefits of preventing serious material hardship. If the premise were valid—that federal entitlements go to the poor—this argument might justify our federal deficits and foreign borrowing. There is nothing wrong, after all, in borrowing to finance an investment.

Unfortunately, the premise is in error. We have already seen that of the $466 billion in entitlements dispensed from the federal budget in fiscal year 1986, only 15.1 percent was means-tested—in other words, was targeted specifically at persons on the basis of financial need. Including benefits funded by state and local governments, which administer a relatively large share of genuine poverty programs, the figure is hardly any less lopsided. Of the $525 billion in benefit payments paid out by all levels of government in fiscal year 1986, no more than about 20.0 percent, or $105 billion, was earmarked toward programs whose benefits are means-tested.

The distinction between "means-tested" and "non-means-tested" entitlements, of course, does not constitute an exact dividing line between benefits that do and do not help the poor. A means-tested program such as Guaranteed Student Loans, for instance, helps many families who are far above the poverty level. A non-means-tested program such as Social Security, on the other hand, assists many elderly, disabled, and widowed persons who are in poverty even if "need" is not the reason they are eligible.

Do we have a more precise way of looking at this problem? Luckily, we do. Every few years, poverty experts make various calculations of the "poverty gap," the total amount of extra income that would be required to push all poor U.S. households up above the official poverty line.* Not counting any benefits, generous estimates would

---

*To be "poor" or "in poverty" became a statistical fact in 1963 when a federal task force (rather arbitrarily) defined it as applying to anyone living in a household receiving cash income that is less than three times a hypothetical "food budget." This dollar threshold was then given a few standard adjustments (for size of household, rural or urban residence, age, and so on); in each year since it has been moved upward according to changes in the Consumer Price Index. Using this threshold, the Census Bureau can count the "poor" and measure the "poverty gap" on the basis of its household surveys. For several reasons—understatement by reporting households, excessive growth in the CPI, and exclusion of noncash "in-kind" income—these numbers have often been attacked for overstating the extent of poverty. The numbers we cite here are corrected for only one of these biases: they adjust the "official" cash-income measure to include in-kind benefit income.

place the poverty gap at about $130 billion in 1986. After all cash and in-kind benefits are included, most estimates would reposition it somewhere near $30 billion. The difference, about $100 billion, is the amount of benefits that actually went to the poor.* One implication of these numbers is that our government allocates considerable resources toward the alleviation of poverty. This $100 billion effectively reduces the number of poor Americans from about 50 million (in the absence of these benefits) to about 20 million (after receiving them). For all those who would be poor without any benefits, the $100 billion translates into an *average* of $2,000 for every adult or child. A still more striking implication of these numbers, however, is that the vast majority of entitlements—again, about 80 percent of all benefit outlays from every level of government and about 85 percent from the federal government—do not go to the poor. If they did, we would have entirely eradicated poverty in America several times over.

If the poor receive only a small share of entitlement benefits, which groups receive the rest? No one knows precisely, but a fair guess could be made by examining the $396.5 billion in non-means-tested benefits dispensed by the federal government in fiscal year 1986. By and large, these went to those Americans *least* likely to be poor. The lion's share ($274.8 billion) consisted of Social Security and Medicare benefits, which went indiscriminately to nearly every elderly person. Far from targeting the poor, Social Security cash benefits are actually regressive in the sense that those with the highest lifetime incomes receive the highest monthly payments. In 1986, for instance, families on Social Security with annual cash incomes over $45,000 received monthly benefit checks that were on average 42 percent larger than those received by families with cash incomes under $15,000. (And remember, this regressivity is accentuated on the revenue side by Social Security's flat-rate payroll taxes, whose burden falls disproportionately on low and middle wage earners.)

Another $41.7 billion in non-means-tested benefits was spent on the two most generous pension systems in America: the civil service and military retirement programs. Among the beneficiaries of these programs, poverty is practically unheard-of: most are not "retired" at all but working at another job and earning a second pension. (The average annual income for a federal pensioner is now more than

---

*The pre-benefit poverty numbers are based on unpublished data from the Congressional Research Service; they are consistent with (or higher than) other estimates. The post-benefit numbers are calculated by the Census Bureau.

$35,000.) Still another $25.8 billion went to agricultural subsidies. Although this sum is the equivalent of $18,000 for every person working in agriculture, federal subsidies fail to help many farm workers. Instead, the money goes primarily to the owners of the farms with the largest sales and to the banks that service farm debt. Among the remaining non-means-tested entitlement programs, it is worth calling attention to veterans' health care, which in fiscal year 1986 disbursed some $9.9 billion in benefits, mostly to elderly people with higher-than-average incomes and without service-related illnesses. Unemployment compensation, amounting to $17.8 billion in 1986, almost gets lost in this sea of money.

The administration and Congress have often boasted of "cutting back" on excessive benefit spending. Unfortunately, nearly all the painful and most visible cuts have been made in the 15 percent of all benefit programs that are means-tested. As we have seen, one result is that (excluding Medicaid) means-tested benefits have actually shrunk in real dollars during the 1980s. Another result is that such benefits target the poor even better now than they did during the 1970s, since spending cuts have effectively excluded many near-poor beneficiaries—those whom, apparently, we no longer consider truly needy. Meanwhile, our huge non-means-tested programs, protected by powerful middle- and upper-class lobbies and automatically linked 100 percent with the Consumer Price Index (CPI)—have continued their uncontrolled growth. Since benefits in these programs, as we will see, bear no clear relation to contributions, it is time we recognized they are not pension or insurance systems but social welfare programs. And since benefits also bear no relation to need, it is time to seriously reconsider their underlying policy rationale.

Myth Two: "The Elderly Are, by Definition, Needy and Dependent"

Because well over half of all federal entitlements flow to the 12 percent of Americans aged sixty-five or over, the notion that most entitlements are dispensed on the basis of need is grounded firmly in the myth that the elderly are, almost by definition, destitute, and thus require substantial cash and in-kind support. To be sure, the massive senior lobbies occasionally reinforce this myth in order to consolidate political support for programs benefiting the elderly. To Washington politicians, the phrase "poor, dependent, and elderly" is repeated so often that the last term almost seems a redundancy. Yet the real strength of this perception lies in its prevalance among all age-groups, even outside Washington. Polls invariably show that most of us think old people are very poor. In 1981, for instance, a Harris Poll found that 65 percent of those under age sixty-five believe that "not having enough money to live on" is a serious problem for most of the elderly, and that 54 percent believe that the elderly are worse off than they were twenty years ago.* As time passes, we might expect that the true facts about the economic status of the elderly would begin to eclipse such perceptions. Popular myths die hard,† however, and there is no guarantee that this one will perish before it has done permanent damage to our economy.

Just what are the facts about the economic well-being of the elderly? We can begin with the radical disparity (already noted in the last chapter) between the trends in real cash income for the nonelderly and elderly over the past fifteen years. For the nonelderly, real income growth has stagnated; for the elderly, it has remained vigorous. From 1960 to 1980, the official median income for elderly families grew by 28 percent relative to nonelderly families; for elderly individuals living alone it grew by 34 percent. This growth was especially rapid in the mid- and late 1970s, when elderly benefit levels (as we will see later) were shooting upward and when nonelderly families were actually losing ground in real dollars. But even since 1980, the trend has continued apace: between 1980 and 1985, the median income for elderly families has gained another 13 percent on nonelderly families. Remarkably, the trend favoring the elderly seems to be occurring at all income levels and for all household types.

Today, as a result, many income measures indicate that the elderly are now better off as a group than the nonelderly. *Per household,* it is true that the reported cash income for the elderly (as measured by the Census Bureau) still averages considerably less than cash income for the nonelderly—about 38 percent less in 1986. But this may not seem all that surprising, since elderly households (very few of which consist of more than a married couple) tend to be considerably smaller than nonelderly households. The typical elderly household consists of 1.8 persons; the typical nonelderly household consists of 2.9 persons. *Per*

Aging in the Eighties: America in Transition (Harris and Associates, 1981).

†A more recent survey conducted by the *Los Angeles Times* in April 1985, for instance, showed that two-thirds of all respondents believed that poverty among the elderly was *increasing.*

capita, therefore, the elderly by comparison do much better. In fact, per capita cash income is now for the first time edging higher for Americans over sixty-five years of age. In 1984, the last year for which comparable Census data are available, the elderly came out on top by 1 or 2 percent ($10,316 versus $10,190).

These figures, moreover, refer to pretax income. After subtracting out all forms of taxation (including state, local, and property taxes), the elderly did better still in 1984: $8,886 versus $7,876, or a 13 percent advantage over the nonelderly. The large discrepancy between pre- and post-tax comparisons reflects an equivalent difference between relative tax burdens. Much of the elderly's income is not taxable at all (most cash benefits and a large share of income from private pensions and assets, for example); and much of their income and real estate is taxed more lightly (due to age-based exemptions, outdated property-tax assessment values, and the small share of all elderly income subject to payroll taxes).* In 1984 the average tax bill for the elderly amounted to about 14 percent of their income, versus 23 percent of income for the nonelderly. Incredibly, as of 1982 about 57 percent of the elderly paid no individual income taxes at all (compared with 13 percent of the nonelderly population), and over 40 percent of elderly households did not even file income tax returns.

Taxes change the picture quite a bit, but other adjustments change it even more. First, we need to take into account noncash income. For the elderly, this primarily means in-kind public benefits such as Medicare. On average, each American aged sixty-five and over received over $2,500 in in-kind benefits in 1984, while only one-tenth of this amount, or about $250, went to each American aged sixty-four and under. (Many younger workers also receive employer-paid health care and related fringes, but this works out to no more than $450 per capita.) Second, we need to adjust the official cash income figures for a well-known phenomenon known as "underreporting." The Census Bureau gathers its information through questionnaires answered by self-reporting heads of households; it has no independent means of verifying each response. After comparing the aggregate response for all households with known figures for total personal income and budget outlays, however, the Bureau is well aware that certain types of income are routinely underreported. Which types of income?

*The 1986 tax reform eliminates the exemptions for over-sixty-five tax filers and replaces them with higher standard deductions. The change resulted in a net revenue loss, but it at least had the merit of denying this age-based preference to upper-income elderly who itemize.

Precisely the same types—government cash benefits and asset income—that go disproportionately to elderly households. All told, it seems that the elderly underreport their cash income by at least 30 percent. Persons aged sixty-four and under, on the other hand, underreport their cash income by no more than about 5 percent.*

Finally, there remains the question of net assets, which, as we all know, can be just as important as income in determining living standards. Consider, for example, a person with zero net worth who makes $20,000 yearly from employment, rents an apartment, and pays interest on student and car loans. Then consider a person making $20,000 yearly in pensions, interest, and dividends, who lives in a paid-off home and is entirely debt-free. They have the same income, but they enjoy very different degrees of economic well-being.

Needless to say, it is the elderly who fall most often into the latter category, quite simply because they are in the dominant wealth-holding age bracket. In 1984, 56 percent of all elderly households had a net worth of at least $50,000; only 7 percent had a zero or negative net worth. By contrast, only 23 percent of households headed by persons under forty-five exceeded the $50,000 mark; and 15 percent had a zero or negative net worth. Much of the difference lies in home ownership. Fully three-quarters of all elderly householders are home owners, of whom 84 percent own their homes free and clear; about half of all householders under age forty-five are home owners, of whom nearly all owe mortgages.

But the difference is also reflected in financial assets, where the elderly's median exceeds that of every other age-group for every type of asset—stocks, bonds, and mutual funds, as well as checking, savings, and money-market accounts. For the last two decades, reported cash income from financial or real property has been one of the elderly's fastest-growing sources of income. It has risen from 15 percent of total elderly income in 1967 to 28 percent in 1984. The comparable figure for the nonelderly is about 5 percent over age forty and almost nil under age forty.

---

*This remarkable concentration of underreporting in the over-sixty-five age bracket is well known to experts acquainted with the Census data. The figures cited here are simple adjustments of the 1983 survey by type of income; detailed earlier studies indicate that the true cash income of the elderly may be as much as 40 percent higher on average than what is reported, while young householders may actually overreport their income (see articles by Daniel Radner and Melinda Upp in the July 1982 and January 1983 issues of *Social Security Bulletin*). The single most important reason for this discrepancy is the elderly's high level of asset income —by far the most underreported income type.

Given so many different perspectives on comparative affluence, it may be impossible to quantify the relative economic status of the elderly with precision. Weighing all the evidence, however, it is also impossible to defend the claim that on average the elderly are in greater financial need than younger age-groups. Their after-tax income is significantly higher on a per capita basis; after adjustment for noncash benefits and underreporting, it is no doubt higher on a per-household basis; and the high net worth typical of elderly households affords a measure of financial security generally unknown among younger households.

None of these facts, it is worth pointing out, are lost to the private marketers who advise retail corporations where to direct their sales pitches. Indeed, since the late 1970s and early 1980s there has been a veritable explosion of literature in trade and marketing publications (*American Demographics* comes first to mind) that seeks to define, describe, and analyze the "booming new senior market." Ironically, even *Modern Maturity*, the life-styles magazine of the American Association of Retired Persons, runs pieces on the affluence of the new senior market side by side with articles that perpetuate the myth of elderly poverty.*

The objection is often raised that measures of per capita income do not reflect the unique economic burdens facing many of the elderly, such as the higher per capita cost of running a small household, the loss of control over income due to retirement, and much larger medical bills. This objection has some merit, though it must be qualified. Elderly households also enjoy unique advantages. The retired elderly, for instance, do not bear job-related expenses, and typically their advantage in leisure time enables them to avoid purchasing services (home repairs and dining out, for example) that younger full-time workers often cannot avoid.

More fundamentally, we must reflect on how many of the elderly's unique burdens are a direct reflection of their newfound affluence. A higher income, for instance, today offers nearly all the elderly, either

---

*Most revealing of all is a recent media kit circulated by *Modern Maturity* magazine to attract advertisers. Outside: "50 & Over people... They've got clout! Affluent... Aware... Active Buyers with over $500 Billion to spend." Inside: "50 & Over People are putting into practice the credo of 'Living for Today'! They're spending on self-fulfillment *now* (Hedonism vs. Puritanism), rather than leaving large sums behind." Cited by Phillip Longman, "Justice Between Generations," *The Atlantic Monthly* (June 1985).

as singles or as couples, the option of living alone apart from their families. This option is now chosen by 9 out of 10 of the elderly (up from 7 out of 10 in the mid-1960s), which is why the elderly now live in smaller households. A higher income also makes possible "early retirement" on Social Security before age sixty-five, an option now chosen by 7 out of 10 Americans (up from 4 out of 10 in the mid-1960s), which is why the elderly have little earned income. As for expensive medical bills, the critical factor here has been the growing national demand for health care, in no small part triggered (as we shall see in Chapter 5) by the explosive rise in health-care benefits to the elderly.

To assess how the elderly are doing, perhaps in the end we can do no better than to ask them directly and return to the Harris Poll mentioned earlier. Interestingly enough, the same poll showing that two-thirds of Americans under sixty-five believe the elderly are destitute also showed that most elderly themselves view their own condition very differently. *In fact, only 17 percent of the elderly respondents regarded low income as a serious problem for them personally, and 58 percent thought it was hardly any problem at all.* Only 1 in 10 elderly respondents agreed that "I can't make ends meet with the income I have now," while 1 in 8 of the nonelderly respondents agreed with this statement.

Most other surveys have reached the same basic conclusion: everyone thinks the elderly are vastly poorer than the elderly themselves report being (even the elderly believe this about other elderly households). Similarly, everyone thinks that the typical elderly person is older, frailer, and more dependent than he or she actually is. With this perception, we have set out over the last two decades to grant the elderly as a group, with no distinction between the needs of individuals, a plethora of reverse endowments: not just public benefits and tax breaks, but a multiplying array of business favors that we witness in our daily life, from discounts on life, health, and auto insurance to "senior packages" at banks, "Silver Savers passports" for phone service, and "Gray Eagle" bargains for air travel and vacations.

It appears that we face a classic case of cognitive dissonance: a hardy myth that stubbornly refuses to give way to reality, even among the group to whom it applies. Later we will argue that this negative "old equals poor and feeble" perception is a force that threatens our national future. Reversing it would be good for everyone concerned:

for the expectations of our kids, for the health of our economy, for the respect and self-confidence of the elderly themselves, and eventually—as our society ages—for our very self-image as a nation.

Myth Three: "Averages Are Deceiving; Beneath Them Are a Large Number of Needy Elderly"

Nowadays it is a cardinal rule among gerontologists and other experts on aging never to say the elderly are . . . *anything*. The elderly, argue the professionals, are a collection of 27 million individuals so diverse in their income, assets, age, health, prior career experiences, and family relations that any statement true about some of them will be dead wrong about the rest. This diversity, in turn, is often cited to imply that "averages" or "medians" say little about how many elderly need government assistance, or how much assistance is appropriate.

The claim that the elderly are heterogeneous is of course accurate. Experts have long observed that as people grow older, they become increasingly unlike each other—most importantly in their health and sociability, but also, especially around retirement, in their economic well-being. Some elderly find themselves entering their seventies or eighties in excellent health, still married, surrounded by an affluent and caring family, and well provided with pension and savings income at the end of a well-planned (or just lucky) career. Some, at the other extreme, find themselves in poor health, unmarried or widowed, largely isolated from their family or community, and forced to live off meager incomes. This widening "spread" in life experiences is reflected in a similarly widening spread in income distribution. The elderly population has a somewhat higher percentage of upper-income people living above two or three times the median income than do younger age-groups. It also has a somewhat higher percentage of people living below half the median than do younger age-groups.

But the key word is "somewhat." Many experts have cited such diversity to try to conjure up an image of the elderly divided, like Czarist Russia, into one half living in high-life affluence and the other living in desperate penury. After all, this imagery can be used as one more argument to justify our current system of entitlements.

The real picture is quite different. To begin with, the greater income spread shows up only in the cash income received by the richest and poorest quarters of the elderly population. The middle half of all elderly households is just as tightly packed around the median income as the middle half of nonelderly households. More important, the poorest quarter of elderly households, while generally lying further beneath the median than younger households, does not extend disproportionately to the very lowest income brackets. As a result, the nearly universal rise in the relative income of the elderly over the past twenty-five years has led to a commensurate decline in their relative incidence of poverty. In 1970 the poverty rate for Americans sixty-five and over (24.6 percent) was still double the rate for younger Americans (11.3 percent). But in 1982, for the first time since poverty rates have been measured, the elderly's rate dipped slightly below the national average. Today it is still dropping, even though the overall poverty rate for all age-groups has been climbing during the 1980s. *By 1986 the elderly enjoyed an official poverty rate significantly below the national average: 12.4 percent, versus 13.8 percent for all persons under sixty-five.* It is still slightly higher than the poverty rate for most younger adults, but well below the rate for the 15–24 age bracket (16.0 percent) and only slightly more than half the rate for children under age 14 (21.2 percent).

Again, the official "cash income" measure of poverty undoubtedly understates the improvement. According to the Census "total-income" calculation of poverty, which includes in-kind public benefits as part of total household income, the shift has been far more dramatic.* By this measure, the elderly's poverty rate fell beneath the national average as early as 1979, and since then has plunged to a mere fraction of the rate for other age-groups. *In 1986, in fact, the total-income poverty rate for the elderly was 3.0 percent—less than a third of the 9.8 percent rate for the nonelderly.* As Figure 2-2 shows, it was also less than half the poverty rate for any other age-group, and a mere one-sixth the equivalent poverty rate for children under six (16.2 percent). The absolute numbers of persons living in poverty generated by this measure (see Figure 2-3) are stunning: *fewer than 0.8 million Americans aged sixty-five and over versus 12.2 million under twenty-five and another 8.5 million between twenty-five and sixty-four.* Put more starkly: 96 percent of the poor are *not* elderly. The popular belief that a relatively large number of the elderly are poor is an anachronism, rooted in the realities of bygone decades. Today we should not be surprised at the growing anecdotal and journalistic evidence that the

---

*We use here the Census "market valuation" (i.e., cash equivalent value) of in-kind benefits. Those who criticize this measure as excessive are in the awkward position of concluding that the poor would be better off if we replaced these in-kind benefits with straight cash—a switch that would also save on administrative costs. In fact, due to cost shifting, "market valuation" undoubtedly underestimates the insurance value of health-care benefits such as Medicare and Medicaid (an issue to which we return in Chapter 9).

FIGURE 2-2 **Poverty Rates by Age-Group, 1986**

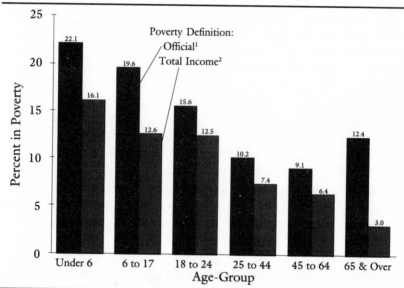

[1]Based on self-reported cash income ("official" definition).
[2]Based on self-reported cash income *plus* public in-kind benefits such as Medicare, Food Stamps, and rental subsidies.
Source: Current Population Reports (Series P-60, No. 157, and Technical Paper 57, Census)

FIGURE 2-3 **Persons Living in Poverty by Age-Group, 1986**

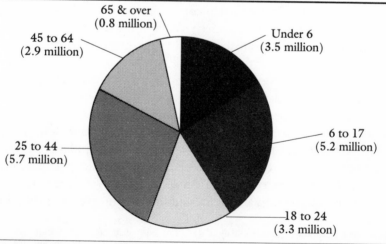

Based on self-reported cash income *plus* public in-kind benefits such as Medicare, Food Stamps, and rental subsidies.
Source: See Figure 2-2

problem of poverty in America is becoming most closely associated with young families and childhood.

We need not belabor the point with further adjustments of the poverty rate for taxes, underreporting, and household wealth. Let us simply note that such adjustments would heighten the disparity further. In particular, the fact that relatively few retirees are subject to regressive payroll taxes (which must be paid on the first dollar of income even by millions of younger workers who live beneath the poverty level) increases the overall advantage for the elderly. As for household wealth, surveys have found that about one-quarter of all elderly households officially in poverty own homes in which the owners have at least $50,000 in equity. It remains true that the greater income spread in the bottom quarter of elderly households translates into a relatively higher concentration of elderly living on near-poverty incomes. Even here, though, the greater spread is overwhelmed by the effect of generally higher incomes. In 1982, for instance, raising the threshold to 150 percent of the official poverty line would have quadrupled the total-income elderly poverty rate, from 4.5 to 18.5 percent. But it also would have more than doubled the nonelderly poverty rate, from 11.8 to 27.2 percent. Even by this measure, the elderly are still better off, though certainly not by as much as before.

Our intention is not to deny that some of the elderly are indeed poor, very poor. As we mentioned earlier, this is particularly true for those elderly who are older, in poor health, female, widowed or divorced, without a private pension, and nonwhite. Aging expert Stephen Crystal has called them "multiple jeopardy" groups.* In 1984, for example, widowed females over seventy-two were *twice* as likely to live beneath the official poverty level (21 percent did so) than the rest of the elderly population. Similarly, Hispanics over seventy-five were *two and one-half* times more likely to live in poverty (over 25 percent did so) than the rest of the elderly population. At the same time, of course, let us not forget that children, as well as the elderly, can belong to "multiple jeopardy" groups: in that same year, fatherless black children under the age of six were *five* times more likely to live in poverty (over 70 percent did so) than all other Americans.

But it is ludicrous to claim that our existing system of age-based entitlements constitutes a systematic attempt to relieve genuine poverty among the elderly. Consider that in 1986 we spent $270 billion, at the federal level alone, on benefits to the elderly. Yet with only an

*In *America's Old Age Crisis* (Basic Books, 1982).

additional $4 billion, properly targeted, we could raise every elderly household over the poverty level,* and with another $4 billion (including, perhaps, state and local aid), we could go very far in alleviating the isolation, chronic health problems, and general hardship afflicting many of the near-poor elderly. The tragedy, unfortunately, is that there is no political pressure to enact such patently desirable assistance. And even if there were, we could not afford it, precisely because we cannot presently afford the untargeted assistance we are handing out to middle- and upper-income Americans in such large dollops.

It might be argued, of course, that even if our expensive entitlements system leaves some of the elderly in poverty, our spending at least helps to narrow the overall distribution of income among elderly households. Even this claim, however, is by no means easy to verify. Of one fact we are certain: non-means-tested benefits constitute the vast majority (over 90 percent) of federal entitlements flowing to the elderly, and the overall impact of this flow is unquestionably regressive. In 1986, for example, 14 percent of all Social Security cash benefits went to the 12 percent of all recipient households that had annual reported cash incomes *above* 600 percent of the poverty level. More remarkable, only 25 percent of all benefits went to the 34 percent of all recipient households whose cash incomes were *beneath* 200 percent of the official poverty level. In 1984 households with annual incomes of more than $24,000 received two out of every three civil service retirement dollars and five out of every six military retirement dollars. Meanwhile, the insurance value of Medicare was about evenly distributed among all elderly households, rich and poor. To be sure, the remaining small share of benefits for the elderly that are means-tested does tend to narrow the income distribution. But the net progressivity of all federal benefit income is surprisingly uncertain.

It is often emphasized that benefits comprise an increasingly large share of the elderly's income, and that to take away all benefits would devastate their overall living standards. Both points are undeniable. Since the unprecedented growth in the elderly's relative income has occurred during a period when ever-fewer elderly are employed, it would be surprising indeed if benefits did not at least have something to do with it. It is also true that eliminating all benefits would have unthinkable and catastrophic results. A stop on all monthly Social

---

*Or at least we could offer, for this price, cash benefits equal to 100 percent of the poverty level to every elderly household that applied for means-tested Supplemental Security Income. Elderly households in poverty often refuse to apply no matter how low their income (see Chapter 7).

Security checks, for example, would quickly throw about nine million elderly into poverty, quadrupling the official poverty rate for Americans over sixty-five.

But obviously it does not follow from this that our current entitlement programs are inviolable. Even the wealthiest man could be impoverished if all his income were cut off, just as the tree in worst need of trimming would die if it were chopped off at its roots. The conclusions we draw are different: first, that most benefits for the elderly have nothing to do with alleviating poverty; second, that vast resources could be saved by modest, structural reductions in benefits flowing to middle- and upper-income groups; and finally, that even a small share of such savings, properly targeted, could at the same time achieve unprecedented relief for those who really are in need.

Myth Four: "You Just Get Back What You Paid In"

Perhaps the most common of all the myths about nonpoverty entitlements is that beneficiaries have funded their retirement through payroll "contributions" made over the course of their working lives—in short, that they have "paid" for them. This myth is of course most closely associated with Social Security cash benefits, but also surfaces in connection with Medicare "Part A" and the Civil Service Retirement System.

Many Americans innocently assume that retirement and disability entitlements function exactly like private-sector annuities; that payroll taxes are a type of savings and that "contributions" are simply deposited in interest-yielding "bank accounts" until beneficiaries reach retirement age. In this sense, it is thought that Social Security and other payroll-financed entitlements resemble fully funded private pension plans in which money is saved, invested, and then returned to the individual beneficiary. Alternatively, another misconception is that entitlement programs are a true form of "insurance" in which payroll taxes are a premium and the event being insured against is retirement or disability.

In keeping with the notion that what workers "purchase" through payroll taxes is either an annuity or an insurance policy, it is widely believed that beneficiaries—at least on the average—receive a return that is roughly equal to their contributions plus interest, or that is at least commensurate with the premiums they have paid. In other words, "you just get back what you paid in." The logical corollary is that Social Security, Medicare, and a variety of other federal retirement benefits in some sense "belong" to the entitled recipient.

The truth of the matter, however, is that payroll taxes bear virtually no relation to entitlement benefits, either for individuals or for entire generations of beneficiaries. For different individuals, the lack of correspondence between taxes paid and benefits received should be obvious to anyone who has applied for Social Security benefits. For example, what must we think of an annuity that grants (as Social Security does) a married couple an extra 50 percent monthly benefit for the rest of their life together just because the retiring worker has a nonworking spouse? This is equivalent to an entirely unearned $50,000 "nonworking spouse bounty" handed out to the typical couple retiring today at age sixty-five.* Or what must we think of an annuity that entirely ignores how many years you have been paying for it (as Social Security does) but instead looks only at how much you earned during those years? The Social Security Administration keeps no direct record of your contributions; indeed, it gives no consideration to whether you paid into the system at high or low tax rates, to whether you paid most early or late in your career, or (for many workers now retired, as we will see in Chapter 7) whether you paid anything at all until late in your career.

As for different generations, here the inequities are far more grievous—although they have occasioned fewer complaints since evidently we care less about them. The general rule for Social Security (though there are exceptions†) is as follows: the earlier you were born, the better deal you get. Most Americans who were born before the turn of the century and retired in the 1950s, for instance, received lifetime OASI benefits that were *ten to fifty times greater* than the actuarial value of prior contributions—including both employee and employer contributions plus interest. Most Americans retired today are receiving OASI benefits that are *two to five times greater* than the actuarial value of prior contributions, while the payback for Medicare's HI is *five to twenty times greater* (since HI is still today, as OASI once was, a relatively young program). And what about elderly Americans tomorrow? The best that retirees can hope for forty years from now is to break even on the value of their prior contributions.

---

*Alternatively, this is a "working spouse penalty," since a spouse must have earned monthly benefits at least equal to 50 percent of her husband's in order receive *any* return on prior contributions. Since dual-earning couples are becoming ever more prevalent, this provision also adds—in the aggregate—to the penalty against future generations of retirees.

†See discussion of pre-Notch "Bonanza Babies" in Chapters 6 and 7.

More realistically, most of them probably will *not* break even, meaning that they would have been better off had they been able to excuse themselves from the system altogether.

As for the Civil Service Retirement System, we are told that it is a genuine pension program in which workers and federal agencies each contribute a percentage of payroll to a trust fund that is earmarked for benefit payments. Yet the pension level is so high (averaging 56 percent of preretirement pay after thirty years), the retirement age so young (two out of every five civil servants retire before age fifty-five), and the disability criteria so lenient (one-quarter of all civil service pensioners are "disabled") that every outside actuary has found that benefits far exceed contributions—usually by two to three times. By any objective standard, however, it is military retirement that is the ultimate bonanza. The serviceman contributes nothing to a trust fund, yet upon completing twenty to thirty years of service (the median retirement age is forty-one) is entitled to 50 to 75 percent of preretirement pay, indexed yearly, for life. Typically, military pensioners—including many of the most valuable members of the armed forces—spend more years collecting benefits than they spent in the service. Only a quarter are over sixty-five, all are eligible for Social Security, and most pursue second careers in order to earn a "triple-dip" private pension.

As we will see in later chapters, the widespread confusion about the nature of Social Security and Medicare (and to a lesser extent the other nonpoverty entitlements) reflects real ambiguities in the structure and purpose of the programs themselves. While the lack of direct correspondence between payroll taxes and benefits makes it meaningless to think of Social Security as a pension or insurance plan in any conventional sense, the program does have elements of an annuity (benefits, for instance, are actuarially reduced for early retirement) and is cloaked in the metaphors of private insurance. This confusion aside, if Social Security is not a conventional annuity, an insurance plan, or a means-tested poverty benefit, what is it?

It is, of course, a system of *social insurance*, and just like similar systems abroad it is funded out of the government's current revenues, not by "drawing down" the past contributions of beneficiaries.* In

---

*Although citizens abroad are generally aware that their social insurance systems do not "save" their contributions, many of these systems keep current surpluses in accounts that are separate from the general budget and are formally integrated with private pension systems that are fully funded. Ironically, while we alone remain convinced that our contributions are saved, our system has had one of the purest pay-as-you-go track records—that is, it has been one of the poorest in actually generating savings.

reality, Social Security, Medicare (HI), and civil service and military retirement were never intended to function like fully funded pension systems. They all largely or entirely operate on a "pay-as-you-go" basis, meaning that current benefits are paid by the contributions (taxes) of current workers. That all these entitlement programs maintain trust funds into which payroll taxes or contributions are deposited is in this respect irrelevant, since the so-called funds have historically served as no more than temporary repositories for revenues that are first collected from workers and then redistributed to beneficiaries. In fiscal year 1986, for instance, the income to the Old-Age, Survivors, and Disability Insurance trust funds was $215.5 billion, and outlays amounted to $198.9 billion, but assets at year's end totaled only $39.7 billion, barely enough to pay for two months of future benefit spending.

In pay-as-you-go social insurance, there is no necessary link between contributions and benefits. This is particularly true in the start-up phase of a pay-as-you-go program, which often entails huge windfalls for the first generations of beneficiaries. Workers begin paying into the system immediately, but since taxes are not saved, they can be used to pay full benefits to potential beneficiaries at or near retirement who have paid in little or nothing. Moreover, since contributing workers in the start-up phase greatly outnumber potential beneficiaries, this can be accomplished with relatively low initial tax rates. The dynamics of the start-up phase can later be repeated by raising benefit levels or by bringing additional participants into the system. As we will see in Chapter 7, this is precisely what has happened with Social Security.

The assertion that Social Security retirees today are enjoying huge, unearned windfalls so often encounters skepticism that we will illustrate our point in Figure 2-4 and Table 2-3 by means of a typical example. Consider the payback of benefits to taxes for a man who was born in January 1916, began work at age 21 (in January 1937), and earned average wages in Social Security-covered employment throughout his life. He chose to retire at age 65 in January 1981, and from then on has been receiving OASI cash benefits and Medicare, both for himself and for his nonworking wife. We expect him to live until age 79 and his wife until age 84 (the average 1981 life expectancies at age 65 for males and females). Table 2-3 indicates how he fares in terms of total taxes paid (both by himself and his employer) versus benefits received. We compare all amounts in terms of *discounted*

1981 dollars—meaning that we *add* the interest on taxes paid before 1981 and *subtract* the interest on benefits to be received after 1981.

How does this couple make out? Very well indeed. Note that the 1981 value of all Social Security taxes paid (including HI) is about $39,000, while the 1981 value of all benefits to be received is about $178,000. In other words, for every $1.00 the couple supposedly "earned" in benefits (even this of course was never actually saved), they are receiving a $4.40 donation from younger workers. For OASI alone, the ratio is 4 to 1, and for HI alone, it is 10 to 1—both about standard ratios for this couple's generation. Figure 2-4 makes the same point a bit more dramatically by showing how long it takes this couple to recoup their prior tax contributions. Only four months after retirement, they have already gotten back all HI taxes plus interest, and by three and one-half years after retirement, they have also gotten back all OASDI taxes plus interest.

But consider yet another calculation. Six years and three months after retirement, these two Americans are reimbursed *for all their lifetime federal income taxes* (prior to retirement), and just before twelve years, they are reimbursed for *all of the lost interest* on those federal income taxes. Before their retirement is over, in short, they will have been repaid for virtually everything they have ever given to the federal government. What they paid for Lend Lease and TVA, Inchon Landing and NATO, Model Cities and the space missions, CETA programs and cruise missles—their lifelong public endowment is returned to them before their retirement is over.

To be sure, not everyone retiring in the late 1970s or early 1980s is doing as well as this couple. Many are doing somewhat worse (for example, those who are unmarried, or who had working spouses, or who made higher-than-average incomes); on the other hand, many are doing somewhat better.* A more interesting question is whether future generations will do anywhere near as well. And here we must give a firmly negative answer. Just consider the numbers: as recently as 1959, halfway through the working career of the couple retiring in 1981, the *maximum* yearly FICA tax was $240. In 1990, at the beginning of a career for today's young adults, the maximum yearly

---

*Aside from the advantage of the nonworking spouse, this couple was born in an unusually good year for receiving Social Security benefits (as we will see in Chapter 6). But it also experienced certain disadvantages: the husband, for instance, began paying FICA taxes in 1937—whereas many Americans born the same year did not have to start paying until the 1950s (with no loss in ultimate benefits). Note as well that we included neither what the "average" couple receives in disability (DI) benefits, nor the large federal subsidy for SMI medical benefits.

FIGURE 2-4 **Social Security Benefit Payback on Contributions for Couple Retiring at Age 65 in January 1981**

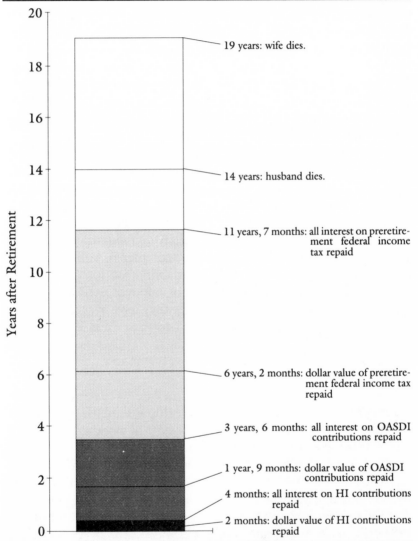

Assumptions: Man born in Jan. 1916; began work in Social Security-covered employment in Jan. 1937; retired with nonworking spouse in Jan. 1981; earnings each year equal to average earnings for all Social Security-covered workers; federal income tax applied to these earnings only; husband dies at age 79; wife dies at age 84. Initial Primary Insurance Amount (PIA) equals $529.86; initial HI cost per enrollee equals $79.82 per month. Discount (interest) rate through 1981 equal to yearly interest rate on OASDI trust-fund assets; after 1981 equal to inflation rate plus 2 percent. Yearly cash benefits are indexed to inflation rate for all future years; yearly value of HI benefits per enrollee rises at inflation rate plus 4 percent for all future years.

Source: Authors' calculations

TABLE 2-3 **Social Security Benefit Payback for Couple Retiring at Age 65 in January 1981**

Average Yearly Taxes Paid	OASDI	HI	Federal	Total	Total as Percent of Income
1937–39	$19	$0	$0	$19	2.0%
1940–49	31	0	178	209	13.3
1950–59	126	0	541	666	20.6
1960–69	345	22	807	1,174	24.7
1970–80	868	159	1,283	2,310	26.0
Total Lifetime Taxes Paid	14,619	1,971	29,372	45,962	15.0
Total Accrued Interest	20,854	1,657	55,904	78,417	—
1981 Discounted Value of Lifetime Taxes (Principal Plus Interest)	35,473	3,630	85,276	124,379	21.6
Average Yearly Benefits in Retirement	9,742	2,291	0	12,033	—
1981 Discounted Value of Lifetime Benefits	140,939	36,757	0	177,695	30.8
Memo: Ratio of Lifetime Benefits to Lifetime Taxes	4.0	10.1	0.0	1.4	—

Assumptions: Same as for Figure 2-4.

Source: Authors' calculations

FICA tax will be $7,524. That is an increase of more than eight times the price level and nearly six times the average wage level over the past thirty years. Young adults must pay all this, and for future benefits that will not be not much greater (and may ultimately be less) than those enjoyed by current retirees.

Imagine—by analogy—a college that promised each graduating senior a lump-sum payment greater than all of his or her previous four years of tuition plus interest. Could it fund its operations and stay solvent while fulfilling such a promise? For a time, yes: during the first four years it will do fine, and after that it can always resort to enrolling more freshmen or raising the tuition to keep its cash flow going. Clearly, however, the time will come when the game is up. For future Social Security retirees, that time has arrived. We can no longer enroll any new "freshmen" (all candidates are already enrolled, and the supply of future young adults is now shrinking); nor can we raise the tuition much higher (we will already have to raise it just to keep from defaulting on the "seniors" now due to graduate early in the next century).

In the end, when a pay-as-you-go social insurance system matures, the number of beneficiaries will climb relative to the number of current workers, tax rates will rise, and the discounted ratio of benefits to contributions will fall for younger generations of participants. For Social Security, these inequities are being greatly compounded by our slowdown in productivity (and real wage) growth, by the demographics of an aging society, and by the coming retirement of the Baby Boom. Here there is both irony and cause for moral concern. Current beneficiaries are by and large convinced that their huge windfalls are no more than a legitimate return on what they paid into the system; future retirees will not even cash in on the value of their contributions plus interest. Such disparities must eventually call the rationale of our entitlements system into question.

Myth Five: "Retirement Benefits Constitute a 'Social Contract' Between the Young and Old"

Once it is established that Social Security contributions are not "saved" in an "account" and that the system is not analogous to a private pension or insurance plan, apologists for our entitlements status quo fall back on the "generational contract" myth. Here they admit up-front that Social Security is financed through transfers of income between generations, but argue that the benefit and tax provisions of the system should nonetheless be regarded as inviolable, since all Americans, taxpayers and beneficiaries alike, have somehow agreed to the rules of the game beforehand. And even if all Americans have not agreed, it is socially useful for us to pretend they have. Thus Social Security is a "contract" or "compact" between generations, and as such is no less binding than a private-sector pension agreement between workers and their employer.

The power of this self-defining myth to explain away any of the system's economic as well as ethical problems is nothing short of miraculous. According to one typical account: "Social Security is often referred to as a compact between citizens and the government, and is often considered an intergenerational compact as well. These perspectives help explain why pay-as-you-go financing is generally sufficient to guarantee the continuity and stability of the program."*

---

* *Ties that Bind: The Interdependence of Generations* by Eric R. Kingson, Barbara A. Hirshorn, and John M. Cornman (Seven Locks Press, 1986).

A common defense of this public "generational contract" is that in its absence there would exist in society a vast private transfer of resources from the young to the old, since most children would have to care for their parents in old age. Therefore, it is claimed, the social insurance "contract" has no generational losers, at least not among younger workers as a group, and assuming that they would all want to live up to their obligations. Instead, it merely replaces a *private* transfer with a *public* transfer, and it does so in a manner ensuring that the pre-existing burden will be more equitably distributed among society's members. This is the claim that legitimizes Social Security as a "floor of protection" for all the elderly, regardless of their individual economic circumstances or the ethical instincts of their children.

This floor-of-protection argument may indeed be a valid defense of Social Security. It does not, however, justify any given level or distribution of benefits as an immutable "contract." If it were true that our existing system merely replaced a customary floor of private, intrafamily transfers, we might expect elderly and nonelderly incomes to follow the same general trends over time. Clearly, as we saw earlier, this is not the case. We might also expect that, if the system is not overcompensating for the private transfers it is replacing, we should still observe some net private transfer of resources within families from children to their parents. Whatever may have been the case back in the early decades of Social Security, there exist no data today that bear out this expectation.

In fact, all the evidence indicates that the opposite is true—which is what we might have supposed given the elderly's growing relative affluence. According to one recent poll, people below the age of sixty-five estimate that about 30 percent of the aged receive income from their children. But of all elderly who report on their own condition, only 1 percent say they receive their principal support from children or relatives; more than 95 percent say they do not receive any help that could be considered income; furthermore, *twice as many say they are providing help to their children as receiving it.** Significantly, 13 percent of families headed by individuals aged fifty-five and over report that children who had moved away from home find that financial difficulties require them to move back in with their parents (about the same proportion of elderly who live with their adult children). Catastrophic health-care costs are often cited as perhaps the major reason

*See *America's Old Age Crisis* by Stephen Crystal (op. cit.).

why adult children give financial support to their elderly parents. Of course, many do, but even here the transfer of resources is by no means a one-way street. In terms of the absolute number of families affected, catastrophic out-of-pocket health-care costs are three to four times more prevalent among nonelderly households.*

Even when it is conceded that current levels of social insurance are not substituting for private transfers, it is often argued that this "social contract" is justified if viewed in terms of "life cycles" rather than of "competing" generational needs. According to this life-cycle theory, the point is not that one generation is giving and another is getting, but that over the course of each generation's life span individuals both pay into and receive benefits from our social insurance system. In the end, we all come out even (your parents may be taking money from you today, but tomorrow it will be your turn to take money from your children).

To be sure, so long as the outcome achieved is socially desirable, the life-cycle theory may be a good argument. We might, for example, make a legitimate public decision to force individuals to save for their old age even if they are not inclined to do so. To avoid a pernicious outcome, however, such a decision would have to guarantee that each successive generation enjoy comparable expectations as it passes through its life cycle. This is impossible in a pay-as-you-go retirement system such as ours in which no resources are actually saved and no endowment is passed on. As things stand with Social Security, planned benefit levels for future beneficiaries are backed by nothing more certain than highly optimistic projections about the productive powers and tax-pain thresholds of our children. The problem, again, lies neither in the "private transfer replacement" theory nor in the "life cycle" model. Rather, it lies in the belief that such notions can justify a fictive *contract* guaranteeing some level of income transfer from one generation to another.

That the alleged contract is fictive there can be no doubt. One does not have to be a legal expert to know that in law a genuine contract between two parties assumes a mutual agreement on its binding terms, a full awareness of all obligations, and voluntary consent. In terms of

*According to *Catastrophic Illness Expenses* (Department of Health and Human Services, 1986), this approximate ratio holds no matter how we choose to define "catastrophic" out-of-pocket costs. Although the per-household rate of catastrophic health costs remains higher for the elderly, this fact is overwhelmed by the much-larger number of nonelderly households and the large share of such households that lack any health insurance.

these most basic guidelines, the Social Security "contract" fails on all counts. First of all, children and the unborn (those who will bear the brunt of the system's future financing) were obviously not present as parties to the original contract; even most adults are entirely uninformed about its true terms. In addition, as we will see in Chapter 7, the original contract has been repeatedly altered over the past half-century without the consent of the affected parties. Finally, our social insurance system is not voluntary: the universal and legally binding nature of Social Security leaves no room for individual choice in deciding to enter into the contract.

An agreement between the individual and the state that is not subject to the process of democratic review and change is alien both to our national heritage and to the ethical instincts of most Americans. This is precisely why the "social contract" argument is cited as a "deeper" rationale for Social Security. To Americans at large, public retirement pensions remain money-back "insurance," a concept with which we all feel comfortable. Only among those who know that this argument is indefensible do they become "generational contracts."

The only sense in which Social Security might be considered a contract is in Rousseauian terms: a "social contract" that lies beyond choice, voluntary agreement, or conscious reasoning. As such, it would be exempt from the process of democratic choice. It is worth noting that the binding of the unborn was anathema to our Founding Fathers. We might recall Thomas Jefferson's remark that the earth belongs to the generation of the living and that the "dead hand" of prior generations should not encumber the decisions of generations that follow. In his day, contracts that bound posterity were associated with involuntary servitude, laws of entail, and (last but not least) excessive public debt.*

In conclusion, we should reemphasize that Social Security is indeed social insurance financed through intergenerational transfers—nothing more and nothing less. It is perfectly legitimate for Americans to make an informed decision to achieve public goals through such a

---

*To Jefferson, a generation that incurred a public debt without paying it was in violation of natural law, for it raised "the question whether one generation of men has a right to bind another." He wrote: "What is true of every member of the society, individually, is true of them all collectively.... Then I say, the earth belongs to each of these generations during its course, fully, and in its own right. The second generation receives it clear of the debts and incumbrances of the first, the third of the second, and so on. For if the first could charge it with a debt, then the earth would belong to the dead and not to the living generation. Then, no generation can contract debts greater than may be paid during the course of its own existence." (Letter to James Madison, 1789.)

program and to mandate that all citizens must be participants. It is not legitimate to consider Social Security an inviolable contract, exempt from the democratic process that governs all of our other public decisions about how we allocate our national resources.

A tragic irony in the myth of the "generational contract" or "compact" is that its application is so partial and one-sided. When it comes to immediate benefits for a small body of mature voters, we find that appeals to such a contract are both loud and popular. But when it comes to delayed benefits to the potentially infinite number of those unborn or too young to vote, we wait in vain to hear reference to any reciprocal obligation. Where is the congressional leader who reminds us of what we owe to posterity? Who quotes the terms of the contract that guarantees to our children an effective educational system, the rebuilding of our decaying roads and bridges, the preservation of our natural environment, or the technological breakthroughs in the next century with which future working families will compete in the world economy? Such issues, of course, do not only raise questions about the equity of the Social Security "contract"; they also point directly back to the question of its economic sustainability.

Myth Six: "The Social Security Surplus"—or, "Whatever Problems Once Existed Have Now Been Solved"

After a decade of crises in which Social Security teetered on the edge of bankruptcy, we have witnessed in the wake of the 1983 reform act the rise of a new myth: mounting trust-fund "surpluses" will guarantee the solvency of the OASDI system until the middle of the next century. Accordingly, not only have Social Security's past financing problems been cured, but the program's excess revenues now have a net positive effect on our national balance sheet by offsetting deficits in the rest of the federal budget. Social Security, we hear, could hardly be in better financial shape.

Unfortunately, this renewed faith in Social Security's eternal solvency rests on a stunning series of shaky assumptions and misunderstandings: it takes for granted a future payroll tax hike yet to be enacted, it ignores certain fiscal disaster just beyond a self-imposed seventy-five-year time horizon, it presupposes highly optimistic changes in nearly every economic and demographic trend underlying the system's future financial balance, it deliberately neglects the grim prognosis for its health-care benefit component (Medicare), and it

114

"double counts" its trust-fund surpluses in the unified federal budget. Quite apart from these errors, moreover, this newfound faith refuses to acknowledge that pay-as-you-go financing burdens the federal balance sheet with multitrillion-dollar unfunded liabilities. These in turn suppress the incentive of households to save. The fact that our system of entitlements will be unaffordable tomorrow, in other words, is already undermining our ability to save today.

Let us examine the evidence on which the solvency myth is based. According to the actuarial definitions used by the Social Security Administration (SSA), it is technically correct that the cash benefit programs (OASDI) are solvent or in "close actuarial balance." What this means is that, *averaged* over the next seventy-five years and using "official" (meaning favorable) economic and demographic assumptions, the costs of the OASDI programs will not exceed 105 percent of expected revenues.

This observation, though it might reassure an actuary, in fact conceals the contingent and roller-coaster path that the SSA is projecting for Social Security's financial future. The revenues needed to pay for OASDI benefits in the next century will have to be generated by higher payroll tax rates that have already been legislated but not yet enacted (the "last" tax hike is due to arrive on January 1, 1990). Thereafter, in what amounts to a partial exception to traditional pay-as-you-go financing, the system's trust funds are supposed to run surpluses for the next thirty years while a large (Baby Boom) generation is working and a small (Silent) generation is retiring. By means of these yearly surpluses, the OASDI trust funds are projected to accumulate sizable cash reserves, peaking at over $12 trillion in the year 2030.* But beginning about 2015, as the Baby Boom becomes the Senior Boom, the OASDI surpluses will narrow; eventually, after 2030, they will turn into ever-larger deficits—meaning that benefits will have to be funded by "drawing down" the accumulated reserve. Though the official projection says the trust funds will still be able to pay benefits for another two decades, they are scheduled to run out of money in the year 2051. Forever after—and not just through the end of today's seventy-five-year projection period, which ends ten years later in 2061—the continued solvency of OASDI will require one of

---

*Adjusting this $12.41 trillion figure for forty-two years of projected inflation makes it seem a bit less spectacular. In 1988 dollars, it will amount to about $2.35 trillion.

two options: either a steady decline in benefit levels or an equivalent rise in payroll tax rates.

Accepting this scenario at face value, we run into two questions at the outset. The first concerns our willingness to enact (in 1990) a Social Security payroll tax hike solely for the purpose of accumulating a trust-fund surplus. Never before in the history of Social Security has Congress agreed to enact such a measure—though often it has reneged on previously declared *intentions* to do so.* The second concerns the fate of Social Security after the year 2051. Is history simply supposed to come to an end on that date? Are we invited to use the same approach in formulating our policies toward infrastructure and the environment? The federal government enforces many laws prohibiting financial scams (such as chain letters) whose attractiveness depends upon slamming the books shut after a certain prearranged date. Here, perhaps, is a case in which the law should be applied to the enforcer.

The year 2051, of course, is a very long way off, and we might be excused for gazing at it with some complacency were it not for a further disquieting fact: the "official" economic and demographic assumptions on which the above scenario rests are almost certainly too optimistic. Far more probable are what the SSA calls its "pessimistic" assumptions. In later chapters, we will defend the prudence as well as the plausibility of the "pessimistic" assumptions in some detail. For the moment, we will simply call attention to the bottom line. *According to the SSA's "pessimistic" scenario, the combined OASDI trust funds begin running deficits in 2015 and are bankrupt by 2025—well within the expected life span of every American now under age forty-five.* Opinion polls have revealed a growing skepticism among young workers about the future ability of our current Social Security system to pay them benefits through their retirement—skepticism, we will argue, that is well founded.

Then we come to the problem of Medicare, where even the optimists admit the solvency prospects are bleak indeed. According to HI's 1987 Annual Report, under "official" assumptions Medicare's Hospital Insurance trust fund will be bankrupt in 2002 (fourteen years from now); under "pessimistic" assumptions, it will be bankrupt in 1996 (eight years from now). Clearly no one would want history to

---

*The history of Congress' repeated failure to follow through with its plans to build up a sizable Social Security trust fund ought to be an omen to those who are banking on the 1990 tax hike. It is a story to which we return in Chapter 7.

116

come to an end as soon as this.

Defenders of the solvency myth now argue that Medicare is a special case and that its financial difficulties must be dealt with independently from the rest of Social Security. The rationale for this, however, is not easy to fathom. Medicare was originally designed as a integral supplement to Social Security, and in fact the population of Medicare beneficiaries is nearly identical to the population of those who receive (or are eligible for) OASDI cash benefits. Is it likely that OASDI and Medicare will be allowed to follow their separate courses toward bankruptcy? Not if history is any guide. When OASDI was in trouble before the 1983 reform act, after all, OASDI was allowed to borrow from HI in order to keep itself afloat; and even later, borrowing between the system's three trust funds (OASI, DI, and HI) was authorized through 1987. If this authorization is extended indefinitely, much of the near-term surpluses in OASDI will be diverted to finance widening deficits in HI. According to "official" assumptions, the combined OASDHI trust funds would begin running deficits in 2015; according to "pessimistic" assumptions, *they would already be running deficits as early as 1993*. The huge expected trust-fund reserve, in short, would disappear completely.

A. Haeworth Robertson, former chief actuary of Social Security, once employed a striking image to illustrate the absurdity of assessing the financial status of the cash benefit programs without taking into account the imminent bankruptcy faced by Medicare: it's like the patient who goes to the doctor and is told that his cardiovascular system is in fine shape, but is not informed that his lungs are about to give out.

As we have seen, both Medicare "Part A" (HI) and Social Security cash benefits (OASDI) are largely pay-as-you-go benefit plans; what "bankruptcy" of their trust funds means—simply put—is that outlays are scheduled to exceed revenues plus any remaining assets. The sooner bankruptcy becomes imminent, therefore, the sooner we must either raise payroll taxes further than already scheduled or cut benefits. As for the other major pension and health programs—Medicare "Part B" (SMI), civil service retirement, and military retirement—a discussion of trust-fund "solvency" would be irrelevant since none of them make any real pretense of self-funding. Beneficiary premiums pay for less than 25 percent of SMI benefits. And the civil service and military pension trust funds neither possess assets equivalent to more than a small fraction of their future benefit liabilities, nor are able to keep the

U.S. Treasury from borrowing and spending "off the books" what little they do have.

Returning to the OASDI cash benefit trust funds and accepting for a moment the "official" scenarios offered by SSA, there remains a further problem with the solvency myth. Even if all goes well, it leaves us with the false impression that the enormous reserves accumulated by these trust funds by the early twenty-first century will painlessly finance mounting OASDI deficits for decades thereafter. Unfortunately, it cannot happen this way. Because all OASDI surpluses must (by law) be invested in IOUs from the U.S. Treasury (bonds and notes of varying maturities), the trust funds will find themselves sitting on top of a mountain of Treasury debt when the time finally arrives, in the year 2020 or so, to start "spending down." For OASDI to reclaim this debt, the trustees will have to present their IOUs to the Treasury for payment in cash.

But where will the Treasury find the cash? Needless to say, the cash the Treasury originally received from the OASDI surpluses (for which it gave the trust funds IOUs) will have long since been spent. There will remain only two options: the Treasury will have to get the cash by borrowing from the public in amounts equal to the trust-fund deficits; or the Treasury will have to raise more revenue. Either way, the whole purpose of the vaunted trust-fund reserves will be vitiated. If the Treasury borrows the cash from the public, we will in effect be funding Social Security through deficits; if the Treasury resorts to more revenue, we will merely be replacing a higher payroll tax with a higher personal or corporate income tax.

To Americans who expect still to be taxpayers in the third or fourth decade of the next century, it may of course seem unfair that the Treasury has already spent the surpluses entrusted to it. But what else can it do with the growing cash surpluses it receives from the trust funds? It can hardly just sit on the money. What about allowing the surpluses to be invested in private-sector securities? We might, for example, invest them in high-quality state, corporate, and municipal bonds. This would indeed get around the dilemma so far as the trust funds are concerned. But it would also mean that the Treasury would receive less revenue and thus would have to borrow more from the private sector. What one hand would be giving, another would be taking away in precisely equal amounts.

Some distinct separation of the trust-fund accounts from the rest of the federal budget would, however, at least constitute a conceptual reform: it would force us to face the truth about how much we are borrowing.* Currently, the official numbers veil the truth. At the end of fiscal year 1986, for instance, everyone "knew" that the federal budget deficit weighed in at $220 billion; only a few specialists understood that this figure was the sum of a $240 billion deficit excluding OASDI and a $20 billion surplus for OASDI. As this surplus grows in the 1990s, our perception will become even more warped. Consider the CBO's current (recession-free) forecast, which projects a $134 billion federal deficit by fiscal year 1993; unmentioned is that this figure is generated by a $231 billion *deficit* excluding OASDI and a $97 billion *surplus* for OASDI.

The problem is of course one of "double counting." The anticipated OASDI surplus cannot simultaneously serve both as a credit to the Social Security trust funds *and* to the unified federal budget. So long as the system was designed to function on a purely pay-as-you-go basis, it no doubt made sense to treat Social Security as part of the unified budget; but now that OASDI is ostensibly "prefunding" part of the Baby Boom's retirement, its inclusion mocks the whole purpose of a trust-fund reserve. Ironically, our current accounting practice amounts to using the OASDI surplus—financed by high and regressive payroll taxes shouldered almost entirely by working-age adults—to fund general-purpose federal outlays. Perhaps an analogy will help to clarify the nature of this double counting. We can all appreciate the consternation a young man would experience if his parents persuaded him to buy them a house, promised him that it was for his own future and that they would never sell it, but then proceeded to mortgage every bit of equity he paid into it.†

As the "double counting" problem makes clear, what matters is not

---

*Where the trust-fund surpluses are invested (in Treasury bonds or in the private sector) is really beside the point. Either way, the effective size of the federal budget deficit will have to be measured independently from the trust funds. If we want a "balanced" budget, therefore, we will have to run a surplus on our official budget—a point made by Fed Chairman Alan Greenspan in recent testimony to Congress. It may have seemed that Congress was moving in this direction when it decided in 1983 to move Social Security "off budget" by 1993. Incredibly, subsequent legislation (including Gramm-Rudman) has interpreted this to mean *off* budget for the purpose of changing benefits, but *on* budget for the purpose of calculating the federal deficit.

†Or in the words of John C. Hambor, Director of Economic Research at the Social Security Administration, if deficits in the rest of the budget offset the Social Security surpluses, "the trust fund more accurately represents a stack of IOUs to be presented to future generations for payment, rather than a buildup of resources to fund future payments. In this case, the cost of the baby-boom's retirement is borne fully by future workers...." ("Economic Policy, Intergenerational Equity, and the Social Security Trust Fund Buildup," *Social Security Bulletin*, October 1987).

the long-term health of any individual benefit trust fund; instead, what really matters is the long-term health of the entire federal balance sheet and its effect on national savings. This leads us to the final and most fundamental question that must be asked of those who defend the solvency myth: What overall effect does our entitlements system have on the federal balance sheet? We can begin with the observation that most of our pay-as-you-go entitlement programs are promises to pay for *our own* consumption later in life when we are elderly or disabled. To the extent that we are not prefunding these future benefits, therefore, we are implicitly assuming that future Americans are going to bear *our* burden.

The parallel with financial debt is obvious. In the case of our budget deficits, we finance current consumption by issuing Treasury bonds— in other words, by writing IOUs that tomorrow's taxpayers will be obligated to redeem. In the case of entitlement programs such as Social Security, Medicare, and civil service or military retirement, we issue promises to current workers that they have a claim on future benefits—claims that also constitute obligations for tomorrow's taxpayers.*

The chief difference between these two types of obligation is simply the degree of formality involved. The former involves an explicit bond issue with a contractual right to interest payments that can be defended in a court of law. The latter involves implicit promises with language that sometimes (for instance, when "social contracts" are mentioned) comes stikingly close to the same thing. Senator Russell Long, former chairman of the Senate Finance Committee, once put it simply: "Social Security is nothing more than a promise to a group of people that their children will be taxed for that group's benefit." Though rarely recognized by either policymakers or the public, this has profound implications for our nation's future. The truth of the matter is that we have silently accumulated an informal federal debt— payable in promised entitlement benefits—whose magnitude dwarfs our already huge "official" national debt.

Our official publicly held debt can be measured precisely: at the end of fiscal year 1986, it amounted to $1.745 trillion, triple what it had

---

*Unlike benefit promises, which cost the taxpayer nothing until they "come due," interest is payable on Treasury bonds starting on the date they are issued. But this is only a difference in financial convention. If, for example, the Treasury issued its debt in the form of "zero-coupon" bonds (where all the interest is paid on the date of redemption), there would be no difference in timing.

been when the 1980s began. Unfortunately, our informal debt cannot be measured with such precision, since total future benefit obligations and available revenues will vary according to future demographic and economic trends. Nonetheless, if we limit ourselves to those federal retirement and health-care programs where individual benefit levels and (in most cases) payroll tax rates are already established by law, we can arrive at a good estimate. According to calculations made by the General Accounting Office (GAO) and independent actuaries,* the informal debt for these programs (most important, Social Security, Medicare, and civil service and military retirement) almost certainly exceeded $10 trillion at the end of fiscal year 1986. Technically, this sum is known as an "unfunded liability" and refers to the present value of all benefits today's workers and retirees are scheduled to receive minus both our current trust-fund reserves *and* the present value of all future payroll taxes today's workers are slated to pay in.[†] It amounts to a hidden debt of $100,000 for every American worker—a debt that we have decided will be borne by our children.

Because the federal government persists in using a system of "cash in–cash out" accounting, the burden of this informal debt appears nowhere in our official federal budget. But if the federal government were a private organization, it would be required by law (ironically, by *federal* law) to publish the full extent of its unfunded liabilities and "amortize" them (in other words, write them off as losses) over a thirty-year period.[‡] It is estimated that if this practice had been followed by the federal government for cash retirement benefits alone, our annual federal budget deficits would have been about $150 billion higher than our "official" deficits each year throughout most of the 1970s and 1980s.

Figure 2-5 presents an overall balance sheet for the federal government that has been drawn up according to the norms that an actuary would follow if employed by a private corporation. As is readily apparent, not only does our informal borrowing outweigh our formal

---

*Each year, the GAO report is prepared for the Treasury Department and published as the "Consolidated Financial Statement of the U.S. Government." The accounting firm of Arthur Anderson & Co. has also periodically prepared such a balance sheet.

†"Present value" is a financial computation that discounts the dollar value of future receipts and outlays to compensate for the future interest we could earn (or would pay) if we received (or spent) the money today.

‡The Employee Retirement Income Security Act of 1974 (ERISA).

FIGURE 2-5   **Federal Assets and Liabilities, End of Fiscal Year 1986**

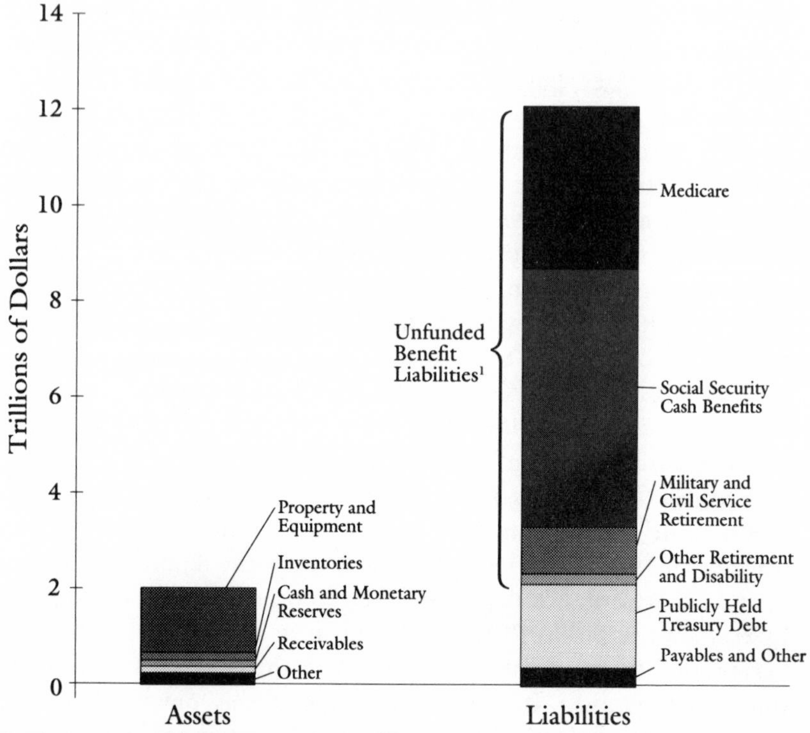

[1]In general, the present value of future benefit payments to current workers and participants *minus* both trust-fund assets *and* the present value of future taxes to be paid in by the same individuals.

Source: FY 1986 Prototype U.S. Consolidated Financial Statement (Treasury) and authors' calculations (see Notes)

borrowing by a ratio of 5 to 1, it also outweighs the total owned assets of the federal government (including land, plant, equipment, military hardware, and all financial assets, valued at cost) by 5 to 1. Just as our formal Treasury borrowing "crowds out" real investment in credit markets, it is reasonable to infer that much of our informal federal debt crowds out private savings that would have occurred in its absence. In other words, if adult Americans today did not assume that federal benefits would someday pay for their retirement, we would all be doing a lot more private savings. In fact, these hidden federal liabilities may help to explain why our net private savings rate is now the *lowest* of all industrial countries; ordinarily, one would expect that a relatively younger population such as ours would have the *highest* savings rate.

To be sure, opinions differ as to whether these unfunded liabilities have a large or small effect on private savings behavior. A few experts have claimed that they have no effect at all.* But this is unlikely. If it were true, we should be surprised to find nearly universal agreement that any reforms that reduce benefit levels must be phased in gradually to allow beneficiaries time to "adjust" to the change. It is hard to imagine what this adjustment might mean if not the opportunity to save more. Alternatively, if the "no effect" argument is correct, we might wonder why we do not allow all private-sector pension plans to function on a pay-as-you-go basis. If this method of financing had no effect on savings rates, what reason would there be to deny an entire generation of private pensioners the opportunity to enjoy windfall benefits?†

The bottom line, once again, is the savings endowment we leave behind us. It is not just an economic question of poorer children in the twenty-first century being unable to *afford* ample benefits for us, their elders. It is also a cultural and political question of poorer children being *unwilling* to return a favor they never received. In the long term, to put it simply, it will be too late to play with shell-game accounting. It will make no difference what politicians once promised or what "earned" benefit number, for which real resources were never allocated, lies buried in some Baltimore computer. Whatever is available for consumption tomorrow must be produced tomorrow. Nothing we do today can change that equation, except to the extent we dedicate resources, through savings, toward helping tomorrow's producers at their task.

Myth Seven: "We Can Balance the Budget Without Touching Entitlements"

We have already seen that explosive growth in entitlements is the driving force behind federal spending, and have argued that cutting

---

*Most economists agree, in theory, that they should have an effect; where they disagree is on the magnitude. The empirical evidence persuades some (such as Martin Feldstein) that there is a large effect, others (such as Alicia Munnell) that there is some effect, and still others (such as Henry Aaron) that there is little effect. Only a few—mainly Robert Barro and the "rational expectations" school—argue that in theory there should be no effect at all.

†We could, of course, continue to protect the beneficiary from corporate bankruptcy as we do now—through the federal Pension Benefit Guarantee Corporation.

nonpoverty benefit programs offers the only means of closing our massive budget deficits. Further reductions in the small nondefense discretionary corner of the federal budget cannot possibly achieve significant savings, and they may even be counterproductive to the extent such programs represent investment. Slashing $600 million from the Environmental Protection Agency, as the administration has proposed in its fiscal year 1989 budget, will have an entirely negligible impact on overall federal spending, though it may adversely effect our future environment. Similarly, adding $400 million to the Energy Department's budget for the "superconducting supercollider" atom smasher will not break the bank, though it may make possible a whole new generation of productive technologies. Those who earn Washington reputations as "fiscally responsible" display their zeal by a perverse skepticism about programs that are not only too small to matter, but often number among those few remaining federal activities that leave something behind when the fiscal year is over. Simply to dismiss them as "pork barrel" is to miss a larger point: dollars that promise future payoffs may actually justify deficit financing.

What about the other budget categories? As already noted, net interest payments on the national debt are mandatory; and, even if the entire procurement, testing, and R&D portion of defense spending were eliminated, we would still be saddled with yawning federal deficits. That, it would seem, leaves entitlements. Yet perhaps, some argue, the budget can be balanced without touching benefits. One school of thought holds that raising taxes is the answer; another maintains that future increases in productivity will allow us to grow our way out of our current deficit problem without taking additional concrete actions. Both lines of reasoning fail to appreciate the magnitude of our problem.

The tax-raisers introduce their case by pointing to the huge chunk of federal revenue we supposedly lost during the 1980s as a result of the 1981 tax reform act. What they fail to add is that much of the 1981 tax cuts, which were to be phased in over several years, was never allowed to take effect. Instead, the 1981 tax cuts were largely neutralized by the tax hikes of 1982 and 1984. Total federal revenue stood at 18.3 percent of GNP in fiscal year 1986, exactly on par with the average percentage for the 1970s decade and only 0.6 percentage points less than revenue in 1979. More important, the tax reform act of 1986 has already raised revenue to 19.4 percent of GNP in fiscal year 1987, and *current deficit projections are based on the assumption that* *federal revenues will remain at 19.4 percent (or higher) from 1988 through 1993 and beyond.* To put this figure in perspective, from the end of World War II through 1979, federal revenues have averaged 17.9 percent of GNP. Postwar federal revenues, in fact, have exceeded 19.4 percent of GNP on only four occasions—all of which brought forth a prompt and passionate voter outcry that the level be reduced.*

One might argue that voters should accept a level of taxation that is permanently higher than what they have accepted in the past. Yet this begs the question, how much higher? In the next chapter, we will show that acceptable tax hikes can raise nowhere near the revenue needed to fund the projected growth in federal entitlement spending. Between 1986 and the year 2025—according to prudent economic and demographic assumptions—the cost of our federal entitlements system will climb by a colossal 11.5 percentage points of GNP. In other words, just to pay for benefits already promised to entitled beneficiaries (and not to make any more room for public investment), it would be necessary to increase federal revenues by *twenty times* the amount they have actually fallen as a share of GNP between 1979 and 1986. Quite aside from the impact such a tax increase would have on economic growth, it is fair to say that the American public, no matter how sympathetically inclined to cutting deficits, would not pay even a major part of this tax hike before a taxpayers' revolt of unprecedented proportions erupted.

The hope that economic growth alone will enable us to grow our way out of our current difficulties is equally illusory. Those who argue this sometimes imply that current deficit projections assume no future growth in our economy. This of course is untrue. Consider, for example, the current CBO projection: not only does it assume no new programs and an actual reduction in real-dollar defense spending, but it also assumes that our GNP will grow at rates considerably higher than it has in recent history. This projection still shows deficits exceeding $100 billion by the mid-1990s. And if we were to exclude the surpluses in our Social Security and federal pension trust funds (as

---

*To be sure, the "mix" of taxes is changing. The first time federal revenues exceeded 19.4 percent of GNP (in 1970), 9.4 percent was raised in personal income taxes and 4.2 percent in payroll taxes. By 1993 the projected levels will be 8.8 percent and 7.1 percent, respectively. Since most Americans judge taxes by their total burden, however, it is doubtful whether this gives us much "room" to raise more through personal income taxes. Indeed, the "income tax" revolts of the late 1970s cannot be understood without looking at payroll taxes: over the entire postwar era, increases in FICA tax revenue have more than accounted for all of the rise in federal revenue as a share of GNP.

proper accounting would require), the projected deficits would be even higher: about $280 billion by fiscal year 1993. Far from gaining on a balanced budget, the CBO's current projection—based on a premise of robust growth—shows that we actually lose ground.

We might, of course, hope that our productivity performance will steadily improve in the 1990s. And as productivity growth accelerates, it would not be unreasonable to imagine that GNP growth would do the same—the happy consequence being an ever-larger flow of tax revenue (at current tax rates) that would ultimately foil the projections and balance the budget.

While hope is commendable, blind confidence is not. Those who place their faith in this sort of extreme good fortune may not fully understand what their faith is up against. Let us make two specific caveats. First, the CBO and similar projections (such as the "official" SSA scenario) *already* assume future productivity growth rates that are—like the assumed GNP growth rates—higher than those in recent history. This optimism is based on the assumption, typically made in these projections, that recessions have been forever banished from our future.

Second, it must be emphasized that the growth of our labor force will be *decelerating* in the 1990s (as a much-smaller generation, born after the mid-1960s, will account for most new workers). It follows, therefore, that *we will have to achieve higher productivity growth rates in the future simply to generate the same real GNP growth.* Alternatively, a constant productivity growth rate must generate a declining rate of GNP growth. Largely as a result of this demographic twist, every SSA projection now shows that our yearly real GNP growth rate will fall dramatically during the 1990–2000 decade, and fall further during the 2000–2010 decade.* After 2010, our GNP growth rate may hold steady. But by then, if our policies have not changed, it won't be worth bothering about the effects of GNP growth on federal revenue. We will be too busy worrying about the far more awesome effect of our coming Senior Boom on federal spending.

In the long run, simply put, current policy leaves us in the position of having to run ever faster just to stay in place. Consider the following numbers, which are borrowed from the SSA projections and will be discussed more fully in the next chapter. If gross real output per worker-hour *increases* from the 0.9 percent per-year growth rate we

---

*According to the "official" (II-B) scenario, for instance, the average annual growth rate in real GNP by the year 2010 will sink to only two-thirds of what it has been during the 1980s.

126

have enjoyed over the 1976–1985 decade to 1.5 percent per year over the course of the coming decades, we will be running budget deficits equivalent to almost 40 percent of GNP in the year 2025 (ten times greater than the deficit levels we are experiencing today). Even if this productivity growth rate were to climb all the way back to 1.7 percent per year, we would still be facing deficits on the order of 15 percent of GNP a generation from now.

Again, the problem with the optimistic "growth" school is not that it is hopeful; we all hope our productivity performance improves—and the more it improves, the better. The problem is that it makes hope the foundation of prudent decision making. As a political gesture, hope often comes across as courage, but as a policy choice it rarely amounts to more than complacency. Ironically enough, the certain expectation that we can "always grow out of it"—by making us believe that we need do nothing about the crippling consumption bias of our economy—is just the thing that will best guarantee that we never will. The argument that painless increases in productivity will close our budget deficits over the next generation is simply the supply-side fallacy of the 1980s projected onto a larger historical canvas. What we failed to achieve during a single decade, apparently, we will be able to engineer over the course of the next fifty or seventy-five years. If former Senator Howard Baker called Reaganomics a "riverboat gamble," what would he call this?

3

A Fiscal Nightmare

"For which of you, intending to build a tower, sitteth
not down first, and counteth the cost, whether he hath
sufficient to finish it?"

— Luke 14:28

THE ENTITLEMENTS PROBLEM will not cure itself.
Indeed, there is no economist or budgetary expert who has
carefully extrapolated the long-term course of our fiscal
policy without rejecting the possibility of "self-cure." The reason is
simple: entitlement expenditures will rise rapidly as our elderly population explodes, and at the same time will become less affordable as the
ratio of taxpaying workers to beneficiaries declines. No matter how
reluctant we may be to accept its consequence, the aging of the U.S.
population is a process that cannot be reversed in the foreseeable
future. "Demography is destiny," as Richard Easterland, one of that
quantitative art's most famous students, once observed.

In this chapter we consider a single key question: If present fiscal
and benefit policies remain unaltered and demographic and economic
developments unfold according to prudent assumptions, what share
of our national resources will federal expenditures—and in particular
entitlement spending—consume fifteen or fifty years from now? This
is an exercise in fiscal "projection," not "prediction." A *prediction* is
a flat assertion that a future event will happen. A *projection* is simply

an if-then statement: *if* current policies remain unchanged, *then* a future event will happen. As we will see, it is doubtful that our nation will honor the long-term spending commitments—or "contracts"—projected in this chapter. Long before entitlement expenditures reach such astronomical levels, we will alter our policies and cut federal spending. If we do not do so now, voluntarily, we will do so later, involuntarily—probably in the midst of economic and financial crisis, and perhaps under the threat of a taxpayer revolt.

As a preview, just consider the following numbers. If current federal budgetary policies are projected into the indefinite future, total federal expenditures—which averaged 20.8 percent of Gross National Product—in the 1970s and hit 23.6 percent in 1986—may reach 30.2 percent of GNP by the year 2000. Entitlement spending alone will climb from 11.1 percent to 14.3 percent of GNP. Similarly, total federal deficits—which averaged 1.9 percent of GNP in the 1970s and rose to 5.3 percent in 1986—may widen to 11.2 percent of GNP by the year 2000. Should we obstinately continue on this same course until the year 2040, our federal budget will be consuming 86.1 percent of GNP, with entitlement spending and interest on the national debt accounting for more than three-quarters of the total. Meanwhile, yearly budget deficits will be running at about two-thirds of GNP.

If you find such projections unsettling, read on. We begin by reviewing the efforts of the Social Security Administration to make long-term projections. Later, we expand these efforts to include projections for all federal entitlement programs and speculate on what these numbers imply for the political and economic future that many of us can expect to inherit in our own old age, and that our children and grandchildren can expect to inherit with much of their lives still ahead of them.

Optimistic, Pessimistic, and Prudent Assumptions

Back in the 1930s, actuaries and social scientists at the Social Security Administration (SSA) began making what still remain the only official long-term fiscal projections used by the federal government—the only projections that attempt to plot the course of a program's expected revenues and outlays beyond the next four or five years.* For Social

*Since 1986, the military retirement system (see Chapter 8) has also started to calculate long-term outlay projections. But unlike Social Security, it calculates only a single projection each year and makes no attempt to analyze its sensitivity to different economic and demographic assumptions.

Security, the need to develop long-term cost projections was self-evident from the beginning. After all, a program that promises benefits payable as much as seventy-five years into the future can only function smoothly if it is reasonably certain that income will always be adequate to cover costs.

Since Social Security is a pay-as-you-go program financed through payroll taxes, its ability to pay promised benefits depends on both future demographic and economic trends. Demographic trends determine how many future taxpayers and beneficiaries there will be; economic trends determine the average taxable income of each future worker and the average monthly benefit of each future beneficiary. Once SSA directors agree on plausible assumptions about these future trends, actuaries can figure how much future benefits will cost as a share of future workers' taxable income. This number is equivalent to the future payroll tax rate needed to keep the system's income at least on par with its outlays.

Throughout the early decades of the system's existence, the SSA limited itself by and large to making demographic projections—in other words, to asking the question: Given certain future assumptions about fertility rates, immigration, longevity, and retirement, how many taxpaying workers and beneficiaries will there be in the years to come? Every few years, a "high-cost" and "low-cost" pair of long-term projections were generated using these assumptions.*

In 1971 the SSA decided to include "dynamic" assumptions about future economic performance (including inflation, wage growth, and unemployment rates) in its projections. When the first "dynamic" projection appeared in 1972, the SSA also chose to abandon its high-low range and instead publish "a single, best estimate, derived from a single set of assumptions that reflect likely future changes."† Chastened by the unexpectedly dismal economic events of the next few years, however, the SSA soon went back to publishing a high-low range. In 1975 it began to calculate three scenarios (I, II, and III, of which II was the "official intermediate" projection). And since 1980, it has calculated four scenarios (I, II-A, II-B, and III, of which II-B

---

*In the "static" projection model, it was simply assumed that average dollar wages would forever remain unchanged (that there would be neither productivity growth nor inflation). Since benefits were unindexed, a couple of years of buoyant wage growth was enough to turn an actuarial surplus, which Congress would then rebalance by granting an "ad hoc" benefit increase (see Chapter 7).

† *The 1972 Annual Report of the Board of Trustees of the Federal Old-Age and Survivors Insurance and the Federal Disability Insurance Trust Funds* (1972).

remains the "official intermediate" projection.* The results of these actuarial computations appear faithfully in the SSA's *Annual Report of the Board of Trustees,* which by law must be presented to Congress by the first of April each year.

The business of making long-term projections when many variables are involved is a tricky one, and over the seventy-five year period for which the SSA is required to crank out numbers, even slight alterations in the underlying demographic and economic assumptions will compound to produce dramatically different results. This is the reason the Social Security trustees calculate future financial trends according to several distinct scenarios. In all four of the SSA's current scenarios, most of the key assumptions fluctuate in the near term before stabilizing at some projected "ultimate" rate some twenty or twenty-five years from now.

Of all the economic assumptions, *productivity growth* is by far the most important in determining the future cost of the system.† The reason is straightforward: over the long term, productivity growth directly determines *real wage growth,* which in turn establishes the future real tax revenue available (at given payroll tax rates) to pay benefits.‡ Assumptions about *inflation* and *unemployment,* on the other hand, are only marginally important in and of themselves. Interestingly, higher future inflation is slightly beneficial to Social Security's future solvency.§ Higher unemployment, of course, hurts by reducing total future taxable earnings—but again, in the long term, its effect is trivial next to productivity and real wage growth.

Among the demographic assumptions, two are of almost equal importance: the *fertility rate,* which determines how many future

---

*Scenarios I, II, and III have always differed in all of their future assumptions, economic and demographic. Scenarios II-A and II-B are identical demographically, but employ somewhat different economic assumptions—most important, faster real wage growth in II-A and slower real wage growth in II-B.

†Defined by the SSA as the average annual increase in gross real output per worker-hour.

‡Real wages and labor productivity are connected through several "linkages" (such as worker compensation as a share of GNP and wages as a share of compensation) which may be loose in the near term but, historically, have kept their respective growth rates nearly identical over the long term.

§This is because the positive impact of inflation on payroll tax revenue (through rising wages) takes place immediately, whereas the positive impact of inflation on benefit outlays (through annual COLA adjustments) takes place with a lag. The overall effect is slight, however, and is usually overwhelmed by the slower real wage growth that normally accompanies higher inflation.

workers there will be paying into the system;* and *longevity at age 65* (both male and female), which determines how long benefits must be paid on average over the lifetime of each beneficiary. Of somewhat less importance is the *labor-force participation rate* for the elderly; to the extent it is higher (or lower) there will be fewer (or more) retirees receiving benefits.† Across the entire reach of the next seventy-five years, the demographic assumptions exercise about the same influence on Social Security's solvency as the economic assumptions. Over time, however, the relative importance of the two change dramatically. During the next couple decades, a change in the demographic scenario can do little to affect our fiscal direction. (A change in this year's fertility rate, after all, will have no impact on the size of the labor force until well after the year 2000.) Further into the future, the demographic assumptions rise rapidly in influence; forty years from now, in fact, they begin to exercise decidedly more control over our fiscal future than the economic assumptions.

Table 3-1 presents actual historical and projected "ultimate" values (from the SSA's 1987 Annual Report) for the major demographic and economic assumptions in scenario II-B and scenario III.‡ As for the first two scenarios ("I" and "II-A"), they have both been omitted from Table 3-1 entirely—not only to save space, but also to avoid needless confusion. Scenarios I and II-A are formally described by the SSA as "optimistic." "Absurd" might be a more appropriate word. Both, for example, posit higher rates of long-term productivity growth (2.4 percent and 2.1 percent per year for generations) than our nation has ever sustained historically. Consequently, they are almost always dismissed in any serious discussion of OASDI's future solvency. Following convention, we will dismiss them at this point as well.

The third scenario ("II-B") embodies the SSA's so-called "most likely" or "intermediate" assumptions, and is customarily used as the official benchmark against which the system's financial health is measured. As we will see, far from being "most likely," scenario II-B is also highly optimistic in light of recent historical experience. Finally, the SSA calculates a fourth, "pessimistic" scenario ("III"), presumably

---

*Fertility is measured here by the "total fertility rate": roughly, the average number of children currently being born to each woman throughout her lifetime (see Notes).

†A higher rate also means there will be more elderly workers paying payroll taxes and adding to trust-fund revenue. The different scenarios use varying assumptions about the labor force participation rate for other age-groups as well, but this one is certainly the most important.

‡The most recent SSA projections and scenarios referred to in this book are those of the 1987 Annual Report. For changes made in the 1988 Annual Report, see Notes.

Table 3-1   Selected Indicators of Economic and
Demographic Trends: Past Experience and
Long-Term Future Projections According
to SSA Scenarios II-B and III

	Historical Values		Projections to 2060	
	1951–71	1972–86	II-B "most likely"	III "pessimistic"
Productivity Growth (avg. % yrly. & ultimate)	2.32%	0.88%	1.70%	1.51%
Real Wage Growth (avg. % yrly. & ultimate)[a]	2.10%	0.27%	1.50%	1.00%
Inflation Rate (avg. % yrly. & ultimate)	2.25%	6.81%	4.00%	5.00%
Unemployment Rate (avg. % yrly. & ultimate)	4.50%	7.00%	6.00%	7.00%
Real Interest Rate[b] (avg. % yrly. & ultimate)	2.07%	2.57%[c]	2.00%	1.50%
Longevity at 65, Women (yrs. increase per decade)	1.2 yrs	1.1 yrs	0.9 yrs	1.0 yrs
Longevity at 65, Men (yrs. increase per decade)	0.3	1.0	0.4	0.9
Labor Force Participation Rate for Elderly Men (percentage point change per decade)	–9.5	–6.2	–0.6	–0.9
Total Fertility Rate (avg. yrly. & ultimate)	3.15	1.82	2.00	1.60

"Ultimate" values for real wage growth, inflation, unemployment, and real interest rates are all reached by 2010; the "ultimate" fertility rate is reached in 2020. Average decennial changes in longevity and labor force participation are calculated from the end years 1951, 1971, and 1986.

[a]The annual increase in average wages (excluding all fringe benefits) in employment covered by Social Security minus the annual increase in the Consumer Price Index.

[b]Interest rates on long-term U.S. Treasury notes (OASDI "Special Issue") minus the annual increase in the Consumer Price Index.

[c]This average, however, conceals a steady rise; in 1986 the real long-term interest rate stood at 6.4%.

Source: Office of the Actuary (SSA) and authors' calculations

FIGURE 3-1   **Average Annual 10-Year Change in Real Wages:**
Official Projections in Retrospect

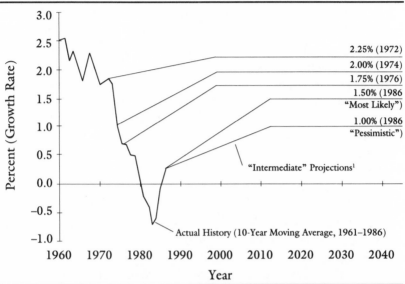

Ten-year moving average of SSA's real wage differential, defined as the percent increase in the average wage of workers covered by OASDI minus the percent increase in the CPI-W.

[1]Except for the "most likely" and "pessimistic" projections, noted for 1986; before 1986, "intermediate" means an average of all SSA scenarios.

Source: Office of the Actuary (SSA)

based on worst-case assumptions, but which in certain respects posits more optimistic developments than we have any prudent reason to expect.

In the next chapter, we will return to SSA's demographic projections when we examine the different factors that are contributing to the rapid aging and earlier retirement of the American population. Here a brief word about overoptimistic economic projections will suffice. A glance at Table 3-1 reveals that for the four major economic variables (productivity, real wage growth, inflation, and unemployment), "ultimate" rates in the "pessimistic" scenario III actually reflect our experience over the past fifteen years *much more closely* than the corresponding rates in the "most likely" scenario II-B. This is especially true for productivity growth and its companion, real wage growth. As we have mentioned, these are by far the most

135

important of all the economic assumptions.* From an average annual growth rate of 0.27 percent from 1971 to 1986, we see that it is "pessimistic" to assume that real wage growth will gradually climb back up to a steady 1.0 percent; and that it is "most likely" to assume that it will rebound all the way to 1.5 percent. Does the SSA know something about our economic future that the rest of us do not? Figure 3-1, which plots past SSA projections of real wage growth against actual experience over the past fifteen years, is not encouraging. Indeed, it reveals how the persistent "optimism" of SSA's past "official" economic assumptions has been continually betrayed by reality.

There is, of course, something bizarre about the choice of words "optimistic" and "pessimistic" to refer to these Social Security scenarios. An "optimistic" future for Social Security's actuarial balance is a world in which many babies are born, in which few of the elderly live very long, and in which those who do live long work rather than retire. The first trend cuts the program's relative cost by broadening the base of future workers who will be paying payroll taxes, while the latter trends directly reduce the benefit expenditures that must be made to the retired elderly. A "pessimistic" future, on the other hand, is one in which relatively fewer babies are born, and in which the elderly retire early and enjoy longer life spans.

"Optimism" and "pessimism" thus refer exclusively to the effects of future developments on Social Security's balance sheet; they do not reflect a coherent set of judgments about the kind of America we look forward to or should like our children to inherit. Not everyone regards many babies and short lives as an optimistic prospect, even if they do brighten the annual reports of the Social Security trustees. Moreover, in light of the vigorous defense of the Social Security status quo made by many Americans who consider themselves "liberals," there is deep irony in the ideological implications of this terminology. The only future that would give the present system even the slightest chance of permanent survival is a future many liberals would find, on the whole, abominable: a future of fantastic economic expansion, buoyant birth rates, working old folks, and stagnant life expectancies. Yet the SSA actuaries tell us that the liberals should be betting on precisely such a future. To be sure, this "optimism" may not be entirely faithful to the "conservative" vision either. But as we reflect on the common cause

---

*The 1987 II-B and III productivity assumptions have already been referred to in Chapter 2.

136

now made by both sides in defense of our current entitlements system, it is hard not to guess that it is the liberals who have wandered furthest from home.

Certainly the most striking characteristic of the SSA's long-term projections is their perennial optimism—an optimism, we should note, that is in large part politically motivated. Simply stated, elected and appointed office holders would much rather preside over a Social Security system whose actuarial balance appears to be improving rather than deteriorating. The former is something that everyone (especially the White House) would like to take credit for. The latter is something that no one (especially Congress) wants to acknowledge, since it might necessitate painful corrective action such as higher tax rates or reduced benefit levels. When the Social Security trustees meet annually to decide on assumptions, therefore, it is clear to the SSA directors and actuaries no less than to the trustees themselves and their staffs (three of the five trustees, the secretaries of Treasury, Labor, and Health and Human Services, are cabinet members who serve on SSA's board ex-officio) that political interests are at stake. Occasionally, SSA's actuaries have been constrained to endorse official, overoptimistic assumptions against their better judgment.*

Since the early 1970s, the politics of overoptimistic projections has caused a curious dialectic to emerge in the SSA's annual reports. Projections are published that reveal OASDI to be "at or near close actuarial balance" over the next seventy-five years. Hardly is the ink dry on the latest report, however, than the revision of one or more of the key actuarial assumptions— almost invariably in the "pessimistic" direction—causes a slow deterioration in Social Security's long-term actuarial balance. After several years of such silent revelations, news of yet another Social Security crisis suddenly surfaces in the press. The president and Congress, having until then avoided the issue, can now come back to the public with "emergency action" to remedy this unplanned "surprise." Revenue-raising or cost-cutting packages are eventually legislated amid assurances that Social Security has been made financially sound "well into the next century"; the SSA actuaries are again obliged to confirm the claim by cranking out a new set of projections—based on only slightly less optimistic demographic and

---

*A case in point was the prudent decision made by SSA actuaries in 1976 to lower the projected "ultimate" fertility rate for scenario II-B to 1.9; the following year, after much behind-the-scenes arm-twisting, the rate was raised once again to 2.1.

economic assumptions than those they used in previous scenarios. At this point the cycle begins again—precisely as it has following the major "reforms" of 1972, 1977, and 1983.

From Assumptions to Projections

Can we know for certain which SSA scenario allows the most accurate projection of future costs? Of course not. What must seem self-evident, however, is that since we are dealing with a program that even under optimistic assumptions is scheduled to consume a growing share of our nation's resources for decades into the future, it is best to be prudent. If, after taking measures now to control long-term costs, future events prove the SSA's "most likely" scenario to be closest to the mark, we should count ourselves lucky. The cost of Social Security including Medicare will still climb steeply, but not to levels that might otherwise have endangered our economy. If the "pessimistic" scenario instead turns out to be the best forecast (this is, after all, the scenario that best describes our current direction), today's caution will have saved both Social Security and our economy from certain crisis in the twenty-first century. Prudence dictates that we prepare for the outcome projected in the "pessimistic" scenario, all the while bearing in mind what experience teaches us: the future may hold still worse in store.

Both the long-term II-B and III cost projections for OASDI are staggering. According to the 1987 II-B assumptions, to be sure, the program is still in "close actuarial balance," with costs over the next seventy-five years averaging 13.51 percent and income averaging 12.89 percent of taxable payroll. This "balance," however, is the result of SSA accounting conventions that allow near-term surpluses to offset ever-widening deficits after the year 2020. Without a fundamental redefinition of federal budget accounting, as we saw in the last chapter, the offsetting surpluses will exist only on paper. After the year 2020, we will in reality be facing rising OASDI trust-fund deficits that will exceed 2.5 percent of payroll from the year 2030 on.

The outlook is much darker if we accept scenario III. According to the 1987 "pessimistic" assumptions, OASDI's average cost rate over the next seventy-five years will be 17.76 percent of payroll, more than 4 percentage points higher than the projected average revenues of 13.07 percent of payroll. There will still be near-term surpluses, but they will be modest; deficits will therefore appear sooner and the trust

---

FIGURE 3-2 **Social Security Income and Outlays as a Percent of Taxable Payroll**

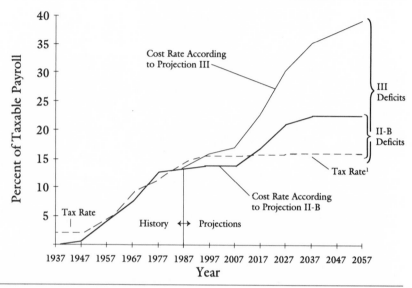

Combined yearly income of OASI, DI, and HI trust funds, expressed as a percent of taxable wages of all workers covered by OASDHI.

[1]Current rate for 1988–90 and "ultimate" legislated rate thereafter; differences between "intermediate" and "pessimistic" projections for the tax rate are negligible.

Source: 1987 OASDI Annual Report

---

funds will be nominally bankrupt by 2025. By the year 2065 annual deficits will amount to 13.14 percent of taxable payroll. At that point, in other words, a balanced budget for the OASDI programs will require nearly *doubling* the current payroll tax rate to 25 percent.

As sobering as these projections are, they refer only to Social Security's cash benefit programs. What about the long-term costs of Medicare, the most rapidly growing of all entitlement programs? For the moment, let us limit ourselves to Medicare "Part A" or Hospital Insurance (HI), since the federal government does not prepare long-term projections for its sister program, Supplementary Medical Insurance (SMI). As recently as 1977, HI was supposed to be solvent indefinitely at a permanent payroll tax rate of 2.9 percent. But today, according to II-B assumptions, HI will pay out medical benefits equivalent to 5.66 percent of payroll by the year 2025 and 6.74

139

percent of payroll by the year 2060. According to scenario III assumptions, HI spending will climb at a still more dizzying pace: to 10.89 percent of payroll by 2025, and to 13.59 percent of payroll by 2060.*

Figure 3-2 provides a comparison of the long-term costs and revenues of the combined OASDHI programs expressed as a percentage of taxable payroll. The difference between costs and revenues is equivalent to the yearly surplus (or deficit). Even according to scenario II-B, the cost of the entire system will reach 22.59 percent of payroll by the year 2060, with yearly deficits amounting to 6.58 percent of payroll. According to the more prudent scenario III, total expenditures will rise to 39.69 percent of payroll in that same year, generating a deficit of 23.22 percent of payroll. Including HI, in other words, the cost of Social Security may consume as much as *one-third* to *one-half* of each worker's taxable compensation.

A. Haeworth Robertson, the former chief actuary of the SSA, concluded recently:

> Of course, in deciding which set of economic and demographic assumptions to rely upon, it is not a question of selecting the "correct assumptions" since that is clearly impossible. The question is this: For the Social Security program, which makes promises about benefits payable as much as 50 to 75 years in the future, what set of assumptions should be used to determine whether or not it seems reasonable to expect that future income will be approximately equal to future outgo and that benefit promises can be fulfilled?
>
> In making this test, it seems to me that the Alternative III assumptions are the most appropriate of the four sets of assumptions shown in the Trustees Reports—and even they may be somewhat optimistic. Based upon these assumptions, it is clear that we have promised substantially more in benefits than can be provided by the scheduled taxes. It is true that taxpayers will be able to pay taxes well above the scheduled future level of 15.3 percent of pay. They will not be able to pay taxes equivalent to 40 or 50 percent of pay, however, since there are many other programs that must be supported by federal, state, and local taxes.[†]

---

*According to the 1987 HI Annual Report, and assuming no interfund borrowing, HI becomes insolvent (goes bankrupt) in 1996 following scenario III, and in 2002 following scenario II-B.

†Speech before the International Society of Certified Employment Benefit Specialists, October 11–14, 1987. That such a message received almost no attention outside a community of specialists is vivid testimony to our careless lack of concern for the bill we are handing to our young.

Projections and the Federal Budget

As Robertson observes, Social Security is not the only public program for which we will have to pay future taxes. More important, it is not the only part of the federal budget (let's leave state and local spending aside) for which the cost will in all likelihood grow much faster than our economy over the next several decades. What about Medicaid and Medicare "Part B" (SMI), which are certain to be buffeted by the explosion in the elderly population and by further real increases in the cost of medical care? Or civil service and military retirement, whose generous and rigidly indexed benefit structure has virtually fixed their future growth trend in concrete? Or veterans' health care and pensions, a set of programs just beginning to feel the burden of the huge crop of retiring World War II GIs?

Finally, what about the growth of interest payments on the federal debt? With deficits averaging 4.1 percent of GNP between 1980 and 1986, in only six years we have already experienced a doubling of interest costs as a share of total federal spending. How long before our Treasury Department, like the Crown of France on the eve of the storming of the Bastille, begins to issue a new bond series just to pay the interest on the one it issued the year before?

To answer these questions, we developed long-term projections for the entire federal budget that would incorporate the same assumptions used by the Social Security actuaries in scenarios II-B and III. The results are shown in Table 3-2 (where all figures are expressed as a share of GNP). In both scenarios, for every future year, the SSA assumptions are faithfully followed for every assumed economic, demographic, and health-care trend. Our sole departure from official SSA assumptions is our decision to use estimates of future interest rates that are more consistent with the overall economic climate projected in the "most likely" and "pessimistic" scenarios.*

In both scenarios, it is of course assumed that no new benefit programs will be added and that no existing programs will be

---

*Because a higher real interest rate makes the trust funds more solvent, the SSA considers it part of a more "optimistic" scenario. Most economists, however, believe it would naturally accompany the more "pessimistic" (slower productivity growth, higher inflation) scenario. We split the difference and use the SSA's II-B "ultimate" real interest rate (2.0 percent) in both scenarios. Note (in Table 3-1) that this projected rate is far beneath recent experience, and thus may considerably understate the compounding growth of interest costs.

modified. Nondefense discretionary spending and all means-tested entitlements other than Medicaid are held constant as a share of GNP. Our handling of defense spending and total revenues, on the other hand, differs according to the scenario. In scenario III, defense spending is assumed to remain unchanged at its fiscal year 1986 level of 6.5 percent of GNP; in our more optimistic scenario II-B, it declines to 6.0 percent of GNP in 1991 and remains at that level thereafter.* Similarly, federal revenue is assumed to stabilize in the long run, at 19.0 percent of GNP in scenario III and at 19.4 percent of GNP (following the current CBO projection until 1993) in scenario II-B. The rationale behind this methodology is straightforward: we want to isolate the effect of entitlement spending on our future fiscal balance if all of our current benefit and tax promises are kept (and no new promises are made).

Now let us turn to the bottom-line numbers for the years 2025 and 2040 in Table 3-2. If they seem to have a nightmarish quality about them, the reason is clear enough: the dramatic increase in the overall cost of non-means-tested benefit payments. From 9.4 percent of GNP in 1986, expenditures for these nonpoverty entitlements will, according to scenario II-B, grow to 13.9 percent of GNP in 2025 and 15.1 percent of GNP by the year 2040. According to scenario III, they will grow to 19.5 percent of GNP in 2025 and 23.3 percent of GNP by 2040 (a sum equivalent to the entire federal budget today).

In the long term, much of this increase is accounted for by Social Security cash benefits (OASDI), which will expand by 1.7 percent of GNP between 1986 and 2040 in scenario II-B and by 3.8 percent of GNP in scenario III. Significantly, nearly all of this growth in cash benefits occurs after 2010, when the Baby Boom generation begins to retire. The cost of health-care benefits, on the other hand, is an explosive force both in the near- and the long term. Over the course of our projection period, HI more than doubles and SMI jumps nearly fivefold as a share of GNP in scenario II-B; in our scenario III, their GNP shares increase at almost twice this rate.

Let us focus for a moment on what our model implies for the cost of health care. According to our more optimistic scenario, total national health-care spending will grow to more than 20 percent of

---

*Since future defense outlays defy any forecasting, the best we can do is suggest a plausible average for the next few decades. The high and low figures chosen here are somewhat higher than the average currently projected by the CBO for the early 1990s (5.6 percent of GNP), but they are considerably lower than our historical average during the 1946–87 postwar era (8.0 percent of GNP).

TABLE 3-2

Federal Budget Outlays and Deficits:
Long-Term Projections as a Percent of GNP

	Actual (percent of GNP)	Projections (percent of GNP)					
	FY 1986	2000 "II-B"[1]	2025 "II-B"[1]	2040 "II-B"[1]	2000 "III"[2]	2025 "III"[2]	2040 "III"[2]
Non-Means-Tested Benefits	9.4	10.7	13.9	15.1	12.3	19.5	23.3
Social Security	6.5	7.6	10.9	12.2	9.0	16.0	19.5
OASDI	4.7	4.4	6.2	6.4	5.0	7.3	8.5
HI	1.2	1.6	2.3	2.9	2.0	4.3	5.5
SMI	0.6	1.6	2.4	2.9	2.0	4.4	5.5
Veterans	0.5	0.8	0.7	0.6	0.9	0.9	0.9
Military Ret.	0.4	0.4	0.4	0.4	0.4	0.5	0.6
Civil Service Ret.	0.6	0.5	0.5	0.6	0.6	0.7	0.9
Other	1.3	1.3	1.3	1.3	1.3	1.3	1.4
Means-Tested Benefits	1.7	1.8	2.2	2.5	2.0	3.1	3.7
Medicaid	0.6	0.8	1.1	1.4	1.0	2.0	2.6
Other	1.1	1.1	1.1	1.1	1.1	1.1	1.1
Total Entitlements	11.1	12.5	16.1	17.6	14.3	22.6	27.0
Nondefense Dom. & Offset	2.8	2.8	2.8	2.8	2.8	2.8	2.8
National Defense	6.5	6.0	6.0	6.0	6.5	6.5	6.5
Net Interest	3.2	3.9	9.4	16.0	6.7	25.6	49.8
TOTAL OUTLAYS	23.6	25.2	34.3	42.3	30.2	57.4	86.1
REVENUES	18.4	19.4	19.4	19.4	19.0	19.0	19.0
BALANCE	-5.3	-5.8	-14.9	-22.9	-11.2	-38.4	-67.1
Balance less Interest	-2.0	-1.8	-5.4	-6.9	-4.6	-12.9	-17.3
Outlays less Interest	20.4	21.2	24.8	26.3	23.6	31.9	36.3
NATIONAL DEBT	41.7	68.5	164.8	277.4	100.8	384.5	745.1

[1] "Most Likely" projection
[2] "Pessimistic" projection
Source: Authors' calculations (see Notes)

GNP by 2040 (up from 11 to 12 percent today); according to our more pessimistic scenario, it may grow as high as 30 percent of GNP. Federal spending on health-care benefits alone will reach 7.2 percent of GNP under scenario II-B and 13.6 percent of GNP under scenario III (more than the federal government spends today on *all* entitlements).* Two specific developments are worth highlighting. Supplementary Medical Insurance (SMI) will grow rapidly until the year 2000, when it will slightly exceed the size of Hospital Insurance (a trend consistent with current concerns about the accelerating cost of physician services). Thereafter, the two programs will grow at about the same rate, although HI will pull slightly ahead as the increased number of "old" elderly begin to use hospitals more intensively than doctors. We should also note the acceleration in Medicaid expenditures after 2015, due entirely to an explosion in the "old" elderly population, those most likely to enter nursing homes.

If these figures alone do not furnish sufficient proof that current policies are unsustainable, consider the effects of unending deficits on the size of federal interest payments. They are nothing less than spectacular. Already by 2025, scenario III projects that interest costs will consume an enormous 25.6 percent of GNP, more than equal to the size of our entire budget today and far larger than the size of any other budget category either then or now. And by 2040, the assumptions underlying the "pessimistic" scenario will push up interest costs to an unthinkable 49.8 percent of GNP. In that year, deficits will consume 67.1 percent of GNP, a sum greater than the likely net savings of all the industrial countries combined.

But what is truly unnerving is that even the "optimistic" II-B scenario—which assumes that all future economic and demographic trends will swing decisively in a favorable direction—nonetheless projects fiscal problems that are considerably more severe than those we face this year or next. What will the prospects for the American Dream be in 2025 when federal deficits are equivalent to 14.9 percent of all the goods and services we produce each year, almost triple the

---

*In order to develop long-term projections for the cost of health-care benefit programs other than Medicare's HI, we developed estimates of total national health-care spending consistent with the SSA scenarios. We then linked federal program outlays to national health-care spending using projection data developed by the Health Care Financing Administration (see Notes). Our current-law figures for the long-term cost of federal health-care programs are roughly consistent with the findings of other researchers. They are, for instance, somewhat lower than the recent projections of John L. Palmer and Barbara Boyle Torrey (in *Federal Budget Policy in the 1980s*, edited by Mills and Palmer; Urban Institute, 1984).

percentage in 1986? (Assuming our nonfederal savings behavior is unchanged, that will also be more than twice the combined net savings of all state and local governments plus all private-sector businesses and households; the rest, presumably, we would have to borrow abroad).* Already by 2015, publicly held debt will have climbed to 110 percent of GNP, equivalent to its twentieth-century high point reached in late 1945, just after the end of World War II.

Perhaps the most significant series of projections in Table 3-2, however, is the entry for federal expenditures minus interest, which simply reflects the underlying programmatic growth in entitlement spending. Under scenario II-B, this measure grows by 0.8 percent of GNP by the year 2000 (despite the assumed reduction in defense spending); by 4.4 percent of GNP by the year 2025 (when the Senior Boom will have arrived in full force); and by 5.9 percent of GNP by the year 2040. The figures for scenario III are commensurately larger and grow by 15.9 percent of GNP by 2040.

If prudence persuades us to accept the assumptions of scenario III, we can now reflect for a moment on the implications of this projection as a fiscal forecast. Could we possibly live with it? If we had no other choice, of course, the first thing we would want to do is to raise taxes—swiftly—in order to prevent interest costs from growing, and to keep raising taxes in line with outlays in the years that follow. Let us suppose that we did so and thereby prevented interest costs from ever rising above their 1986 level (3.2 percent of GNP). That would contain all spending increases to entitlements alone, but between 1986 and 2040 we would still see federal outlays grow from 24 to about 40 percent of GNP. Throwing in state and local spending, and assuming it remains fixed at today's level,† we are looking at total U.S. public-sector outlays of well over 50 percent of GNP.

Let us recall, moreover, that this scenario is designed only to project the future cost of *current* programs. As a forecast of actual future spending, it is therefore highly optimistic in its assumption that programmatic additions or changes will never again add to the level of

---

*According to the Commerce Department, the 1 percent of GNP surplus currently run by state and local governments will gradually disappear in the 1990s (as their pension fund outlays catch up to revenues). But in any case, numbers of this magnitude would clearly make us an economic basket case: while borrowing 9.3 percent of GNP abroad (nearly *triple* today's current-account deficit), we would still have no savings left to make *any* net domestic investment.

†Again, this is a highly optimistic assumption. State and local governments face the same demographic forces closing in on their own underfunded pension plans and the same health-cost forces pushing up their half of the total Medicaid budget.

federal spending. Despite the current mood of "fiscal austerity" in Washington, the likelihood of major expansions in Medicare over the next several years* renders this assumption implausible even for entitlements. As for the rest of the budget, the assumption is even less believable. It means that federal spending on virtually every problem or danger that concerns Americans as citizens—from poverty, the environment, or space exploration to education, infrastructure, or unrest abroad—would be frozen forever at today's levels. Is such an approach feasible? Even if we chose to put all discretionary and defense agencies in a "reactive" mode— spending for new purposes only when forced—the likelihood that we will be hit by one or more expensive emergency over the next several decades (from the Persian Gulf to AIDS) seems overwhelming.

It is difficult, of course, to speculate on the eventual size of public spending with any precision. But it is reasonable to conclude that current policies, pursued indefinitely, will almost certainly leave our children with a level of public spending far higher than anything we have experienced before. All things considered, a rise of 16 percentage points of GNP in U.S. public spending, to about 50 percent of GNP, even seems a conservative guess.

That brings us to the final question: Even assuming that the American public could be persuaded to tax itself sufficiently to pay for such growth in our public sector, could our economy and political system sustain it? One would have to be skeptical. We often hear the argument that, by international standards, the size of the U.S. public sector is really quite small and thus has plenty of room left for more spending and taxing. But the more closely this argument is examined, the less plausible it appears. Let us be generous and ignore the relevant political and cultural differences separating Americans from the French, Canadians, or Swedes. Let us focus only on the official numbers themselves as they appear in the national accounts. When we exclude business activities and capital investment (and focus, as we should, on government's role as a consumer), the official numbers tell us that total public outlays in the United States now weigh in at only 3 to 4 percent of GNP less than the average of all other industrial

---

*Indeed, the *certainty* of major expansions, given the June 1988 passage of the "catastrophic protection" benefit addition to Medicare (the cost of which is not included in our projections). For other proposed expansions, see Chapter 9.

nations*—a significant margin, to be sure, but a far cry from the extra 16 percentage points of GNP we would face at the end of scenario III.

And these are the official figures. For several reasons, these figures tend to overestimate the relative budgetary size of government abroad. To begin with, most of the other industrial countries (unlike the United States) treat cash benefits as taxable income. A sizable share of their benefit spending is, as a result, automatically recycled into state coffers, making the "net" or "after-tax" cost of benefits considerably smaller than the official gross spending figure.† Second, health care is largely nationalized in the other industrial countries. This means that public-sector health budgets in the European welfare states are necessarily larger than in the United States—although, as we shall see, it is highly questionable whether our own heavily regulated "private" health-care system is more efficient (there is no question it costs a lot more). Finally, these countries rely much more heavily on direct benefit payments (such as the massive child subsidy in France), whereas we rely on tax exemptions and deductions that do not show up in our official budget numbers.‡ All told, we must wonder whether America's public sector is indeed sizably smaller than most of those abroad.

Aside from the purely quantitative question of which country truly spends most on benefits, moreover, there remains a qualitative question: To what extent does such spending reflect an investment ethos, a future-oriented public purpose? Here we will simply repeat what so many others have observed: that "socialist" systems in Europe tend to distribute resources far more equitably between the young and

*The figures referred to here are "current disbursements of government" as calculated by the Organization for Economic Cooperation and Development: in 1985, U.S. public spending was an estimated 36.7 percent of GNP; public spending in all other industrial countries averaged 40.2 percent of GNP. The latter average, of course, covers a considerable range among the major countries, from 26.7 percent of GNP in Japan to 49.1 percent of GNP in France. All of these figures include defense. Excluding defense, we would have (in 1987) to take about 6 percentage points away from the United States and about 3 percentage points from the other countries, which would increase the total public spending gap between the United States and the other industrial countries from 3–4 percent of GNP to 6–7 percent of GNP.

†Even where they are wholly or partially exempt from income tax, some share of the benefits are recovered in sales or value-added consumption taxes. Only in the United States are cash benefits largely tax free both in the receiving and in the spending.

‡Consider, for example, just three major U.S. tax breaks: the full deductibility of mortgage interest and property taxes for home owners (unheard-of outside the United States) and the full exemption for employer-paid health benefits (nonexistent or limited in most other countries). These alone were equivalent to about $120 billion in U.S. public outlays (at every level of government) in fiscal year 1987—or an "off-budget" middle- and upper-class entitlement worth nearly 3 percent of GNP.

the old than our "entitlements" system in the United States. The fact that health care abroad is nationalized (whatever the griping or queuing) does make this expensive public subsidy available on equal terms to people of all ages. The fact that cash benefits abroad are generally taxable does mean that retired beneficiaries abroad are subject to the same means-tested tax system as all other citizens. And the fact that these countries' family subsidies are directed progressively toward children and education (while our tax breaks are directed regressively toward owner-occupied houses and generous corporate health plans) does reflect an intent by these countries to impute a certain value to investment as well as consumption.

One last observation is also in order. None of the European industrial countries experienced a postwar Baby Boom as large as our own. Consequently, their work forces are already smaller relative to their elderly populations than in the United States. Even if the per capita level of benefit spending in the European welfare states were no higher than in the United States, these countries would still be spending more than us as a percent of GNP. In terms of demographics, at least, Europe is already several steps ahead of us on the road to tomorrow. Here in America, we are still awaiting the Senior Boom with trepidation: it will arrive much later, and much more suddenly.*

Our purpose here is not to attempt a full international comparison of public benefit spending. Instead, we are simply pointing out that international comparisons are not as simple or straightforward as they might appear in a global summary of budget statistics. For all we know, it may be quite legitimate to argue that the governments of certain nations—Sweden, for example—spend quite as much today as the U.S. public sector is likely to be spending at the end of our scenario III. Yet even this argument, if it were made openly, would add enormously to the honesty and clarity of our current discussion of entitlements. Are the American people aware that in order to fulfill our own expectations of future "entitled" consumption we may ultimately require a public sector of Swedish proportions? Is this an informed choice that any American political leader is willing to address? Or, for that matter, are any of us prepared to contemplate the economic,

---

*Japan is still the youngest of all the industrial countries, but it will be "graying" very rapidly during the 1990s and may (with its extraordinary longevity) become the oldest twenty years from now. The United States and Canada are the next youngest of all industrial countries. North America will not "catch up" in age to Europe until the retiring of our Baby Boom thirty years from now.

political, and cultural transformation the United States would need to undergo in order to manage such a public sector successfully?

For the time being, it must be acknowledged that Americans have no popular desire to embark on such a course. And even if they had, it is unthinkable that they would be willing to pay for this extra public consumption, and pay as well for the resources we will need to allocate toward additional public and private investment—all told, at least *one-quarter* of our GNP—if they realized that all of it must come out of private consumption. The real question, therefore, is not whether we change our entitlements system, but when, in what manner, and after how many more years of damage to our economy—damage that will be especially serious the longer we neither reform our system nor pay for it. Today, current wisdom says that it is "politically impossible" to change entitlements. Tomorrow, we may have to relearn—quickly and painfully—the true meaning of impossibility.

II

The Forces Driving the Projections

4

Driving the Projections:
An Aging Society

"Americans in their sixties and seventies are surely the
first generation of healthy, economically independent
retired people in history—and in the absence of
significant economic growth, they may well be the last."
                                        —*Frances FitzGerald*

DURING THE PAST TWENTY YEARS, America has been
quietly overtaken by two demographic revolutions: an
unprecedented decline in fertility rates and an explosion in
longevity. Neither shows any signs of abating soon. Demography, in
short, will soon hand us an event we are already calling the "aging of
America." The implications of an aging population are of course social
and cultural as well as economic, but for the moment our main interest
lies in its long-term impact on federal entitlement spending. The
numbers speak clearly for themselves and should cause all of us—no
matter what our political leanings—to experience grave doubts about
the ability of our current system to meet the changing needs of the
American people. Indeed, the first public figure to identify and
estimate the magnitude of the problem may well have been Joseph
Califano, a lifelong Democrat and President Carter's Secretary of
Health, Education and Welfare. "When the senior boom hits in
2025..." he wrote a decade ago, the share of the federal budget
consumed by spending on the elderly "will hit about 65 percent."*

Governing America by Joseph A. Califano, Jr. (Simon & Schuster, 1981).

153

FIGURE 4-1 **Federal Benefit Outlays per Elderly Person in 1986 Dollars, Fiscal Years 1960–86**

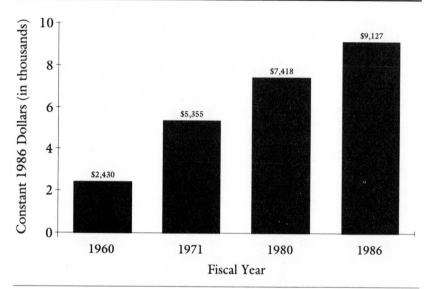

For precise definition of outlays per elderly person, see Figure 4-2.
Source: OMB

Before following Joe Califano into the future, it is worth pausing to review the impressive growth in federal spending on the elderly that has already occurred over the past generation. Since 1960 benefits to persons over sixty-five have risen from 14 percent to 27 percent of all federal spending, and now constitute 57 percent of all federal benefit outlays. As a share of the federal budget, in other words, spending on the elderly has more than doubled in a little over twenty-five years and is still growing. Or look at it another way: between 1960 and 1986, federal benefits per elderly person, in real 1986 dollars, rose from $2,430 to $9,130 (see Figure 4-1). Moreover, what is most telling is that this growth proceeded almost as rapidly during the 1970s and 1980s, when the nonelderly experienced virtual stagnation in their real per capita living standards, as it did during the prosperous 1960s.

Already today, long before the Senior Boom will hit with full force, the share of our resources devoted to the elderly has begun to raise serious questions of equity between generations. One way to assess the relative size of federal per capita expenditures on the elderly is to compare them with total federal domestic spending, *excluding elderly benefits,* for each *nonelderly* person. Today this amounts to $1,470, up modestly from $990 (in 1986 dollars) fifteen years earlier. Not only does this figure include many expenditures that benefit both elderly and nonelderly alike (everything from the National Institutes of Health to our national parks), but it has actually experienced a slight drop during the 1980s. Between 1980 and 1986, in constant dollars, federal per capita benefits to the elderly rose by $1,710, while all other spending per nonelderly person *declined* by $230—a development that is a telling commentary on the composition of recent budget cuts.

Another way to highlight the magnitude of federal expenditures on the elderly is to compare them with public spending directed to America's children (see Figure 4-2). In 1986 federal benefits per elderly person (again, about $9,130) were *eleven times larger* than benefits plus education aid per child (about $810). Even if all state and local benefits plus all public spending on education are included, the ratio is still at least 3 to 1 in favor of the elderly.* It is no accident that between 1969 and 1986 the official poverty rate for children has climbed from 14 percent to 20 percent; meanwhile, the official poverty rate for the elderly has declined from 25 percent to 12 percent. (If noncash benefits are included as income, as we mentioned in Chapter 2, the elderly poverty rate now stands at 3 percent.) Nor is it an accident that the United States now has the dubious reputation of being the only developed country—and perhaps the only country, period— in which children are significantly more likely to be living in poverty than the elderly.

Two additional comparisons should make our point. Consider, for example, that *total* federal spending on net infrastructure investment and on nondefense research and development—the benefits of which will last several generations—amounted to only $357 per American child in 1986. That is less than the *increase* in average federal benefits to each elderly household that now occurs in the span of six months. Or again, consider that *total* federal health-care spending (through Medicaid) for each child in poverty averaged less than $200 in 1986. That is less than the *increase* in federal health-care spending (through

---

*This 3-to-1 ratio is the result of a detailed calculation by Robert L. Clark in "The Influence of Low Fertility Rates and Retirement Policy on Dependency Costs" (North Carolina State University, unpublished, 1976). Over the last decade, this ratio has doubtless shifted further in favor of the elderly.

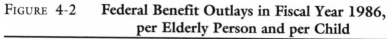

Figure 4-2   **Federal Benefit Outlays in Fiscal Year 1986,
per Elderly Person and per Child**

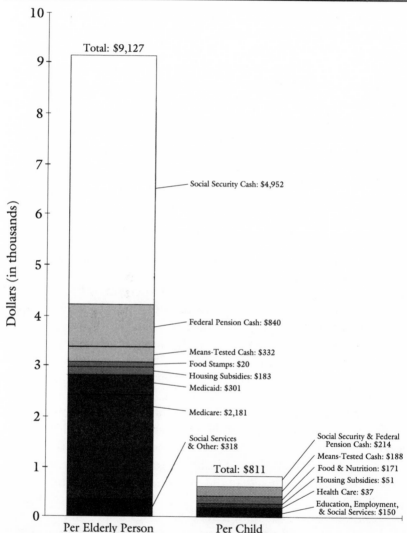

"Per Elderly Person" includes only benefits received directly by persons aged 65 and over, plus small block grants ("Social Services") to states to provide services for the elderly; "Per Child" refers to benefits received directly or on behalf of children under age 18, plus benefits received by adults because they have depedent children (Social Security and AFDC benefits for parents, for instance), plus all federal grants for elementary and primary education, for summer youth employment, for foster care and adoption services, and one-half of the social services block grant to states.

Source: OMB and authors' calculations (see Notes)

Medicaid and Medicare) for each elderly household, rich as well as poor, that now occurs over one year.

What has caused this boom in spending on the elderly? One factor, to be sure, has been the relative increase in the proportion of elderly in the total population. In 1960 there were about 17 elderly persons per 100 working-age adults; by 1986 there were about 20. But the lion's share of the increase—as the per capita spending figures demonstrate—is due rather to enormous hikes in real federal expenditures per elderly beneficiary. In other words, over the past twenty-five years the increase in the share of public resources we devote to the elderly has far outstripped the growth we might have expected simply from the aging of our population.

Most of these benefit hikes, as we will see in later chapters, seemed to be modest at the time, but ultimately led to far greater expenditures than had been anticipated. Some, such as the increase in Social Security payments to widows from 75 percent to 100 percent of their deceased husbands' benefits, involved higher benefit levels for specific groups. Some involved the creation of new benefit categories such as the "disabled dependent" or "Special Age 72" groups. Others were due to across-the-board cost-of-living raises (such as the enormous 20 percent hike in 1972 or the wildly excessive "double" indexing of the mid-1970s). And finally, there was the establishment of entirely new programs, the most important of which was Medicare. When President Johnson signed the Medicare act in 1965, he defended the program by saying an extra $500 million in spending would present "no problem"; today Medicare costs more than 150 times that original estimate.*

Now we can return to Joe Califano's awesome prophesy. What Califano foresaw was that not only would many of the past causes of per capita benefit hikes—medical-cost hyperinflation, for instance, or the full 100-percent-of-CPI indexing of cash benefits—persist into the indefinite future, but that in addition we will certainly face an unprecedented explosion in the numbers of the elderly. What makes the projection especially troubling is that it does not assume any new benefit legislation. If our current benefit policies are simply left on "autopilot," demography will do the rest.

---

*To be fair, Joseph Califano reports that later on LBJ began to worry about Medicare's rapidly growing cost. In 1968 he warned that without reform Medicare would push total national health-care spending to $100 billion by 1975. At the time, Congress ridiculed his warning—although it later turned out that the official cost figure for 1975 was $133 billion. We will return to this subject in the next chapter.

Measuring the Senior Boom

Somewhere among Parkinson's Laws it is written that whenever several things go wrong, they all go wrong in mutually reinforcing ways. Such is the case with the approaching demographic transformation of the American population. All three of the most important demographic trends—longevity, retirement age, and fertility—are now driving us in the same direction. They are all working to increase the future cost of benefit spending on the elderly to unaffordable levels. Though of course we retain the option of curbing future benefit growth by restructuring our entitlements system, the age composition of our population will continue its inexorable shift regardless of what policy measures we adopt.

How will this shift unfold? According to the Census Bureau's "pessimistic" scenario, perhaps the most striking aspect of America's demographic transformation is that the peak population years for different age-groups will be decades apart.* We already know that the peak year for American children (1972) is already fifteen years behind us. The U.S. labor force, however, will continue to expand until around the year 2007. At present, with a torrent of women as well as the tail end of the Baby Boom looking for first jobs, our labor force has been growing by about 1.5 million per year. By the turn of the century, the growth will slow to about 500,000 yearly, or just about the level of annual immigration. Five or ten years later, even our immigration margin will be unable to close the widening gap between retiring workers and new native-born job seekers. Sometime near the year 2007 our total labor force will hit its historic high and thereafter begin an inexorable decline.

Twenty years later, around the year 2027 assuming our demographic engine remains on steady course, the total U.S. population will reach its all-time high of about 283 million and then enter a gathering decline. For decades afterward, however, *more* than the entire decline will be due to ever-fewer numbers of children and working-age adults. The population over age sixty-five will keep rising until it reaches its peak in the year 2060—just ten years before our total population will have fallen back to its level in 1987.

The magnitude of this demographic shift is difficult to grasp, but consider the following numbers. During most of America's colonial

*The numbers here and in the following paragraph are taken from the Census Bureau's detailed projections of its "low mortality, low fertility, middle immigration" scenario until the year 2080 (1984), which approximately correspond to the SSA's scenario III.

era, through the Revolution, and until about 1820, the median age of the American population held steady at about sixteen years of age. Thereafter, due mainly to falling fertility, it rose more or less continuously until it reached thirty by 1950. The advent of the Baby Boom temporarily reversed the trend and pushed the median age back down to twenty-five by 1965. But in 1980 the earlier high point of thirty was passed. By about 2010 the median age of the American population will reach forty; twenty years further on it will reach forty-five. Today about 32 percent of our population is over age forty-five, a share that will rise sharply to 43 percent during the first decade of the next century, as the Baby Boom matures, and hit 49 percent by the year 2025. At that point, there will be six adults over age sixty for every ten adults under age sixty.

The Senior Boom is often explained exclusively in terms of the Baby Boom's coming retirement. To be sure, when the Baby Boom—the huge generation of children born during the postwar surge in birth rates between about 1946 and 1964—begins to retire around 2010, all projections of the elderly population and Social Security expenditures show an explosive rise. This simple explanation, however, overlooks equally important trends, such as a smaller future work force due to declining fertility rates, ongoing gains in longevity, and earlier retirement—trends that alone would force a Senior Boom regardless of when the Baby Boom retires.

An example will illustrate this point. From about 1930 until the end of World War II, birth rates fell to a relatively low level. If senior booms and busts were simply the delayed consequences of prior baby booms and busts, we should expect that between about 1995 and 2010, when the small, "Silent" generation of children born during the Depression will reach retirement age, the retired population will shrink relative to the working population. But nothing like this is expected to happen. Even according to the SSA's "most likely" assumptions, over the course of these fifteen years the elderly population will grow by 6.1 million, or by 18 percent. In contrast, the population of working-age adults will meanwhile grow by only about 12 percent. For a period that has been dubbed Social Security's "Indian summer"—an era when mounting trust-fund surpluses are supposed to accumulate in preparation for the Baby Boom's retirement—these numbers fail to inspire much confidence.

The Senior Boom, in short, is much more than a distant echo of the Baby Boom. It is a relentless structural change in the age distribution of the American population whose effects we are already registering. Certainly the pace of change will become far more rapid early in the next century, when the huge generation now working and paying taxes will retire and begin to receive benefits. But the Baby Boom itself, as we will see, was actually a unique aberration in a secular trend toward lower birth rates. Beginning in about 2010, instead of "leaning against" the forces that are aging our population, the Baby Boom will simply be reinforcing them.

How much worse are things likely to get? It depends on which demographic assumptions we accept. According to the "most likely" (II-B) projection, the working-age population will grow by 13 percent between 1990 and 2040 while the elderly population will grow by 116 percent. According to the "pessimistic" (III) projection, over the same period the number of working-age adults will *shrink* by 3 percent while the number of elderly will grow by 140 percent. After reaching a peak of about 174 million in the year 2010, the number of Americans between the ages of twenty and sixty-four will decline to 126 million by the year 2060; meanwhile the number of elderly will explode from 32 million in 1990 and 44 million in 2010 to an incredible 80 million in 2060.

To put these numbers into a form that more directly reflects future Social Security tax burdens (other entitlement programs for the elderly will face roughly the same sort of arithmetic), Figure 4-3 divides the number of Social Security recipients by the number of payroll-tax-paying or "covered" workers. The resulting quotient, multiplied by 100, represents the number of beneficiaries who must be supported by each 100 workers. Today the number stands at about 30, but according to the "most likely" scenario it will rise to over 53 by the year 2040. According to the "pessimistic" scenario the number will increase indefinitely throughout the next century, to 70 by the year 2040 and to 84 by the year 2060. In other words, even according to the more optimistic scenario, by the middle of the next century *every working couple* will be responsible—through the medium of their payroll taxes—for the public support of one elderly person.

Both the "most likely" and "pessimistic" scenarios project that by around the year 2010 the elderly as a percentage of the entire U.S. population will be equivalent to the percentage of elderly in Florida today. By the year 2040, as Figure 4-4 illustrates, the percentage increase in the elderly population will be from five to forty times greater than the increase in the working-age population. For those

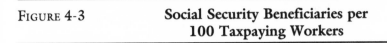

FIGURE 4-3   **Social Security Beneficiaries per**
100 Taxpaying Workers

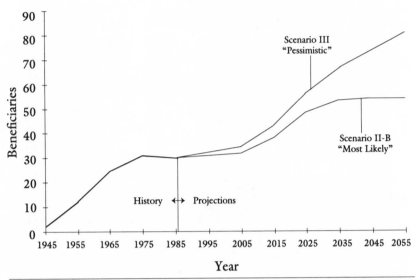

Total number of OASI and DI beneficiaries per 100 workers subject to OASDI payroll taxes.
Source: 1987 OASDI Annual Report

who dare to look forward to the year 2060 as portrayed by the "pessimistic" scenario, it would be difficult to find any adequate analogy. Imagine the entire current U.S. population west of the Mississippi consisting only of elderly persons, and then subtract a New England filled with taxpayers. Is there any chance that our current system of entitlements will continue to function smoothly under these future demographic conditions? The answer, quite simply, is no.

Now let us look a bit more closely at the three major forces—increased longevity, earlier retirement age, and lower fertility—that are bringing about this dramatic Senior Boom.

More Elderly at the Far End: Longer Life Spans

It is common knowledge that the life expectancy of the average American has been increasing steadily over the last century. What is less well known is that, until recent decades, most of this increase came from improvements in treating the diseases of infancy and childhood,

FIGURE 4-4   **Projected Population Growth by Age-Group, 1985–2040**

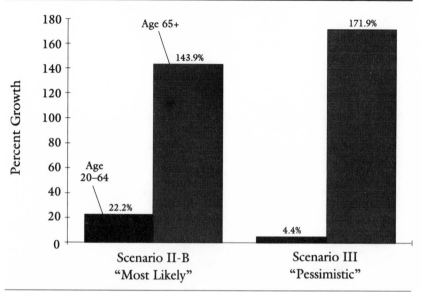

Source: Office of the Actuary (SSA)

not from improvements in the health of the elderly. Vaccination, water purification, antibiotics, and healthier diets pushed life expectancy at birth up from 47.8 years in 1900 to 63.1 years in 1940—a 32 percent gain. Over the same period of time, life expectancy at age 65 grew only slightly, from 11.7 years to 12.7 years—a mere 9 percent gain. As infant and child mortality approached zero, it seemed clear to many observers that further dramatic gains in longevity could not be expected. Since the 1950s, however, changes in life-styles and remarkable advances in treating the diseases of old age have proved such pessimism to have been unfounded.

Between 1940 and 1985, the life expectancy of men at age sixty-five climbed from 11.9 years to 14.4 years; for women it flew upward even more swiftly, from 13.4 years to 18.8 years. Furthermore, the rate of improvement has been accelerating with each passing decade. Indeed, the increase has been so rapid that it has repeatedly caught the agencies responsible for demographic forecasts—from the Census Bureau to the Social Security Administration—by surprise. In 1964, for example, the National Center for Health Statistics was reporting that U.S. death rates for all age-groups have "reached the point where

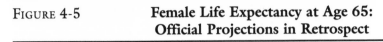

FIGURE 4-5   **Female Life Expectancy at Age 65:**
                    Official Projections in Retrospect

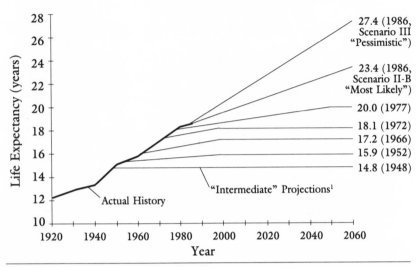

[1] Except for the "most likely" and "pessimistic" projections noted for 1986; before 1986, "intermediate" means an average of all SSA scenarios.

Source: Office of the Actuary (SSA)

further decreases as experienced in the past cannot be anticipated." Some agencies in 1965 were more optimistic and assumed a straight-line extrapolation of 1935–65 trends. This projection indicated that combined male-female elderly life expectancy might reach 15.8 years by the year 1980—fifteen years into the future. Amazingly, this figure was already surpassed in 1974, only nine years later.

Figures 4-5 and 4-6 not only illustrate the magnitude of the recent acceleration in elderly longevity, but also highlight the consistent underestimation of future improvement by past Social Security projections. Especially dramatic is the case of elderly female longevity, where each average "ultimate" forecast from 1948 through 1972 has been surpassed only a few years later. The 1977 average "ultimate" forecast of a life expectancy of 20.0 years for women at age sixty-five may be broken as soon as 1990.

This improvement in elderly longevity, of course, has had an enormous impact on entitlement spending. The original designers of Social Security really had no idea how longer life spans might add to the cost of their system of retirement benefits. Indeed, when federal

163

FIGURE 4-6   **Male Life Expectancy at Age 65:
                     Official Projections in Retrospect**

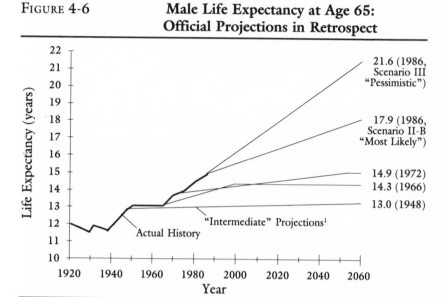

¹Except for the "most likely" and "pessimistic" projections noted for 1986; before 1986, "intermediate" means an average of all SSA scenarios.

Source: Office of the Actuary (SSA)

actuaries first worked out long-term spending projections in the late 1930s, they not only considered retirement to be a rather short episode (lasting little longer than a decade for those who survived to age sixty-five), but also had no reason to believe that the average duration of retirement would lengthen very much in the future.* But consider this calculation: in order for the duration of retirement to be the same as it was in 1940, a working person today would have to wait until age seventy-two before retiring. In the year 2060, he or she would have to wait until age *seventy-seven* before retiring.† In reality, as we shall see,

---

*In the long run, the added cost of OASI (Social Security retirement and survivors benefits) and Medicare—as a percent of payroll for a static population—will be roughly proportionate to the added life expectancy after retirement. By not projecting the future revolution in elderly life expectancy, therefore, the original designers of Social Security missed about 40 to 50 percent of the ultimate payroll cost of retirement according to last year's II-B scenario.

†To be exact, 72.2 years of age in 1990 and 77.2 years of age in 2060, according to scenario II-B (as calculated by the SSA actuaries in 1986). Scenario III would give us an even later equivalent retirement age—well over 80 years of age—for 2060. Note that equivalency is interpreted here to mean the same *duration of retirement in years*. It could also be interpreted to mean the same *ratio of retirement years to working years*. Imagine, in other words, that we divvy up longer life spans between more work and more leisure so that their relative durations remain unchanged; this would still yield an equivalent retirement age of 69.9 years in 1990 and 73.2 years in 2060 according to scenario II-B.

Americans are not retiring later, but sooner.

Even more to the point, these rapid past gains in elderly longevity force us to reconsider how fast such gains might continue into the future. Here we return to the question of the "most likely" versus "pessimistic" scenarios. Over the last ten years, Social Security's actuaries have been forced to revise upward their projections of elderly longevity; despite these revisions, however, their current projections remain conservative. According to the "most likely" (II-B) scenario, increases in elderly longevity will continue in the future, but at a much slower rate than during the 1970s. Even according to the "pessimistic" (III) scenario, future increases will continue at a somewhat slower rate than we have experienced in the recent past.

In Figures 4-5 and 4-6, we can see that the 1987 projection of the increase per decade of elderly life expectancy from 1986 to 2060 is slightly lower in the "pessimistic" scenario (for both sexes) than the historical increase per decade during either the 1960s or the 1970s.* Thus even the worst-case official projection for public spending implies a rate of longevity growth that is slower than our recent experience. Once again we must ask ourselves: Do SSA's official numbers truly reflect a balanced set of expectations? Or in this case is "pessimism" not only something we should hope for, but something we should prudently expect?

Health statistics indicate that the recent improvement in elderly longevity has stemmed almost entirely from reduced mortality rates in two major disease areas: heart disease and strokes. One important reason for the reduction in both areas is a great revolution in medical treatment: earlier detection of these conditions through testing; better diagnosis with recently invented technology; more effective drugs, especially for high blood pressure and irregular heartbeat; and superior methods of surgical intervention. Another important reason has been the steady improvement in elderly life-styles, including healthier diets and more recreational exercise.

There are few physicians who believe that either of these trends is likely to decelerate in the foreseeable future. Some advances can already be counted on. "Borderline" hypertension, for example, is a condition about whose dangers we have only recently learned. As most elderly undergo routine testing for this condition, we can expect a further steep decline in stroke and heart-disease fatalities related to

---

*For a quantitative comparison of the 1972–86 period with scenarios II-B and III, refer again to Table 3-1.

hypertension. New anticholesterol drugs (for chronic treatment) and anticoagulants (for acute treatment) will of course make the rates decline even more swiftly.

International comparisons also reveal that there is much room for improvement. Americans remain considerably more prone to heart disease than the citizens of most other industrial countries. The mortality rate from heart disease among the Japanese elderly, for instance, is only about one-third of the mortality rate among the American elderly. Health experts generally agree that most of this discrepancy has been due to differences in national diets, not to differences in medical practice.

Along with heart disease and strokes (which account for just over 60 percent of all elderly deaths), cancer (which accounts for an additional 15 percent) remains a major killer. Unlike mortality rates for most other diseases, those for cancer have actually risen slightly among the elderly over the past several decades. This overall rise, however, masks two contrary trends: a dramatic increase in lung cancer deaths, from 13 percent of all elderly cancer deaths in 1950 to 36 percent today, and a decline in deaths from most other forms of cancer. We now possess indisputable evidence that the incidence of lung cancer is directly correlated with the per capita consumption of tobacco, and generally shows up with a twenty-to-thirty-year lag. Since the popularity of smoking peaked in the United States during the 1960s and has been falling steeply ever since, we can expect that cancer mortality among tomorrow's elderly will follow this downward trend in the decades to come.

Moreover, improvements in the treatment of cancer may come at a swifter rate in the near future than they have over the recent past. Since the 1950s, the basic options for cancer therapy—surgery, chemotherapy, and radiotherapy—have changed surprisingly little. But most health experts believe that crucial research breakthroughs in the 1980s are for the first time giving us an understanding of cancer's underlying biology and genetics. The results of this research may soon pay off in entirely new forms of cancer treatment and prevention, from designer antibodies, genetically acting chemicals, and mass-produced hormones to Nuclear Magnetic Resonance (NMR) testing and dietary prevention.

Nonetheless, despite serious underestimates in their previous forecasts and the bright outlook for future improvements in longevity on so many fronts, Social Security's actuaries continue to assume that the

166

best we can hope for in the future will be worse than what we have achieved over the last twenty years. To the extent there is any justification for this official "pessimism," it lies in the seemingly reasonable conviction that longevity simply cannot keep climbing at a rapid pace indefinitely. At some point, we feel instinctively, medical progress must eventually push us up against the natural limit to the human life span. The conventional wisdom among biologists and health experts holds that this is indeed the case. It is well known that many measures of the efficiency of human organs (such as kidney blood flow, nerve conductivity, heart output, and lung capacity) decline linearly after about age thirty regardless of an individual's general health. Given this fact, it is reasonable to assume that everyone's reserve physiological strength must eventually reach a level at which even a minor trauma or illness will become life threatening. If fatal, we call this "dying of old age." Either because genetic material becomes damaged over time or because it is "preprogrammed" to reproduce itself with accumulating imperfections, many experts believe that medicine will never be able to alter the fundamentals of the aging process.

Over the last decade, however, other health experts have begun to ask searching questions about this assumption. One school of thought accepts a fixed genetic limit to life spans (though given recent advances in genetic engineering, even this barrier may not be impermeable in the long run), but stresses the difference between knowing that a theoretical limit exists and understanding at what age, precisely, such a limit is of practical significance. The fact that the elderly keep living longer, in other words, may simply suggest that the limit to the average life span is considerably higher than we once assumed—instead of the biblical "three-score and ten," perhaps around eighty-five years or even higher.

Another school of thought rejects the so-called fixity thesis altogether, since its acceptance—the school argues—would imply a number of specific and necessary consequences that are not borne out by observation. The fixity thesis would imply, for instance, that we should be making far less improvement in the longevity of those elderly who live beyond eighty-five (and who have thus passed or at least are much nearer to the average life-span limit) than in the longevity of the elderly who are under eighty-five. It would also imply that the variation in the life span of the elderly should narrow as they begin to "bunch up" against this limit.

Significantly, over the last couple of decades, neither of these consequences has been borne out. From 1960 through 1982, the mortality rates of the oldest elderly age brackets (including centenarians) have shown just as much percentage improvement as the mortality rates of the 65–85 age brackets. The chances of a 95-year-old living to 105, in other words, have risen by the same percentage as the chances of a 65-year-old living to 75. At the same time, the overall variation in life spans among the elderly has remained almost entirely unchanged.

While there may well be some sort of ultimate limit to the human life span, recent statistics and research have shown that such a limit works in a far more complex fashion that we once thought. The limit seems to vary with heredity and to interact in subtle ways with the lifelong health, diet, life-style, and environment of the people involved. Most important, it is certainly set at a much older age than we once thought, since there is little statistical evidence that we are yet approaching it.

The Age-Related Health-Care Multiplier

The ongoing demographic transformation of the American population will have its most explosive fiscal effects in the area of public health-care spending on behalf of the elderly. Here we face not only the arithmetic of retirement—longer life spans and fewer working adults—but an arithmetic accelerated by three other multipliers: the rising number of treatable acute and chronic illnesses; the rising real cost of skilled labor and technology per treatment; and, perhaps most important, the rising incidence of illness among the elderly due to the "aging" of the elderly themselves. Before looking at how this age-related health-care multiplier will affect future spending, however, we must first understand how much health care for the elderly already costs.

Here the statistics speak for themselves: an elderly person consumes on average nearly four times as much health care as the typical nonelderly person. In 1984 (the most recent year for which statistics are available), the average American over the age of sixty-five spent (or had spent on his or her behalf) $4,100 on health care—three times as much as a nonelderly adult ($1,300) and eight times as much as a child ($500). So wide is the difference in health-care consumption between age-groups that even though children today outnumber the elderly by 2.5 to 1, the elderly outspend them on health care by 3.5 to 1. In fact, typical Americans must reach their late sixties before incurring *half* of

TABLE 4-1	Growth Rates in Real Health-Care Spending per Capita for the Elderly, Nonelderly, and Children, 1965–84			
	1965–70	1970–76	1976–84	1965–84
Aged 65 and older	7.5%	4.5%	5.2%	5.6%
Under Age 65	5.6	4.1	3.6	4.3
Aged 18 and under	5.7	1.7	3.1	3.3
Memo: Real GNP Per Capita	2.1%	2.0%	1.9%	2.0%

Source: HCFA (published and unpublished data)

their lifetime health-care costs.

Furthermore, the age-related differential in health-care spending has been steadily widening in recent decades. While in 1965 the per capita cost ratio of spending by the elderly to spending by children was 5.7, in 1970 it was 6.2; in 1976 it was 7.0; and in 1984 it was 8.2. Table 4-1 puts these changes into perspective by tracking the growth in health-care costs for different age-groups in real dollars. Since the real per capita growth rate of health-care spending for the under sixty-five age-group weighs in at over twice the real per capita growth rate in GNP, it is already a powerful force behind the expansion in national health-care spending relative to the size of our economy. Health-care spending on the elderly has been further accelerating this expansion, both because *per capita* costs for the elderly have been rising 1.3 percentage points faster than per capita costs for the nonelderly over the entire 1965–86 period, and because the *number* of elderly has been rising faster than the numbers in other age-groups.

The aggregate dollar figures are stunning. Between 1977 and 1984 alone, health-care spending by or on behalf of the elderly more than tripled, from $38 billion to about $117 billion. Since a large and rising share of all elderly health-care costs are paid out of public budgets— 67 percent of the total in 1984, including state outlays—the impact of this growth on public-sector spending is quite direct. Between 1977 and 1984, for example, just the growth in *real* public health-care

169

spending per elderly person added about $48 billion to our total public budget outlays, and nearly $40 billion to federal outlays alone. Indeed, federal spending on elderly health care has been growing even more swiftly than overall federal spending on the elderly: health benefits amounted to fully 25 percent of all such spending in 1984, up from 20 percent in 1970.

If this blistering growth rate in real per capita elderly health costs persists into future decades, the total elderly health-care bill will become unmanageable under the impact of the accelerating rise in the number of elderly persons. In the next chapter, we will discuss the reasons why we can as yet expect little change in the rapid growth of national per capita health-care spending for *all* age-groups. Here our task is more specific: to explain why demographic and social forces virtually guarantee that we will continue to experience an *even more rapid* growth in per capita health-care spending for the elderly.

The explanation has two parts. First, there is a direct relationship between longer life expectancies and a higher average age for the elderly as a group. In other words, as the elderly population itself ages, there will be a disproportionate increase in the number of the "old elderly." From 1985 to 2040, the entire elderly population will grow by between 144 percent and 172 percent.* As Figure 4-7 reveals, however, these overall numbers mask widely variant growth levels, which range from 83.4 percent to 88.3 percent for the 65–74 age-group to 349.2 percent to 498.5 percent for the over-85 age-group. While those over age 80 currently comprise less than one-quarter of the elderly, the growth in their numbers will account for one-half to two-thirds of the growth in the total elderly population between now and 2040. Today octogenarians and their elders number 6.5 million; by 2040 they may number as many as 30 million.

The second part to the explanation involves the age-related health-care multiplier. It is well documented that every measure of health-care utilization rises sharply with age even among different elderly age brackets. The old elderly visit the hospital more often: in 1982 hospital stays averaged 306 per 1,000 people in the 65–74 age-group, but 507 per 1,000 in the over-85 age-group. They also have more surgery and longer hospital stays: in 1980 those aged 65 to 74 averaged 3.1 hospital days per person; those aged 85 and over averaged 7.0 hospital days per person. Such figures, of course, translate directly into higher

---

*The ranges here refer to the SSA II-B and III scenarios, respectively.

170

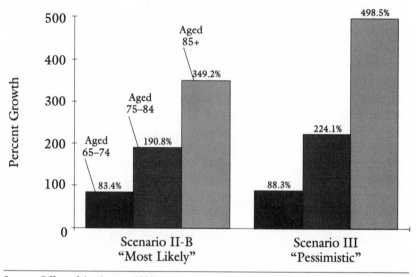

FIGURE 4-7   **Projected Population Growth by Age-Group, 1985–2040**

Source: Office of the Actuary (SSA)

costs. In 1984, for instance, the average reimbursed hospital cost for Medicare enrollees over 80 ($1,781) was more than double the cost for enrollees aged 65 to 74.

Aging also brings with it higher disability rates, which in turn entail a greater need for care of long-term chronic illness—not just more hospital stays, but more doctor visits, pharmaceuticals, physical aids, and skilled personal services. A recent national survey of disabilities that limit "activities of daily living" (ADLs) revealed that about 13 percent of the 65–74 age-group suffer from at least one such disability, but that the figure rises to 25 percent for the 75–84 age-group and to 46 percent for those over age 85. Disability due to chronic illness rises with age not only because of a higher incidence of illness, but also because it is more likely that a given illness will impair the way the body functions. At older ages, for instance, more people have heart disease, and among those who do, a greater proportion are disabled by the condition. Or consider Alzheimer's disease, as yet incurable and now recognized as the most common cause of debilitating senility. It is estimated that about 2 million elderly suffer from Alzheimer's; this number, however, includes less than 5 percent of the population aged

171

65 to 79 but more than 20 percent of the population aged 80 or older. Alzheimer's victims ultimately become dependent on round-the-clock nursing care, an expensive, labor-intensive treatment that no technology is likely to make more efficient.

Extreme disability is of course a primary consideration when an elderly person decides to receive long-term care at a nursing home. Another is whether a spouse or a child can provide adequate care. Unfortunately, here too the odds are stacked against the old elderly. With increasing age, the likelihood rises that an elderly person will be widowed, will be living alone, will be physically separated from his or her children, or will have children who are themselves elderly and disabled. As a consequence, nursing home residency climbs dramatically with advancing age. Overall, only about 5.0 percent of the elderly live in nursing homes, but the percentage rises from 1.3 percent for men and 1.6 percent for women in the 65–74 age-group to 14.0 percent and 25.2 percent respectively for men and women over 85 years of age.

Nursing home care is of course expensive—$22,000 per year per resident in 1986—and, once again, the cost rises with age due to the greater incidence of disabilities. Among nursing home residents over age eighty-five, fully 37 percent are bedfast or chairfast, 35 percent have heart disease, 32 percent are senile, and 26 percent are incontinent. Most elderly who enter nursing homes—even middle-income elderly who initially finance their own care—sooner or later become dependent on public funding. About 50 percent of the $25 billion paid to nursing homes in 1984 on behalf of the elderly came directly from public-sector budgets.

But what is especially significant about nursing home care is that use rates for the oldest age brackets have been rising steadily over the past few decades. Since 1950 nursing home residency for those aged sixty-five to seventy-four has remained constant (at a rate beneath 2.0 percent); but for the elderly aged eighty-five and older, the rate has risen from 9 percent in 1950 to 22 percent in 1985. In other words, the overall number of nursing home residents in this age bracket has increased twice as fast as the underlying population.* A major contri-

---

*Since a major 1977 survey, it is true that the rate has stabilized for all age brackets. But it is likely that this has been a short-term plateau, induced by regulatory limits on the construction of new nursing home beds in many regions and (partly as a result) huge real hikes in the per-diem cost of nursing home care. Moreover, even if the *rate* for the eighty-five-plus age bracket has remained unchanged from 1977 to 1985, the *absolute number* of residents has risen from about 450,000 to 600,000—a 33 percent increase in only eight years.

buting cause of the explosion of the nursing home population has been the fact that women, traditionally the providers of home care for the elderly, have now entered the work force and are often geographically separated from their parents.

The nursing home, of course, is by no means the only way long-term care is managed. Most disabled elderly, even at an advanced age, get along with the help of family, neighbors, or a paid home-care professional. Indeed, most experts believe that for every disabled elderly person who enters a nursing home there are three or four others who rely on noninstitutional care. Although these are always less expensive (and often happier) options than the nursing home, their economic cost—especially in terms of uncompensated hours—is considerable. One specialist estimates that the quantity of informal care delivered to those elderly who are over eighty-five alone amounts to some 23 million hours per week. As for paid home care, 1.1 million elderly (about the same number who reside in nursing homes) reported receiving it in 1982.

Figure 4-8 summarizes the effects of many of the age-cost multipliers we have discussed on per capita federal spending. In general, the elderly over age eighty receive more than twice as much in federal health-care benefits as those between ages sixty-five and seventy, though there are substantial variations in different programs. The differential between the "old elderly" and the "young elderly" is least (1.3 times) for physician services under Supplementary Medical Insurance (SMI), more (2.0 times) for hospital care under the Hospital Insurance (HI) program, and dramatically higher (14.4 times) for long-term nursing home care.

What does the future hold? Table 4-2 presents the results of a study that attempts to project the impact of the aging of the elderly on future health-care utilization.* Even using "most likely" (and therefore "optimistic") demographic assumptions, the authors of this study reach some sobering conclusions. From 1980 to 2040—according to this scenario—our elderly population will increase by almost 160 percent, but health-care use by the elderly will climb at an even faster rate than the growth in their total numbers. Elderly hospital days will increase by 197 percent; the number of "activity-limited" elderly by 232 percent; and elderly nursing home residents by 279 percent. The

---

*Dorothy P. Rice and Jacob Feldman in "Living Longer in the United States: Demographic Changes and Health Needs of the Elderly," *Milbank Memorial Fund Quarterly* (Summer 1983).

FIGURE 4-8   **Federal Health-Care Benefits to the Elderly in 1984: Per Capita Cost by Age-Group**

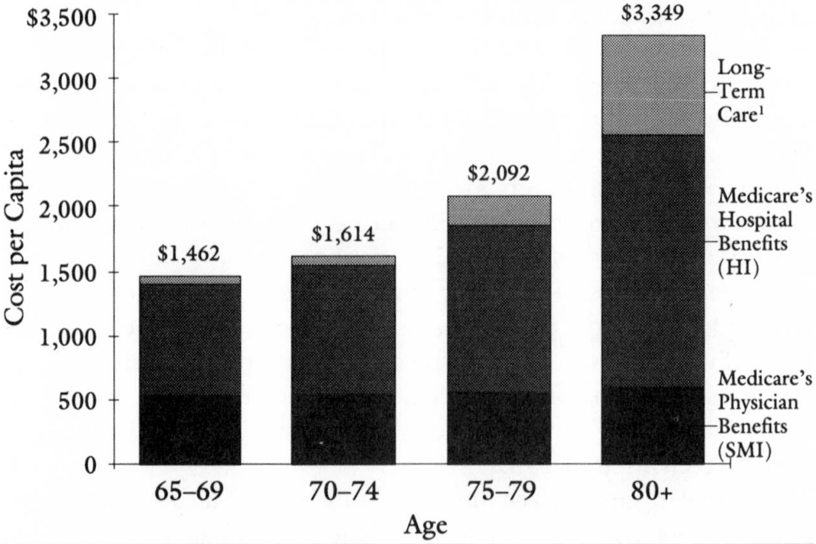

¹Federal cost only (primarily Medicaid and VA benefits).

Source: Barbara Boyle Torrey, "The Visible Dilemma of the Invisible Aged," *Milbank Memorial Fund Quarterly* (Spring 1985)

driving force behind this acceleration, of course, is the headlong increase in health-care use by the elderly in the bracket over age eighty-five. The number of elderly over eighty-five in nursing homes, for instance, will more than double by the year 2000; by the year 2040, it will have more than quintupled.

Dramatic as these numbers may seem, they only tell part of the story. Table 4-2 provides a crude measure of the quantity of future health-care services that the elderly will consume; it does not reflect increases in the real price per service for health care—increases that will undoubtedly grow at a faster rate than our economy for decades to come. Moreover, the projections in Table 4-2 are based on "most likely" demographic assumptions; if "pessimistic" assumptions were adopted instead, the overall increase in the use of health-care services by the elderly would be about 20 percent higher between 1980 and the year 2000 and about 30 percent higher between 1980 and the year 2040.

TABLE 4-2 **Selected Projections of U.S. Population, Health, and Health-Care Utilization by Age-Group, 1980–2040**

	1980 Actual Base	Projections		Percent Change 1980– 2000	Percent Change 1980– 2040
		2000	2040		
U.S. Population (millions)					
Working-Age	132.7	160.7	177.0	21.1%	33.4%
All Elderly	25.9	36.3	67.3	40.2	159.8
Aged 75 and Over	10.3	17.9	37.8	73.8	267.0
Aged 85 and Over	2.6	7.7	13.3	196.2	411.5
Persons with "Activity of Daily Living" Limitation (millions)					
All Ages	3.14	4.51	7.92	43.5%	152.1%
All Elderly	1.78	2.78	5.92	55.9	232.6
Aged 75 and Over	1.13	1.99	4.63	75.9	309.2
Physician Visits (billions)					
All Ages	1.10	1.31	1.62	19.3%	47.2%
All Elderly	0.17	0.23	0.43	39.2	157.8
Aged 75 and Over	0.07	0.12	0.24	74.2	265.2
Short-Stay Hospital Days (millions)					
All Ages	274.5	370.6	548.7	35.0%	99.9%
All Elderly	105.3	159.9	312.3	51.9	196.6
Aged 75 and Over	56.1	102.1	219.4	82.0	291.1
Nursing Home Residents (millions)					
All Ages	1.51	2.54	5.23	68.2%	245.9%
All Elderly	1.32	2.32	4.98	76.1	278.6
Aged 75 and Over	1.09	2.05	4.56	88.5	318.7
Aged 85 and Over	0.56	1.20	2.90	113.3	415.6

Projections assume the II-B economic and demographic scenario.

Source: See citation on page 173.

Finally, Table 4-2 assumes a constant per capita use rate of health-care services for each age bracket. Is this an optimistic or pessimistic assumption? In light of the elderly's growing longevity, this might seem pessimistic. After all, if fewer of those in each age bracket will be dying, it might be reasonable to assume that fewer will be getting sick. Health experts who take this position believe that longer life spans will lead to a "compression of morbidity"—longer "health spans" followed by a rapid and less costly disintegration of health just before death. Yet many other health experts have taken just the opposite position. They argue that most health care has little to do

175

with mortality, and that even when improvement in medical practice does lengthen lives, survivors are prone to more—not fewer—disabling illnesses. Supporting their first argument are data showing that only 36 to 41 percent of all disabilities are related to potentially fatal diseases. Supporting their second argument are numerous instances (from brain trauma and heart attacks to diabetes and kidney failure) where victims who would have died young or quickly in the past now live on through years or decades of expensive treatment for the resulting complications.*

The verdict is still out on which position best describes our current direction. Some experts split the difference and conclude that the impact of longer lives and better medicine will have a neutral effect on the future, age-specific demand for health care.† Turning from acute "cure" to chronic "care," however, it is hard to believe that the demand will not grow. We have already seen, for example, how fast the use rate for nursing home services (to take one example) has risen among the old elderly over the last few decades. It would be unreasonable to believe that this trend will not continue. Consider the three most important predictors of nursing home residency besides age: being female, being widowed, and living alone. From 1950 to 1980, the number of elderly widows more than doubled, from 3.5 million to 8.2 million. At the same time, the proportion of elderly widows living alone increased from only one out of four in 1950 (the other three-quarters lived with relatives or friends) to two out of three in 1980. The total number of elderly widows living alone thus rose by over 500 percent. What about the future? Demographers tell us that the number of widows and single elderly will necessarily keep rising faster than the overall number of the elderly. They also say that the odds that these single old elderly have children able or willing to care for them at home will continue to decline.‡

*The classic exposition of the "compression of morbidity" thesis has been presented by James F. Fries in "Aging, Natural Death, and the Compression of Morbidity," *New England Journal of Medicine*, 303 (1980) and in "The Compression of Morbidity," *Milbank Memorial Fund Quarterly* (Summer 1983). The alternative "failure of success" thesis is defended by E.M. Gruenberg in "The Failure of Success," *Milbank Memorial Fund Quarterly* (Summer 1977) and by Lois M. Verbrugge in "Longer Life but Worsening Health?" *Milbank Memorial Fund Quarterly* (Summer 1984).

†See Kenneth G. Manton in "Changing Concepts of Morbidity and Mortality in the Elderly Population," *Milbank Memorial Fund Quarterly* (Spring 1982) and James M. Poterba and Lawrence H. Summers in "Public Policy Implications of Declining Old-Age Mortality" (National Bureau of Economic Research, 1986, unpublished).

‡See discussion in Chapter 9.

If we begin to prepare for the aging of the U.S. population now, there will be no need to deny the exploding number of dependent elderly—those who are very old, in poor health, and living alone—the care they require. But few Americans have faced up to the fact that affording these costs will necessarily involve distinguishing between the self-evident need of these elderly and the vast array of less legitimate "entitlements" enjoyed by those who are healthier, wealthier, or more self-sufficient. The explosive impact of the age-related health-care multiplier will force us to come to terms with this fundamental fact.

More Elderly at the Near End: Earlier Retirement

Just as recent gains in longevity have been lengthening the typical American's retirement years, so has the decision to leave the work force earlier. At the time of the New Deal, when "retirement" was first proposed as a possible means of relieving the labor glut of the Great Depression, the very idea seemed novel, since it was still generally accepted that men should work as long as their health allowed. Only fifty years later, retirement has practically come to be regarded as a right that derives from citizenship. Even as recently as the early 1950s, nearly half of all elderly men were working. By 1986 less than one out of every six were working. Figure 4-9 illustrates this steep decline in labor force participation among elderly men.

The fact that the majority of Americans can afford to leave the work force by the time they reach their early sixties (the average retirement age for men today is sixty-two, and two-thirds of all workers retire before age sixty-five) is of course a testament to the impressive rise in U.S. living standards since the Depression. Whether or not the seeming boon of retirement actually has beneficial effects on the physical and psychological health of the elderly is a matter that is still being debated among gerontologists. For our purposes, however, it is enough to note that the twin trends toward greater longevity and earlier retirement have pushed up the cost of our major entitlement programs far beyond levels that could have been envisioned when they were instituted.

Indeed, the original designers of Social Security could not have foreseen that savings from higher real wage levels, appreciated property values, and the spread of private pension plans would make retirement an increasingly feasible—and, in time, a socially

177

FIGURE 4-9 **Labor Force Participation Rates for Men Aged 65 and Over, 1940–1986**

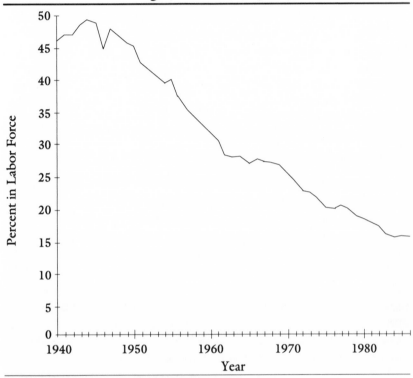

Source: Employment and Earnings (BLS, Labor)

fashionable—option. Nor, it seems, did later legislators foresee that increasing benefit levels and creating special provisions for "early retirement" would themselves strongly reinforce the decision to retire earlier. Today we know better. What is most remarkable about the long-term trend toward earlier retirement is that it has proceeded so rapidly despite the clear weakening of the two strongest forces that formerly pushed aging employees out of the work force involuntarily: poor health and mandatory retirement.* During the 1960s, the labor

---

*As for poor health, the share of workers retiring for this reason has certainly declined since 1950, though the extent of the decline is unclear since subjective opinions about "health reasons" and pension rules defining "disability" have no doubt shifted over time. According to data recently released from the 1984 National Health Interview Survey (National Center for Health Statistics release; May 8, 1987), only 27 percent of all retirees over age 65 report "health" as the main reason for their retirement. Among retirees under age 65, the share was higher: 34 percent (aged 60 to 64), and 44 percent (aged 55 to 59). As for mandatory retirement, although

force participation rate for elderly men fell from 33 to 27 percent. During the 1970s, it plummeted further to 20 percent. By 1986 it had dropped to 16 percent. A steep drop has also occurred among mature, nonelderly men since 1950—from 87 to 68 percent among men aged 55 to 64, and from 96 to 91 percent among men aged 45 to 54—with most of the drop occurring since 1970.[†]

Will the trend toward earlier retirement continue into the future? Without a major restructuring of our entitlement programs—together with the creation of positive incentives to retain greater numbers of the young elderly in the work force—it is an almost foregone conclusion that it will. According to the "most likely" (II-B) scenario, the labor force participation rate for elderly men will decline to 12.9 percent by the year 2060; according to the "pessimistic" (III) scenario, it will decline to 10.3 percent. Both of these projections actually seem rather optimistic, especially if one takes into account the fact that the elderly population itself will be aging.

Although the labor force participation rate for all males over the age of sixty-five in 1986 was 16.0 percent, for males seventy and over it was a much-lower 11.5 percent. One might suppose that the eventual increase in the age at which a retiree can receive full Social Security benefits (plus other reforms favoring later retirement legislated in the 1983 Social Security act) would slow this trend in the future, but the consensus among experts is that this change will have little effect.[‡] Survey data support the same conclusion. According to one recent poll, 72 percent of Baby Boomers surveyed said that they planned to retire before sixty.[§]

Whether this will ultimately prove to be feasible for today's young

the practice may have once been common, the federal Age Discrimination in Employment Act (ADEA), first passed in 1967, has been interpreted as prohibiting it on the basis of age (with very few exceptions) for all employees from age 40 to age 70. In 1986 Congress got rid of the age 70 limit and further prohibited any age bias (such as a "cap") in private pension benefits. Even under the original law, the National Longitudinal Survey (see article by Gloria J. Brazzoli in *The Journal of Human Resources;* Spring 1985) reported that fewer than 3 percent of all retirees were "retired mandatorily."

†After rising slightly in the 1950s and 1960s, the labor force participation (LFP) rate for women over age 54 has also declined. The only distinct countervailing trend among mature workers has been for women aged 45 to 54, whose LFP rate (like that of younger women) has climbed strongly—from 38 percent in 1950, to 54 percent in 1970, to 64 percent in 1984. The net result is that the much-heralded rise in the overall U.S. LFP rate has been more than entirely accounted for by the declining relative size of today's child population and the rising LFP rates of younger adults (especially younger adult women).

‡See Chapter 7.

§Poll conducted in 1987 by the Del Webb Corporation (Phoenix, Arizona) among Californians born between 1946 and 1964.

workers is of course another question entirely. Indeed, before the Senior Boom arrives in full force early in the next century, it will become essential to forge a new vision of "old age" as a period of productivity and continued contribution to society. For the youngest elderly (those between sixty-five and seventy), most of whom are in good health, this will almost certainly involve a significantly postponed retirement.

Fewer Workers in the Future: Declining Fertility

Thus far we have discussed the demographic forces that will tend to increase the number of elderly receiving federal entitlement benefits. But what about the workers who will be around to pay for those benefits? For the next twenty years (barring a significant change in net immigration), we know with reasonable precision what the size of the U.S. work force will be, since its potential members have all been born and most are already gainfully employed. Further into the future, however, our vision gets cloudier. For instance, half of those who will be working in the year 2030 have not yet been born.

Unfortunately, there is no way to predict future fertility rates with certainty—and indeed, past predictions have proved to be wildly mistaken just about as often as they have proved to be correct. During the mid-1960s, for instance, Social Security's actuaries—along with most other Americans—were taken entirely by surprise when the postwar Baby Boom suddenly ended. Surely, they reasoned, this sharp fall in fertility rates must soon reverse itself.* By the mid-1970s, however, it became apparent that much of the decline in fertility rates that had occurred since 1957 (the peak year of the Baby Boom) might be permanent. As a consequence, the SSA actuaries grudgingly began to lower their official estimates of future fertility—with instant and devastating results for Social Security's long-term actuarial balance. Figure 4-10 contrasts recent historical data on U.S. total fertility rates with the overoptimistic SSA and Census Bureau projections.

Today the consensus has shifted. Rather than regard the last two decades as a period of abnormally low fertility, most experts have instead come to believe it was the Baby Boom that was highly unusual. As Figure 4-11 demonstrates, the Baby Boom indeed represents the

*Ironically, much of the reluctance among Census and SSA experts to lower their fertility projections came from the erroneously *low* forecasts they made back in the late 1930s. Most demographers had been burned by failing entirely to predict the Baby Boom (and later by being slow to acknowledge it in the 1950s); no one wanted to be embarrassed twice by prematurely advocating a return to the 1930s "birth pessimism."

180

FIGURE 4-10 **Official Projections in Retrospect: Total Fertility Rates**

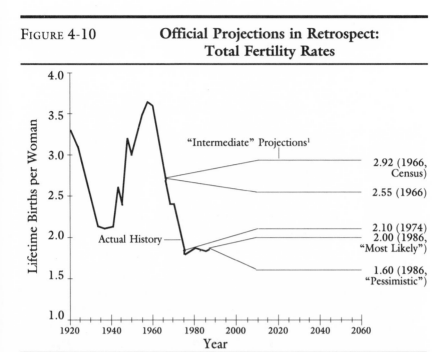

The total fertility rate in each year is the number of children that would be born per woman, throughout her lifetime, at that year's age-specific birth rates.

[1]Except for the "most likely" and "pessimistic" projections noted for 1986; before 1986, "intermediate" means an average of all SSA or Census scenarios.

Source: Office of the Actuary (SSA)

only significant interruption in a long-term historical trend that stretches out over the last two centuries: a trend toward ever-fewer children born per American woman over the course of her lifetime. From well over 7.0 through the eighteenth and early nineteenth century, the U.S. total fertility rate declined fairly steadily to 2.53 in 1930, and then dropped much more rapidly to a low of 2.15 during the so-called baby bust years of the Great Depression. Beginning in 1946 and 1947, the long-term historical trend toward ever-lower birth rates was dramatically reversed, and by 1957 the total fertility rate had shot up to 3.68—the highest it had been in any year since 1900. But from its twentieth-century peak in 1957, the U.S. fertility rate declined slowly to 3.17 in 1964 (the last year of the Baby Boom), and then fell rapidly to an all-time low of 1.74 in 1976, far beneath its earlier nadir in the 1930s baby bust. Since that time, despite the surge from late-birthing Baby Boomers, it has risen only slightly, to 1.86.

181

FIGURE 4-11　　　　U.S. Total Fertility Rates, 1800–1985

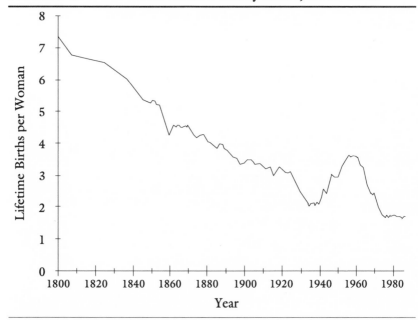

For definition of total fertility rate, see Figure 4-10.

Source: 1800–1916, Ansley J. Coale and Melvin Zelnick, *New Estimates of Fertility and Population in the U.S.* (Princeton, 1963); 1917–1919, NCHS; 1920–85, Office of the Actuary (SSA)

What do these numbers mean? They mean a great deal to our nation's future. Low fertility rates are just as important as increased longevity in driving up the future costs of our entitlements system. But the implications are more than fiscal. Absent a large stream of immigrants, any fertility rate beneath about 2.1 children per woman (the so-called replacement rate) must inevitably lead to a decline in total population. The consequences, as Ben Wattenberg has persuasively argued in *The Birth Dearth*,* may well be a decline in U.S. cultural and political influence in world affairs during the next century—especially if these consequences are compounded by a low-investment, low-growth economy.

---

*_The Birth Dearth: What Happens When People in Free Countries Don't Have Enough Babies?_ by Ben J. Wattenberg (Pharos Books, 1987). Wattenberg summarizes the cultural impact of the "birth dearth" by citing a pithy description from the French demographer Alfred Sauvy: "A society of old people, living in old houses, and ruminating about old ideas"—to which, Wattenberg remarks, Sauvy might have added: "And waging political warfare with younger people about who pays the bills for old people's pensions."

What are the current projections of future U.S. fertility rates? According to the "most likely" assumptions in SSA's 1987 Annual Report, the total fertility rate will rise slightly and then stabilize at an "ultimate" level of 2.0.* According to the "pessimistic" scenario, the U.S. fertility rate will drop slightly before eventually stabilizing at 1.6. Once again, we must ask ourselves: Are these assumptions prudent?

Given the volatility of American family life (U.S. divorce rates are at least double those of any country in Western Europe), the growing numbers of married women in the work force (currently 70 percent of those between the ages of twenty and forty-four are employed), and the widespread availability of contraception, it would seem that the "ultimate" fertility rate of 1.6 projected in the "pessimistic" scenario is probably the best outcome for which we can prudently hope.† This pessimism, moreover, is further justified by the recent experience of other industrial countries. The *average* total fertility rate in Western Europe, to take the most useful parallel, now stands at 1.5—a *lower* figure, in other words, than the "ultimate" rate projected in SSA's "pessimistic" scenario. And in West Germany—a country where many of the same social and cultural forces are at work as in our own—the most recent statistics reveal that the fertility rate has sunk to an alarming 1.3.

In Part One of this book we argued that an "optimistic" economic future—one in which a healthy rate of productivity growth can be sustained over several generations—presupposes an ample rate of domestically financed capital formation. In a similar fashion, it seems likely that higher fertility rates depend in part upon the prospect of rising real after-tax income per family. Indeed, most experts in demography now tell us that stagnating economies quickly translate into stagnating fertility rates (the Great Depression is an example). This observation in turn raises an obvious question: Given their poor expectations about future income levels, is it at all realistic to suppose that today's young families will decide to reverse what is now a three-

---

*During late 1987 and early 1988, a proposal that the II-B "ultimate" fertility rate be revised downward to 1.9 in the 1988 Annual Report became the focus of a heated behind-the-scenes debate at the Social Security Administration.

†It is, in fact, sobering to realize that we are witnessing a positive movement in virtually every socioeconomic variable that historical evidence indicates is negatively correlated with fertility: female labor-force participation, average female age at first marriage, share of female population never married, female educational attainment, and divorce rates (though recently this last variable has been stabilizing). Meanwhile, the use of oral contraceptives is rebounding (after a 50 percent decline from 1973 to 1982) now that the widely publicized reports on their adverse side-effects, such as an increased risk of cancer, are being disproved.

decades-long decline in U.S. fertility rates?

As we have seen, Census Bureau and Labor Department statistics plainly show that the drop in real personal income per U.S. family during the 1970s and 1980s has been especially steep for young families. To be sure, since the size of young families has also declined, this age bracket has fared somewhat better in terms of per capita income. But on the other hand, we must remember that per capita gains in family income have only been possible because the proportion of wives in this age-group who are working has more than doubled since the early 1960s. Are these the young women from whom we should expect an abundant crop of future taxpayers?

Historically, we know that parents' decisions about whether to have few or many children are critically affected by three conditions: (1) the cost in time and money of raising a child; (2) the chance a child will have of enjoying a higher standard of living than his or her parents; and (3) the extent to which parents will have to rely on a child to assume personal responsibility for their security in old age. It is not hard to see that each of these conditions is currently shifting in a direction that argues against higher future fertility rates. In particular, the third one has undergone an unprecedented reversal over the past few decades. For centuries, most parents who survived to old age counted on their own children to help support them financially. Today, as we saw in Chapter 2, many surveys report that net voluntary transfers within families are heading in the opposite direction, from elderly parents to their adult children.

While our public entitlement programs have effectively subsidized much of the cost of being old, we have subsidized very little of the cost of being young (after all, a child's room, board, health, and education must be paid for directly by his or her parents). As a consequence, raising children is coming to be regarded as a personal economic decision entailing growing and obvious costs along with shrinking and dimly perceived benefits. This is not to say that having children is purely an economic decision (or that Social Security per se is a bad idea). Rather, it is simply to point out that economic conditions and incentives have a well-documented impact on choices about how many children to raise.

Many policy experts seem to hope that future young families will offer up ever more children to work at zero-growth real wages while bearing ever-higher payroll tax rates. In this way, it is supposed, the

Baby Boom's retirement may be adequately financed.* But history shows that such hopes must be ill-founded. And so, for that matter, do contemporary surveys and opinion polls.† Surveys of young women all indicate that a very small and declining proportion of them want to have more than two children. While changing attitudes about family life and about the intrinsic value of a career help explain this trend, the attitudes themselves reflect a new mood of caution among young people about their economic future. No one wants to end up at the wrong end of a chain-letter scam; few of us want our own children to end up there, either.

Coming to Grips with the Aging of America

Even if the "optimistic" assumptions embodied in the SSA's "most likely" scenario prove to be correct in every way, the total impact of an aging population will still mean that we will face an endless future of considerably higher federal spending levels. The purpose of contemplating the "pessimistic" scenario—whether or not the reader agrees with us that it represents the most likely outcome given current policy—is to prepare for the future prudently by keeping in mind the potential dimensions of our problem.

There are three strong reasons why we should begin to prepare for the future now. The first reason is equity. If we delay fundamental entitlements reform for many more years, we will be closing in on the time when the Baby Boom's retirement will turn the trend in real benefit costs from a steady slope to a steep wall. By the year 2010, it will be too late to make gradual adjustments around which individu-

---

*The notion that tomorrow's birth choices will grind on like some autonomous machine may be inferred from the 1987 SSA Annual Report's coldly worded defense of the II-B fertility assumption: "Future fertility rates may be expected to exceed the present low level, because such a low level has never been experienced in the U.S. for a long period, and because such a level is well below that needed to maintain the size of the population. . . ."

†From 1959 to 1985, for instance, the Gallup Poll found that those who believed that the "ideal size of a family" included four or more children dropped from 47 to 11 percent of all Americans; meanwhile, those preferring only two children climbed from 16 percent to 56 percent. The Census Bureau conducts similar surveys of young women (aged 18 to 24) to find out how many children they expect to have. Since the mid-1970s, the numerical average generated by these surveys has been well below 2.1 children. Experience indicates, moreover, that women end up having fewer children than they earlier expect. The Census Bureau recently concluded that no birth cohort born after 1946 is likely to have an average completed family size of over 1.9 children, although many initially expected to have an average family size of well over 2.1 children.

als can plan their futures. "Reform" will instead have to come abruptly—violating the principle of gradualism and raising the very real specter of draconian benefit cuts, huge tax hikes, and debilitating generational strife.

The second reason is economic. Only by instituting measures that will encourage young families to save a greater portion of their income over the course of their working lives can we ensure higher levels of private-sector savings, smaller federal deficits, an investment renewal, and a generous standard of living for the future elderly. The proper mix of incentives, if put into place now, could transform our vicious circle of deficit-financed retirement into a virtuous circle of savings-financed retirement. And it could do this while raising the future standard of living for all Americans.

The final reason is frankly political. If we wait until that vast Baby Boom generation is about to retire before facing up to entitlements reform, questions of equity and politics are bound to become inextricably confused. In the year 2010, the Baby Boomers will dominate the electorate. As the first generation in U.S. history to spend their entire working lives paying into Social Security at total payroll-tax rates of more than 10 percent, they may well experience a legitimate sense of grievance at becoming the first generation to be asked to make major sacrifices in benefits. What about the generation that is retiring today, a generation that for much of their working lives paid little or no payroll taxes at all? Is theirs the attitude of Louis XV, "Après moi, le déluge"? When such questions are asked twenty or twenty-five years from now, how will they be answered?

It is hard to overemphasize the key role the Baby Boom's retirement will play in shaping policy in the year 2010. If the cost of investing in our children and our economy seems onerous to our society today, as a "boom" generation is working and a "bust" generation is retiring, we can only imagine how unaffordable it will seem thirty years from now when the situation is reversed. Will the Baby Boom accept the necessity of sacrifice, or will the full burden of our insufficient productivity growth be forced to fall on the shoulders of still younger age-groups? If the latter, then the present vicious circle of declining opportunities will be perpetuated into the indefinite future with predictable results: more poor young families, still fewer and less productive children, and ever-darker prospects for new generations of workers and retirees alike.

"The prophesying business," wrote H. L. Mencken, "is like writing fugues; it is fatal to everyone save the man of absolute genius." But that depends on what one is trying to prophesy. In this chapter, we have sketched the constraints demography will impose on our future. Of course, no one can foretell "surprise" events that may improve or worsen this scenario, or more important, how Americans will respond to these constraints. It is certain, however, that ultimately we will be forced to make momentous choices that will in large part determine America's economy, its politics, and its culture.

5

Driving the Projections: Health-Care Hyperinflation

"May you become fabulously rich, and then spend all your money on doctors."
—*Ancient Chinese Curse*

DURING THE EARLY YEARS of the Reagan administration, most Americans were hopeful that new federal policies could control the explosive growth of national health-care spending. When novel cost-saving reforms were legislated by Congress in the early 1980s (such as the prospective pricing system now used by Medicare's Hospital Insurance), this hope turned into sunny confidence. By 1984 then Health and Human Services Secretary Margaret Heckler could announce that we had "broken the back of the health-care inflation monster."

Today both the confidence and the hope have faded. Although total U.S. health-care spending as a share of Gross National Product fell slightly in 1984, from 10.5 to 10.3 percent, it rose anew to an unprecedented 10.7 percent in 1985 and further—with monthly health-care inflation racing seven times faster than the Consumer Price Index—to 10.9 percent of GNP in 1986. The data for 1987 will certainly show that it is now over 11 percent and perhaps closing in on 12 percent. We are now spending at least *double* the share of our GNP on health care that we spent in 1965. Optimistic projections made just

189

TABLE 5-1	Personal Health-Care Spending by Sector, Selected Years		
	1965	1980	1986
	Billions of Dollars		
Public	$7.9	$86.5	$160.0
Federal	3.6	62.5	121.8
State & Local	4.3	24.0	38.1
Private	$28.0	$133.2	$244.0
Total	$35.9	$219.7	$404.0
	Percent Distribution		
Public	22.0%	39.4%	39.6%
Federal	10.1	28.5	30.2
State & Local	12.0	10.9	9.4
Private	78.0	60.6	60.4

Source: HCFA

a few years ago by federal health officials are in shreds. As the Health Care Financing Administration (HCFA) admitted in a 1986 report: "Little relief appears to be in sight. . . . The decline in the share of GNP going to health in 1984 appears to be a one-time blip in the historic trend rather than the start of a new trend."[*] In the judgment of Uwe Reinhardt, a prominent health economist at Princeton: "I can't imagine how anyone could conclude from the available data that the 1980s have produced any health-care cost containment. On the contrary, the spigot has opened."[†]

Indeed, despite all the talk about cost containment, we now know that the chief effect of federal policy remains today what it was in the 1960s and 1970s: to drive up total national health-care spending. During the 1980s, health-care benefits as a share of the federal budget did not show even a one-year dip. They have risen every year and now amount to about $120 billion annually, or 25 percent of all federal benefit spending. The explosion in federal health-care spending has been responsible for a disproportionate share of the spiraling growth in total national health-care costs. In 1965 federal expenditures accounted for

[*]"National Health Expenditures, 1985" by Daniel R. Waldo et al., *National Health Care Financing Review* (Fall 1986).
[†]Uwe E. Reinhardt, cited in *Medical Economics* (August 14, 1987).

only 10.1 percent of the dollars Americans spent on health care; in 1986 federal expenditures accounted for 30.2 percent of the total. Table 5-1 illustrates this historical trend.

Much of the growth in federal health-care spending reflects the deliberate decisions Congress made during the 1960s to create new health-benefit programs, to expand old health-benefit categories, and to multiply the number of federal grants passed out to state and local health authorities. The most important year in the history of this benefit expansion was 1965, when President Johnson and the Eighty-ninth Congress established Medicare for elderly persons covered by Social Security, and Medicaid for the disabled, elderly, and "welfare" poor covered by various state-administered programs. Medicare and Medicaid began their first full year of operation in 1967; between 1966 and 1968, federal health-care spending more than doubled.

Another important year was 1972, when Medicare benefits were extended to disabled persons covered by Social Security as well as to special groups requiring costly or acute care (patients with kidney failure who require dialysis, for example). Between 1968 and 1973, federal health-care spending once again nearly doubled. But even in more recent years, when legislated additions to federal health programs have been few (and regulations aimed at curbing costs have proliferated), this growth has continued. From 1973 to 1986, federal health-care spending kept expanding at more than twice the national rate of inflation.

A critical factor in the steep upward course of federal health-care spending has been the open-ended basis on which personal health benefits have been disbursed. The legislation behind these programs, in other words, has generally covered each beneficiary for all or most of whatever acute-care health services he or she consumes. It is true that federal reimbursements to doctors and hospitals are subject to complicated limits on price per service; a health-care "service," however, is difficult to define, and in any case there are no effective limits on the number of services rendered per beneficiary. The result has been an explosion in the cost of federal health programs that vastly exceeds any increase attributable to growth in the numbers of beneficiaries. Take the case of Medicare. Real spending since 1970 has risen about twice as fast as total federal outlays and *three times as fast as the number of Medicare enrollees.*

Federal health benefits are thus "uncontrollable" in an even more fundamental sense than federal cash benefits. Growth in cash benefit levels, though driven upward by indexing, is at least constrained by the limits of a price formula. Health benefits have no predetermined boundaries. Within certain (largely ineffective) regulatory guidelines, they are simply the sum of what each beneficiary—with the advice of his or her physician—decides to purchase in a market for ever more sophisticated, varied, and expensive forms of medical treatment.

The direct cost of open-ended federal benefits, however, is only part of our health-care cost problem. Even more worrisome are the expansionary pressures exerted by federal policies on spending in other sectors—in hundreds of state and local governments and in millions of homes and businesses having little or no connection with the federal purse. On the one hand, our federal tax and regulatory structure has been expressly designed to encourage or mandate health-care spending by nonfederal buyers; it does so, for example, by exempting employee fringe benefits from taxation, and by specifying the type of care that participants in federal programs such as Medicare must provide to all comers. On the other hand, the sheer size of direct federal health-care outlays, which finance nearly one-third of total national health-care consumption, has served to "bid up" the price of medical services for other buyers. The result is that all Americans, not just the federal government, must directly pay more for health care.

Total health-care spending by state and local governments, for instance, has also been increasing at a breakneck pace. In 1960 state and local authorities spent $3.6 billion on health care; by 1986 they were spending $55.0 billion—a smaller growth rate than in the federal sector, but nonetheless a fourfold rise in real terms. State and local governments have been spared the enormous costs of Medicare. But they subsidize the costs of thousands of community hospitals and clinics and provide health care for a much larger population of public employees. And since the states must pay for more than half the cost of Medicaid—for which the federal government designs the general administrative rules—much of the rise in state health-care spending has been beyond the effective control of locally elected officials. As a result of these pressures, the share of all state and local budgets devoted to health-care spending has risen from 12 percent in the early 1970s to 18 percent today. As New Jersey Governor Thomas Kean once quipped, "Health spending is the Pac-Man of my budget."

Nor has private-sector spending on health care been standing still. Here the dollar flow has widened from $20.3 billion in 1960 to $268.5 billion in 1986, more than a threefold increase in real terms.

The prime force behind this growth has been the continuous expansion in employer-sponsored health insurance (encouraged by the tax-exempt status of employee fringe benefits) and in the demand by employees for insured health-care services available at little or no user cost. In 1986 total private health-plan premiums paid by employers amounted to $108 billion; this is greater than the total after-tax profits of all U.S. corporations and about double what employers spent on health care as recently as 1980. Relative to the take-home wages of all civilian workers, employee health benefits have risen from about 1.7 percent in 1960 to 5.3 percent today. And this average includes many workers who are not covered at all. In many high-wage, high-benefit industries the premium level is a great deal higher—as much as $4 of a production worker's hourly compensation costs.

So while federal and state legislators worry about the effect of health-benefit payments on their budget deficits, business leaders have now become equally alarmed at the impact of insurance premiums on the competitiveness of their goods. The Chrysler Corporation, according to its chairman Lee Iacocca, now pays more money to Blue Cross and Blue Shield of Michigan every year than it does to any other single supplier—including any steel manufacturer. But current costs are only the tip of the iceberg. U.S. corporations have also accumulated over $1 trillion in unfunded liabilities for retiree health-benefit plans.* In the future, the federal government may have to assume much of this cost by guaranteeing these plans (just as it already guarantees pensions).

When we add up all these numbers, we are looking at what the media have dubbed our "national health-care crisis." Some critics argue that concerns over rising health-care costs are exaggerated, since economic growth will allow us to bear any future health-care burden. It is of course true that many things—including more and better health care—will become affordable if U.S. living standards rise swiftly over the next ten or fifteen years. But as we have seen, real family

---

*Estimates of private-sector retiree health-care liabilities vary widely, from at least $300 billion (according to a soon-to-be-released GAO study) to $2 trillion (according to former HEW Secretary Joseph A. Califano). What is certain is that the number is growing rapidly, especially since the work force in so many large companies is aging in place. In 1974, for instance, the average Fortune 500 company had twelve active employees for each retiree; today it has three. Currently, only 1 percent of all companies "prefund" their retiree health-benefit plans. Nonetheless, recent court rulings, which imply that these benefits cannot easily be cut, have this year prompted the Financial Accounting Standards Board to determine that unfunded plan liabilities must be accounted for on the corporate balance sheet—a step that may have devasting repercussions for many firms.

income has hardly moved for more than a decade now and is likely to remain stagnant until our domestic and international debt problems are resolved. Current federal policy, while doing much to ensure that real health-care spending will double by the year 2000, can unfortunately make no such guarantee about the size of our future economy. Indeed, an endless climb in the share of our national resources allocated to health care is the best way to guarantee that vigorous economic growth will *not* occur.

Other critics believe that it is just a matter of time before we stem the onrushing health-cost tide, and cite evidence that doctor visits, hospital admissions, and hospital patient-days per capita have all dropped sharply since 1983, partly in response to stricter rules introduced by Medicare and private insurers. It is important to note, however, that the long-term trend in visits, admissions, and patient-days has been stagnant or nearly stagnant for the last couple of decades. The reason health-care costs have been rising rapidly, in other words, has never been an increase in the number of encounters between patients and providers; rather, it has been the mounting volume of technology, skill, and labor devoted to each patient that arrives at a doctor's office or spends a day in a hospital bed.

Is it reasonable to assume that the growth rate in real health-care expenditures per person will fall significantly in the years to come? Few experts dare to predict this. In the first place, we can count on continuing acceleration in the sophistication and variety of available health-care treatments. Much of this acceleration comes from pioneering research and technology, the results of which are the stuff of newspaper headlines: artificial skin, bones, and joints for the victims of burns, accidents, and arthritis; organ transplantation to replace diseased kidneys, livers, hearts, or arteries; angioplasty; multimillion-dollar electromagnetic, X-ray, and acoustic detection devices; CAT and PET scans; nuclear imaging; advanced pharmaceuticals to treat hypertension and arrythmia; electrophysiological testing for heart drugs; customized and genetically coded antibodies to destroy or control cancer; computerized monitoring of vital signs; genetic screening for marriage or employment; laser therapy and microsurgery. The list of recent or soon-to-be-offered treatments and diagnostic tools is long and growing. Nowhere has their impact been more expensive than in the hospital. The HCFA has estimated that the introduction of new technologies accounts for fully 40 percent of the historical growth in real hospital spending.

194

The cost of new technology, however, is not the only reason for the increase in the number of health-care services per capita. A second impetus comes from a growing per capita use of services that have always been available, such as routine testing (to further check a diagnosis or assuage patient anxiety), specialist consultation (to ensure that the most expert opinion is obtained, especially in view of proliferating malpractice suits), assorted personal services (such as psychiatry), and pain alleviation therapies (such as chiropractic). It is possible that patients are becoming more knowledgeable about available treatments or simply that the long-standing correlation between educational level and health-care consumption is making itself felt as the educational background of the general population (especially in the older age-groups) rises.

In any event, it is interesting to note that despite the so-called doctor glut (an issue to which we will return), physician shortages remain most acute in psychiatry and rehabilitation, not in the technology-intensive specialties. Comparison of Medicare records from 1977 and 1982 shows that the greatest percentage increases in visits to physicians between those two years were in chiropractic, emergency care, initial eye examinations, psychiatry, and podiatry (in that order). Moreover, the same records reveal that the composition of visits to physicians shifted dramatically toward initial visits (which are 20 percent more costly than follow-up visits) and toward specialist visits (which are 50 percent more costly than general and family practice visits). Thus even though the per capita number of visits is not changing, each one typically involves more testing, labor, and specialized education—quite independently of any intensification in the use of new technologies.

Finally, we must face up to the dramatic health-care consequences of our aging population. The elderly will keep growing as a proportion of the total population, while the numbers of the "old elderly" will continue to climb even faster as a proportion of all aged Americans. As we saw in the previous chapter, the expansionary effects of these demographic changes alone will cause a rapid acceleration in real health-care spending on the elderly. Continued advances in medical technologies, together with the growing demand for more specialized and expensive services, will further compound this trend.

If we have not yet stemmed the tide of surging health-care costs, how much worse can we expect things to get? Experts at the Health Care Financing Administration now expect that health-care spending in the United States will hit 15 percent of GNP by the year 2000.* And in Chapter 3, we concluded that the figure would rise much further by the year 2040 if current policies remain unchanged. According to our more optimistic scenario, the reader will recall, health-care spending will rise to more than one-fifth of GNP by the time today's young children are contemplating retirement. If the future unfolds according to "official" HCFA projections, the health-care industry will be gargantuan only twenty years from now: several times larger than defense; bigger than farming, energy, utilities, transportation, and construction combined. Do we really think that we can once again become competitive in trade while allocating an ever-larger proportion of our scarce supply of capital and skilled labor toward health-care consumption? Just to mention the health-benefit costs generated by our "pessimistic" scenario for the year 2040 is to conclude that we will be forced to implement drastic reforms of our health-care system.

Thus far, however, we have refused to contemplate how such reform might unfold. Will it be belated, sudden, and demoralizing, enacted in the midst of economic crisis and crunching down inequitably on health care for those who need it most? Or will we move gradually and with forethought toward reforms that control costs with the least pain or waste—and quite possibly improve the quality and equity of our current system? Let us emphasize that America has no time to lose. Near-term reform of our publicly funded cash entitlements is necessary to allow us time to adjust before the adverse demographics hit early in the next century. Near-term reform of publicly funded and regulated health-care spending is necessary for an even more compelling reason: the cost explosion is advancing so rapidly that it will not wait for adverse demographics. Recall the optimistic official projection cited above: 15 percent of GNP will be spent on health care by the turn of the century—that is, less than halfway between now and the beginning of the Baby Boom's retirement.

To be sure, federal health-care spending poses the same problem we face in other areas of our entitlement budget: growing deficits generated by outlays that rise beyond what the public is willing to pay in taxes. It also reflects our deeper entitlement ethos at work. Like the

---

*This is the best-case scenario (*Health Care Financing Review;* Summer 1987) prepared by the HCFA and incorporated in our II-B projection in Chapter 3. Its economic and health-care (price and utilization) assumptions are, therefore, an optimistic improvement on current trends. Perhaps most optimistic of all—given this year's flurry of congressional activity over new health-benefit proposals—is the political assumption that no new public benefits will be added to current law.

FIGURE 5-1 **Public Health-Care Spending per Capita on the Elderly as a Percent of Spending per Capita on the Nonelderly in 1980**

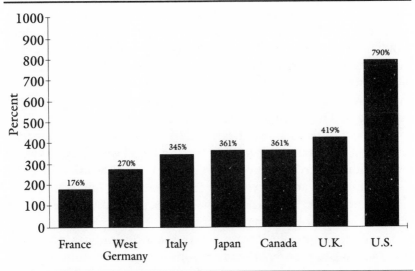

Spending by all levels of government. Elderly, aged 65 and over; nonelderly, aged 0 through 64.

Source: See footnote citation on this page.

unrealistic dream of unfunded pensions—ever-more leisure for everyone at the far end of life—the equally unrealistic dream of endless health-care consumption is in essence a willful negation of the future that lies beyond our own lives. Both dreams constitute a personal and collective refusal to age responsibly and accept mortality; both reflect the denial of the spirit of endowment and hence the importance of investment.

Perhaps it seems unfair to suggest that Americans have become the quixotic heirs of Ponce de Leon, in search of a "fountain of youth" no matter what the cost. Yet consider: U.S. public spending on health-care benefits for the elderly is *eight times greater* per capita than for the nonelderly(see Figure 5-1) and *fifteen times greater* than for children.*

*Based on 1980 data in *Aging and Social Expenditures in the Major Industrial Countries, 1980–2025* (Occasional Paper 47 of the International Monetary Fund; September 1986). These ratios are for all levels of government. According to these estimates, the 1980 per capita spending ratio between the elderly and nonelderly was 7.9 to 1 in the United States; in no other major industrial country was it higher than 4.2 to1. The per capita spending ratio between the elderly and children was 14.7 to 1 in the United States; in no other major industrial country was it higher than 7.3 to 1.

America is the only society in the world (indeed, in history) to sanction a collective solicitude toward the health of its oldest members that is so vastly greater than toward the health of its youngest members.

Such age-group differences are what we might expect from a society not accustomed, at the macro level, to giving investment a high priority in its allocation of public resources. Yet there is also a deeper problem here: our mistaken belief that health is not an investment at all, but rather a finite and purchasable consumption item. From this premise we have moved to the conclusion that it is possible, through an assortment of indiscriminate subsidies, to make health a deliverable public right. This conclusion, as we will see shortly, has shaped nearly every aspect of federal health-care policy—program design, supervision, regulation, tax structure, and law. To begin with, it has allowed our public policy to be twisted in favor of the politically powerful. After all, if health is regarded merely as consumption and not as an investment in the future, there is no reason to expect that the young will fare very well in the political marketplace.

Yet what is equally disturbing, this conclusion has generated enormous waste precisely where the subsidies have been most generous. It has persuaded us to insulate both the consumer (the patient) and the provider (the doctor or hospital) from the costs of their consumption choices. It has led us to relegate the very definition of our choices to the group interests of the providers themselves, thus making our policy an "entitlement" for health-care professionals as well as for their favored patients. And it has blinded us to the meaningful resource trade-offs—between those who need subsidies and those who do not, between where health care is likely to deliver health and where it is not, between the cost of retrieving health and the cost of maintaining health, and between health defined as prolonged life and health defined as prolonged death. Our obsession with health as a politically malleable consumption right has left its imprint upon our entire system of health-care provision, a system that funnels most of its income to the marginal and often questionable acts of heroic, acute-care intervention (health on instant demand) and leaves the vast benefits of preventative approaches (health as deferred reward) starved for public funding.

In short, we are dealing once again with a skewed cultural outlook, not just with a set of mistaken public policies. "Good health" is not of course a finite consumption item any more than "good retirement" or "good housing." In fact, health is not by nature a consumption item at all. In the opinion of nearly all medical experts, by far the most important determinants of good health are the delayed and nonpurchasable benefits of personal life choices (regarding diet, sleep, exercise, toxic drugs, and work), plus certain collective investments (in sanitation, vaccination, general medical practice, and ongoing research on major killing diseases), the cost of which is very modest. Most of the rest of what we call "health care" is indeed consumption, in the sense that its justification lies more in our personal desire for it—rather than in cost-effective paybacks to either ourselves or others. This consumption rationale, enshrined in public policy, remains the propelling force behind our national health-care cost explosion.

Our basic attitudes toward the public role of medicine in our lives will have to change radically over the course of the next generation. In Chapter 9, we will outline a few of the new and painful trade-offs we soon will face, and will examine some of the specific policy options already (and unsuccessfully) tried, as well as those yet available to us. This chapter explains how we reached this crossroads and why our current course is absolutely unaffordable. The theme is one that policymakers in Washington, still preoccupied with enlarging the limitless health-equals-consumption equation, have yet to grasp.

Are We Getting Our Money's Worth?

To the extent that the steep climb in our national health-care costs over the past few decades has been a response to political demand (in the case of government spending) and consumer demand (in the case of private spending), we might suppose that the public is well satisfied with our health-care system. The truth, as we all know, is otherwise. The public is profoundly worried about how much it must regularly pay—in taxes or in insurance premiums—for the care it receives. Opinion polls show that although most Americans believe that the "quality" of U.S. health care has been improving, they are increasingly dubious of its "worth" as a return on their money.

Of all industrial countries, the United States now spends the most on health care as a share of GNP (see Figure 5-2).* As of 1985, U.S. health-care spending stood at 10.6 percent of GNP. No other nation exceeded 10 percent and only Sweden exceeded 9 percent; moreover,

---

*The international health-care cost figures are calculated by the Organization for Economic Cooperation and Development (see *Financing and Delivering Health Care*, Social Policy Study Number 4, OECD, 1987).

FIGURE 5-2   **Health-Care Expenditures as a Percent of GNP in 1985**

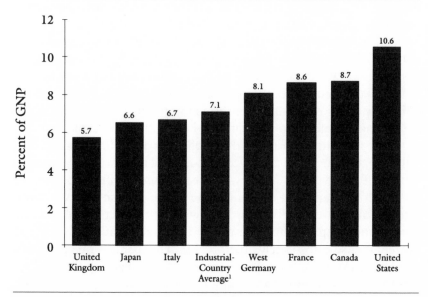

[1]Average of 17 major industrial countries, excluding the United States.
Source: OECD (Paris)

the per-GNP spending level in most other industrial countries has stabilized or fallen during the 1980s. Relative to the average for all other industrial countries, U.S. health-care spending per GNP in 1985 stood 50 percent higher than the norm (7.1 percent of GNP).*

Considering how much we spend on health care relative to the rest of the developed world, one might legitimately wonder: What are we getting out of it? Are we any healthier? The statistics are far from comforting. According to most indicators of health status, the United States is just about average with respect to all other industrial countries. In terms of age-adjusted mortality rates, we are slightly worse than average for the young and slightly better than average for the old (and slightly worse than average for men, slightly better for women). Moreover, when the United States is compared to the other most affluent industrial countries (which may be the most relevant

*Since real per capita GNP remains greater in the United States than abroad, the absolute dollar comparisons for 1985 are even more stunning: $1,770 in average health-care spending per capita in the United States, versus $990 in West Germany, $780 in Japan, and $620 in Britain (using BLS purchasing-power parity exchange rates).

measure), it comes out considerably below average in nearly all indicators of health. Japan, for instance, spends a relatively low 6.6 percent of GNP on health care, yet life expectancy in Japan is longer than in the United States—at birth, at age fifty-five, and at age sixty-five.*

Given the skewed age distribution of U.S. public health-care spending, perhaps the most illuminating comparisons are those that monitor health at the extreme ends of life. For the very young, we are the *least healthy.* As of 1985, the United States had the highest infant mortality rate (10.6 deaths per thousand births) of all industrial nations.† In fact, if we had experienced the same incidence of infant mortality that year as Japan (5.5 deaths per thousand births, about half our rate), 19,000 fewer U.S. babies would have died. For the very old, on the other hand, we are the *most healthy.* Although our life expectancy at age sixty-five is only slightly better than average, at age eighty-five it is the highest in the world.‡ America has become the last place in the industrial world you would want to be born, but the first place where you would want to live (or travel to for treatment) when you are an octogenarian.

In addition to disappointing health outcomes, there is another fundamental problem with the U.S. health-care system: despite its high cost, it fails to provide even minimal coverage to millions of Americans. We read of elderly patients who receive a second heart transplant at a cost of several hundred thousand dollars, yet we may also know of parents who cannot afford dental care for their children. Many wealthy families (which are the most likely to be well insured) are often able to weather a health crisis while spending hardly a dime. Less affluent families (which are frequently without any insurance) are brought to the edge of financial ruin by one serious illness.

The spottiness of health-care coverage in the United States today is, again, largely a generational problem. Almost 100 percent of the elderly are covered by Medicare (or by a more generous public-

---

* The 1983 figures for Japan and the United States respectively (with simple averages of male and female) are 77.0 versus 74.7 years at birth; 25.1 versus 24.1 years at age fifty-five; and 16.8 versus 16.7 years at age sixty-five.

†The 1985 rate of infant mortality in the United States was just a bit worse than Spain's 10.5. West Germany, Belgium, and the United Kingdom were the only other industrial countries in which the rate exceeded 9.0. The rate for U.S. blacks is 18.0 per 1,000 live births. (See the recent 1988 report by the U.S. Office of Technology Assessment.)

‡The most recent data from the National Center for Health Statistics show that U.S. life expectancy for men at age eighty-five (5.1 years) is matched only by Canada; for women at age eighty-five (6.6 years), it is considerably longer than in any other country.

employee plan); of these, fully 80 percent supplement their Medicare coverage with private insurance (employer-paid retiree plans or individually purchased "medigap" policies) or some other public entitlement (either Medicaid or Veterans Administration benefits). Significantly, the number of elderly who receive means-tested benefits under Medicaid (3.2 million in 1986) is nearly equal to the number of elderly officially in poverty (3.5 million in 1986).* The result is that virtually the entire elderly population is insured once—and the vast majority are insured at least twice—for a substantial share of their health-care expenses.

Now consider the nonelderly population. Although about three-quarters are covered privately by a group plan or an individually purchased policy, many of these policies are considerably less extensive than Medicare. According to one recent survey, 17 percent of all privately covered workers lack any major medical coverage and an additional 34 percent have no limit on major medical out-of-pocket costs. Of the one-quarter of nonelderly Americans not covered by private-sector insurance, less than one-third receive Medicaid. The rest, variously estimated at about 30 to 40 million (a number greater than the total elderly population) have no health insurance at all, either public or private. Figure 5-3 summarizes the results of one recent survey conducted by the Census Bureau. Overall, about 13 percent of the entire U.S. population was not covered by any health insurance in 1985, but beneath this average we find that this rate declines dramatically with age. For Americans under age twenty-five, nearly one in six were not covered; for Americans sixty-five and over, one in two-hundred were not covered. In terms of absolute numbers, Figure 5-4 shows that the former group comprises 16.3 million people, or more than half of all persons not covered; the latter group comprises 147,000 people, or only about six-hundredths of one percent of all persons not covered.

Many of the 30 to 40 million uninsured younger Americans, moreover, are officially in poverty. According to the most recent surveys, about half of all nonelderly families in poverty (14 million persons in

---

*To be sure, these two populations do not exactly match each other—for much the same reason that they do not match each other for Supplemental Security Insurance (SSI), the program through which most elderly become eligible for Medicaid. As explained later (see footnote on page 303), many poor elderly persons either cannot or do not receive SSI; those who do not often avoid applying until they encounter a sizable medical expense. The Commonwealth Fund Commission estimates that 29 percent of the poor elderly get by on Medicare alone. On the other hand, some elderly persons above the poverty line (depending on the state) receive SSI and Medicaid.

FIGURE 5-3 **Health Insurance, Rate of Uncovered Population by Age-Group in 1985**

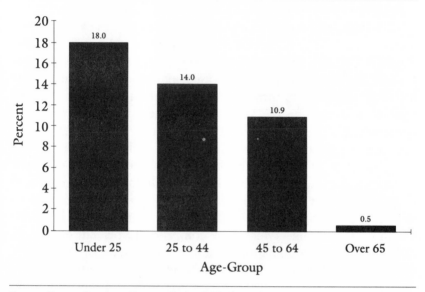

Source: Current Populaton Reports (Series P-70, Census)

FIGURE 5-4 **Health Insurance, Total Number of Uncovered Persons by Age-Group in 1985**

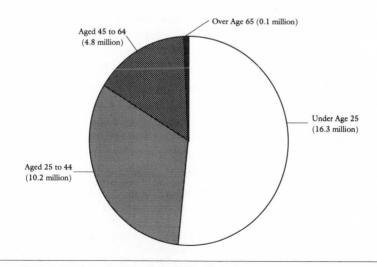

Source: Current Populaton Reports (Series P-70, Census)

1986) were entirely uncovered by insurance in any given month, and about one-third were entirely uncovered throughout the year. Contrary to popular impression, most poor Americans under sixty-five are *not* eligible for publicly funded health care. The reason is straightforward: federal law requires that states offer Medicaid to participants in just two means-tested cash benefit programs, Aid to Families with Dependent Children (for poor mothers) and Supplemental Security Income (for elderly or disabled poor persons). Since many states limit Medicaid eligibility to these groups alone, most of the poor do not receive Medicaid for the same reasons they do not receive cash benefits: they do not apply; they are categorically disallowed (because they are nonelderly and without dependent children); or, even if categorically allowed, they are not poor enough—meaning that their income or assets surpass AFDC or SSI thresholds, which are set well below the poverty line in most states.*

It may seem paradoxical that the tremendous growth in public health-care spending—which now comprises 40 percent of our national total—has resulted in such indifferent coverage for the millions of Americans, especially the young, beneath the poverty level. But once again we find that alleviating poverty really has very little to do with the rationale behind entitlements. Only 20 percent of all federal expenditures on health-care benefits goes for Medicaid, the one health-care program that categorically targets families in financial need. Of all Medicaid benefits, moreover, 70 percent currently flows to the elderly or totally disabled, who comprise only 23 percent of Medicaid beneficiaries. Only 30 percent flows to all other families and children, who comprise the other 77 percent of Medicaid beneficiaries. Where do the rest of our federal health-care benefit dollars go, aside from Medicaid? In 1986 about 62 percent of the total was spent on Medicare (where poverty is never an eligibility issue), and most of the remainder went to veterans' and military health-care programs (where poverty is very rarely an eligibility issue).

In order to gain some perspective on the huge cost, poor results, and haphazard public targeting of American health care, we should return to the example of Japan. Japan's overall spending on health care relative to the size of its economy is so low that the Japanese public sector can pay for three-quarters of the cost of all health services,

---

*Thirty-two states provide Medicaid to low-income persons who incur heavy medical expenses and would be eligible for AFDC or SSI if they did not slightly exceed the program's income criteria. This "medically needy" category, however, represented only about 15 percent of all Medicaid recipients in 1984.

including 90 percent of hospital, physician, and pharmaceutical bills, while spending no more than the American public sector relative to GNP. Because virtually the entire Japanese population is covered (primarily through a payroll-tax-financed "sickness fund"), poor Japanese families are rarely if ever at risk of financial collapse due to illness. Yet the real cost per person of health care in Japan is about one-half of what it is in the United States. This disparity apparently has had neither bad consequences for Japanese health nor measurably positive consequences for our own.

Most Americans now past middle age grew up at a time when health care consisted of casual family practitioners and a rare and brief visit to a community hospital. Today we encounter a vast health-care industry employing 8 million workers and grossing well over $1 billion daily. Why has it become such a bad investment? Why does it fail to give us effective, equitable, and affordable care?

Health Care: A Market Gone Haywire

Among all the perverse disincentives that riddle our expensive and consumption-oriented approach to health care, most experts agree on the fundamental importance of one underlying malady: the growing predominance of "third-party payments" combined with unrestricted "fee-for-service" pricing. The term "third-party payments" refers to health-care purchases for which neither the first party receiving the service (the patient) nor the second party providing the service (the physician or hospital) bears any of the cost of the purchase. Instead, the cost is borne by a distant third party (the government or a private insurer). "Fee-for-service" refers to the method of pricing whereby the total price is determined by adding up the real or presumed costs of whatever services the patient and the provider agree are necessary.

Although there has been a marked movement toward alternative systems of pricing over the past few years (such as "health maintenance organizations," a development we will discuss later), traditional fee-for-service pricing linked to third-party payments still shapes the basic contours of the American health-care system. These pricing and insurance mechanisms can generate practically unlimited increases in costs. Since health-care providers have a direct incentive to increase the amount of medical services purchased, and since the patient has little incentive to limit the amount, total costs tend to follow incentives—upward. If a large proportion of all patients had to bear the cost of health care out of their own pockets, or, alternatively, if providers' fees were fixed in advance regardless of eventual services rendered ("prospective" payment), then upward pressures on costs would meet a downward pressure from patients (or providers). The market would thus be kept honest. One salutary result would be that patients would turn away from higher-priced physicians and hospitals and instead be attracted to providers offering quality care at lower prices.

Over the last few decades, however, the U.S. health-care market has been steadily losing its most important source of downward pressure. As Figure 5-5 illustrates, the share of all personal health-care expenditures paid "out of pocket" (that is, directly) by patients has declined from 66 percent in 1950 to about 28 percent today. As a share of all physician income, direct patient spending has fallen from 62 percent as recently as 1965 to about 26 percent today; and as a share of all hospital payments (by far the most expensive health-care category), patient out-of-pocket spending now accounts for an almost negligible 9 percent. Significantly, nursing home expenditures represent the only major exception to this sharp downward trend; here the share of direct patient spending has merely fallen from 65 percent to 51 percent over the past twenty years.

Increased health-care spending has undoubtedly saved lives and comforted millions. That fact is not in dispute. The point is that a system of third-party payments and fee-for-service financing is just as likely to generate increased spending for redundant, superfluous, or entirely counterproductive services. When patients bear little or none of their own medical costs directly, they will seek not the most economical care available, but the care that is perceived as having the "highest quality." The problem, as Uwe Reinhardt has observed, is that "the American is conditioned to think quality is having fancy equipment and doing fancy procedures." As more patients seek "quality" regardless of cost, physicians respond by adorning themselves with expensive "selling points" (such as specialized licensures, high-tech machines, and plush facilities). Once they settle on the physician or hospital of their choice, patients heedless of cost will have little reason to monitor the number of services provided to them. This might be in their own best interest (since extensive testing, for example, might help identify their illnesses); then again it might well be entirely wasteful or dangerous, since fee-for-service medical providers have the incentive to raise their income by increasing the number of services they render whether necessary or not.

The fundamental problem with third-party payment and fee-for-

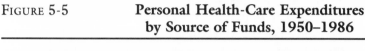

FIGURE 5-5 **Personal Health-Care Expenditures by Source of Funds, 1950–1986**

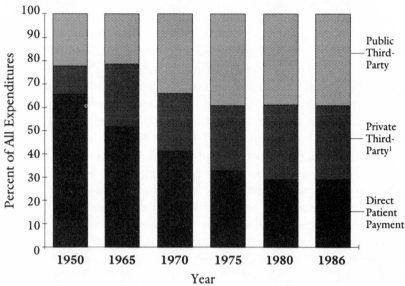

[1]Primarily employer-provided or individually purchased health insurance.
Source: HCFA

service pricing is that no one has a compelling incentive to distinguish the objectively positive effects of additional services and procedures from simple waste or redundancy. Patients and physicians are told to seek and provide "quality" care regardless of its cost. All of us collectively end up paying for the resources consumed by this perverse system of financing, either through higher taxes or through higher insurance premiums. But for each individual patient, the incremental cost of extra tests or treatments is of course negligible.

The resulting symptoms of waste and inefficiency in our market for health-care services have been well documented. One symptom is an extreme variability of price for identical services, even within the same city or county. To pick random examples: in 1981 the hospital charge for treatment of angina in Essex County, New Jersey, varied between about $1,800 and $3,650 depending on the hospital; in 1982 the physician charge for a normal birth in Los Angeles, California, varied between $500 and $1,150, depending on the doctor. In fact, for most medical services, price disparities of 100 to 200 percent are common—

and very little of this can be explained by differences in the provider's success rate or the type of patient treated.

Another symptom of markets gone haywire is a remarkably wide variation between regions in the amount of health care consumed. The average hospital stay in the Northeast, for example, is nearly 50 percent longer than in the West. The average yearly number of hospital days per Medicare beneficiary (according to 1977 data) reveals a similarly odd regional pattern, varying from a high of 4.0 days (in the Northeast) to a low of 2.8 days (in the West). It has long been observed that per capita visits to physicians occur in urban areas at over twice the rate in rural areas. Indeed, nearly everywhere the experts look—whether at surgical rates, lab tests, hospital beds per capita, length of hospital stay, or cost per hospital admission—they have found wide variations between regions and even wider variations between individual doctors and hospitals. Almost none of these discrepancies seems to be correlated with the age, sex, or most important, the health status of the population served.

Systematic analyses of regions and treatment methods have come to even more remarkable conclusions. A couple of years ago, a study by the National Academy of Sciences (NAS) found the following variations among cities in rates for major surgery: tonsillectomy by age fifteen, 7 to 70 percent; hysterectomy for a woman by age fifty-five, 40 to 60 percent; prostate operation for a man by age eighty, 7 to 40 percent. The NAS study also concluded that 27 percent of all hospital days and 19 percent of all spending for Medicare beneficiaries may be medically "unnecessary." Another study by a team of university health-care experts found that up to 30 percent of surgical operations performed may be unnecessary (which explains why many insurers now insist that patients get second opinions). International comparisons, moreover, show that U.S. doctors are vastly more inclined than their peers abroad to perform such lucrative operations as Caesarean sections (at $1,000 each), pacemaker implants (at $12,000 each), and coronary bypasses (at $25,000 each). Independent studies show that at least half of such operations are medically unnecessary. The total extra bill for these three examples alone is about $6 billion this year.*

Perhaps the most telling indictment of third-party payment and fee-for-service financing, however, is supplied by cost and health-

---

*Another dramatic case in point was revealed in a recent review by the Chrysler Corporation of its employees' use of insured health coverage: it found that 2,264 out of 2,677 days spent in hospitals for lower-back pain were "inappropriate" to actual medical need.

outcome comparisons with alternative modes of health-care delivery in which either patients or providers assume much of the cost themselves. Such alternative arrangements fall into two categories. One is "first-party" payment, the old-fashioned system whereby patients finance their medical expenses out of their own pocket. (This does not necessarily mean that the patient is entirely uninsured, but rather that the insurance compels him or her to bear a significant share of the spending—up to a "stop-loss" limit—through deductibles and copayments.) The second category includes various forms of "prepaid group practice." Here a person or family pays a preset monthly or yearly premium to become a member of an institutional provider, and in return for this "prospective capitation payment" the provider agrees to render whatever health-care services the member may need at no (or a negligible) additional charge. The largest and oldest prepaid group practices are the "health maintenance organizations" (HMOs) in which physicians generally serve as salaried employees; thus the HMO is responsible for covering the cost of all services rendered. In recent years, smaller HMO-type practices have sprung up under a variety of alternative acronyms: "individual practice associations" (IPAs), "foundations for medical practice" (FMAs), and "primary care networks" (PCNs).* What they all have in common is that most of the services are provided in exchange for a "prospective" premium, which gives the providers a direct incentive to keep costs down.

According to all indications, both first-party payment and prepaid group practice provide health care at a much lower cost per person than the U.S. norm—and do so with no measurable ill effects to the health of those served. The most comprehensive study of first-party payment (conducted by the RAND Corporation†) carefully monitored the amount of health-care services consumed by randomly selected groups of patients insured for 100 percent, 75 percent, 50 percent, and 5 percent of their initial health costs; above $1,000 per year, all patients were insured for 100 percent of costs. Despite this relatively low "catastrophic" ceiling, the study found that health-care spending decreased dramatically as the level of required copayments increased. Compared with persons insured at the 100 percent rate

---

*The working arrangements of these newer HMOs can be quite complex. Some allow physicians to maintain their own personal practices on the side, some share with the physicians part of the profit and risk, and some may combine elements of capitation with fee-for-service pricing.

†The "RAND Health Experiment" has been an ongoing project since the late 1970s. These results were first published in a now-famous article by J.P. Newhouse et al., "Some Interim Results from a Controlled Trial of Cost-Sharing in Health Insurance," *New England Journal of Medicine* (1981).

(that is, the ones receiving free care), persons who had to make 25 percent out-of-pocket copayments spent 19 percent less on health care; those whose copayments were 95 percent spent 31 percent less on health care.

Most studies of prepaid group practice have come to equally impressive conclusions. The consensus is that persons enrolled in HMOs and IPAs consume between 10 percent and 40 percent less in health services than the U.S. average. Whereas in first-party payment the incentive to economize rests with the patient as consumer, in prepaid group practice the incentive rests firmly with physicians (and plan administrators) as providers. HMOs have an interest in seeing that patients do not get sick to begin with, and when they do, HMOs think twice before testing, operating, and (most important) hospitalizing.

Not one scientifically based study of health outcomes in HMOs (or other forms of prepaid group practice) has concluded that the quality of care provided is inferior to that in traditional fee-for-service medicine.* Surveys designed to measure consumer satisfaction, however, have come up with mixed results. Americans, after all, are by and large accustomed to a lavish style of medicine. It is fair to conclude that it will take time, even with compelling incentives, for long-standing habits and attitudes to change and for patients to feel comfortable with cost-conscious medicine. The same may be said of the habits and attitudes of physicians, many of whom (especially those who are older) remain hostile to prepaid group practice because of the limitations it places on their professional and economic autonomy.

To what extent have these new modes of health-care delivery changed the fee-for-service and third-party financing tradition? Not nearly enough, as yet. As for first-party payment, significant deductibles and cost-sharing (as we will see shortly) remain the exception rather than the rule for most persons who are publicly or privately insured. Sadly, by far the most prevalent first-party savings incentive today is the brutal "everything-out-of-pocket" gauntlet faced by 30 to 40 million Americans who are entirely uninsured. Yet even here, we

---

*RAND concluded (see article in *The Lancet;* May 3, 1986) that the "initially sick" poor in its "Health Experiment" may not have done as well with HMO treatment as with fee-for-service treatment. This has been attributed, however, to two flaws in the study. First, fee-for-service physicians treating RAND's control group were all reimbursed at a higher rate than under Medicaid—which means that the experiment did not compare HMOs with the only fee-for-service option usually available to the poor. Second, and more important, these "initially sick" poor were not enrolled in the prepaid group's outreach program designed to orient patients to HMO care.

waste rather than save money. An uninsured person typically avoids any encounter with a physician until the last possible moment—at which point he or she resorts to expensive acute (often emergency) care for a condition that might have been prevented at little cost. Ordinarily, this charge goes down in the hospital books as "charity" or "bad debt," an accounting entry (estimated at $13 billion in 1986) that the rest of us pay through our insurance premiums, taxes, or voluntary donations.

Prospective capitation, on the other hand, has shown some signs of rising popularity. After a disappointing performance throughout the 1970s, when HMOs were first promoted as an obvious means of cost containment, prepaid group practice made rapid advances during the first half of this decade. In 1980 only 9 million Americans belonged to HMOs; today the figure stands at about 24 million, or 10 percent of our total population. But recently these advances have slowed and there are reasons to doubt that an autonomous trend toward prospective capitation will alone be able to control costs in the long run. Most important, so long as federal policy continues to encourage the fee-for-service approach, there will be strict boundaries on the savings prospective payment will be able to achieve. These boundaries will keep HMO enrollment small, relative to the total health-care market, and will maintain the expensive provider practices (and expensive patient expectations) of the fee-for-service approach as the professional norm even within the HMO community. HMOs can always attempt to "underbid" the norm, of course, but those who do risk a no-win choice between fleeing patients and plunging profit margins.

Today we face a health-care market gone haywire from lack of clear cost incentives for either the buyer or the seller. It is typical of market failure that one can witness feast and famine side by side, and this is what we see in the health-care industry today. On the one hand there are organized lobbies that castigate the health professions for "force feeding" us with too much care—too many Caesareans and hysterectomies, for example. On the other hand there are patients bankrupted by a month of uninsured intensive care, the price of which could buy a small home.

Root Causes: The Structure of Public Health-Care Benefits

How did America get hooked on a system of health-care financing that has brought us such indifferent results? For the federal sector, which now pays for nearly one-third of our total national health-care bill, the answer is simple: we legislated it. Most federal health benefits are provided by law on an open-ended fee-for-service basis. The means-tested Medicaid program, for instance, covers all health expenses from the first dollar on for about 30 million people. While most states have placed stringent limits on the price Medicaid will pay per discrete service, no patient cost sharing is required. Moreover, no limit is placed on the volume of obtainable services, including many that few other insurance policies cover, such as dental work, psychiatric care, and nursing home residency.

These same open-ended principles generally apply to the military health-care system, which not only covers over 2 million active-duty personnel, but also provides care to about 7 million other individuals—dependents of active-duty personnel, military retirees, and their dependents and survivors. Dependents and retirees pay nothing for outpatient care and next to nothing (about $5 per day) for hospital care at military facilities; if they seek outpatient care from civilian providers, they are 75 or 80 percent insured (respectively) for any costs over a $100 family deductible.*

Similarly, the Veterans Administration operates clinics, hospitals, and nursing homes that provide health care to about 3 million patients annually, most of whom pay nothing for the services they receive. Veterans Administration medical care cost $9.9 billion in fiscal year 1986, and was for the most part distributed to individuals who have higher-than-average family incomes and who do not have service-related disabilities or illnesses (only 30 percent of veterans treated each year fall into this latter category). Moreover, it is widely acknowledged that the system itself is wasteful and inefficient. A major National Academy of Sciences study has recommended, for example, that VA hospitals be disbanded and their functions merged with those of military and community facilities.

Medicare is of course far and away the largest federal health-care benefit program. Medicare's coverage undeniably leaves large gaps, especially for chronic and long-term care and (perversely) for very catastrophic acute care. But where it does provide coverage, it is generous. For each hospital stay, Medicare's HI program pays all

---

*Or a $50 deductible for an individual. For over half of these covered families, however, such deductibles and copayments are picked up by private insurance (often obtained through a spouse's civilian employer). At civilian hospitals, perversely, dependents of active-service personnel can receive care at the same negligible fee as at military hospitals. The result is a strong incentive to choose hospitalization over outpatient care, especially for those not covered by private insurance.

hospital costs up to sixty days after a one-shot deductible—$544 in 1988. (Only one-half of one percent of the elderly exceed this time limit in any given year.) For the next thirty days it pays 75 percent of all hospital costs. (Even fewer, about one-twentieth of one percent of the elderly exceed this second limit in any given year.) Thereafter, it pays nothing, although it does grant every beneficiary a ninety-day "lifetime reserve."* Up until 1983, HI reimbursed hospitals essentially by means of fee-for-service billing. Since 1983 HI has switched to a "diagnosis related group" (DRG) reimbursement method which pays the hospital a fixed fee per patient depending on his or her "diagnosis group" when admitted. As yet, DRGs do not represent effective capitation. They have succeeded in dampening hospital costs, but they have not succeeded in cutting the overall growth rate in Medicare spending, as we will see in Chapter 9.

About one-quarter of the cost of Medicare's SMI program is offset by premiums from each SMI beneficiary (this premium, $24.80 per month in 1988, is normally subtracted from his or her Social Security check). Otherwise, like HI, the insurance coverage is "free." After an annual deductible of $75, SMI reimburses physicians for 80 percent of all bills for services rendered; the beneficiary pays the other 20 percent. There is no limit on reimbursements. And though there are fixed or "assigned" limits on the price a physician may bill SMI for each service, beneficiaries can avoid extra charge by choosing a "participating" physician who has agreed to accept SMI's rates. (On about one-third to one-half of all SMI claims, physicians charge a higher price and bill patients separately for the difference.)

Again, putting HI and SMI together, Medicare offers good coverage for most acute-care treatment: not only hospitals and doctors, but also skilled nursing facilities and home care, so long as it is related to acute care. These covered services make up 65 percent of the cost of all elderly health care. Medicare coverage is very limited in other areas: it does not cover prescription drugs,† dental care, most physical aids,

---

*Lifetime reserve days pay for 50 percent of hospital charges. Very few elderly persons—only a couple thousand each year—enter this perverse and costly zone without supplementary private insurance to pick up the copayments. But clearly it can be a nightmare for those who do. With the enactment of the "catastrophic cost" amendment to Medicare in June 1988, Hospital Insurance will cover all hospital care after a single deductible of $564 beginning in 1989. The purpose of this law—to reshape HI to provide greater rather than less coverage for lengthy hospital stays—has long been urged by reformers. But Congress of course understands reshaping to mean adding, never subtracting, from existing benefit provisions (see Chapter 9).

†This too will soon change. Beginning in 1989, the new catastrophic benefit package will pay for a large share (rising from 50 percent in 1989 to 80 percent in 1993 and thereafter) of any beneficiary's prescription-drug purchases over an annual deductible ($600 in 1989).

or home care for chronic illnesses. Most important, it does not cover institutional chronic care, which makes up another 20 percent of health-care spending by or on behalf of the elderly (but even here we should note that Medicaid eventually picks up the tab for about half of the elderly's nursing-home bills).

At first glance, it may seem that Medicare's modest deductible and cost-sharing provisions would give beneficiaries at least some incentive to keep costs down. But these incentives are vitiated by one crucial fact: the program does not adjust its coverage in the presence of supplementary private insurance designed to pay for whatever Medicare does not. Such "medigap" insurance (either provided by former employers or purchased individually for a yearly premium of about $500*) covers fully two-thirds of the elderly. Another 12 to 15 percent do not need supplementary insurance, since Medicaid or some other comprehensive public program already provides them with medigap coverage. The net result is that at least four-fifths of the elderly face negligable deductibles and copayments for care from physicians or hospitals.† The "first-party" effects of premiums and cost-sharing were no doubt intended to form part of Medicare's original benefit structure; since then, however, it is clear that any such incentives have largely evaporated.

At this point we should step back a bit and look at the results of these public-policy decisions. Over the past couple decades, we have done nothing less than engineer a revolution in the financing of health care for the elderly. The figures in Table 5-2 tell the story clearly: a dramatic shift from privately financed health care to a system of publicly financed third-party payments in most major elderly spending categories. Overall, the public sector paid for less than a third of elderly health care in 1965; in 1984, the last year for which data are available, it paid for over two-thirds.

*According to a survey of major carriers by the Health Insurance Association of America, virtually all purchased medigap policies cover the HI deductible, 84 percent offer unlimited coverage of all HI copayments, and 92 percent offer unlimited coverage of all SMI copayments. A recent national survey of Blue Cross/Blue Shield plans (about half the market) reached similar conclusions. In addition, nearly 50 percent of the plans provide some protection against physician fees in excess of the SMI ceiling; 43 percent include prescription-drug insurance; 36 percent include skilled nursing care not covered by Medicare; and 29 percent include vision-care coverage. In 1985 three-quarters of these policies charged less than $516 per year (although the cost is now rising rapidly).

†For the 20 percent of the elderly lacking any supplementary insurance, moreover, an estimated 40 percent of physicians do not attempt to collect any SMI copayments (see "Acute Health Care Costs for the Aged Medicare Population: Overview and Policy Options" by Sandra Christensen et al., *The Milbank Memorial Fund Quarterly;* Summer 1987).

TABLE 5-2	Elderly Health-Care Spending by Category and Source of Funds, 1965 and 1984	
	Percent from Each Source	
	1965	1984
Total		
All Public	30.0%	67.2%
Medicare	0.0	48.8
Private	70.0	32.8
Hospital		
All Public	49.1%	87.7%
Medicare	0.0	74.5
Private	50.9	12.3
Physician		
All Public	6.9%	57.3%
Medicare	0.0	53.4
Private	93.1	42.7
Nursing Homes		
All Public	35.0%	48.1%
Medicare	0.0	2.1
Private	65.0	51.9
Other Care		
All Public	13.9%	34.7%
Medicare	0.0	19.9
Private	86.1	65.3

Source: HCFA

It is often said that real health-care costs borne by the elderly themselves are greater today on average than they were when Medicare was founded. Data from the Health Care Financing Administration bear this out: private health-care spending per elderly person rose from $1,005 to $1,378 (in constant 1984 dollars) between 1965 and 1984—a 37 percent increase. This growth, however, is only a small fraction of the much faster rise in total health-care consumption by the elderly. Public health-care spending per elderly person (again in constant 1984 dollars) was $425 in 1965 and $2,762 in 1984—a 550 percent increase. In other words, despite the fact that the publicly covered share of elderly health-care consumption has risen from 30 to 67 percent over the past two decades, the growth in total spending has been so rapid that the remainder (private insurance and out-of-pocket expenditures) has risen slightly rather than fallen in real terms.

But does this mean that the private spending burden is actually heavier for the elderly today than before Medicare began? Not at all. Remember, the real per capita income of the elderly has also been rising strongly—by two-thirds—over this same period, so that the burden has declined relative to income. In 1965 private health-care spending amounted to about 16 percent of the elderly's reported cash income; in 1984 it amounted to about 13 percent.*

Even more remarkable, however, is the highly skewed distribution of the real spending increase. Almost none of it occurred in spending for doctors or hospitals (the areas best covered by Medicare), which means that private spending on these services plummeted even more dramatically relative to income (from about 8 to 5 percent). Most of it occurred instead in nursing-home care, a "treatment" that was not often available in the mid-1960s and even today is used by only 5 percent of the elderly. Nonetheless, the share of *total* elderly out-of-pocket spending accounted for by nursing homes has doubled from a bit more than 20 percent in 1965 to 42 percent in 1985. Behind today's averages, therefore, lie two very different elderly populations: about one in twenty who pay nearly all of their income—sooner or later, as a rule, spending themselves into poverty—for nursing-home care or (much less frequently) catastrophic medical care; and the other nineteen in twenty for whom out-of-pocket medical spending is no big deal.† Feast and famine yet again. The many who do get public insurance generally do not need it on such generous terms; the few who most need minimal public protection do not get it until they go broke, at which point the public sector ends up picking up the bill anyway.

Part of the explosion in elderly health-care spending, as we have seen, is the result of changing demographics and costlier medical

---

*Using HCFA estimates for private spending by age-group that include premiums for private insurance. Not surprisingly, despite the popularity of medigap policies, the elderly spend less today than before on private coverage. Looking only at "first-party" private spending, therefore, the decline is small and (given the imprecision of our data) might support the claim that the elderly's out-of-pocket spending has not declined significantly as a share of income. But the often-heard claim that it has risen sharply is indefensible.

†According to 1980 household survey data, for the 90 percent of the elderly who neither died nor spent part of the year in a nursing home, average health-care spending amounted to $1,327 per person, of which $239 (or 4.2 percent of reported cash income) was paid out of pocket; half paid less than $156 out of pocket. (See "Expenditures for the Medical Care of Elderly People Living in the Community in 1980" by Mary Grace Kovar, *The Milbank Memorial Fund Quarterly;* Winter 1986.) For the 10 percent who died or spent at least part of the year in a nursing home, on the other hand, total health-care spending ranged from $13,000 per person overall to over $20,000 for those in institutions all year—most of which was paid for out-of-pocket or by Medicaid.

technologies. Yet part of it has also been due to the design of our federal benefit programs. Rarely do they give the patient incentives to seek cost-effective care; only recently have they attempted to give the provider such incentives, and as yet they are not working. Moreover, the rigidly uniform, "front-end" protection of Medicare fails to make common-sense distinctions between patients with different incomes and health problems—calling into question not just the efficiency of our elderly health-care entitlement, but its equity as well.

Root Causes: The Nontaxability of Employee Benefits

When we turn to the private sector, we are confronted with a seeming riddle: If third-party payments and fee-for-service financing generate wasteful spending, why, until recently, haven't more insurers and employers switched to other methods of paying for health care? Unlike the public sector, after all, the private sector tends to be intolerant of inefficiency. If waste can be reduced, why haven't all parties concerned—insurers and employers as well as policyholders and employees—been powerfully motivated to share in the potential savings?

To find one important answer we need look no further than federal tax policy. In the late 1940s, the federal government determined as a general principle that employee fringe benefits (that is, noncash compensation) should not be subject to federal income or payroll taxes. No one thought much about this at the time, since tax rates were low and fringe benefits were usually meager. Since then, however, fringe benefits have consistently grown more rapidly than take-home wages—over 50 percent faster per year on average since 1950. And they grew especially rapidly during the 1960s and 1970s, as higher tax rates made tax-free benefits an increasingly desirable alternative to taxable income. By now a river $200 billion wide, these fringe benefits today constitute by far the largest single category of tax-free personal income. Over half of this river consists of employer premiums for health insurance. Not taxing these premiums will cost the federal government an estimated $40 billion in 1989.* This sum is greater than the $32 billion it will lose due to a far better-known subsidy: the deductibility of mortgage interest on owner-occupied homes.

---

*As estimated by the CBO. About $28 billion is lost to federal personal income taxes and another $12 billion is lost to Social Security payroll taxes. Since most state and local governments also honor this exemption, they lost another $10 billion in revenue. And this does not include the $2 billion lost to personal federal income taxes due to the individual deductibility of large health-care expenses (the benefits of which go almost entirely to households in above-average income-tax brackets).

There are two ways to look at this figure. On the one hand, we can view it as a $40-billion addition to the federal deficit; on the other, we can consider it a $40-billion subsidy for employer-paid health insurance. Most health-care experts agree that it is both. As a subsidy, moreover, it explicitly encourages employees to "overconsume" health insurance. Employees, that is, are encouraged to "purchase" more comprehensive policies than they would otherwise be willing to pay for in the absence of a subsidy. How much does our current tax structure encourage excess insurance coverage? Estimates vary, but many economists maintain that, as a direct result of our tax structure, between 15 and 25 percent of current employer-sponsored insurance coverage may be excessive.

Exemption of health benefits from taxation adds to the federal deficit and encourages excess insurance coverage, but this does not exhaust the list of its ill effects. The exemption is also a steeply regressive subsidy, since its value increases along with the marginal tax rate (and the current health-care coverage) of the employee. For an employee earning less than $20,000, its yearly value is less than $100; for an employee earning more than $50,000, its yearly value is more than $500.* Perversely enough, it offers the greatest incentive for additional insurance coverage to those workers who are in high tax brackets and are already best insured. It offers the least incentive for additional coverage to workers in lower tax brackets who are likely to have substandard insurance; and it offers no incentive at all to the poorest workers who are most likely to have no employer-paid insurance coverage. One might have hoped that such a wasteful tax policy would at least have the saving grace of encouraging better insurance coverage for those working families truly in need. Once again, however, we are confronted with the sure sign of market failure: feast and famine side by side.

Even if employee health-care benefits are tax favored, they do of course represent a bottom-line loss, especially once company executives figure their high price tag is no longer buying much worker satisfaction. Over the last several years, therefore, businesses have begun sporadic and well-publicized efforts to control the exploding costs of their health benefits. One strategy is to reduce the demand for

---

*According to a CBO estimate, the average yearly value of the tax subsidy in 1983 was $83 for an employee earning $15,000 to $20,000 and $622 for an employee earning $50,000 to $100,000. (See P. Ginsburg, *Containing Medical Costs Through Market Forces;* Congressional Budget Office, 1982).

acute care (and sick-leave time) by improving the general health of workers through voluntary "wellness" and "health promotion" programs. A second strategy is to give workers more choice in how they are compensated, either by reducing employee-paid premiums or by increasing other fringes (through so-called cafeteria plans) for employees who choose lower-cost health insurance.

A third strategy—and by far the most widely used—is to reorient traditional insurance incentives toward lower-cost treatment options. Many companies, for instance, now require nominal deductibles (to avoid excessive initial doctor visits) and disallow full 100 percent reimbursement unless the employee is a "prudent" consumer. Prudence may simply mean getting a second opinion before surgery or choosing outpatient settings for certain medical procedures; or it may mean going to the company's "preferred provider organization" (PPO), a selected group of doctors and hospitals with whom the company (or insurer) has bargained a special price and whose treatment costs the company carefully monitors.

This surge of innovation is swiftly reorganizing the health-care marketplace. On the one hand, the number of health-care purchasers is multiplying as businesses expand the variety of their insurance options and begin to bargain directly with providers. On the other hand, as providers band together in self-defense, the old, atomistic independence of hospitals and doctors is being replaced with larger and more integrated health-service organizations. Purchasers and insurers are becoming more sophisticated in managing cost and price information; providers are fast learning the art of marketing different services to different buyers and of combining to sell services at high-volume group discounts. The hospital industry is being turned inside out by these forces. Together with DRGs, private-purchaser "gatekeeper" devices are forcing many independent nonprofit hospitals either to make money off their outpatient and community services or to sell themselves to large and growing for-profit chains, who can offer total "managed care" packages directly to companies or insurers. The marketplace for physicians is also changing. Few young doctors can any longer begin their career alone by just putting out a shingle; most must now start out in some form of group practice, either in an HMO or "managed care" chain or as a member of a PPO.

For all this marketplace bustle, however, we should not conclude that it necessarily adds up to effective control of private-sector health-care spending. Although many of the new business initiatives—such as promoting health and discouraging gross acute-care waste—are clearly steps in the right direction, they have not altered the fundamental cost-free attitude with which patients approach treatment choices. As far as first-party incentives are concerned, few employers yet give workers a compelling reason to select plans that have behaviorally significant deductibles or copayments.* The same is true for fully capitated plans, now offered by a growing number of employers. As we have already seen, HMO enrollment has grown very rapidly over the last few years, but still stands at only 10 percent of all employees. And since they must compete directly with generous fee-for-service plans in most company benefit menus, many HMOs are more inclined to advertise their convenience and "boutique" coverage than to sell their full cost-cutting potential. Even the promising move toward PPOs must be viewed with caution. Much of it, to be honest, simply reflects bargain hunting in a fast-changing market—and the result is that one shrewd purchaser can pay less by shifting the cost onto another purchaser, who must pay more.

So once again we come back to the tax subsidy. It is only fair to ask: How much greater would the incentives for savings be if employer premiums for health insurance were taxed? What might employees tell their bosses if employer contributions to their health plans were prominently displayed on their W-2 forms? It is suggestive to look at some of the most popular commercial policies now offered to individuals who are *not* members of subsidized company plans; most have $1,000 annual deductibles and 20 percent cost sharing for *any* choice of provider. Very few employees face such terms. If they did, we would certainly find them asking their doctors critical questions about testing and treatment or, alternatively, turning to HMOs whose main emphasis is premium savings.

Root Causes: Protective Regulation

Thus far we have said very little about the character of the main actor in this drama, the health-care industry itself. Vitriolic complaints about the rapacity of doctors and hospitals are perennial, and we

---

*Although the share of all insured workers facing very small deductibles ($50 or less) has dropped dramatically in the 1980s, most deductibles still remain quite modest. The Bureau of Labor Statistics reports that in 1986 only 6 percent of all insured workers had annual deductibles higher than $200; 57 percent had annual deductibles of $100 or less.

would be amiss not to remark at the outset that many of the charges are misguided. One often hears, for instance, that health-care costs are rising because doctors or drug companies are gouging the public. This is untrue. The net income of all physicians comprises less than 20 percent of total health-care spending. Their average income may be high, but even if it were reduced by 25 percent, the effect on our national health bill would be less than 5 percent. As for pharmaceuticals, their average real price has actually fallen over the last fifteen years.

That being said, we should note some basic failures in the way we allow our health-care industry to function—failures that systematically suppress cost-saving innovation and exacerbate the waste of open-ended fee-for-service financing. Some of these failures may indeed explain why the popular misconceptions about doctors and drug companies have gained credence. It may be true that physicians' income now accounts for a bit less than 20 percent of all health-care spending, but physicians' decisions—about testing, hospitalization, medication, and other aspects of care—determine over 75 percent of all spending. The attitudes of physicians toward cost and efficiency, therefore, set the tone for the entire health-care industry. As for pharmaceuticals, there remains the question of why, despite patients' obvious preference to spend less (drugs are not covered under Medicare and most private insurance), providers still routinely prescribe brand name potions that are 25 percent more expensive than their precise generic equivalents.

What are the factors that have shaped the professional culture of the American medical establishment in ways that fuel our health-care crisis? Entrenched and excessive regulation comes most readily to mind. Overregulation is one of those issues that no one likes to talk about with regard to health care for fear of being called a quack or a friend of butchers. Health care is an exact and expert practice; no one wants to see it bought and sold like cattle at an auction. Strong regulation on behalf of the patient's health and safety is therefore a self-evident necessity. The closer one looks, however, at the multilayered jungle of laws and regulations actually in force, the more one is impressed by how little of it explicitly protects the patient. Much of it, instead, focuses far more directly on provider markets and professional livelihoods: from school accreditation, licensure, certification boards, and scope-of-practice rules to peer review, ethical prohibitions, insurance regulation, and tort law.

Education. The transformation of American medicine from a relatively unorganized, laissez-faire body of practitioners in the late nineteenth century into a tightly organized, self-selecting, and increasingly specialized profession in the decades following World War I has attracted the attention of many scholars. Perhaps preeminent among these is Paul Starr, author of the Pulitzer Prize-winning *The Social Transformation of American Medicine.** Most historians would agree with Starr that a key instrument in this transformation was the ability of professional medical organizations to accredit only those medical schools that met their qualifications—and then to persuade the states to make "accredited" education a necessary prerequisite to licensure. Many would also argue that organized medicine has deliberately used school accreditation as a means of cartelizing the supply of doctors and dentists, and thus of driving up the price of medical services. Consider: in 1906 there were 162 medical schools in the United States, a number that dropped to around 76 in the 1930s and still has not been surpassed today; in 1904 there were more than 28,000 medical students, a number not again surpassed until 1954. The number of doctors per 100,000 persons reached a peak of 157 in 1900, plummeted thereafter, and did not again reach the earlier level (despite huge advances in medical capability) until 1967. Not surprisingly, the average net income of physicians has risen quite swiftly over the last several decades, from twice the average worker's salary in the 1940s to about five times that amount since the late 1970s.

Public alarm over the "doctor shortage" in the mid-1960s led the federal government to subsidize the operation and expansion of medical schools. From the late 1960s until today, the size of graduating classes has doubled, from 8,000 to more than 17,000, and the population per doctor has fallen from 650 to 450. Since the late 1970s, accordingly, the federal subsidies to medical education have been drastically scaled back.[†] But the often-heard opinion that we now face a "doctor glut"—an opinion voiced emphatically by the American

---

*Basic Books, 1982.

[†]Federal policies initiated in the 1960s to expand the supply of physicians culminated in the Comprehensive Health Manpower Training Act of 1971, which directly funded medical school construction, programs, and student loans and scholarships. The cutbacks, however, began in 1976 and accelerated after the appearance of the 1980 Graduate Medical Education National Advisory Committee (GMENAC) Report, which forecasted a future oversupply of physicians. In 1981 Congress eliminated most of the remaining subsidies.

Medical Association—may be premature.* Supply is rising, but so too is demand. The average net income of physicians continues to keep pace with that of other professionals. In fact, American physicians remain the most highly paid of all professionals—not only in this country but in the world.†

To be sure, cuts in federal student-loan subsidies and uncertainty about the future of the medical profession have recently squeezed the number of young people aspiring to be doctors. But the competition remains intense. Only the most talented college graduates apply to U.S. medical schools, half of these applicants are rejected, and many then go abroad to get around the bottleneck. The number of American graduates from foreign medical schools who take qualifying examinations to practice in the United States increased from less than 1,000 in 1970 to over 6,000 in 1983— one graduate from abroad for every three graduates educated within the United States. Another symptom of tight supply (or healthy demand) is a continuing increase in the ratio of allied health professionals to physicians, which has risen to more than 7 to 1. These allied professions are now showing signs of acute shortage themselves, not only in nursing but also in a variety of specialties ranging from lab technicians to therapists. The wages for these professions are due to rise at an especially fast clip over the next few years—adding billions of dollars to our national health-care bill.

The Federal Trade Commission (FTC) has long challenged the American Medical Association's role in determining medical accreditation as a possible antitrust violation. However, as health-care regulation expert Clark Havighurst has pointed out, the consequences of centralized professional control over medical education are not limited to the number of doctors accredited; the monopoly over the *type* of medicine taught may be equally important. But as Havighurst notes, the FTC cannot challenge how the AMA influences "the

---

*In order to eliminate the "doctor glut," a 1986 report by the AMA advocates (again) tightening medical-school enrollments and limiting the inflow of foreign-trained doctors; otherwise, it implies, the public will suffer worse and costlier treatment. Others challenge the premise of this inverted economic logic. A recent study by William B. Schwartz, Frank A. Sloan, and Daniel Mendelson, published in the April 7, 1988 issue of the *New England Journal of Medicine*, argues on the contrary that current technology and insurance trends are pushing up demand faster than supply and will leave us with a doctor shortage in the year 2000.

†The average net income of physicians in 1986 was $119,500, as reported by the AMA—up from $112,200 in 1985 and still a higher multiple of average wages than in any other industrial country. The fact that HMO physicians are earning less is due to their younger age; holding constant age, specialty, and location, physicians' earnings in different types of practice are (as we would expect) about the same.

medical schools' strong emphasis on specialization and high-cost acute care, their inattention to cost-effectiveness and efficiency, and their devaluation of primary and preventative care."*

Licensure. In the case of physicians and dentists (and an increasing variety of other fields, from registered nursing to social work), state licensure is dependent upon "accredited" education, which in turn is dependent upon the judgment of the organized health professions. The professions thus can exercise indirect control over the number of practitioners in their fields. Licensure testing strengthens such control, since state tests are almost always terminology-oriented (which would ensure that the applicant has undergone a specific course of education), rather than task-oriented (which would simply ensure that the applicant has the skill to provide expert care). It has been shown conclusively (and this should not be surprising) that states having the strictest tests also have the highest-paid health-care professionals. This is especially true in fields such as dentistry and optometry, where licensure qualifications can vary widely from state to state.

State licensure laws also establish in minute detail which types of care particular professional groups may and may not legally render. As a result, each health-care specialty is frequently lobbying to have these laws restructured in ways that expand its own turf and effectively prevent trespassing by outsiders. The resulting internecine feuding is intense: registered nurses against physicians, practical nurses against registered nurses, dental hygienists against dentists, and nurse practitioners against physicians' aides. Ordinarily, the only feasible way to arrange a lasting truce is to multiply the number of legally recognized health professions. Some states now have more than ten, from podiatry to psychiatric social work, each overseen by a board friendly to its own practitioners. The outcome is that state laws routinely require patients to be treated by vastly overqualified personnel. Most physicians' aides (PAs), for example, would be capable of handling a large share of all doctor visits at one-third the hourly cost of an M.D. But state laws generally prohibit PAs from receiving fees, or from initiating any treatment, without a supervision arrangement that has been approved by the local medical profession. A similar situation confronts pediatric nurses, who—according to one study—have the

---

*These views are developed at greater length in *Deregulating the Health Care Industry* by Clark C. Havighurst (Ballinger, 1982).

skills to treat 95 percent of first-time infant visits without the direct supervision of a physician.

State licensure laws and scope-of-practice rules are ostensibly designed to prevent inexpert care and gross malpractice. If this is indeed their purpose, one might legitimately wonder why retesting or relicensure is almost never required of any health-care professional (no matter how many years ago his or her original license was issued), and why probation or license revocation is exceedingly rare in most states even in cases of gross and repeated malpractice.* Professions that decide to upgrade the educational requirements and testing qualifications in their fields nearly always exempt current practitioners by means of a grandfather clause. Clearly, then, one purpose of licensure laws is to frustrate vertical and horizontal mobility among health professionals—and thereby prevent the fee level in each profession from being lowered by an influx of new practitioners. An ophthalmologist who was licensed thirty years ago may legally charge a patient for setting a broken arm; a physician's aid who sets broken arms every day may not.

Specialty Certification and Quality Controls. While state licensure law establishes the parameters of the basic health fields, professional "certifying" boards chop up each field into a vast multitude of subdivisions. An M.D., for instance, may choose from twenty-three overall specialties (from dermatology to internal medicine) and at least eighty subspecialties (within internal medicine these range from nephrology to hematology). Once again, the effect of such specialization is to raise the cost of treatment: by creating bottlenecks where a specialty is undermanned; by discouraging physicians from efficiently substituting for each other; by encouraging expensive "single-use" technologies; and, according to some critics, by making it easier for physicians to agree informally on the price of particular treatments.[†]

The trend toward specialization is accelerating. Well over half of all subspecialties have been created over the last fifteen years. As recently as 1973, only half of all doctors were specialty-certified; today, nearly every resident trains for a specialty exam. Although specialty certifica-

---

*Although the enforcement is improving, in 1985 there were only 1,132 serious disciplinary actions by all state boards for over 400,000 physicians.

†Although the total number of U.S. physicians per capita is about the same as in most other industrial countries, the distribution of U.S. physicians is tellingly odd: we have by far the most specialists (who are also the best paid) and by far the fewest general practitioners (who are also the least paid).

tion has no legal status, a doctor who practices in a specialty without it may be denied reimbursement from Medicare or insurance companies, will probably be denied hospital privileges, and will likely face hostility from his peers.*

In addition, the health-care industry is governed by a bewildering multitude of "quality control" laws ostensibly designed to enhance the quality of care. One of their side effects, however, is to tempt providers to cartelize their market by agreeing informally on services and prices. In the early 1970s, Congress established "professional standards review organizations" (PSROs, or later just PROs) to ensure that patients (especially those receiving Medicaid or Medicare) receive the best possible care. Whatever goes on in PROs, however, disciplining providers for ineptitude clearly gets a low priority; in twenty-three states these PROs have yet to impose a single sanction. Much procedural regulation has the same questionable result. Nursing homes are required to have a fixed quota of registered nurses and dietary consultants per resident. Many types of medical equipment must be attended by certified technical assistants. Equipment manufacturers welcome federal regulation that prevents clinics from substituting "substandard" (that is, lower-priced) machines for the ones they produce. Even construction companies have gotten into the act. State safety codes for health-care buildings (often drafted in close cooperation with major contractors) have typically been so strict that by 1980 it cost hospitals an estimated $120,000 for each new bed they added to their existing supply.

Ethical Prohibitions. One method the health professions have traditionally employed in protecting their collective interests is the enforcement of strict "professional" codes of conduct. In general, these codes have sought to prohibit advertising and discourage the public's evaluation of professional work, whether in terms of its competitive pricing or relative quality. The thrust of these codes, in short, is to create a professional mystique that isolates health-care practitioners from the marketplace.

The controversy over whether advertising is "professional" has been especially fierce, since it is in effect the only means by which patients (and insurers) can choose among health-care providers on the

---

*To return to our earlier example of the ophthalmologist, though he could legally set arms, he would rarely be allowed to do so in most large hospitals, even if he were excellent at it.

basis of price. Until the 1970s, societies of doctors, dentists, pharmacists, and hospital administrators were successful in persuading their members to refrain from advertising. After numerous studies demonstrated that such agreements inevitably raise prices, however, the FTC began to challenge them as antitrust violations. In 1982 the FTC finally won its case in a landmark decision by the Supreme Court. Since then, of course, we have gradually become accustomed to hard-sell ad campaigns launched by HMOs, PPOs (preferred provider organizations), and physician-controlled IPAs. Nonetheless, despite this seemingly complete defeat of guild prohibitions against advertising, the health-care professions are still lobbying to have advertising restrictions written into state law—a move that would render them immune to attacks on antitrust grounds. Quite apart from the issue of advertising, consumer groups are asking that the extensive comparative data on the quality of clinics and hospitals accumulated by federally sponsored "professional review organizations" (PROs) be made public. Hospitals and physicians are loudly objecting on the grounds that such data would be misunderstood by an inexpert public.

Another long-standing ethical rule that many medical societies successfully enforced in the past is the prohibition on "contract practice." So long as it remained in effect, this prohibition meant that doctors could not work other than on a traditional fee-for-service basis—in other words, they could not work for a salary—or participate in any insurance reimbursement scheme that discriminated between high-cost and low-cost providers. During the 1930s, the AMA succeeded in having "contract" or "corporate practice" banned in a score of states; and as recently as the 1950s, physicians affiliated with HMOs were routinely ostracized from local medical societies, black-listed, and denied hospital admitting privileges. Since passage in 1973 of the HMO act (an early federal attempt to promote prepaid group practice), however, the AMA has been forced to assume a position of official, if guarded neutrality on the issue of "contract practice." And over the past few years, the fear of losing patients has actually prompted a growing number of state and county medical societies to launch their own HMOs modeled on individual practice associations. Nonetheless, radical fee-for-service physician action groups, including, among many others, the Independent Doctors of America, maintain an implacable hostility toward any form of prepaid group practice, which is often considered a pernicious form of "socialized" medicine.

Insurance Regulation. Over the years, the health-care professions have naturally taken a keen interest in the practices of private third-party payers, the dominant source of their private-sector income. Indeed, state regulation of health insurance companies—regulation that was originally set up under the supervision of physicians' groups—has almost everywhere served to protect the interests of doctors and other health-care professionals. In the first place, existing regulations discriminate sharply against commercial insurers and in favor of nonprofit insurers, that is, the state Blue Cross and Blue Shield plans, which often have physician majorities on their boards of directors. Second, insurers have often been discouraged from offering policies that require patients to make use of a limited selection of low-cost providers (usually called "closed-panel arrangements"). Third, new regulations steadily expand the number of "mandated benefits" and services that insurers must cover (the most recent additions range from orthotics, psychiatry, and in vitro fertilization to treatment for drug abuse and alcoholism). Finally, it is worth pointing out that, just as with much insurance regulation in general, lively competition is restrained in many states by laws that limit the rate at which any one company can change its premium market share.

The burden of state taxation and regulation of the health-insurance industry has become so onerous that many large employers have decided to set up their own insurance plans (federal regulation under the 1974 Employee Retirement Income Security Act exempts such plans from most state laws). Premiums raised by self-insuring companies have risen from 10 percent of the health-insurance market in the early 1970s to about 22 percent today. By the end of the 1980s, they may exceed 30 percent, a share equal to all the nonprofit insurers and only somewhat less than all the commercial insurers combined. Unfortunately, only the largest employers can afford the sort of innovative price and quality monitoring that might ensure cost-effective health care. The vexing problem with this fast-growing and largely regulation-free form of health insurance, in other words, is that it can only be run by firms whose business is not insurance.

Malpractice Law. The ramshackle condition of that venerable house of jurisprudence called "medical malpractice law" is both a sorry testament to our litigious society and another force behind rising national health-care costs. Here, of course, the beneficiaries are lawyers rather than doctors. Doctors don't like malpractice law—not so much because it affects their income (most of the costs can be passed

228

on to third-party payers), but because what it adds to the total cost of health care brings political heat to bear on the entire system.

Average malpractice settlements today vary wildly from state to state, ranging from some $20,000 to $40,000 in most midwestern states to nearly $1 million in California. Lured by the prospect of enormous contingency fees, malpractice lawyers file an ever-growing number of claims each year. In 1975 they filed 5 claims for every 100 doctors; in 1983 they filed 16. To pay for it all, physicians in 1983 spent about $1.5 billion on malpractice insurance—nearly double what they had spent in 1975. In certain specialties, the statistics are mind-numbing. Nearly 60 percent of all obstetricians and gynecologists have been sued at least once; 20 percent of them have been sued three or more times. Many now pay as much as $100,000 per year in malpractice insurance.

The inflationary impact of physicians' insurance premiums on the total cost of health care, however, is just the tip of the iceberg. Far more important is how the threat of malpractice suits has altered the way medicine is practiced. On a routine basis, health-care professionals recommend tests, perform surgery, call in consultants, withhold opinions, prescribe drugs, and order hospitalization—even when, in their best professional judgment, they know these steps are entirely unnecessary. In case anything goes wrong, no doctor wants the patient to be able to claim that any conceivable stone was left unturned (especially since turning these stones usually costs the individual patient, not to mention the doctor, little or nothing). The result is that most doctors protect their backsides—or, to use the professional jargon, practice "defensive medicine." According to one knowledgeable estimate, excess use of health-care services induced by our system of malpractice law currently adds between $15 billion and $40 billion to the nation's health-care costs every year.*

Another unfortunate effect of malpractice law is that it entrenches "customary" standards of practice that are unnecessarily costly to begin with. Given the risks of eventual lawsuits, physicians are much more likely to introduce a new service than to abandon an old one, lest the elimination of the old one be construed as defective medicine. Several HMOs, for example, have wanted to discontinue fetal monitoring for most expectant mothers, not only to save costs, but because many experts have concluded that the procedure is more likely to be

*See the findings of *The American Medical Association Special Task Force on Professional Liability and Insurance* (1984).

harmful than helpful in all but high-risk situations. After considering their potential liability under malpractice law, however, most of these HMOs have decided to continue fetal monitoring on a universal basis. Precisely because cost-blind fee-for-service medicine has made fetal monitoring a standard practice, they correctly reasoned, any deviation from that practice might be grounds for suit. Not even an advance notification to enrollees would change this fact, since professional standards would take precedence in a court of law over any contract between provider and patient.

As currently interpreted and enforced, the most serious defect of state malpractice law is not that it encourages wasteful or redundant medical procedures in specific cases, but that it inflates the cost of customary practice in all cases. In short, it serves to reinforce among medical practitioners a conformist aversion to innovations that foster efficiency—an aversion that may be strong to begin with in any profession, regardless of the legal environment. Totally apart from its questionable value in protecting patients from incompetent doctors, it is a system we can simply no longer afford.

Bribing the Providers, Blinding Ourselves

If much of our regulatory structure serves to bolster the established positions of health-care providers, it is because we have systematically allowed the organized health-care professions to dictate the terms of their own competition. To a degree unequaled in any other nation, we have allowed health professionals to regulate their own standards of care. We have allowed them privately to exercise strong collective influence over decisions about who will be allowed to practice, how, with what facilities, where, with which patients, and in return for what means of payment. We have also allowed them publicly to design the very legislation and to dominate the very state boards and federal committees by which we attempt to "oversee" their behavior.

Consider the case of private health insurance. Physicians and hospitals no doubt did this country a great service in setting up hundreds of Blue Cross and Blue Shield plans in the late 1930s and 1940s; for the first time, millions of American families were offered access to insurance against the catastrophic costs of health care. In the years since, however, the public has looked the other way as state after state endowed many of the "Blues" with powerful tax and regulatory advantages, allowed them to agree not to compete with each other, and thus effectively discriminated against commercial insurers that attempted to introduce more cost-conscious policies (by limiting reimbursements to high-priced providers, for example). Supported and administered by the same groups of professionals to whom they make payments, the "Blues" still control about one-third of the national market in private health insurance. Tax policy alone cannot explain why most Americans still purchase open-ended fee-for-service policies, or why until a few years ago HMOs were nothing more than an obscure alternative to traditional medicine. Part of the explanation lies in the history of the "Blues," and, more generally, in the physician-dictated structure of much of our insurance regulation.

Or consider the case of Medicare. When an overwhelmingly Democratic Congress debated the pros and cons of various elderly health-benefit proposals in the spring and summer of 1965, the idea of financing such a program on any basis other than open-ended fee-for-service reimbursement was never even seriously considered. Why not? One reason, to be sure, was that few legislators at the time had the slightest inkling what Medicare would cost ten or twenty years down the road. But there was certainly another reason: the implacable hostility of the American Medical Association and the American Hospital Association to any program that impinged on the "freedom" of their members to treat any beneficiary or to charge for services in their customary manner. The proponents of the new health-benefit program worried not only that the AMA might rally enough support to block their legislation, but also that health-care providers might turn their new program into a fiasco by means of organized resistance (such as a boycott of beneficiaries). In the past, providers had often effectively resisted "intrusive" insurance firms or the incursions of "socialist" HMOs.

Medicare's reimbursement policy has thus been described by critics as the outcome of a great "bribe." Legislators got what they wanted: acceptance of Medicare by the medical profession. And doctors and hospitals got what they wanted: freedom to practice health care in return for public money just as they had always practiced it in return for private money. They didn't even have to deal with new insurers, since Medicare's legislation carefully stipulated that reimbursements would be channeled though private "financial intermediaries"— meaning, in most cases, the "Blues." The distinction between Medicare's Hospital Insurance (HI) and Supplementary Medical Insurance (SMI), providers found to their pleasure, coincided almost perfectly with the familiar distinction between Blue Cross and Blue Shield. As Social Security Commissioner Robert Ball explained to Congress in 1965, the "main principle" of HI was that "per diem costs will differ depending on the hospital from place to place, and we will reimburse whatever it turns out to be."

Much has changed since 1965. Many physicians complain bitterly about the loss of "professional autonomy" they suffer in today's "managed-health-care systems" and, by way of justification, warn that any infringement of their traditional prerogatives will have decidedly negative effects on the quality of care their patients receive. We would be naive not to realize, however, that much of this treasured "professional autonomy" actually involves control over markets. The media never tire of calling attention to "today's increasingly competitive health-care marketplace." But compared with any other industry, we would have to judge this degree of competition to be about on par with the medieval guild system.

Others who note the unique power that providers exercise over U.S. health-care policy conclude that cost containment must begin with a vengeful assault on the health-care professions. That would miss the point entirely. What the health-care professions have tried to accomplish is no different than what any other profession has tried to accomplish. The only difference is that we—the public—have allowed them to succeed, and this acquiescence, in turn, is but a sign of the fundamental unreality that clouds our whole approach to health-care policymaking. Quite simply, our goal has been to shelter everyone from making any meaningful cost trade-off between competing needs. We had no direct intention of creating an entitlement for providers; we simply found that we could not create the illusion of a cost-free health entitlement without "bribing" the providers to come along with us.

The result has been a system that satisfies no one. It rewards wasteful treatment along with effective treatment. It indulges acute-care consumption at the expense of preventative investment. It allows those who are healthy to enter expensive institutions free of charge (because this is a "right"), while categorically denying modest at-home assistance for those who are chronically ill (because this is not a "right"). It lavishes universal subsidies on those who do not generally need them (especially the aged and the well-off), while playing Scrooge to those who often do need them (especially the young and the poor). And ultimately it crowds out other national goals—without commensurate payback—by devouring a rising share of our budgetary and overall economic resources.

Our present system is unaffordable today, and the combined impact of demographics and technology is certain to make it even more unaffordable tomorrow. Radical reform is therefore inevitable. We would do well to act now before reform is thrust unwillingly upon us. But this will mean opening our eyes and facing painful choices—not only political choices about where we can save money, but cultural choices about what share of the American Dream involves "the pursuit of happiness" for our own personal lives only, and what share should be bequeathed to those who live beyond us.

6

Driving the Projections:
Indexing

"The fight against inflation must be on the basis of the
equality of sacrifice, not the sacrifice of equality."
— *George Meany*

A LONG WITH AGING and health-care inflation, indexing is
the third fundamental force driving up federally financed
consumption. Twenty-five years ago, "indexing" was a technical term known only to economists. Today it has become a household word, and from time to time we hear heated debate over
proposals to reform "cost-of-living adjustments" (COLAs), which the
Congressional Budget Office projects will add an extra $14 billion to
the cost of entitlements each year by the early 1990s—increments that
could easily add up to as much as $200 billion in annual federal outlays
by the year 2000. That sum is twenty times greater than what the
federal budget now spends (directly or indirectly) on net infrastructure investment, or forty times greater than what it now spends on aid
to child education.

As we will see, the triumph of indexing during the 1970s marked
a dramatic revolution in public policy. Although the consequences of
this revolution may seem less apparent today, during a period of
relatively modest inflation, the cumulative costs of years of benefit
indexing have slowly brought about profound—and largely unintend-

FIGURE 6-1   **Indexed Federal Benefits as a Percent of Domestic Spending, Fiscal Years 1960–1986**

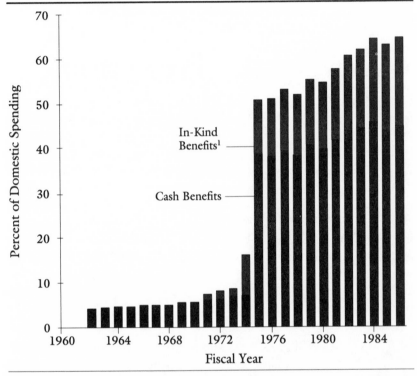

Domestic spending is total federal spending excluding defense and net interest payments.

[1]Yearly increase either open-ended or guided by special indexes for cost of food and health care.

Source: OMB and CBO

ed—changes in the current level and composition of federal spending. And if most economists are correct in observing that greater inflation is on its way back, it is very likely that the pace of such changes will speed up again in the near future.

Although policy solutions to the indexing problem might seem straightforward, the political and cultural obstacles to effective reform are formidable. Many Americans have come to expect as a matter of right that public-sector benefit payments to individuals will be automatically adjusted or "indexed" in accordance with changes in the national price level. As Figure 6-1 illustrates, the shift toward indexing within the federal budget has been dramatic over the past twenty-five years. As recently as the late 1960s, only about 5 to 6 percent of all federal domestic outlays* were automatically indexed to prices. By the end of the 1970s, this share had exploded to about 55 percent. Today, it stands at about 65 percent. The driving force behind this shift was of course the decision to index our major entitlement programs. In the late 1960s, only 8 percent of all federal benefits were indexed; today more than 80 percent of all benefits are indexed, including nearly every non-means-tested cash benefit.

During the 1970s, automatic indexing effectively tied the hands of both Congress and the president while driving up benefit spending far faster than our economy was growing. Part of the problem, obviously, was that our economy was slowing down. But the real culprits (between the early 1970s and the early 1980s) were a Consumer Price Index (CPI) that exaggerated the true rate of inflation and a flawed "double indexing" formula for all Social Security cash benefits. To-gether, they conspired to drive up benefit levels much faster than either inflation or average wages. The cumulative effect of overindex-ing since the early 1970s *now costs the federal government over $25 billion per year.* And even though Social Security's double indexing was eliminated in 1977 and the CPI has recently been revised, automatic indexing continues to lock this entirely unintended windfall of benefits into our entitlement budget for the indefinite future.

Since the flaws that led to overindexing during the 1970s have been largely corrected, the reader may wonder whether there is still a serious problem with our system of COLAs. There is. Any automatic index-ing system poses grave problems by preventing elected policymakers from reordering their spending priorities. If indexing were not auto-matic, they could gradually allow real benefit levels in some programs to fall behind inflation in order to commit new resources to new national concerns.

Back in the early 1970s when our major entitlement programs were first indexed, none of this seemed to matter. Since real federal spending, real GNP, and real wage levels were all still growing rapidly, an automatic link between benefit levels and prices did not seriously constrain our budgetary options. Today our situation is different. Facing as we do the prospect of declining or (at best) stagnant real consumption per worker over the next ten or fifteen years, it follows almost by definition that during many of these years we will see prices rising faster than after-tax wages. Each year this occurs, indexing will

---

*Federal domestic outlays are defined as total federal outlays minus defense and net interest payments.

automatically cause benefit spending to grow faster than wages (which is precisely what happened in the late 1970s). The very nature of indexing will then pose a genuine question of equity: To what extent should beneficiaries not in poverty be "held harmless" from downward jolts in the standard of living that affect all other Americans?

In this chapter, we will examine the past effects of automatic indexing on federal benefit spending. More than any other single policy measure, it is indexing that allows us to project the future course our entitlement programs will follow. If Congress had not decided to place the federal budget on "automatic pilot," we could not have made the long-term projections for federal benefit spending presented in Chapter 3. Without automatic indexing, it would be impossible to project how future Congresses might respond to trade-offs between old and new priorities during renewed episodes of stagflation. With indexing, such projections can be made with great confidence: the old priorities will always win.

The Overheated CPI

It will no doubt come as a surprise to many readers to learn that the Consumer Price Index, despite its official role in indexing federal cash benefits, is rarely used by economists.* Instead, when experts analyze consumer spending, most prefer an entirely different price index known as the Personal Consumption Expenditure Deflator, or PCE deflator. As it turns out, the growth in the CPI over the last two decades has been significantly more rapid than the growth in this PCE deflator. The CPI, in short, has a long reputation among economists as a mistakenly buoyant price index—one that the careful expert should stay away from.

The major conceptual problem with the CPI is that the statistical weights the Bureau of Labor Statistics (BLS) employs in translating yearly price data into index numbers are based on a prior year and are "rebased" only once every decade or so. In averaging raw price data to arrive at an index number, the CPI—like most other indexes—

---

*To clear up the arcana, let us point out that the "CPI" (used internally by the SSA and by all federal agencies to index benefits) is now known as the "CPI-W" (W for "Urban Wage Earners and Clerical Earners"). It is essentially the same as the original CPI, published monthly by the Bureau of Labor Statistics (BLS) since 1913. But when the BLS introduced a new "CPI-U" in 1978 (U for "All Urban Consumers"), it became necessary to give each a unique acronym. Although the BLS has actively promoted the CPI-U as more accurate since it uses a broader population base, indexing law remains attached to the CPI-W. In practice, the two indexes have been almost identical over the past decade.

238

"weights" the price of each item in its "market basket" of selected goods and services according to the percentage share of total spending represented by that item during the course of a base year. But unlike the PCE deflator and other price indexes, which update their weights each year, the CPI as recently as 1986 was still using weights that reflected patterns of consumer spending prevalent in 1972 and 1973—the last year these "fixed" weights had been updated.

Perhaps an illustration will best clarify the reason prior-year fixed weights tend to give an upward bias to any price index. Suppose that our market basket contains only two products, flounder and tuna, each of which costs $1 per pound and each of which consumers purchase in equal amounts. Let us call the year in which we make these observations our base year, and assign it an index number of "100." Each of the products in our market basket would thus have a fixed weight of 50 percent. Let us further suppose that after a number of years we find that flounder has become relatively scarce and now costs $3 per pound, while the price of tuna has remained unchanged. If we retain the original fixed weights of 50 percent that were calculated for each product in our base year, we will obtain a new index number of "200." All this means is that if consumers still wished to purchase the same amounts, they would now have to spend $4 where they had previously spent only $2. Inflation according to this index thus would have been 100 percent. Most consumers, however, will respond to those new prices by shifting some of their purchases from flounder to tuna. If consumers' income—in the form of cash benefit payments—has been fully indexed to changes in the price of our fixed-weight market basket, consumers will be wealthier, since they can purchase more with $4 at the new prices than with $2 at the old. The true increase in the price level, in other words, will be much less than 100 percent.

The best way to reduce such upwardly biased distortions in a consumer price index is to provide a yearly update for the weights assigned to the different products in the market basket. Indeed, if we had done this for the market basket in our example, the less flounder that people bought with each passing year the less its price would have been weighted, and the less effect its increased cost would have had on the overall upward movement of our index.*

*Economists agree that there is in theory no perfect solution to what they technically refer to as the "indexing problem." By using prior-year weights, any fixed-weight index such as the CPI (a Laspeyres index) always overstates inflation; by using current-year weights, any deflator such as the PCE deflator (a Paasche index) always understates inflation. But because the CPI's weights are changed so infrequently, its overstatement is large; because the PCE deflator's weights are changed yearly, its understatement is small.

The distortions of fixed-weight indexing have always been recognized in theory, but so long as the overall inflation rate was low and relative price shifts were moderate it was long assumed that they had little practical significance. The enormous increase that occurred in the relative price of energy during the 1970s, however, has shown that these distortions can indeed be consequential. As we have seen, a fixed-weight index such as the CPI works well only if the average consumer maintains the same spending patterns over time. As far as the cost of energy is concerned, this means that the CPI in 1985 would have reflected its relative price today only if Americans still bought gas-guzzling cars and left their doors open in the winter. But given the level of income required to continue past spending behavior at today's prices, most of us realize (just as in our flounder and tuna example) that we are considerably better off when we choose to spend our money in alternative ways. This is precisely what has happened. Relative to their incomes, Americans in 1985 consumed 25 percent less oil and natural gas than they did in 1973.

Another specific problem with the CPI has been its past treatment of housing purchases. The problem arose because a consumer price index is by nature designed to treat all purchased items as though they were immediately and entirely consumed. But when we purchase an item that is in reality an asset, such as an owner-occupied home, some method must be found for separating the item's consumption cost from its investment function. Economists agree that the best way to isolate the current consumption cost of housing is to measure the equivalent rent that houses either do or could charge—which is precisely how the PCE deflator has always handled this problem.

Before January 1985, however, when the BLS finally adopted a rental equivalency measure, the CPI had consistently exaggerated the cost of housing by measuring its full purchase price.* It did not figure that when the price of a home as an asset is pushed up by inflation expectations and by increasingly favorable tax treatment, much of the price increase does not represent a consumption cost. Rather, it reflects an increase in the home's expected resale price and its tax-shelter value—all of which can be sooner or later recaptured by the

---

*Although the BLS had known about this problem for years, it moved very slowly. It switched the CPI-U to a rental equivalency measure in January 1983; it did not make the same switch for the CPI-W (the indexing CPI) until January 1985.

owner.* Nor was this the CPI's only mistake in handling homes. It also "overweighted" home prices by counting both their full purchase price and half of all future mortgage interest payments immediately upon sale. The impact of the CPI's total confusion of the investment and consumption aspects of home ownership has been considerable. According to the CPI, the price of housing rose by 173 percent between 1970 and 1982. According to the PCE deflator, it rose by only 124 percent.

We should note in passing a curious irony in the CPI's exaggeration of housing costs. Very few recipients of indexed benefits are first-time buyers of new homes. This is not because they are poor, but because the lion's share of all these indexed benefits goes to the retired or elderly. As we have seen, three-quarters of the elderly already own homes and two-thirds own homes on which the mortgage has been entirely paid off; half of all adults between age fifty-five and sixty-five own a fully paid-off home. In contrast, only 12 percent of all adults under fifty-five own a fully paid-off home. The excessive housing "push" to the CPI has thus benefited precisely those Americans least likely to be paying for a first-time home, while of course no price index—not even a realistic one—protects the incomes of the younger Americans who really are making most of these purchases.†

Altogether, the cumulative effect of overindexing on federal spending has been enormous. From 1970 through 1982, the CPI rose about 21 percent faster than the PCE deflator, which means that all cash beneficiaries who began collecting in 1970 saw their monthly benefit checks go up by an extra one-fifth by 1982. Consider this micro example: with the CPI, a typical monthly benefit payment of $300 in January 1975 was actually raised to $583 by January 1983; if the PCE deflator had been used instead, it would have climbed only to $516. In macro terms, the cumulative effects of overindexing to the CPI

---

*In other words, using today's full purchase price means incorporating today's expectations about decades of *future* inflation into this year's price index. As for the rising value of home interest deductions as a tax shelter, it is enough simply to contemplate the interaction of rising marginal income tax rates with exploding mortgage interest rates. In the mid-1960s, the tax implications of debt-financed home ownership seldom mattered; today, for many families, it translates into an effortless 15 percent of after-tax income.

†It is sometimes claimed that inflation is especially high for the elderly due to their unique pattern of consumption. The most recent and exhaustive examination of this question concludes, however, that inflation for the elderly has been about the same as for younger Americans—and that inflation for both groups has been overstated by the pre-1983 CPI-U. See article by Michael Boskin and Michael Hurd in *Public Finance Quarterly* (October 1985).

since the early 1970s now cost the federal government at least $13 billion each year.* In defense of this estimate, it is worth pointing out that it does not rest solely on a comparison of the CPI with the PCE deflator. A comparison with any other general measure of inflation would show a similar disparity.†

During a period of zero productivity growth and zero real wage growth, widespread benefit indexing to an accurate measure of prices would alone have caused serious fiscal and inflationary problems; indexing to an exaggerated measure of prices throughout the 1970s and early 1980s simply made matters much worse. In 1987 the BLS finally introduced a new series of fixed weights to replace the ones that had been in use since the early 1970s. Will this at least improve the accuracy of the CPI? Perhaps for a time, but the index will sooner or later become skewed again as consumer spending patterns change in response to future trends in the real costs of goods and services. The crowning irony would of course be if energy costs were once more to climb steeply during the early 1990s—a trend that many economists are now predicting. In that case, only a few years after its belated "reweighting" to take into account consumers' responses to the oil shocks of the mid-1970s, the CPI would once again quickly find itself in need of radical revision.

A Short History of Indexing—and Double Indexing

As incredible as it may seem, the upward bias of the Consumer Price Index during the 1970s and early 1980s was itself further exaggerated by a terrible flaw in the raw mechanics of computing Social Security benefits. In order to appreciate how this came about, we must step back for a moment and take a brief look at the history of indexing. The origins of indexing date back to the early 1960s, an era when most policymakers were confident that high rates of productivity growth and low rates of inflation would endure indefinitely. Before the introduction of automatic indexing, when creeping prices periodically threatened to erode the real value of benefits, Congress simply responded with ad hoc hikes in benefit levels. Because the size of all

---

*This conservative estimate is based on SSA research (see "Notes and Brief Reports" in the *Social Security Bulletin;* August 1982) showing that the CPI's housing mismeasurement since 1974 was alone costing Social Security an extra $7.5 billion yearly by 1981.

†For instance, the price deflators for Gross National Product, Gross Domestic Product, Net National Product, and so on.

entitlement spending was then much smaller than it is today, and because the economy was growing much more swiftly, it often turned out that Congress was able to raise benefit levels for popular programs by more than the increase in the cost of living.

As a consequence, the first legislative decisions to index benefits aroused very little public attention, except for scattered complaints that automatic indexing might serve to hamper the customary generosity of Congress. When the Kennedy administration first succeeded in indexing federal civil service and military retirement benefits in 1962, for instance, there was vocal disappointment that the complicated new formula failed to produce any benefit increases in the first few years (inflation rates at the time were very low). Congress responded to this outcry by enacting a more generous, twice-per-year indexing formula in 1965, and then tacked on an extra one percent "kicker" to the formula in 1969. The "kicker"—whose peculiar rationale we will explain in Chapter 8—was not repealed until seven years later in 1976.

Attitudes had not changed appreciably by the early 1970s, when Congress—prompted by rising inflation rates—decided to protect the major entitlement programs by making automatic indexing of benefits the rule rather than the exception. In the case of Social Security cash benefits, the decision to shift to a system of automatic indexing actually came right on the heels of enormous ad hoc increases in benefit levels. In any event, both fiscal liberals and fiscal conservatives made common cause in supporting the decision. Liberals, of course, wanted to protect newly won benefit increases against the ravages of future inflation. Conservatives believed that they had at last found a means of neutralizing the political pressures that periodically persuaded Congress to grant overly generous ad hoc adjustments.

No sooner had Congress finished its handiwork, however, than the gathering storm clouds of stagflation broke over the American economic landscape. With the oil embargo of late 1973 and the worldwide recession of 1974–75, U.S. productivity growth stagnated. At the same time, inflation began to soar to rates never before imagined.

For every CPI-indexed entitlement, stagflation began to generate benefit increases that for the first time approached (and in some years greatly exceeded) increases in average wage levels. But for Social Security, which in 1975 represented three-quarters of all indexed cash benefits, it acted on a flawed benefit formula to generate huge benefit leaps for new beneficiaries that were entirely unintentional and outpaced anything that even the CPI could justify. Between 1973 and the early 1980s, this computational quirk alone added several billion dollars to Social Security spending each year. And even after widespread panic about Social Security's impending bankruptcy forced Congress to correct the flawed benefit formula in 1977, these runaway benefit hikes continued to threaten the near-term solvency of the system. The accident of double indexing, as it has sometimes been described, forms such an important chapter in the history of entitlement spending that it deserves special attention.

Throughout most of Social Security's history, the initial monthly benefit payments to new retirees—known as Primary Insurance Amounts, or PIAs—were calculated on the basis of their past "unindexed" (that is, dollar-value) Average Monthly Wages, or AMWs. The amount that a new beneficiary received as a PIA was determined by applying a bracketed PIA percentage formula to that person's AMW. In 1952, for instance, the initial monthly benefit of a new retiree was equivalent to 55 percent of his or her first $100 in Average Monthly Wages plus 15 percent of the next $200.

The system was originally conceived in the 1930s when it was generally assumed that wage levels would not change much over time in terms of dollars. During subsequent decades, of course, it soon became clear that dollar wages did tend to rise significantly from year to year, in part due to inflation and in part because of productivity improvement or "real" wage growth. As a consequence, in order to keep benefits to current retirees from falling behind prices, Congress repeatedly increased the benefit formula by a bit more than the increase in the price level (that is, it increased the percentages by which all AMWs for all retirees were translated into monthly benefit payments). From 1950 until 1972, Congress performed this ad hoc formula adjustment about every two years or so.

This brings us to the peculiar problem of "coupled" indexing. What "coupling" meant was this: whenever Congress decided to increase the benefit formula by a certain percentage, such increases applied not only to all *current* retirees; they applied equally to all *new* retirees, even though the ones just leaving the work force had more recent and hence somewhat higher AMW histories than the current beneficiaries. Policymakers found, as a general rule, that this "coupled" method of indexing succeeded in keeping both current benefits on a par with inflation and new beneficiaries on a par with rising wage levels, so long as the rate of inflation was equal to slightly more than half the rise in the wage level. By happy historical accident, these were in fact the conditions that prevailed during the 1950s and 1960s.

Although the 1972 Social Security act replaced the original ad hoc system of benefit hikes with an indexing rule that automatically equated percentage changes in the PIA formula with percentage changes in the CPI, it retained the traditional system's "coupling" mechanism. At just about this time, however, the fortuitous relationship between inflation and wage growth, which alone had allowed the coupling mechanism to function, suddenly collapsed. From 1973 on, prices soared and real wage growth screeched to a halt. While automatic indexing kept all current beneficiaries on a par with rising prices, new retirees cashed in on both the rising percentages in their PIA formulas and the fact that their AMWs were already being driven up by accelerating inflation. As a result, each year new beneficiaries were retiring with much higher real benefits than those who had retired the year before, even though no one's real wages before retirement were rising at all.

Figure 6-2 illustrates this leapfrogging behavior of initial benefit levels after the late 1960s—a behavior so inappropriate in view of stagnating real wages that "coupled" indexing soon became known as double indexing. To appreciate how badly the system had gone awry, consider the trend in new retirement benefits at age sixty-five as a percent of earnings in the year prior to retirement. From the early 1950s through the late 1960s, this so-called replacement ratio held steady at about 31 or 32 percent. After a series of steep benefit hikes enacted by Congress in the late 1960s and early 1970s (which, as we will see in Chapter 7, caused a sharp rise in benefit levels that may or may not have been deliberate), the replacement ratio had risen to 38 percent by 1974. The next year came the first of the automatic, "double-indexed" COLAs mandated by the 1972 act. From then on, the giant jumps in the replacement ratio were entirely inadvertent: to 45 percent in 1979, to 47 percent in 1980, and to 51 percent in 1981 (the best year ever to retire at age sixty-five on Social Security).

Since 1981 the reforms enacted in 1977 have been pushing the average replacement ratios back down again. But the 1977 act ensures that the ratios will forever remain substantially higher than they were before the advent of double indexing.* There is, of course, no protest

---

*According to the 1977 act, the replacement rate for an average-earning worker retiring at age sixty-five will ultimately stabilize at 40.8 percent of prior-year earnings. Relative to where the rate stood in 1974, on the eve of indexing, this represents a permanent 6.6 percent increase in the benefit level.

FIGURE 6-2 **Real Value of Average Monthly OASI Retirement Pension for Men Retiring in Different Years, in 1986 Dollars**

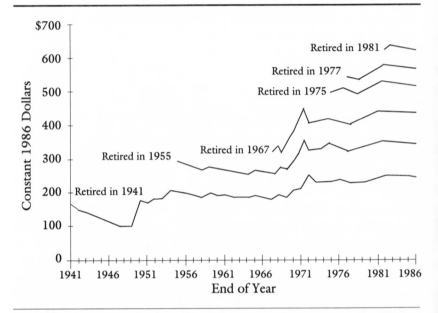

Average for all men, assuming they retired exactly at age sixty-five (at end of year) so that their "Primary Insurance Amount" is unadjusted for early or late retirement; also excluding any spouse benefit. Dollars deflated with fourth-quarter PCE deflator.

Source: Annual Statistical Supplements, *Social Security Bulletin* (SSA) and BEA

that millions of beneficiaries with lucky birth years are receiving monthly Social Security checks 25 percent higher than they ought to be as a result of this mishap. There is, instead, organized outrage from those born just a bit too late (the so-called Notch Babies) to be dealt the perfect hand.*

The history of indexing is altogether one of the sorriest stories in federal policymaking, and the history of double indexing is perhaps

---

*The term "Notch Babies" refers to the 7 million elderly Americans born between 1917 and 1921. Since they reach age sixty-two after 1978, the 1977 act grants them progressively lower PIAs relative to earlier age-cohorts in order to repeal part of the lofty (and unaffordable) replacement-rate increase generated by double indexing. In recent years, the "Notch" has lobbied Congress and presidential candidates in an effort to get this "injustice" corrected. But as Robert Myers, former SSA chief actuary, has remarked, it would be more appropriate to think of those born just before 1917 as "Bonanza Babies."

246

the most flagrant case in point. This single, colossal error that hyperinflated initial Social Security benefit checks from the mid-1970s to the early 1980s is forever scheduled to spill more money out of the federal budget—we estimate a minimum of $12 billion yearly*—than total federal spending on AFDC benefits to welfare families. Yet it represented, much like the misguided CPI, a fundamental allocation of resources about which the public was neither informed nor consulted. Its only legitimacy came from the collective vow of silence that enshrouds our public-sector consumption ethos. Moreover, unlike our problematic CPI, which at least involved subtle errors that unfolded over many years, double indexing was an obvious mistake from the very beginning. By 1973 policy experts both inside and outside the SSA were well aware of it. But though Congress and the President took only a couple days in 1972 to debate, pass, and sign double indexing into law, it took five years—and the imminent threat of Social Security's bankruptcy—to dismantle it.† Even then, Congress failed to scale back most of the unintended benefit increases, and the effects of double indexing remain locked into our entitlements system today.

The Economics and Ethics of Indexing

Before the introduction of automatic indexing, Congress always retained the option of curtailing entitlement expenditures during periods of relative austerity by allowing real benefits per person to fall as needed. During World War II, for instance, inflation accomplished this task without any special action on the part of Congress. The result was that a common national hardship was generally shared by beneficiaries and nonbeneficiaries alike. Ever since the introduction of automatic indexing, however, Congress has lost its traditional control over benefit levels. During the 1970s and early 1980s, a combination of overindexing to 100 percent of the CPI, "stagflation," and (in the

---

*This is a conservative estimate that applies only the ultimate extra cost legislated by the 1977 act to actual 1986 Social Security outlays. It entirely excludes both the effect of any of the ad hoc benefit increases through 1972 as well as the temporary extra costs of those who have retired since 1974 with replacement rates higher than 40.8 percent (though they will be with us well past the year 2000).

†On June 30, 1972, the Senate added the indexing provision (together with first a 5 percent and then a 20 percent across-the-board benefit increase) to a House-passed bill raising the ceiling on the national debt. After a rushed Senate-House conference, Wilbur Mills obtained the consent of the House before a midnight deadline. President Nixon signed H.R. 15390 into law on July 1, 1972. See discussion in Chapter 7.

FIGURE 6-3 **Real Value of Benefits and Wages;
End of 1965 = 100**

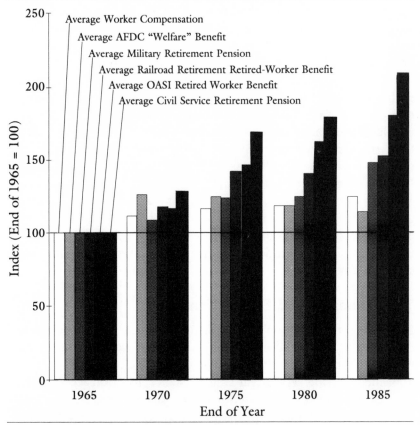

All values deflated to 1965 dollars with fourth-quarter PCE deflator.

Source: Worker compensation and deflators: BEA (Commerce); military pensions: *Selected Manpower Statistics* (Defense); CSRS pensions: *Compensation Report* (OPM); others: Annual Statistical Supplements, *Social Security Bulletin* (SSA) and authors' calculations

case of Social Security) double indexing caused real benefit levels to rise much faster than real wage levels.

Figure 6-3 illustrates the impact of this development on selected entitlement programs. Between 1965 and 1985, we can see that the average benefit level for every major indexed federal program grew considerably faster than the average private-sector wage level. For the largest program, Social Security Old-Age Insurance, that growth was especially swift. By 1985 the average monthly Social Security check for a retired worker was 81 percent higher in real dollars than it had been twenty years earlier. For the two next-largest cash benefit programs, federal civil service and military retirement, the cumulative real growth figures between 1965 and 1985 were 110 percent and 53 percent respectively.

During the same years, however, growth in real wages gradually slowed to a halt. During the late 1960s, total worker compensation per hour was still rising at a moderate pace, and by 1970 had climbed 12 percent above its 1965 level. But during the next fifteen years, real pay growth stagnated, reaching a level by 1985 only 25 percent higher than 1965. Excluding fringe benefits and employer pension contributions from total compensation would cut this growth by half. And counting only the disposable pay left over after rising income taxes and payroll deductions would, for most workers, cut this growth to virtually nil. The zero-growth experience of most wage earners during the 1970s and early 1980s provides a striking contrast with the windfalls experienced by most federal beneficiaries. In some years, the contrast between wage growth and benefit growth was particularly striking. From 1974 to 1975, for example, while average weekly wages rose by 5.7 percent (before taxes) in current dollars, most federal benefits were indexed upward by 8.0 percent. That fiscal year the federal deficit climbed from $6 billion to $53 billion. The transition from 1979 to 1980 was equally dramatic: average pretax weekly wages rose by 9.0 percent in current dollars, while most indexed (and tax-free) cash benefits were jacked up by 14.3 percent; predictably, the federal deficit rose from $40 billion to $74 billion.

During most years since 1981, real wage growth has again turned positive, thanks more to falling energy prices and a flood of federal and foreign debt than to swifter productivity growth. Such good fortune appears to be coming to an end.* But while it lasted—and for the first time since Social Security indexing went into effect in 1975—inflation rates fell close to (in 1984 and 1985) or beneath (in 1986) the 3 percent COLA "trigger" specified by the indexing law. According to the original 1972 act, Congress was not bound to grant any COLA if the year-to-year CPI weighed in under three percent; the idea was to allow Congress to use its own discretion when the inflation rate was low. Since the federal budget now faced deficits of unprecedented size, one might suppose that political leaders would have used this discre-

---

*With the CPI again rising, many measures of real wage growth have already turned negative in 1987 and all (including the official SSA measure) are likely to do so in 1988.

tion to trim where earlier they had so often added. Nothing like this ever happened. President Reagan, campaigning for reelection in the summer of 1984, announced that he was in favor of granting all Social Security beneficiaries full COLAs even if the CPI came in under 3 percent. Congress responded by passing a similar resolution. In 1986, when the trigger line was again about to be crossed, Congress not only granted the full COLA for that year, but also passed a law repealing the 3 percent trigger for all future years.*

Today, it seems, we have come to accept as a matter of right that however fast (or slow) inflation rates rise, all those who receive federal benefits must be "held harmless" from the consequences. Everyone else is left to manage as best they can in the private sector, where no more than a tiny proportion of all workers and pension-plan retirees enjoy even partially indexed contracts. The consequences of this discrepancy are illustrated in Figure 6-4, which compares real benefit levels for public retirement and typical private pension plans over the past two decades.

Consider the case of two workers who retired in December 1964 with identical initial monthly benefits. One received cash benefits in the form of Social Security Old-Age Insurance, while the other received them in the form of a company pension. The contrast between their subsequent benefit histories is dramatic. Thanks to ad hoc benefit hikes and full CPI indexing, the real value of Social Security benefits soared to 136 percent of their initial value by the end of 1972. By the end of 1986, that figure still stood at 135 percent. In contrast, the real value of the monthly private pension plummeted like a stone to between 58 and 76 percent of its initial value by the end of 1975, and to between 30 and 58 percent of its initial value by the end of 1986. The reason why private pension benefits have fared so poorly is that a sizable portion of them—about 40 percent of the total—has received no adjustment at all. And of the remaining private pensions that have received some cost-of-living adjustment, less than one-fifth provide even a partial indexing to the CPI. We have yet to find even one private pension that offers 100-percent-of-CPI indexing—which is the standard practice for all federal pensions (and a few state and local ones as well).

Since it is retired Americans living off private-sector fixed incomes

---

*However revealing, the commotion in the summer of 1984 turned out to be technically unnecessary since the CPI later came in at 3.5 percent—over the trigger. In 1986 the CPI came in at 1.7 percent, which quickly forced Congress to take formal action.

FIGURE 6-4   **Real Value of Pension Benefit for Person**
Retired in 1964; End of 1964=100

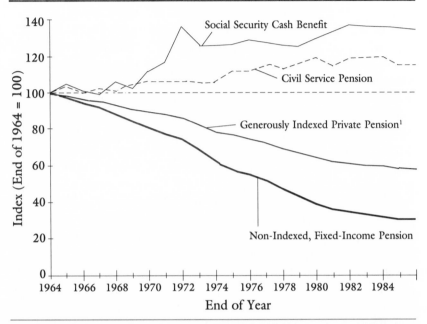

With retirement at the end of 1964; all values deflated with fourth-quarter PCE deflator.

[1]Assuming yearly adjustment equivalent to 50 percent of the CPI.

Source: BEA (Commerce), CRS (Congress), and authors' calculations

who suffer most from inflation, it is ironic that apologists for our current system of entitlements indexing routinely appeal to principles of equity. The gist of their argument seems to be that "it is only fair" to maintain the real value of benefits unchanged during periods of inflation. But is it? The problem is that this argument treats inflation as though it were an entirely external event, whereas inflation, almost by definition, occurs when both our private and public sectors place demands on our economy greater than it is able to satisfy through either production or trade. As a consequence, no one can purchase what he wants during periods of inflation without having his dollar income appropriately devalued. If, as a matter of public policy, we decide to hold one favored group exempt from this devaluation, we simply ensure that inflation will hit everyone else that much harder.

The most unambiguous illustrations of this principle were the

251

inflationary surges of 1974 and 1980, both of which were largely attributable to the sudden and sizable hikes in the world price of petroleum. Apart from any other changes in our domestic production, these oil-price hikes meant that the real purchasing power of our exports had declined, and that the U.S. economy was thus suddenly somewhat poorer than before in terms of real income. The component of inflation during the surges of 1974 and 1980 that was due to the increased cost of energy simply registered our relative impoverishment. Is there some principle of equity mandating that federal beneficiaries alone should be spared from bearing the shared burden of national misfortunes? In most other industrial countries, it is worth pointing out, governments retain and use the administrative authority to grant cost-of-living increases that are *less* than inflation when conditions warrant.* In at least one case, energy imports are deliberately left out of the price index used to adjust benefit levels.†

An equity defense of automatic indexing might be more compelling if the recipients of indexed benefits were generally below the poverty line. As it turns out, however, *the vast majority of indexed benefits are disbursed through non-means-tested programs,* and hence are not targeted at individuals or families in poverty. Figure 6-5 illustrates this point. Out of $259.7 billion in indexed cash benefits issued by the federal government in fiscal year 1986, $245.5 billion (or 94.5 percent) were non-means-tested, while only $14.2 billion (or 5.5 percent, accounted for entirely by Veterans Pensions and SSI) were either partly or strictly means-tested.

It is hardly an accident that during the 1970s and 1980s the benefit levels for our primary means-tested cash program—Aid to Families with Dependent Children—rose far more slowly than the benefit levels for non-means-tested programs. Indeed, the average AFDC payment has failed even to keep up with worker compensation (see again Figure 6-3). Unlike public retirement benefits, AFDC payments in most states are not indexed at all, but depend on legislative discretion for cost-of-living adjustments. Despite the rapid growth in the number of poor, single-parent families during the 1980s, stricter

---

*Including Finland, Sweden, West Germany, the United Kingdom, and Canada. In addition, most other industrial countries have *always* used rental equivalency to measure the price of housing.

†The Swedish government—interestingly, the first to institute price-indexed benefit COLAs (in 1948)—decided as of January 1981 to omit energy prices, import duties, and indirect taxes from its COLA.

FIGURE 6-5 **Indexed Federal Cash Benefits
by Type in Fiscal Year 1986**

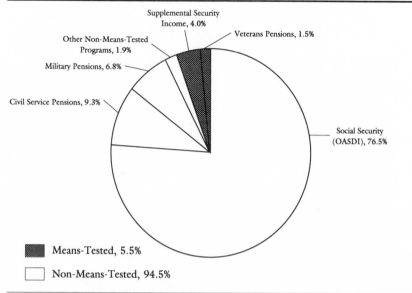

Source: OMB and CBO

---

eligibility rules have prevented any growth in the number of families receiving AFDC. Meanwhile, between 1980 and 1985 total federal and state spending on AFDC has declined by 6 percent (or about $1 billion) in real 1986 dollars. The fact that poverty programs are by and large unindexed goes a long way toward explaining their vulnerability to budget cuts in recent years.* Nonpoverty entitlements, on the other hand, have been exempted from the budgetary process altogether. While episodically chopping away at the small "discretionary" programs that serve the destitute, politicians can tell their constituents that the indexed growth in the much larger middle- and upper-class entitlements—and the budget deficits they generate—are simply "uncontrollable," an act of God for which no one need be responsible.

*Even the indexing of SSI—the next-largest means-tested cash benefit program—bears little similarity to the generous indexing of Social Security. To begin with, the "asset" test and "set-aside" earnings test for an SSI beneficiary have remained fixed in unindexed dollars since 1974 and thus have become stricter over time. SSI's basic *federally financed* benefit, though indexed to the CPI, does not change (like Social Security) to reflect higher real wage levels; new beneficiaries do no better than old beneficiaries. SSI's *state-financed* supplement (about 20 percent of total SSI benefits in 1986) is not indexed at all, and in fact it has dropped from $2.9 billion in 1975 to $2.1 billion in 1986—a drastic real cut of 50 percent since the federally financed portion of SSI was first indexed.

TABLE 6-1   **Real Cost Growth of Federal Non-Means-Tested Benefits Between 1970 and 1985: Breakdown of Components in 1985 Dollars**

	1970	1985	Percent Growth
Real Benefit Payments[1]	$139.1	$333.0	139.4%
Real GNP[1]	2,695.9	3,998.1	48.3
Benefits as Percent of GNP	**5.2%**	**8.3%**	**61.4**
Beneficiaries (millions)	31.5	44.5	41.2
Workers (millions)	78.3	103.0	31.6
Beneficiaries as Percent of Workers	**40.2%**	**43.2%**	**7.3**
Real Benefits per Beneficiary[1]	**$4,417**	**$7,490**	**69.6**
Real GNP per Worker[1]	**34,450**	**38,833**	**12.7**

	(1) Change in Real Benefits per Beneficiary	+ 69.6%
combined with	(2) Change in Beneficiaries per Worker	+ 7.3
combined with	(3) Change in Workers per Real GNP	– 12.7
equals	**(4) Change in Benefits per GNP**	**+ 61.4**

Benefits for most major programs; some estimates used in netting out the number of beneficiaries receiving more than one type of benefit.

[1]All expressed in billions of 1985 dollars.

Source: All citations in Figure 6-3 plus HCFA

Our experience with indexed cash entitlements over the last fifteen years bears one great similarity to our experience with open-ended health-care entitlements: in both cases, we have locked in methods of paying out benefits that offer no stability in benefit levels, and therefore no assurance that the system as a whole will remain affordable. The substantial increase in the cost of federal benefits as a share of GNP since the early 1960s owes little to greater numbers of beneficiaries or to new benefit programs. Instead, it has been driven almost entirely by yearly surges in what we pay, on average, to each beneficiary within the same set of eligibility criteria.

Table 6-1 illustrates this point by breaking down the growth in federal non-means-tested benefits as a share of GNP over the past fifteen years into two components: increases in the number of beneficiaries (relative to the number of workers) and increases in benefits per recipient (relative to GNP per worker).

Between 1970 and 1985, these benefits grew as a share of GNP by a remarkable 61.4 percent. What is even more striking, however, is that of the two components that contributed to this upward trend, the relative growth in the number of beneficiaries (7.3 percent) played a very minor role compared to the growth in real benefit levels (69.6 percent). In fact, if the real benefit levels had not grown at all over this period, the slight growth in beneficiaries per worker would have been more than compensated by the somewhat larger growth in real GNP per worker. *In other words, absent real benefit-level changes, labor force and productivity growth would have actually reduced the size of these benefits as a share of GNP.* In the future, needless to say, we can count on no such offsetting growth in our labor force. During tomorrow's episodes of stagflation, total entitlement spending will skyrocket because of *both* autonomous hikes in cash and health-care benefits per recipient *and* the explosion in the number of elderly beneficiaries relative to the working-age population.

In sum, rather than guarantee the protection of our "social safety net," indexing—like open-ended health-care reimbursement—has instead served to turn our largely middle- and upper-income benefit programs into inflexible "entitlements." We first placed federal spending on automatic pilot back in an optimistic era when we believed that robust economic growth would last forever. Circumstances have long since changed. As we explained in Chapter 1, the next couple of decades could easily bring us many years in which disposable, after-tax pay will shrink moderately in real terms—that is, will not keep up with inflation. Yet excessive and unintended benefit hikes still remain locked into our federal entitlements system. If we wait for the next bout with inflation before taking action, the political resistance to indexing reform will climb right along with the CPI.

III

From
Complacency
to Reform

7

Social Security:
The End of the
Chain Letter

"Social Security will always be a goal, never a finished
thing, because human aspirations are infinitely expand-
able. . . just as human nature is infinitely perfectible."
— *Arthur Altmeyer, Chairman of the*
Social Security Board (1937–46)

O N A BLUSTERY WEDNESDAY in April 1983, President
Reagan signed into law the bipartisan legislation designed to
"rescue" the Social Security system. A good deal of fanfare
marked the event. Prominent congressional leaders clustered round
the President for the ceremony and White House aides solicited
spectators from nearby tourist lines to beef up the crowd on the South
Lawn. "The changes in this legislation will allow Social Security to age
as gracefully as all of us hope to do ourselves, without becoming an
overwhelming burden on generations to come," the President declared as he signed his name to the act.

Senate majority leader Howard Baker, an avid amateur photo-
grapher, moved exuberantly among the notables, taking pictures of
smiling faces and joining in the mutual congratulations. House
Speaker Tip O'Neill joked with the President and declared afterward
that "the system does work" and that it was "a happy day for America." Press reports the following day described the new law as one that

FIGURE 7-1   **Tax and Cost Rates of Social Security
                  (OASDHI) as a Percent of Taxable Payroll**

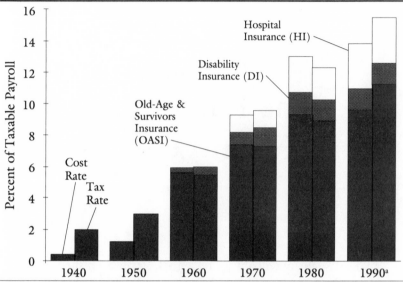

[a]After currently scheduled payroll tax raise goes into effect on January 1, 1990.
Source: 1987 OASDI Annual Report

would assure the solvency of the Social Security system for the next seventy-five years. As they read these reports, Americans across the country heaved an almost audible sigh of relief. With that sigh, Social Security departed from the front pages of the nation's newspapers and was crossed off the national agenda. The crisis had been resolved and Americans were ready to move on to new challenges.

That was a serious mistake.

As we have seen, Social Security's future remains as problematic as ever. Long before the cost of Social Security reaches the prohibitive share of taxable payroll now projected by the Social Security Administration, Congress will be forced to choose between two politically "unacceptable" expedients: tax hikes and benefit cuts. Why is it that Social Security seems to be forever on the verge of a new crisis? The explanation is simple. The cost of Social Security benefits has grown much more rapidly than available tax revenues throughout the program's history, and, after a brief respite over the next decade or two, will continue to do so into the indefinite future. The only way to alter this pattern of explosive benefit growth would be to enact far more fundamental reforms than those that "rescued" the Social

260

FIGURE 7-2   **Cost of Social Security, Including Both Parts of Medicare, as a Percent of All Federal Outlays, 1935–1985**

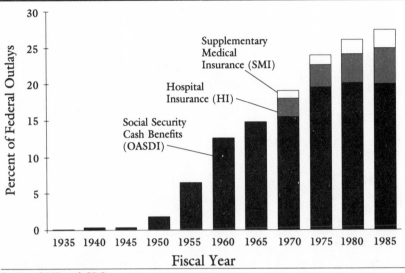

Fiscal Year

Source: OMB and CBO

Security system back in April 1983.

Consider the following numbers: as recently as 1965, Social Security was comfortably funded at a combined employer-employee payroll tax rate of 7.25 percent; today the Social Security system (OASDHI) is being funded at more than double that rate—15.02 percent of taxable payroll (plus a minor tax on benefits)—and yet it still has fewer trust-fund assets, relative to yearly spending, than before. A substantial part of this growth, to be sure, is due to the founding of the payroll-funded Hospital Insurance program (see Figures 7-1 and 7-2). Yet even if we omit HI and keep our focus in this chapter on Old-Age, Survivors, and Disability Insurance, the payroll tax rate has risen by two-thirds since 1965, from 7.25 to 12.12 percent of payroll.

In other words, a 67 percent increase in the payroll tax rate over the last twenty years—an increase more than three times as large as the growth in relative numbers of beneficiaries would have warranted—has only just managed to keep Social Security's cash-benefit trust funds operating. Moreover, even this rate hike would have proved insufficient to keep the system solvent if the "cap" on taxable wages had not also risen considerably faster than the average wage level. In 1965

261

FIGURE 7-3   **Average OASI Retired-Worker Benefit as a Percent of Average Covered Wages, 1940–1984**

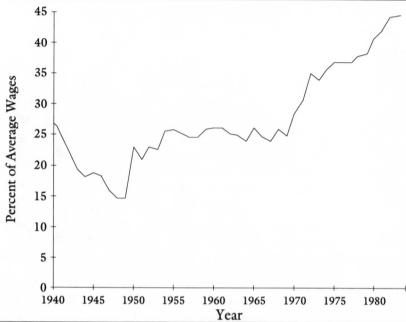

Benefit is unadjusted for early or late retirement and excludes spouse benefit; wages are average salaries and wages of all workers covered by OASI.

Source: Annual Statistical Supplements, *Social Security Bulletin* (SSA) and Office of the Actuary (SSA)

covered wages were taxable only up to $4,800 yearly (about 80 percent of the total pay of covered workers), whereas in 1988 they are taxable up to $45,000 yearly (about 90 percent of the total pay of covered workers). There is only one explanation why the added fiscal burden of higher taxes has far outpaced the added numerical burden of new beneficiaries: average benefits per beneficiary have been rising much faster than average wages per worker.

Figure 7-3 illustrates the magnitude of this increase in Social Security benefits by comparing the average benefit level of retired workers with the average wage level. Here we can see that from the early days of Social Security in 1940 until the late 1960s the average retired-worker benefit rarely exceeded 25 percent of the average wages earned by covered workers. We can also note that between 1967 and 1982 the average retired-worker benefit climbed from 23 percent to 45 percent of average wages. In other words, relative to the wages of workers paying into Social Security, benefits per retiree approximately doubled.

In 1939 the American public was promised a Social Security system that in the long run was designed to cost 6 percent of payroll. Today we know that this same basic package of Old-Age and Survivors Insurance benefits (OASI) may cost more than 21 percent of payroll by the middle of the next century. And together with Disability Insurance and Medicare "Part A" (HI), the total tax burden may weigh in at close to 40 percent of payroll. It is incredible to think that this has happened without any public announcement that the "social contract" between taxpayers and beneficiaries has been redrawn. Perhaps the time has come to take a retrospective look at Social Security and try to measure the full distance we have drifted on a current of mistaken forecasts, unworkable formulas, and political hijinks.

Social Security Comes of Age (1935–1967)

Social Security was conceived in a time of unparalleled economic dis-location and deprivation. The Great Depression had struck a society largely without economic cushions, either private or public, and millions of Americans were battered by the consequences. Tens of thousands of businesses were driven into bankruptcy, hundreds of thousands of home mortgages were foreclosed, and the financial crash shattered the life savings of even the most prudent families. From 1932 through 1935, unemployment as a share of the labor force averaged over 22 percent. The domestic demand for goods and services stagnated; the value of U.S. exports sank to less than half of what it had been before 1930. The needs of the economically dependent—among them the newly urbanized elderly—quickly overwhelmed the ill-prepared relief efforts of state and local authorities. The economy was in a tailspin, and Americans could no longer be confident that a life of hard work would ensure self-respect and material security.

It was in this atmosphere of national crisis that the Social Security act of 1935 first created a vast package of programs designed to shield Americans against future economic deprivations. What we now know as Social Security was just one part of this package, which also included unemployment compensation, aid to the elderly and disabled poor (now Supplemental Security Income), and welfare for women with dependent children (now Aid to Families with

Dependent Children).* When President Roosevelt affixed his signature to this omnibus legislation on August 14, 1935, the words he spoke were hopeful: "We can never insure 100 percent of the population against 100 percent of the hazards and vicissitudes of life, but we have tried to frame a law which will give some measure of protection to the average citizen and to his family against the loss of a job and against poverty-ridden old age."†

From today's vantage point, it is important to keep in mind the vast differences separating the world of the New Deal from our own. First, very few Americans who reached old age in the 1930s had been able to prepare financially for their retirement through pensions, insurance, or personal savings; poverty among the elderly who could neither work nor live with their families was therefore pandemic. Today nearly half the work force is covered by a private pension, many retirees have substantial real and financial assets, and poverty is less frequent among retirees than among young working families. Second, it seemed evident in the mid-1930s that the short life expectancy of the elderly would prevent the overall cost of any public retirement plan from ever rising very high. In 1930 the average person aged sixty-five could expect to live another 12.5 years and the elderly comprised only 5.4 percent of the population. Today these figures are 16.8 years and 12.1 percent; after another half century, they could be as high as 22.3 years and 28.0 percent. Third, health-care spending in the 1930s was not an issue. What little anyone might need could usually be paid for out-of-pocket. Private health insurance was still a novelty, and even minimal public health coverage was nothing more than a "progressive" idea.‡

---

*Not part of the Social Security act—but signed into law just two weeks later—was the Railroad Retirement system, a little-known "pay-as-you-go" federal pension system that still covers most railway employees. It is beyond the scope of this book mainly because of its minor cost (if you can call $6.4 billion in fiscal year 1986 "minor"). In fact, Railroad Retirement today is a nightmare version of Social Security: its benefit level ranges from 60 to over 100 percent of preretirement pay; there are now *three* railroad retirees for every *one* covered worker; it is funded by a 33.3 percent payroll tax plus a general federal subsidy; and even the most optimistic scenario projects bankruptcy within 20 years. Roughly one-sixth of the price of moving freight by rail in the United States goes straight to retired employees—a major reason why in America railroads have become a no-growth industry.

†President's message to Congress, June 8, 1934.

‡In 1929 total national health-care spending amounted to about 3.5 percent of GNP, nearly all of it private and out-of-pocket. Total personal health-care spending by all levels of government barely exceeded $3 per capita (or about $23 per American in 1987 dollars). One reason we spent so little is that we were poorer; another reason is that often there was still little medicine could do to help. In the words of Harvard's Lawrence Henderson, it was not until after World War I that "for the first time in human history, a random patient with a random disease consulting a doctor chosen at random stood better than a 50-50 chance of benefitting from the encounter."

Finally, it was widely believed in the 1930s that our stagnant-demand economy could create only a fixed number of jobs. Allowing an elderly worker to retire was thus not only humanitarian, it "made a place" for a younger family. Today, by contrast, no one believes that there is an effective limit on potential demand or on potential jobs. Indeed, what is scarce today—if anything—is younger families. We cite these changes not to lay blame at the feet of the New Deal planners. They simply coped as best they could with the world as they saw and found it. We find it harder, however, to be as charitable to modern-day defenders of Social Security who—with full knowledge of how our society has changed—continue to look upon the system as though every one of its provisions were chiseled in sacred stone. Such defenders violate the very spirit of flexibility and innovation that attended the system's birth.

But now let us return to our story. Under the original 1935 act, "social security"—its actual name was simply Old-Age Insurance, or OAI—was scheduled to begin making payments out of a single trust fund in 1941. Benefits were to be financed by a flat-rate tax on the payrolls of eventual beneficiaries (that is, current workers). Collection of the payroll tax, which was divided equally between employee and employer, was to commence in 1937 at the rate of 2 percent of the first $3,000 of annual wages. The initial tax rate was then scheduled to increase to 6 percent by 1949, and thereafter remain at that "ultimate" level indefinitely. By today's standards, the initial tax rate was modest; the maximum tax payable by the employee was $30 per year, or about $250 in 1986 dollars.*

According to the Social Security program's original 1935 design, the benefit level for each retired person was to be based on the total (rather than the average) lifetime amount of taxable or "covered" wages he had earned. Here the intention was to reward those individuals with the longest work histories. At the same time, however, the initial benefit formula was also designed to be mildly progressive, since the proportion of covered wages that was translated into monthly cash benefits decreased as the total lifetime amount of those wages increased.† In addition, the original legislation provided

---

*By contrast, in 1990—just two years from now—the employee "max tax" for OASI (again, in constant 1986 dollars) is expected to be $2,600 per covered worker.

†Despite this progressive benefit formula, many economists (most notably, Milton Friedman) have questioned the true progressivity of Social Security retirement over the entire lives of beneficiaries. Negating the effect of a progressive benefit formula, they argue, is the fact that low-

for a "money-back" guarantee on employee taxes: all covered workers or their estates were assured of receiving at least their own contributions plus interest.

Social Security payroll-tax collections began on schedule in 1937, but before the benefit payments even got under way, the system was given the first of its many alterations and expansions. The act of 1939 added Survivors Insurance to the functions of the original trust fund, thus changing its acronym from OAI to OASI. The new benefit was a set of extra monthly payments to certain dependents (primarily the widows) of eligible workers upon their deaths.

In addition, the act of 1939 sharply raised benefit levels for retirees with relatively few years of covered wages—a group that obviously included anyone intending to retire during the first few decades of the system's operation. This was accomplished by calculating initial benefits primarily on the basis of the Average Monthly Wage in covered employment before retirement (AMW), rather than on the basis of total lifetime wages in such employment. The 1939 act also eliminated the "money-back" guarantee and made the benefit schedule more progressive. All in all, the result was that those workers with lower wages, shorter wage histories, and more dependents fared better under the 1939 act than under the original 1935 plan.

Curiously, even at this initial stage in the history of Social Security, the principles underlying the relationship between taxes paid and benefits received were never made entirely clear. Because a worker aged sixty-five or older actually had to retire in order to receive benefits, the system partly resembled an insurance plan where retirement was the event being insured against. On the other hand, the "money-back" plus interest guarantee had given the 1935 plan some of the trappings of an annuity. And although this guarantee was rescinded in 1939, Congress and the public in later years never felt altogether comfortable in abandoning the annuity notion. For instance, when "early" retirement at age sixty-two was introduced (in 1956 for women and 1961 for men), Congress insisted on reducing the benefit level for those who took advantage of this provision. The

income persons start working and paying taxes earlier in life (which, since 1950, has done nothing to increase their benefit levels) plus the fact that they have shorter life expectancies and thus draw out fewer years of benefits. Moreover, whether or not low-income workers receive a lower payback *rate* from Social Security, nearly all economists agree that they have received a smaller *absolute* windfall during the system's generous early decades. To illustrate: a low-income worker might receive a 10-to-1 return off a $1 contribution, but a high-income worker might receive a 5-to-1 return off a $5 contribution.

rationale was that this reduction reflected the lower "value" of early retirees' contributions and compensated the trust fund for the additional years during which benefits would have to be paid. In 1972 and again in 1983, Congress took this notion a step further when it added a "delayed retirement increment" to the monthly benefit of those workers who retired after age sixty-five.

Yet there was still another ambiguity in the relationship between taxes paid and benefits received in the Social Security program. The benefit formula, with its progressive brackets, also had a welfare dimension that made it fundamentally different from either private insurance or a private annuity.* The intention was to ensure a more generous "floor of protection" for the lower-paid worker, even at the expense of equal treatment for the higher-paid worker. As we have seen, the 1939 act enhanced the welfare dimension of the 1935 act by adding an extra twist: much better treatment for workers who had paid taxes for only a few years relative to those who had paid taxes for many years.

Paradoxically, despite these changes in the system, it was in 1939 that the Social Security Administration first began to describe the program to the public in terms of private pension and insurance metaphors.† Payroll taxes became known as "contributions"; the OASI trust fund was where taxes were "kept" in an "account"; and benefit provisions were dubbed "insurance." After decades of this rhetoric, the American people eventually became convinced that they were "buying" future benefits with their own payroll taxes—something that has never been true either for individual retirees or for entire generations of Social Security beneficiaries. To an extent, Social

---

*The basic monthly benefit was determined by a formula that converted the prior Average Monthly Wages (AMW) into a "Primary Insurance Amount" (PIA). For a single worker retiring at age sixty-five, the monthly OASI check was equal to the PIA. But the PIA formula was progressive because the percentages it applied to the AMW declined (between "bend points") as the AMW rose. According to the 1939 act, for instance, the PIA equaled 40 percent of the first $50 in AMW plus 10 percent of anything up to the next $200 in AMW. In this case, there was a formula "bend point" at $50. This is similar to the PIA formula still in use today (although, as we shall see, we now have an "AIME" rather than an "AMW" to measure prior earnings).

†Perhaps it was not so paradoxical. When President Roosevelt signed the original 1935 act, his advisors feared that the Supreme Court would strike down a self-billed retirement-insurance system as uinconstitutional under the Tenth Amendment (granting all powers not specifically ascribed to the federal government "to the States respectively, or to the People"). Their strategy was to enact the payroll tax and the retirement benefit separately (based on the federal government's unquestioned power to tax and spend) and to deny any necessary link between the two. Only after FDR's successful confrontation with the Court in 1937 was it safe to talk explicitly about "federal insurance."

Security's traditional rhetoric—which is still used today—represented a deliberate attempt on the part of New Deal officials to mislead the public about the welfare dimension of the new program. In fact, the very decision to finance Social Security through payroll taxes (rather than through general revenues) may have been designed to foster the impression that this "social insurance" scheme was actually a form of true insurance in which—on the average—benefits directly reflected contributions. As President Roosevelt himself once explained when asked about the economic rationale behind the taxes: ". . . those taxes were never a problem of economics. They are politics all the way through. We put those payroll taxes there so as to give the contributors a legal, moral, and political right to collect their pensions. . . . With those taxes in there, no damn politician can ever scrap my social security program."*

One reason Congress and the public were willing to accept these ambiguities in Social Security lay in the dynamics typical of any "pay-as-you-go" retirement program that has only just started. A pay-as-you-go program, as we have seen, is one in which the benefits of current retirees are paid for by the contributions of current workers; a "funded" program, on the other hand, is one in which workers' contributions are saved, invested, and later returned to them in retirement. During the start-up phase of any pay-as-you-go program, it is possible for retirees to receive benefit payments far in excess of the taxes they have paid. The reason is simple: until the system "matures," there are always far more workers contributing taxes than retirees collecting benefits. In the Social Security program, these "early birds" typically received total retirement benefits that were 50 or 100 times greater than their total payroll-tax contributions plus interest. Consider the case of Mrs. Ida Fuller, the very first Social Security beneficiary, who received check number 00-000-001 back in 1940. Before she retired, Mrs. Fuller had paid $22 in employee taxes; by the time she died at one hundred years of age she had collected over $20,000 in benefits.

These windfalls have of course been the key to Social Security's broad-based popularity throughout the first half-century of its existence. Participants contributed to the system for only a portion of their working lives (and, moreover, at low tax rates), yet in retirement enjoyed generous benefits that they believed they had earned. Perhaps Mrs. Fuller never succumbed to this illusion, but countless

*Cited by Arthur M. Schlesinger, Jr. in *The Coming of the New Deal* (Houghton Mifflin, 1958).

millions of other Americans have. The reality, however, is that over the past fifty years Social Security taxes (including employer contributions) have amounted to only 20 percent of the value of the benefits already paid for or promised.*

Since Social Security seemed to function so smoothly in the near term, it is perhaps understandable that Congress failed to peer decades into the future and reflect upon how the system would fare when, on the average, the taxes each worker paid came to approximate the benefits he received. In a pay-as-you-go retirement system, there is always a strong temptation to reap the rewards of current benefit expansions without worrying about their costs, which are borne later. High benefit levels seem affordable in the present, but can be bought from today's taxpayers only by promising to pay them the same high benefit levels when they retire in the future. In short, future liabilities for higher benefits are issued in exchange for increased current revenues.

Such pay-as-you-go financing has always been a central element of the Social Security system. Contrary to popular mythology (often bolstered by the Social Security Administration itself), OASI was never designed to function like a fully "funded" private pension plan. In the latter, contributions are kept in an inviolable capital fund that is then used to pay each group of retirees the exact value of that group's contributions plus interest. The adoption of such a system for Social Security would have been unacceptable for several reasons. It would have required taxing all covered workers in the start-up phase at the same higher tax rate as that anticipated for the mature phase. At the same time, it would have involved amassing an enormous trust fund during the early decades of the system's operation, and then delaying full benefit payments until covered workers had earned them through a lifetime of tax payments.† Instead, the original Social Security system was expressly designed so that at any given moment future tax receipts would always be necessary to pay off all the benefits that workers had previously earned. It is for this reason that legislators could at the same time afford to keep the initial tax rate relatively low and the initial benefit level relatively high.

*This is similar to the difference between the actuarial values of taxes paid in and benefits promised back—a growing gap that has given rise to the "unfunded benefit liability" described in Chapter 2.

†Alternatively, a "funded" plan might start out by requiring *higher* contribution rates for the earliest workers (since they will pay in for only part of their adult lives) and in return grant them full benefits upon retirement. This start-up procedure has been commonly used by private pension plans.

Despite Social Security's underlying pay-as-you-go structure, however, the original intention was that the system should eventually build up a sizable interest-earning trust fund. According to the 1935 plan, the OASI trust fund was supposed to run continual surpluses and grow to some $47 billion by 1980. Projected as a share of GNP, $47 billion in 1935 would be equivalent to $1.7 trillion in 1980. With this trust-fund surplus, it was anticipated that by 1980 the system would be able to pay benefits equivalent to 9 percent of all covered workers' taxable payroll, while receiving income from an "ultimate" tax rate that amounted to only 6 percent of taxable payroll.* In other words, about one-third of all benefits by 1980 were to be paid for simply by interest on the trust fund. The contrast between intention and outcome is startling. Already by the 1970s (as is apparent in Table 7-1), Social Security had arrived at pay-as you-go financing in its purest form, and its trust funds now functioned as nothing more than temporary repositories for tax income destined for current benefit outlays.

The reasons why Social Security failed to amass a significant trust fund during its early decades are to be found in the inevitable politics of pay-as-you-go benefit plans. Congress slowed the fund's growth repeatedly by enacting expansions in near-term benefits, while at the same time postponing the scheduled hikes in payroll taxes to their "ultimate" levels. (In 1949, for instance, the tax rate was still stuck at 2 percent.) On countless occasions throughout the 1950s and 1960s, Congress attempted to reestablish a significant, interest-earning trust fund by rescheduling steep future increases in tax rates. But it subsequently foiled each of those attempts by enacting new benefit hikes and postponing the scheduled tax increases.

The next milestone in the history of Social Security was reached in 1950, when the original OASI system of retirement and survivor benefits was expanded and revised in several important ways. In the first place, the legislation enacted in 1950 went a long way toward

---

*This original plan to partially "fund" OASI benefits involved none of the budgetary "double counting" (see Chapter 2) that mocks our post-1983 effort once again to build up a sizable trust fund. The reason is that surpluses were then kept entirely separate from all other federal operations; they did not "neutralize" deficits elsewhere in the budget. As early as the recession of 1937, however, policymakers came to fear that large surpluses would be a drag on our economy. This fixation on stimulating aggregate demand later helped persuade the Johnson administration to abandon separate trust-fund accounting and adopt a "consolidated budget" in 1969—a move that also masked growing war deficits. Just three years later, in 1972, popular Keynesianism also helped justify the decision to fund Social Security on a purely pay-as-you-go basis. In theory, the 1983 act has returned us to partial funding, but with our large consolidated budget deficits, such "funding" is of course illusory.

TABLE 7-1	Trust-Fund Assets as a Percent of Yearly Outlays	
Year	OASI	OASDHI[1]
1940	2,781%	2,781%
1950	1,156	1,156
1960	180	186
1970	101	96
1980	23	30
1986	31	41

[1]DI (Disability Insurance) is added for 1960 and after; HI (Hospital Insurance) is added for 1970 and after.

Source: Annual Statistical Supplements, *Social Security Bulletin* (SSA)

making OASI a universal social program by extending coverage to many groups of workers who had originally been excluded from it. Indeed, by the end of the 1950s (after the belated inclusion of a few remaining categories, such as self-employed persons) the share of all workers covered had jumped from an original 65 percent in 1935 to nearly 90 percent—about where it remains today. The only large group still excluded from the system was made up of public-sector workers, namely, all federal employees and many state and local employees.*

The 1950 act also introduced a new benefit formula that once and for all severed the link between benefits received and total lifetime taxes paid. Monthly benefits for retired workers or their survivors were now to be determined solely on the basis of the Average Monthly Wage of the covered worker before retirement (AMW), regardless of how long he had been paying taxes.† Furthermore, in order to make benefits immediately available to those newly covered by the 1950 act, practically all workers—even workers who had been covered for less than a year—were made eligible for full benefits under the new formula. The combined effect of these provisions sharply

---

*Under the 1983 act (see below), all federal workers hired on or after January 1, 1984 are covered by Social Security.

†The 1939 act had still provided for a benefit increment of one percent of AMW for each year of covered employment in which a worker had earned more than a minimal wage.

271

increased Social Security's near-term costs. The notion that full benefit levels should await even a partial "maturation" of the system had been abandoned altogether.

Finally, the 1950 act legislated an ad hoc increase of about 77 percent in the dollar value of benefits to both current and new recipients. This was the first in what was to become a long congressional tradition of "across-the-board" benefit hikes. Indeed, the 1950 benefit hike was soon followed by a second hike in 1952 (12.5 percent) and a third hike in 1954 (13 percent). It should be noted, however, that these 1950s benefit hikes did not raise the long-term cost of Social Security as a percent of payroll beyond the original projections. Most of the increase simply compensated beneficiaries for the rapid rise that had occurred in the national price level since the early 1940s. More important, the increase in the dollar cost of Social Security benefits was nearly matched by an increase in the dollar value of wages, and hence in OASI payroll-tax income.

Nevertheless, the benefit hikes of the 1950s did have a crucial indirect effect on benefit costs by encouraging many more eligible elderly workers to cash in their OASI "insurance" by retiring. Retirement had been made more attractive both by the sudden rise in the monthly benefit level and by the important precedent that it seemed Congress had established: future Social Security benefits would always be raised as least as fast as inflation. It is hardly a coincidence that the long-term trend toward earlier retirement we examined in Chapter 4 accelerated so rapidly during the early 1950s. Between 1930 and 1950, the share of all elderly men who were employed had only decreased from about 48 percent to 46 percent, whereas between 1950 and 1960 it fell off dramatically to 33 percent (and today stands at a mere 16 percent). At the same time, the percentage increase in the numbers of elderly persons actually receiving retirement benefits was even more impressive. In 1945 only 30 percent of all eligible elderly persons were receiving benefits (most of them still chose not to retire); by 1955 this share had risen to over 70 percent. Today it hovers around 93 percent.

It is difficult to overestimate the full economic and social consequences of the legislation of the early 1950s. In terms of sheer size, whether we measure it in dollars or beneficiaries, the Social Security system mushroomed. During the six years between 1949 and 1955, the average retired-worker benefit rose from $26 to $62 per month; the number of families receiving benefits climbed from 1.7 million to

5.5 million; and the total cost of the system grew more than seven-fold, from $721 million to $5.1 billion. Social Security had come of age. Its coverage had become practically universal; its tax rate, now set at 4 percent, had doubled; and its benefits, largely protected against inflation by ad hoc benefit hikes, were pouring out to millions of new retirees, many of whom had contributed virtually no payroll taxes to the system during the course of their working lives. Within the span of a few short years, Social Security had grown into the world's largest social welfare program. In the process it had also become a fundamental American institution.

Such vast changes in Social Security's benefit structure of course required Congress to make some commensurate adjustment in the program's financing. As far as the 1950 act was concerned, the main problem was how to afford the near-term cost of paying full benefits to the armies of new retirees who had hardly contributed any payroll taxes to the system. Congress' solution was to start raising the current payroll-tax rate, while at the same time curtailing the surplus of tax income over benefit expenditures. Smaller tax surpluses, of course, meant a relatively smaller future trust fund. And since Congress remained reluctant to schedule much of an increase in OASI's "ultimate" tax rate, merely nudging it up from the original 6.0 percent to 6.5 percent, a smaller future trust fund also spelled relatively lower benefit levels for workers retiring in future years.

Congress responded to this problem in the same way it had in 1939: once again significant reductions were made in the benefit levels of workers with a greater number of years of covered employment in order to give favorable treatment to workers who had just been brought into the system. This was done by establishing a single target "replacement ratio"—the ratio of a worker's initial monthly benefit level to his monthly wage immediately before retirement—in place of the original variable ratios of the 1935 and 1939 acts. Whereas previously the replacement ratio for workers earning average wages had ranged from about 29 percent to 40 percent, depending on the length of their covered-wage histories, now that replacement ratio was fixed at about 30 to 33 percent regardless of prior taxes paid. The fact that in 1950 no worker had as yet earned more than thirteen years of covered wages certainly helped to make this maneuver politically feasible. Yet once again, Congress had managed to purchase near-term benefits by incurring additional long-term costs.

Who were the real winners and losers in the watershed legislation of the early 1950s? It is easy to identify the winners. They were the workers near the age of sixty-five in 1950, who, after making only a few payments, retired shortly thereafter with full benefits. But what about the losers? What about the workers who had begun covered employment in 1937 at the age of twenty and had planned to retire around 1980? According to the 1939 act, they could expect a combined employee-employer payroll tax no higher than 6 percent throughout their careers, and then retire (if they were average wage earners) with initial benefits pegged at 40 percent of their wage level. During the early 1950s, however, Congress enacted new laws that raised the "ultimate" tax rate and established the eventual benefit level of these workers at considerably less than 40 percent of their wages.

This situation was not unlike the windfall phenomenon that had favored retirees in the early 1940s—with one important difference. For the first time, the rules of the game had been changed in midstream to the detriment of an entire generation of Social Security beneficiaries. The 1950 act had raised the combined "ultimate" payroll tax to 6.5 percent; the 1954 act raised that rate again to 8.0 percent; and the 1965 act pushed it up still further to 9.0 percent—all to maintain the new lower replacement ratios that had been introduced at the beginning of the decade. Each age-group was being short- changed in comparison with the age-group that had preceded it. Either by cutting future benefit levels or by raising and then postponing "ultimate" tax rates, Congress was perpetuating a cascading pattern of inequity between generations. Under such circumstances, one might have expected a political reaction from younger, tax-paying workers against older, newly covered workers and current retirees. What was perhaps most distinctive about Social Security's age-group losers, however, was that no such protest ever arose.

One reason for the almost absolute silence on this generational issue was simple political arithmetic. So long as both the labor force and worker coverage were growing rapidly, the number of younger "losers" was vastly greater than the number of older "winners." This meant that benefit losses in the distant future were spread out among many people, few of whom gave much thought to the matter, whereas benefit gains in the near future were concentrated among a few, each of whom cared a great deal about whether those gains were forthcoming. Indeed, it is this cohesiveness of the elderly as a political constituency—coupled with their high voter-participation rates—that has largely shaped the present structure of our Social Security system.

It is of course understandable that neither Congress nor the Social Security Administration was eager to raise generational issues. After all, the last thing they wished to do was fragment the broad public consensus on which the future of the system rested. But strangely, even outside experts—from whom we might have expected a dispassionate critique—defended the system. Perhaps the most influential argument was made by the economist Paul A. Samuelson in a seminal 1958 article.* Samuelson argued that the generational equity issue was in effect based on a misunderstanding of how Social Security worked. While some workers might receive a better deal than others, he maintained, all covered workers, even in the distant future, would be "winners" in the sense that they would do better by participating in Social Security than in any comparable private system. This would happen because the taxable wages of all covered workers per retired beneficiary tended to grow faster than the rate of interest. Thus, even if the tax rate remained forever constant, average workers would get a better return on their money if they invested it in payroll taxes rather than in their own interest-earning accounts.

In February 1967, Samuelson summarized his influential ideas in a popular news magazine:

> The beauty about social insurance is that it is *actuarially* unsound. Everyone who reaches retirement age is given benefit privileges that far exceed anything he has paid in. And exceed his payments by more than ten times as much (or five times, counting in employer payments)!
>
> How is this possible? It stems from the fact that the national product is growing at compound interest and can be expected to do so for as far ahead as the eye cannot see. Always there are more youths than old folks in a growing population. More important, with real incomes growing at some 3 percent per year, the taxable base upon which benefits rest in any period are [*sic*] much greater than the taxes paid historically by the generation now retired. . . .
>
> Social Security is squarely based on what has been called the eighth wonder of the world—compound interest. A growing nation is the greatest Ponzi game ever contrived. And that is a fact, not a paradox.†

Of course we know today that the conditions on which this "greatest Ponzi game" depended—rapid population and productivity growth "as far as the eye cannot see"—may not be witnessed again

---

*"An Exact Consumption-Loan Model of Interest with or without the Social Contrivance of Money," *Journal of Political Economy* (December 1958).

†*Newsweek* (February 13, 1967).

FIGURE 7-4   **Annual Real Rate of Return on OASI Social Security Contributions by Generation and Income Level**

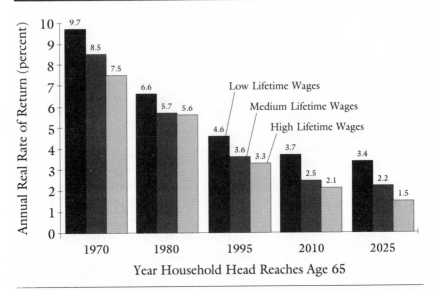

All figures are for married couples with a nonworking spouse. The real rate of return is the interest rate (above inflation) a couple would have to "earn" on its OASI payroll taxes (employer and employee combined) in order for its lifetime taxes to pay exactly for its lifetime OASI benefits.
Source: Michael J. Boskin, *Too Many Promises: The Uncertain Future of Social Security* (Dow-Jones Irwin, 1986)

within the lifetime of any living American. It is already doubtful that most young workers today can expect to receive *anything* more in Social Security benefits than the value of their contributions—even if there are no changes in scheduled tax rates or benefit provisions for the next seventy-five years (see Figure 7-4*). More probably, as we

*The conclusion that succeeding generations are getting (and will continue to get) a sharply declining rate of benefit return on their payroll-tax contributions has been reached by virtually every economist who has examined Social Security. The figures shown in Figure 7-4 are typical—and are consistent with the huge "windfall" results we explained in Chapter 2. Whether or not younger generations are currently slated to get a lower payback rate than they could obtain privately, on the other hand, is open to interpretation. The 8.5 percent real yearly payback rate shown in Figure 7-4 for the couple retiring in 1970 is indeed (as Samuelson suggests) wildly better than anything it could expect in the private sector. But what about the 2.2 percent rate shown for the couple retiring in 2025? The answer is unclear, especially since this one-earner married couple enjoys the very best payback rate its generation can obtain. We could, for example, compare it with the annual real interest rate on OASDI Treasury bonds since 1972: 2.7 percent.

have already seen, looming insolvency will not allow us to enjoy such a carefree future. Instead, we will sooner or later be forced to make substantial cuts in the system's future rate of return (through benefit cuts or tax hikes). And when that happens, today's youth will finally know for certain that they will not only be "losers" compared with the previous generation of Social Security beneficiaries, but will receive far less in benefits than they might have earned by investing their payroll taxes in the private sector.

However mistaken as a forecast, Samuelson's "everyone a winner" argument set the tone for the further rapid expansion of the Social Security system during the rest of the 1950s and 1960s. In 1956 Disability Insurance (DI) was added to Social Security, thus changing the system's acronym to OASDI. And in 1965, the last major addition to Social Security was made in the form of Medicare. (As we noted in Chapter 2, Hospital Insurance [HI], or Medicare "Part A," is usually considered an integral part of Social Security, thus yielding the acronym OASDHI to refer to all the payroll-tax-based components of the system.) Medicare is its own separate subject, and is discussed at length in Chapter 9; here we will limit ourselves to a few words about Disability Insurance.

The new DI program simply provided for the extension of Social Security benefits to workers who become incapacitated due to injury or disease. Under the terms of DI, a disability must be both "medically determinable" and entail "the inability to engage in any gainful activity." In addition to the disabled person's habitual work, "gainful activity" is defined to include "any other kind of substantial gainful work which exists in the national economy." In the original act, DI benefits were limited to workers aged fifty and over; but this restriction was removed by Congress in 1960 under the presumption that the program's long-term cost would be negligible.

In truth, however, these early projections were gross underestimates. Once again—as with early retirement—the program's designers did not figure on later, more liberal eligibility standards. Nor did they figure on "offsetting behavior": the tendency of any new insurance to modify attitudes and incentives in such a way that awards become more frequent over time. The SSA actuaries originally anticipated that by 1980 there would be 1.0 million beneficiaries receiving $860 million in DI benefits. In reality, by 1980 there were 4.8 million beneficiaries receiving $15 billion in benefits. DI was designed to be financed at an "ultimate" tax rate of 0.5 percent of payroll, but the program in 1986 already cost 1.1 percent of taxable payroll and may well exceed 2.0 percent twenty years from now.

The Great Benefit Explosion (1967–1972)

During the *thirteen* years between 1952 and 1965, a series of across-the-board hikes increased benefit levels for Social Security recipients by a cumulative 45.6 percent—an amount roughly sufficient to stabilize current benefits relative to prices and new benefit awards relative to wages. In contrast, during the *five* years between 1967 and 1972, across-the-board legislation pushed up benefit levels by a much steeper 71.5 percent. For the first time in Social Security's history, Congress engineered a major and explicit increase in benefit levels in terms of both real dollars and prevailing wage levels. Moreover, it was persuaded to guarantee the inviolability of these higher benefit levels. Starting in 1975, an automatic "indexing" mechanism was to go into effect that would grant yearly cost-of-living adjustments across-the-board in accordance with subsequent rises in the Consumer Price Index.

All four benefit hikes legislated by Congress between 1967 and 1972 were traditional across-the-board measures in the sense that they raised the level of current benefits and new awards by the same percentage. What was highly unusual about them was rather the magnitude of the benefit increases: 13 percent in 1967; 15 percent in 1969; 10 percent in 1970; and fully 20 percent in 1972. Table 7-2 summarizes the cumulative effects of these hikes on the value of Social Security benefits relative to prevailing prices and wages.

Before the first of these hikes in 1967, the average retired-worker benefit (at $85.36 per month) had been equivalent to 22.3 percent of the average covered wage. By the end of 1972 (at $162.35 per month), it was equivalent to 31.5 percent of the average covered wage—a rise of 41.8 percent relative to wages. Replacement ratios for the average-earning worker, which had previously been expected (since the early 1950s) to remain stable at about 32 percent, had reached 40 percent by 1973. Total OASDI expenditures inevitably surged. From $22.5 billion, or less than 14 percent of all federal spending in 1967, they reached $53.1 billion, or more than 20 percent of spending in 1973. Social Security had suddenly become a juggernaut whose expenditures outpaced those of every other major federal program. And the generation soon to retire—which might have been slighted by earlier changes in the rules of the game (in 1939

278

TABLE 7-2   Cumulative Percentage Increase in
OASDI Benefits, 1967–72

Average Actual Benefit as a Percent of Hypothetical Benefit Indexed...		to Annual Average Price Level[1] (since 1967)		to Annual Average Wage Level (since 1967)	
Legislation	Effective Date	Current Benefits	New Awards	Current Benefits	New Awards
1967 Act	Feb. 1968	108.7%	111.4%	106.2%	108.9%
1969 Act	Jan. 1970	114.4	121.7	109.1	116.1
1970 Act	Jan. 1971	120.6	130.6	114.4	116.1
1972 Act	Sept. 1972	139.6	154.8	127.9	141.8

[1]As measured by the quarterly PCE deflator.

Source: BEA (Commerce) and Annual Statistical Supplements, *Social Security Bulletin* (SSA)

and in the early 1950s)—discovered to their satisfaction that they could recoup much of their lost windfall. But of course they could only do so on the backs of still younger and future generational losers.

Why were these benefit hikes granted? It is hard to say. Since they had the outward look and feel of routine "ad hoc" adjustments, no one responsible for enacting them wanted to draw much attention to the fundamental change they represented.* Perhaps the most important motivating force behind the hikes was simply the mood of the times. Unparalleled prosperity had given rise to a powerful urge to redirect resources toward new social goals. During the Great Society years, new programs and vast initiatives—some stillborn and others ultimately enacted—rose up in spectacular variety: Model Cities, Volunteers in Service to America (VISTA), Food Stamps, the Negative Income Tax, Family Assistance, Community Action, and the Comprehensive Employment and Training Act (CETA), to name some of the more memorable. What could be more natural than to plan for a

---

*As with double indexing, it is surprisingly difficult to find—either in the SSA or in Congress— any explicit consensus on the intention: How much of the hikes was supposed to represent a COLA, and how much was an increase relative to wages? How much was supposed to be permanent, and how much temporary? Even Robert Myers, SSA chief actuary from 1947 to 1970, was unsure. Congress treated them no differently than earlier ad hoc hikes, he wrote later, but considering their magnitude "one can well ask whether the floor-of-protection concept has been abandoned in favor of having OASDI be a virtually complete national retirement system." (*Social Security* by Robert J. Myers, 2nd ed.; McCahan Foundation, 1981.)

large expansion in one of our oldest and most popular benefit programs, Social Security? Moreover, since Samuelson's "everyone a winner" argument still prevailed, no matter what the benefit increases might cost, all covered workers could be assured that they too would come out ahead in the long run.

Election politics were another major factor in encouraging the explosion in Social Security benefits between 1967 and 1972. In this feverishly optimistic climate, the uncontroversial tradition of ad hoc benefit hikes provided temptations that no successful politician could afford to ignore. Take 1967, for example, when President Johnson, preoccupied with the upcoming elections, was approached by Secretary of Health, Education and Welfare Wilbur Cohen with a proposal for a 10 percent across-the-board hike. Johnson's reaction (as Cohen later reported) was a direct, "Come on, Wilbur, you can do better than that." Or again, take 1972, when President Nixon (then seeking reelection) and various congressional leaders, including Congressman Wilbur Mills and Senator George McGovern (both presidential aspirants), all but fell over one another in their efforts to claim credit for ever-larger benefit increases. From Nixon's original 5 percent proposal, the benefit hike reached 20 percent before Congress finally approved it—whereupon, not to be outdone, Nixon not only signed the legislation amid media fanfare, but proposed to send out personal notices with all the benefit checks. The mailing date, naturally, was scheduled to fall just before the 1972 election. The Democratic Congress, furious that it was no longer in the limelight, swiftly passed a resolution barring such notices.

A final factor in the great benefit expansion of the late 1960s and early 1970s is to be found in the policy agenda of the Social Security Administration itself. Executives and policymakers at the SSA, far from being detached and neutral administrators of Social Security, had for decades worked hard to provide their congressional allies with arguments and research that would support expansion of the system. During the early 1950s, they had been busy setting up Disability Insurance; during the late 1950s and early 1960s, their attention had been directed toward establishing Medicare. But by 1967, after Medicare had been enacted, a mood of "what's next?" is reported to have arisen within SSA.* The answer soon became obvious: higher

*To be sure, there was disagreement within the SSA. But from the mid-1960s on, especially after citizen advisory councils began to report directly to Congress, the expansionists had the upper hand. Wilbur Cohen, Secretary of HEW (1968–69), freely admitted that most SSA staff did not regard Social Security as a completed system, but rather (to use his curious phrase) "were strong

cash benefit levels. In presenting its arguments to Congress, the SSA took care to emphasize the effect that higher benefit levels would have on alleviating the poverty rate among the elderly—a rate that during the late 1960s was still higher than that for the population as a whole. Congress was of course accustomed to thinking of Social Security in these terms, and had repeatedly affirmed that the primary purpose of the system was to serve as a "floor of protection" for the destitute elderly.

If the purpose of higher benefit levels was to alleviate poverty, however, many critics outside the SSA wondered why this should require across-the-board increases to all recipients. Perhaps, they suggested, a more progressive benefit structure or an increase in funds spent on specific poverty programs would prove more equitable as well as more economical. But the SSA executives feared that a more progressive benefit structure might weaken middle- and upper-class support for Social Security. In short, poverty relief would have to be bought by concealing it within a massive subsidy to all income brackets. In any event, though the across-the-board hikes of 1967 through 1972 were expensive by any standard, they were ludicrously expensive as an antipoverty measure. The 20 percent increase in 1972 alone, for instance, raised cash benefit outlays by some $8 billion per year. To put this figure into perspective, consider that total federal outlays on poverty relief *for all age-groups* in fiscal year 1973— including all cash benefits and all nonmedical benefits in kind, from food to housing—amounted to less than $15 billion.

As for federal cash benefits specifically targeted at the elderly poor, they were now utterly dwarfed by the entire Social Security program. As recently as 1949, Old Age Assistance—a means-tested welfare program—had outspent Social Security. By fiscal year 1973, Old Age Assistance was allotted a mere $1.1 billion compared with Social Security's $57.8 billion. The hikes of the late 1960s and early 1970s no doubt helped to alleviate poverty in America by dint of the sheer amount of money spent. But it is obvious that the primary effect of the hikes was to transfer income from one generation to another within the ranks of the nonpoor.

believers in the inevitableness of gradualism." As Robert Myers has described it, many on the staff believed in expansion "with almost a religious zeal." Yet he notes, in agreement with Cohen, that "the expansionists, as a matter of strategy, use the 'ratchet approach.' They do not unveil their ultimate goals in their entirety, but advocate only a part . . . . Usually, the ink is scarcely dry on a newly enacted amendment before plans are being developed for the next legislative effort." (Both citations are from *Policymaking for Social Security* by Martha Derthick; Brookings Institution, 1979.)

And what about their affordability? An essential part of the story behind the benefit hikes of 1967 to 1972 is how surprisingly little they seemed to cost at the time. While the value of the average retired-worker benefit relative to the average wage level rose by 41.8 percent over those five years, the OASI tax rate on covered workers increased from 7.1 percent to 8.1 percent of taxable payroll, or only 14.1 percent. Still more surprising, in light of the expected growth in benefit levels, is that the future scheduled tax rate from 1973 until 2011 was actually set at a lower level under the 1972 act than it had been under the 1965 act. The 1965 act had provided that the OASI tax rate should reach an "ultimate" level of 9.0 percent in 1973, whereas the 1972 act planned to set that rate at a lower 8.45 percent in 1973 and not raise it again until 2011 (when it would reach an "ultimate" level of 10.2 percent).

Opponents of these acts argued in vain that the public must inevitably pay a price commensurate with the magnitude of such benefit increases. Perhaps typical was the protest of Congressman John W. Byrnes over the 1972 benefit hike: "The American people will not be fooled. If we are going to pay out 20 percent more in benefit dollars, someone will have to pay 20 percent more in tax dollars than they would otherwise have to pay. It is that simple." All that advocates of the benefit hikes needed to do to refute this commonsense argument, however, was to point to the projections that had been hurriedly prepared for them by the SSA actuaries. According to these projections, the Social Security system would still be in long-term actuarial balance even though benefit levels had been raised and near-term tax rates lowered.

There were several ways in which the apparent cost of these benefit hikes was kept so low. For the first three acts, Congress balanced the books partly by increasing the share of covered wages that was taxable and partly by offsetting outlays against the actuarial surplus that had been projected before 1968. It was the 1972 act, however, that presented the real challenge. Here Congress was able to combine its largest percentage increase in benefit levels—plus an automatic index-ing provision—with a significant reduction in the near-term tax rate. One factor that helped to make this 1972 act feasible was the decision to change OASI's method of financing from the "partial-reserve" system, which had been assumed in every previous act since 1950, to an entirely pay-as-you-go procedure. As a result, the effective date of the "ultimate" tax rate could be pushed many years further into the future—though the tax itself would have to be set at a higher level.

A more important reason for the seeming affordability of the 1972 act, however, was the decision to switch from the traditional "static" method of projecting future costs to a new "dynamic" method. All actuarial projections before 1972 had made rigidly zero-growth assumptions about future economic behavior. In 1972 policymakers for the first time decided to incorporate their economic optimism directly into the official SSA projections. Although everyone was aware, for instance, that the automatic indexing provision would increase the system's future costs, the official assumption was that wages would rise considerably faster than prices—and thus more than compensate for this effect. The consequences of the 1972 switch from "static" to "dynamic" projections were dramatic; at a single stroke, the future seventy-five-year cost of OASI seemed to have been reduced by between 1 and 2 percent of taxable payroll.

Deficits and Rescue Missions (1972–1983)

The 1972 act marked the high tide of Social Security's confident expansion. In retrospect, it is striking how little serious debate accompanied the passage of an act that introduced such sweeping changes into our Social Security system—and in particular, how little controversy arose over the cost-of-living adjustment (COLA) provision, which with broad bipartisan support was rushed through Congress in a matter of days. But even this unprecedented generosity had not exhausted the limits of congressional largess. In addition to the 20 percent across-the-board benefit hike and automatic indexing provision enacted in July 1972, Congress approved a basketful of further benefit liberalizations in September—including Medicare for disabled persons, higher percentages of "primary insurance amounts" (PIAs) for various dependents, and a more lenient earnings test for retirees.

The euphoria was short-lived. Hardly was the ink dry on the September legislation than the Social Security trustees issued a new annual report the following April that raised future cost estimates and concluded that the system's long-term actuarial balance was considerably less sound than had been projected the previous year. Until the end of 1977, the trustees' annual projections of the long-term deficit grew by leaps and bounds. And beginning in 1975, the SSA annual report also began to show a near-term deficit that threatened to exhaust the system's trust funds by the early 1980s.

For the first time in Social Security's history, reports of "bankruptcy" and "runaway deficits" started appearing in the newspapers. Official advisory councils and congressional study groups were appointed to examine the problem, and academics at universities and foundations developed a variety of econometric models forecasting Social Security's uncertain future. Legislators were stunned by how quickly their handiwork was falling to pieces. Fifteen years later, Richard Nixon, who had supported the automatic indexing provision, identified his decision as his gravest fiscal mistake as president.

Part of the reason for the rapid deterioration in Social Security's cost projections lay in a more realistic interpretation of fundamental demographic trends. The final analysis of data from the 1970 Census simply confirmed what most demographers had already suspected: the U.S. fertility rate was falling dramatically. The result was a sharp rise in projected long-term Social Security costs per future worker. But by far the most important factor contributing to the sudden turnabout in SSA cost projections was the overoptimism of the new "dynamic" economic assumptions hammered out in 1972. During 1973 and 1974, U.S. inflation surged to levels that no one had previously thought possible; and by the end of 1974, as the economy slid into its worst recession in decades, the experts were further confounded by the emergence of stagflation. When Social Security's actuaries began to revise their projections to take into account higher long-term rates of inflation and lower long-term rates of real wage growth, they found that the cost of the program rose to astronomical heights.

In the previous chapter, we noted the effects of stagflation on the new system of automatic indexing. Here it is enough to remember that a flaw in the raw mechanics of benefit computation known as "double" indexing had the unintended effect of sharply increasing the level of new benefit awards relative to wages. From 1973 to 1977, when reform legislation finally eliminated this quirk in the system, official forecasts revealed that average benefit levels would continue to rise relative to wage levels virtually without limit during the decades to come.

Had anyone foreseen the consequences of the 1972 act before it was passed? In fact, Social Security's actuaries had foreseen them as a theoretical possibility, but this possibility was widely dismissed at the time as improbable. What this shortsightedness meant, of course, was that by the time Congress braced itself to grapple with reform

TABLE 7-3 **OASDI 75-Year Average:**
Cost and Revenue Projections as a Percent
of Taxable Payroll, 1972–77

Date of Actuarial Estimate	OASI		DI		OASDI Balance
	Benefit Cost	Tax Revenue	Benefit Cost	Tax Revenue	
Dec. 1972	9.32%	9.31%	1.31%	1.32%	0.00%
Apr. 1973	9.81	9.38	1.58	1.50	−0.51
Apr. 1974	11.97	9.39	1.92	1.52	−2.98
Apr. 1975	13.29	9.41	2.97	1.53	−5.32
Apr. 1976	15.42	9.43	3.51	1.54	−7.96
Apr. 1977	15.51	9.45	3.68	1.54	−8.20

Source: OASDI Annual Reports, 1973–77

legislation in 1977, the long-term cost projections facing Social Security seemed hopeless. In the past, Congress had often tried to wiggle out of tight spots on the expenditure side by arranging more income on the revenue side in a way that did not entail raising the tax rate. But since Congress had no longer been planning for major trust-fund surpluses in future years, it could no longer sidestep higher near-term costs by sacrificing those long-term surpluses. The OASDI trust funds were facing disaster, and there seemed to be embarrassingly little that Congress could do about it. Table 7-3 shows the rapid deterioration in Social Security's long-term actuarial outlook during the course of the 1970s.

Closing the long-term deficits in OASDI by raising the tax rate alone—which would have required an immediate hike equivalent to more than 8 percent of taxable payroll—was politically (and economically) out of the question. The perceived balance between the expansion and affordability of benefits thus shifted decisively. Between 1967 and 1972, Congress had raised the Social Security benefit level on terms that seemed entirely affordable. Yet by 1977, that new benefit level, which each year was forced inexorably upward by the

---

TABLE 7-4   **Projected Effect of the 1977 Reforms on the 75-Year OASDI Actuarial Balance as a Percent of Taxable Payroll**

OASDI Actuarial Balance before 1977 Act	−8.20%
Effect of "Decoupling" PIA Formula[1]	+4.85
Effect of Higher Tax Rates	+1.24
Effect of Increase in Taxable Maximum	+0.53
Effect of Other Provisions	+0.12
OASDI Actuarial Balance after 1977 Act	−1.46%

[1]PIA stands for "Primary Insurance Amount."

Source: Michael J. Boskin, *Too Many Promises: The Uncertain Future of Social Security* (Dow-Jones Irwin, 1986)

---

double indexing formula, no longer seemed to be affordable at all. The stage had been set for the passage of the 1977 rescue legislation.

The first order of business was to end the nightmare of double indexing. To achieve this, the 1977 act, though it did preserve the full CPI indexing of current benefits, "decoupled" that indexing from the PIA formulas used to compute the benefit levels of new retirees. Henceforth the Average Monthly Wage, or AMW (which had been expressed in terms of unadjusted dollars), would be replaced by another measure of a worker's wage history: the Average Indexed Monthly Earnings, or AIME. Since past wages were now to be expressed in terms of current wages through a process called "wage indexing," the AIME of the average-earning worker would always be equal to the current average wage—which in turn meant that new benefit awards would remain stable relative to wages.*

But since the "decoupling" reform eliminated only somewhat more than half of the long-term deficit projected in 1977, Congress had no choice but to resort to further tax hikes. The "ultimate" combined tax rate for OASDI was increased from 11.9 percent to 12.4 percent of taxable payroll, and the effective date of the tax was

---

*More precisely, the stability of the *replacement ratio* for the average-earning worker was (and still is) assured by the 1977 act, since the "bend points" of the post-1977 PIA formula are indexed to average wages just as is every worker's AIME. Each passing year, therefore, the rise (inflationary or real) in awarded monthly benefits to all new beneficiaries with average-wage histories will be identical with the rise in the previous year's average wages. It was an obvious and simple solution.

rescheduled from 2011 to 1990. In addition, Congress approved yet another expansion of the taxable wage base, which was now widened from 85 percent to 90 percent of all covered workers' wages.* The effect of these various provisions on the long-term deficit for OASDI is summarized in Table 7-4.

As is readily apparent from the table, the 1977 act failed to close OASDI's long-term actuarial deficit. What is more shocking, however, is that it failed even to solve Social Security's near-term financial crisis. Average new benefit awards continued to rise steadily between 1977 and 1981, largely because Congress delayed the final introduction of the AIME method of wage indexing. At the same time, COLAs for current retirees remained pegged at 100 percent of the CPI, a measure of inflation that continued to give benefit levels a strong upward bias. In 1980 the SSA's annual report announced that by 1983 at the latest, Social Security would once more be facing bankruptcy.

When the Reagan administration moved into the White House in February 1981, the grim specter of Social Security's impending crisis was suddenly eclipsed by yet more urgent agendas. The new leaders arriving in Washington—elated by their landslide electoral victory, but also fearing an "economic Dunkirk"† in the face of soaring inflation and interest rates—looked eagerly for quick victories that would calm the markets and rally the public behind their "supply-side" manifesto. There was much (perhaps too much) to be done in the first few months: tax cuts to be passed, deregulation to be enacted, a defense buildup to plan, "welfare fraud" to be eliminated, and more. For the most part, the Reagan initiatives were moving well by early spring, when someone evidently remembered that something still had to be done about Social Security. The work of a Reagan transition advisory team (which had been studying Social Security reform since the previous November) was quickly finished, and on May 12 the re-

---

*Despite the higher taxes, the higher stable replacement ratios, and the full grandfathering of windfall benefit levels to anyone then over age sixty (no matter how long he or she waits to retire), many senior advocates in the Carter administration complained bitterly about the 1977 act. "You are cutting benefits," insisted the President's counselor on aging to Joseph Califano, then Secretary of HEW. "These benefits are earned rights that people have paid for and are entitled to." (*Governing America* by Joseph A. Califano; Simon & Schuster, 1981.)

†The phrase "economic Dunkirk" was coined in a pre-inaugural memo from David Stockman to President Reagan. Several months later, in conversation with William Greider (see "The Education of David Stockman," *The Atlantic Monthly;* December 1981), Stockman quipped: "I'm not going to spend a lot of political capital solving some other guy's problem in [the year] 2010."

sulting reform recommendations were announced by Richard Schweiker, the newly appointed Secretary of the Department of Health and Human Services.

What followed was the first and still perhaps the most stunning political defeat of the eight-year Reagan administration.

In concept there was nothing especially outrageous about the four-part Schweiker proposal: (1) a 25 percent reduction in benefits for "early" retirement before age sixty-five; (2) tighter eligibility rules for disability and "minimum" benefits; (3) a one-time, three-month delay in the COLA adjustment; and (4) permanent reductions in the PIA percentage formula for future retirees. The administration's fundamental misjudgment, however, was to believe that the sharp benefit reductions embodied in the first three reforms could be enacted, in full, by July 1982—which is to say, almost immediately. Even to sympathetic observers, it seemed as if the administration was tailoring a major structural change in Social Security to help close the next year's widening fiscal deficit. Compounding this error, the administration came forward with these far-reaching reforms at the *end* of its initial budgetary agenda, a time when the public was feeling that the "Reagan Revolution" had perhaps done enough for one year, rather than at the *beginning*. Finally, the administration had consulted no one in Congress—not even the leaders in its own party—before announcing the reforms. Apparently it failed to consider that no elected representative would want to be stuck out alone on the wrong side of such a sensitive issue.

All together, these mistakes spelled disaster. In an instant, Washington was swept by a firestorm of irate letters, phone calls, and telegrams, many from Americans in their early sixties planning to retire shortly. Leaders of senior lobbies quickly rallied the protest and fanned the flames with apocalyptic rhetoric. "Old people are being thrown to the sharks," said the head of the National Council on Aging; it is the "biggest frontal attack on Social Security ever launched," said the president of the National Council of Senior Citizens.* Democratic leaders in Congress, seeing at last a chance to regroup under a popular banner, soon joined in the assault. And despite Secretary Schweiker's assurances that the reforms would not reduce current (nonminimum) checks to any beneficiary, before long

---

*These reactions are cited in *Social Security: Visions and Revisions* by W. Andrew Achenbaum (Twentieth Century, 1986).

even Republican leaders were disavowing—in the words of the conservative Senator William Armstrong—"this masterpiece of bad timing." When it reached the Senate floor, the proposal did not receive a single affirmative vote. The aftermath included a predictable White House shakeout that ended in Schweiker's resignation.

After the crash landing of the May 12 reform package, Congress made only a few minor life-preserving changes in the OASDI system that summer and fall. One change authorized Social Security's trust funds (including HI) to begin borrowing from each other if necessary in order to avert bankruptcy.* All of this still left Social Security where the new presidency first found it: facing a firm solvency deadline in July of 1983. As the year drew to a close, the administration decided it had to take action, but resolved to forswear any further political risks. In December, President Reagan announced the formation of a National Commission on Social Security Reform (better known after its chairman, Alan Greenspan, as the "Greenspan Commission"). The President would appoint Greenspan and four others; the House and Senate leaders would each appoint five members as well.† The resulting balance, eight Republicans and seven Democrats, seemed to assure that all points of view would be represented and that a genuine bipartisan consensus could emerge.

Early in 1982 the Greenspan Commission was off and running. Yet throughout the deliberations, its bipartisan composition turned out to be its biggest problem. Not only did the commission members have very different opinions on what should be done with Social Security, but most were political figures who had previously staked out well-defined positions and who did not want to be associated with an unpopular recommendation. The congressional elections of 1982,

---

*Another change—essentially in agreement with the Schweiker proposal—was to eliminate the "minimum" PIA for all workers not yet eligible to receive benefits. The purpose of the original "minimum" in 1935 ($10 per month) was administrative simplicity. Over the years, as it grew along with ad hoc hikes and double indexing (reaching $183 per month for those retiring at age sixty-five in 1981), it came to be defended as an antipoverty measure. By the late 1970s, however, many experts were pointing out that its primary effect, in practice, was to grant windfalls to upper-income civil service retirees (see Chapter 8).

†Nine were prominent current or former members of Congress: Senators William Armstrong, Bob Dole, John Heinz, and Representatives Bill Archer and Barber Conable (for the Republicans); and Senator Daniel Moynihan and Representatives Martha Keys, Claude Pepper, and Joe Waggoner (for the Democrats). Standing in for business were Robert Beck, chairman of Prudential, and Alexander Trowbridge, president of the National Association of Manufacturers; standing in for labor was Lane Kirkland, president of the AFL-CIO. The expert commission members were Mary Fuller, former SSA commissioner Robert Ball, and former SSA chief actuary Robert Myers.

moreover, reopened partisan wounds that had hardly healed since the Schweiker affair. The Republican National Committee (doing a retake of President Nixon in 1972) produced a television commercial showing a postman delivering a check. "This year's 7.4 percent cost-of-living increase," said the postman, "was signed and delivered by the President." The Democrats' counterattack was a bumper sticker that read: "Save Social Security—Vote Democratic."

By December 31, 1982, the end of the commission's scheduled life span, the members were still deadlocked, though all were quite aware that time was running out for the OASDI trust funds. After a thirty-day extension was requested and received, the members renewed their efforts with the help of congressional and administration leaders—each wanting to make sure that the others would go along before committing himself publicly. Finally, on January 15, a commission vote of 15 to 3 on a package of revenue-raising and benefit-trimming proposals sealed the near-consensus outcome that everyone was looking for. These were the proposals that, with some modifications, were eventually incorporated into the "rescue" legislation signed by President Reagan on that blustery Wednesday in April 1983.

In one respect, the rescue package that grew out of the Greenspan Commission's proposals was an unqualified success: it effectively averted the OASDI trust funds' near-term bankruptcy. Unlike the ill-fated 1977 act, it is very likely that the 1983 act has assured the solvency of OASDI beyond the next one or two recessions. In other respects, however, its success was mixed at best. It failed (as we will see shortly) to balance OASDI over the near term without deepening the system's generational inequity—a tradition that has now run through nearly every Social Security amendment since the 1939 act. More seriously, though its later-retirement and benefit-taxation provisions are important steps in right direction, the package as whole falls far short of resolving the system's long-term deficit. This is especially true when this deficit is viewed in the context of prudent assumptions and of complementary deficits in sister programs (such as Medicare) serving the same beneficiaries. Since HI was deliberately excluded from the commission's deliberations (although its long-term deficit was, even then, larger than that of OASDI), it would not be unfair to surmise that achieving long-term solvency was not the real purpose of the Greenspan Commission. The long-term agenda for Social Security, in short, still awaits consensus, leadership, and action.

Before discussing this Social Security reform agenda in the concluding section of the chapter, a review of the main provisions of the 1983 act will provide a useful frame of reference.

Revenue Increases. In addition to rescheduling the effective date of payroll-tax hikes, the 1983 legislation increased Social Security revenues in three ways. (1) The Treasury was instructed to reimburse the OASDHI trust funds with a lump-sum payment of about $23 billion for Social Security retirement credits granted to military servicemen before they became subject to payroll taxes. (2) As much as one-half of OASDI benefits was included in taxable income for beneficiaries with incomes above certain base amounts. (3) The OASDHI tax rates for self-employed persons were raised to equal the level of the combined employee-employer payroll-tax rates.*

Expanded Coverage. Newly hired federal civil service employees and employees of nonprofit organizations, not previously covered by Social Security, were brought into the system. At the same time, state and local government employees lost their option of withdrawing from Social Security. Both measures added substantially to the system's near-term balance, since for any group's "start-up" phase revenue from payroll taxes comes in long before benefits have to be paid out. Early in the next century, however, the savings will diminish to the vanishing point.

Increased Retirement Age. The act determined that the "normal" retirement age (that is, the youngest age at which full benefits can be received) will be increased by two-month increments starting in 2000 until it reaches sixty-six for individuals turning sixty-two in 2005. A similar increase would then commence in the year 2017 and raise the retirement age to sixty-seven for individuals turning sixty-two in 2022 and later. (Congressman "Jake" Pickle, who deserves the credit for breaking the magic inviolability of the number sixty-five, once acknowledged that he picked the year 2022 since it would affect

---

*Breaking an old precedent, provisions (1) and (3) essentially mandate general federal revenue contributions to the OASDHI trust funds. The self-employed do not actually pay the full combined payroll tax (15.02 percent in 1988); 2.00 percent is paid for them (in 1988) by the Treasury.

relatively few voters alive and working today.)*

Cost of Living Adjustments (COLAs). In addition to a six-month postponement of the July 1983 COLA, Congress also provided for a cost-of-living "stabilizer." According to this measure, whenever the OASDI trust-fund reserves have fallen below a certain minimum level at the beginning of the year, the COLA adjustment on current benefits for that year will be based on the increase in workers' average wages if that amount proves to be less than the increase in the Consumer Price Index.†

Several of the measures in the 1983 act, particularly the partial taxation of benefits in upper-income brackets and the eventual increase in the retirement age to sixty-seven, are at least symbolic steps toward genuine, long-term reform. Close examination, however, reveals that they are inadequate steps, and that on the whole the 1983 act perpetuates the same cascading pattern of generational inequity as before. The reason is simple: although current retirees are enjoying far larger windfall returns on their prior contributions than future retirees can ever expect, the vast majority of the actuarial savings enacted by the 1983 amendments leave current and soon-to-be retired Americans untouched. Instead (and yet once more), the sacrifices are passed on to the future.

In the 1983 amendments, the net reduction in benefit levels that will affect beneficiaries before the year 2000 is trivial—estimated in 1983 to amount to only 0.16 percent of taxable payroll over the next seventy-five years. That is a mere 7.0 percent of the total long-run savings accomplished by the act. On the other hand, program changes that will affect today's workers, or beneficiaries only well after the turn of the next century, were estimated to generate a long-run savings of

---

*After much debate, it was decided to leave early retirement eligibility at age sixty-two unchanged. But as a percent of full benefits at age sixty-six in the year 2005, it will drop from its current 80 percent (at age sixty-five) to 75 percent; as a percent of full benefits at age sixty-seven in the year 2022, it will drop further to 70 percent. Combined with the effects of the two-year delay, the overall benefit reduction for all early retirees is not large, but it certainly exceeds what Schweiker proposed. One need not agree with the May 12 shock-therapy approach to marvel at how a burden so "draconian" when applied to ourselves becomes so "reasonable" when we can pass it on to our children.

†As we mentioned in Chapter 6, inflation is almost certain to outpace wages by 1988. It is unlikely this provision will ever be activated, however, since there is the "catch": it does not apply when OASDI trust-fund assets are sufficiently high relative to outlays (no matter what disaster might be facing HI, SMI, or the rest of the federal budget). Apparently, the rule is that OASDI, when it is in trouble, can lean on the rest of the budget—but not the reverse.

some 1.38 percent of payroll, or 65.0 percent of the total savings. These include, of course, the delayed retirement age. (This provision did not touch anyone over age forty-five in 1983; the entire one-year delay until sixty-six for collecting full benefits affected no one over age forty.) Such changes also include the "expanded coverage" measures reviewed above, rescheduling the payroll-tax hikes, and raising the payroll-tax rate for self-employed workers.

The most important remaining provision, the partial taxation of Social Security benefits, may seem to entail a substantial sacrifice for current beneficiaries. To some extent it does, but what is most significant about this provision is that the income thresholds (set at $25,000 for a single taxpayer and $32,000 for a married couple filing a joint return) are not indexed for inflation. In the near term, consequently, only the relatively well-to-do will be subject to benefit taxation. But as the years pass, even a modest rate of inflation will push an ever-higher proportion of beneficiaries over the tax threshold. As a result, a disproportionate share of the total long-term savings from this provision (0.61 percent of payroll over the next seventy-five years) will come from future, not current, beneficiaries. According to the "most likely"(II-B) projection, for instance, nearly half of the total savings will come from "threshold creep" affecting only beneficiaries after the year 2008 (and more than half according to the "pessimistic" [III] scenario, which assumes swifter inflation).*

Altogether, then, only about 0.37 percent of payroll is saved by a level of benefit taxation that affects all generations equally; the rest is a sacrifice called forth from future beneficiaries alone. Aggregated with the other reform measures, this means that only 24 percent of the total long-term savings of the 1983 act applies to everyone; the other 76 percent is reserved solely for younger generations. Figure 7–5 illustrates how the 1983 act increased the generational inequity of OASI retirement in terms of the lifetime "present-value" costs and benefits for typical covered workers. (Quite clearly, Figure 7–5 also reflects the massive payback inequities, both between and within generations, that were well in place before the 1983 act.)

Like the earlier 1977 "rescue package," the 1983 amendments were greeted on their enactment with projections showing a startling

---

*To illustrate, consider that in 1987 benefit taxation comprises only 1.6 percent of total OASDI revenue. By the year 2030, according to scenario II-B, it will grow to 5.0 percent; according to scenario III, it will grow to 6.3 percent. That is a 300 to 400 percent increase in the relative tax burden for future beneficiaries.

FIGURE 7-5   **Net Social Security Returns for Workers
Aged 55 and 25, with $25,000 Annual
Income, Before and After 1983 Act**

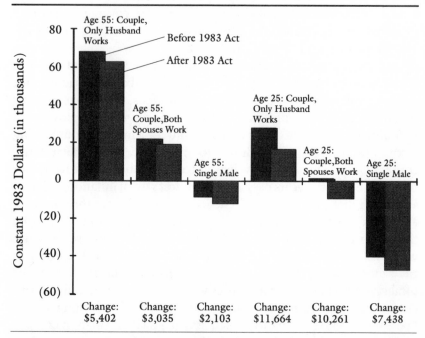

Change:	Change:	Change:	Change:	Change:	Change:
$5,402	$3,035	$2,103	$11,664	$10,261	$7,438

Net returns are calculated by subtracting lifetime payroll-tax contributions (by employer and employee) from OASI benefits for retired workers (with spouse and widow benefit, if applicable). Calculations are for 1983, in that year's present-value dollars, and assume retirement at age 65. Salary was $25,000 taxable in 1983, with prior and later salary growth according to change for average wage earner. All economic variables after 1983 are projected according to the SSA's 1983 "most likely" (II-B) scenario. Rate of return on taxes equals OASDI trust-fund interest rate.

Source: Anthony Pellechio and Gordon Goodfellow, "Individual Gains and Losses from Social Security Before and After the 1983 Amendments," *Cato Journal* (Fall 1983)

improvement in OASDI's long-term actuarial health. The seventy-five-year actuarial balance according to the "most likely" scenario, which showed a deficit of 1.82 percent of taxable payroll in April 1982, bounced back to a perfect 0.00 percent by July 1983. Once again, however, the knots are beginning to unravel. By April 1986, the trustees' annual report indicated that the long-term deficit under this scenario had risen again to 0.44 percent, and by April 1987 to 0.62 percent—already one-third of the level just prior to the 1983 crisis.

The 1983 act may have effectively removed Social Security from our national reform agenda for the rest of the 1980s, but it has not solved the system's very real structural problems. If no one yet anticipates another rescue package in the near future, it is less because OASDI's long-term health is sound than because the retirement of the small "Silent" generation (born from the late 1920s to the early 1940s) promises temporary trust-fund surpluses over the next two decades. In the long-term, as we saw in Chapter 3, the problem remains monumental. And if we look at OASDI and HI together, we should recall the "pessimistic" projection, which shows that benefit outlays will exceed tax revenue as early as 1993 and that the gap will widen to more than 5 percent of payroll as early as 2015. A prudent assessment of the entire payroll-funded Social Security system (OASDHI) would concede, in short, the possibility of a massive solvency crisis many years before the Senior Boom even begins to hit.

After half a century of history, Social Security remains essentially what it was at the outset: a chain letter to the future. With each passing generation, the cost of the program has increased while its expected returns to new participants have diminished. A national social insurance system must continue to reflect the changing needs of the U.S. population as a whole if it is to survive. Under the impact of demographics (longer lives and a smaller work force), technology (ever-higher health-care costs), and economics (stagnating productivity), it will become increasingly inappropriate to divide the productive from the nonproductive population according to an arbitrary formula developed fifty years ago during the Great Depression. Questions of equity between generations—as well as between the rich and the poor, and between workers and retirees—require that Social Security should always be subject to negotiation.

Rewriting the Chain Letter

Perhaps more than any other American institution, Social Security now serves as the defining link between citizens and the state. Almost all workers are required to fund the system through their payroll taxes; almost all older Americans are entitled to receive its benefits. We have collectively decided that the state should make *some* provision for old-age security on a universal basis. There exists no compelling reason why this defining link should be severed, whether by dismantling the system altogether, or (as some policymakers have suggested) by privatizing it.*

At the same time, however, we must recognize that the terms of this "quasi-contract" between citizen and state have evolved considerably over the course of Social Security's history—and must continue to evolve in the future if the program is to retain its legitimacy. As it is currently structured, Social Security is a universal subsidy paid for through intergenerational transfers. Many of its beneficiaries (especially those who are older, unmarried, living alone, or nonwhite) are undeniably needy. But to most, the monthly benefit check is just one component of a middle- or upper-class standard of living. As we saw in Chapter 2, two-thirds of all Social Security cash benefits go to households whose reported annual cash income is at least twice the official poverty level.

It is time we faced up to the fact that we can no longer afford this universal subsidy. Vast savings could be achieved through modest benefit-level reductions that would not affect any household near the poverty level. Indeed, we would argue, some portion of such savings could and should be allocated toward providing better support for those elderly or disabled persons truly facing economic hardship. It seems morally repugnant to claim—as apologists for Social Security do—that it is a political necessity to subsidize *all* older Americans to maintain broad-based support for a program that serves a legitimate welfare function for a few. Benefits to the elderly poor should be sacrosanct. But to make them so—to maintain a sound and meaningful safety net for the poor—we must stop padding the hammocks of the comfortable. Someone, in other words, will have to give up something. If everyone remains on the Social Security bandwagon, there will be nobody left to pull it.

Those who believe that no benefit need ever be touched either point to Social Security's current surpluses, or else suggest that payroll taxes can always be raised. We already explained in Chapter 2 that Social Security's projected surplus at best represents nothing more than paper savings, and as such cannot avert a crashing deficit

---

*Many of the proposals for privatizing Social Security call for "super-IRAs" in which current workers could accumulate "funded" retirement benefits. But who then would pay for current retirees? One way out is to grant current workers tax credits for their super-IRA contributions so that they can still afford payroll taxes. But who then pays for the lost federal income tax? Any privatizing scheme runs into a central dilemma: there is no way to get from a pay-as-you-go system to a funded system without some generation paying for two retirements—its own and its elders'. (Remember that on our way to pay-as-you-go, a previous generation in effect got away with paying for no one's retirement.) The best we can do over the next one or two generations is plan for greater—but still partial—funding of our total retirement income.

sometime early in the next century. As for a substantial hike in payroll taxes, it should be clear by now that additional intergenerational transfers are simply not a solution to the underlying problem. Social Security taxes are already so high that they rob the rest of the budget of much of its revenue-raising capacity. In fact, over the past thirty years hikes in payroll taxes have more than accounted for the increase in total federal revenues as a percentage of GNP. Yet still greater hikes would be necessary to close Social Security's projected long-term deficits in OASDI, which by 2060 will rise to 2.7 percent of taxable payroll under the "most likely" (II-B) scenario and to 12.5 percent of payroll under the "pessimistic" (III) scenario.*

If raising taxes is not the answer, what is to be done? We suggest the following five-point reform program. (1) Reduce cost-of-living adjustments (COLAs) for nonpoor beneficiaries. This will generate substantial long-term savings, scale back prior windfall benefits, and give us some degree of near-term control over our fiscal future. (2) Count all Social Security cash benefits that exceed the actuarial value of each worker's contributions as taxable income. This proposal appeals to principles of generational equity, and has the additional merit of protecting low-income beneficiaries (who would not be burdened, due to our progressive tax system). (3) Cut the initial benefit formula for upper-income beneficiaries. The rationale for this measure is that it reinforces the legitimate welfare dimension of Social Security. (4) Raise the retirement age substantially. This fundamental reform simply recognizes the changing realities of our aging society. (5) Use part of the savings to provide better poverty protection than we currently offer.

Although some of these measures are based on the principle of income equity—those who have the most give up the most—none would require the discomfort of an *explicit* "means test" for households not in poverty. (Most of us feel perfectly comfortable with an *implicit* means test, such as the income brackets of our tax system.) All of these measures, moreover, could be implemented gradually, and thus allow all potential beneficiaries plenty of time to adjust their future plans. Such adjustment will undoubtedly include somewhat higher rates of savings in most households (elderly and nonelderly

---

*The political and economic impossibility of raising payroll taxes much further is a point developed at length in "Social Security: The Coming Crash," "A Plan for Salvation," and "The Great Debate" by Peter G. Peterson, *New York Review of Books* (December 2 and 16, 1982, and March 17, 1983).

alike) in order to replace gradual reductions in entitlement benefits. More savings may take place in a variety of forms: company pensions, tax-favored individual accounts (such as IRAs or Keogh plans), insurance, annuities, family businesses, or ordinary personal savings.* In whatever form, however, we should regard higher private-sector savings rates—in addition to smaller public-sector deficits—as an essential contribution to future economic growth in America. It would thus represent a further collective benefit our proposed reforms would confer to future generations.

To examine the measures in greater detail:

(1) COLA Cuts. One straightforward reform often proposed for Social Security (as well as for the other non-means-tested entitlement programs) is a one-year freeze on automatic cost-of-living adjustments for nonpoor beneficiaries. This measure would scale back some of the windfall gains made by current beneficiaries during the late 1970s and early 1980s when double indexing and an exaggerated Consumer Price Index caused benefits to rise much faster than wages. Savings from even this modest measure would be substantial. According to the Congressional Budget Office (CBO), elimination of the COLA for fiscal year 1989 would bring about an *annual* reduction in Social Security outlays of about $10.5 billion through the early 1990s. These savings would continue past the turn of the century, though thereafter they would gradually diminish upon the deaths of the beneficiaries affected by the freeze.†

Two other frequently discussed COLA reforms would generate substantial long-term savings beyond a temporary freeze: the first is indexing benefits to the CPI minus two percentage points; the second is indexing them to 60 percent of the CPI (a so-called diet COLA). Since both measures would involve a permanent alteration in the

---

*Retirement financing is sometimes described as a four-tiered system (or a "four-legged stool"): (1) an unfunded means-tested minimum benefit (or "floor of protection"), paid exclusively to poor or near-poor retirees; (2) unfunded non-means-tested social insurance, paid generationally through payroll taxes; (3) fully funded group plans; and (4) fully funded individual savings. Our reforms would improve the equity, efficiency, and savings of this system by strengthening (1), (3), and (4)—while reducing the enormous cost of (2).

†Unlike any of the other proposed measures, this one (like the six-month freeze included in the 1983 act) deliberately targets current as opposed to future beneficiaries. Possible rationales include not only the older group's higher basic payback rate on prior tax contributions, but more important, the uniquely high replacement ratios enjoyed by anyone who began collecting benefits from the early 1970s to the early 1980s. The most precise solution to the "Notch" inequity would be to ask the SSA to target a COLA freeze at windfall beneficiaries by their year of birth (say, 1911 to 1917)—but this, of course, would be impolitic.

indexing formula, savings would rapidly compound. Either measure would yield huge long-term reductions in Social Security outlays, though the "CPI minus 2" formula would tend to lose its effectiveness at high levels of inflation.

According to our calculations, holding Social Security COLAs to 60 percent of the CPI (assuming a 6 percent inflation rate) would, by the year 2000, save more than $90 billion *annually;* and even pegging COLAs at 90 percent of the CPI would save about $25 billion annually. If the same measures were adopted for all non-means-tested cash benefits, these savings would rise to $140 billion and $38 billion, respectively. The results for the "CPI minus 2" reform are almost as dramatic. If the inflation rate is 2 percent or more (the "most likely" [II-B] scenario assumes a 4 percent rate), the annual savings in Social Security outlays would be about $65 billion by the year 2000; for all non-means-tested cash programs, the annual savings would be almost $100 billion.*

A complementary reform would be to limit COLA increases to real wage growth whenever this is lower than the CPI (regardless of the status of the Social Security trust funds). None of the other proposals for COLA reform possesses the virtue of forging a direct link between wage and benefit levels, and thereby reducing Social Security's vulnerability to cyclical downturns in the economy. (Wage growth is the primary determinant of how fast income from payroll taxes will increase, while COLAs are the critical factor in determining how fast benefit payments will rise.) If the 1990s prove to be a period of low real wage growth (as we have argued is likely), such a linkage would allow us to avoid replaying the inequities of the 1970s by ensuring that sacrifices are commensurate for beneficiaries and nonbeneficiaries alike.

The major objection to COLA cuts is that they are "regressive" or, in other words, that they reduce the benefits of the poor just as much as those of middle- and upper-class beneficiaries. This regressivity could be mitigated by applying cuts selectively—for instance, by excluding those Social Security beneficiaries whose monthly benefit amounts fall below a minimum threshold or by allowing a refundable

---

*These savings figures are illustrative, not necessarily prescriptive. A permanent switch to a "CPI-2" COLA would cut real benefit levels by 18 percent after ten years of retirement, and by 33 percent after twenty years of retirement—a penalty that would hit the "old elderly" hardest. As part of a balanced reform package that includes a gradual shift to later retirement and lower initial benefit levels, it may be preferable to enact a universal COLA reduction for only ten years, or an individual COLA reduction for only the first ten years in which benefits are received.

tax credit to all low-income beneficiaries.* Alternatively, a part of the huge savings realized through COLA reform could be targeted directly at the poor and nonpoor through means-tested programs such as SSI.†

Another objection to COLA reform is frankly political: any policymaker who advocates it must answer to the powerful "gray lobby." A 1982 survey conducted by Gallup, however, suggests that much of the public does not wholeheartedly endorse automatic indexing. Most respondents in this poll believed that adjustments ought to be annual decisions based on current circumstances. And among those who did favor automatic COLAs, a majority thought that adjustments should be equal to the automatic adjustments made in labor contracts, which historically have averaged only about 60 percent of the increase in the CPI.

(2) Benefit Taxation. Since the 1983 act was passed, beneficiaries whose adjusted gross income (AGI) exceeds certain thresholds ($25,000 for single returns and $32,000 for joint returns) must include up to one-half of their Social Security benefits in that income. Proposals to increase benefit taxation commonly focus on either lowering or eliminating these thresholds (under current law, only about 8 percent of the elderly pay taxes on their Social Security benefits). According to the CBO, if the thresholds were eliminated and 50 percent of all cash benefits were included as taxable income, about $7.5 billion yearly would be added to Social Security revenues from fiscal years 1990 through 1993; if thresholds were eliminated and 85 percent of benefits were taxed, the additional revenues would be $17.5 billion yearly. It should be emphasized that the poor would

---

*Obviously, the first approach presupposes eliminating the minimum benefit for all retirees with substantial "uncovered" pension income (such as many public-employee retirees). The connection between the monthly benefit amount and "need" would admittedly remain uncertain, since some retirees with medium benefit levels (but with no other income) are in poverty. In this respect, the refundable tax credit (which would prevent low-income retirees from losing the cumulative value of their full COLA) would be more equitable. Receiving the tax credit, of course, requires filing a federal income-tax form—but this inconvenience might be regarded as a small civic price for the privilege of enjoying an implicit means test.

†The claim is sometimes made, for instance, that a one-year COLA freeze could cause 300,000 elderly to fall from slightly above to slightly below the official poverty line. Even if this claim were correct, the income lost by these individuals could not average more than about $20 monthly for each, or about $75 million total over a year—*which means we could more than repay all such persons and still retain 99 percent of the $10 billion savings.* In fact, just half of these total savings would be enough to raise the cash income of every elderly household now below the official poverty line by a stunning 50 percent.

automatically be exempted from any burden through the wide zero-bracket of the post-1986 tax code.

Another avenue of tax reform that appeals to equity (and would achieve comparable or greater savings) would be to tax all benefits in excess of employee contributions plus interest (that is, in excess of the actuarial value of all contributions on which workers have previously paid taxes). This would not only bring the tax treatment of Social Security benefits more into line with the treatment of private-sector pension benefits, but would also mitigate the system's generational bias. Large savings would be achieved in the near term, since current retirees receive benefits many times in excess of their past contributions. As younger generations retire, however, the proportion of their benefits subject to taxation will *decrease,* since the present value ratio of their contributions to benefits will be lower.*

We should, indeed, go one step further: for beneficiaries with high incomes, it would be fair not just to apply existing income tax rates to "unearned" benefits, *but to use a sliding-scale rate of up to 100 percent to tax away the full value of cash benefits in excess of total contributions plus interest.* At somewhere between $40,000 and $100,000 in annual adjusted gross income, in other words, we could simply put an end to *any* benefit windfalls during that year.† This reform might not raise a lot of revenue (especially if the income threshold were high). It would, however, help put Social Security on higher moral ground in the minds of all Americans by entirely terminating unearned windfalls to well-off retired families—a shameful transfer now borne, in part, by young workers in poverty through their payroll taxes. In keeping with the spirit of such actuarially based tax rules, we would notify all workers and beneficiaries each year exactly how much they have paid into Social Security and how much their contributions are "worth" at trust-fund interest rates. Even if none of these tax rules is enacted, such notification makes excellent sense simply as political education. All Americans should know how much they have paid in—and how much they can justifiably take back.

---

*For current retirees, this reform would render at least 85 percent of Social Security benefits taxable. The budget savings (as mentioned above) would thus be at least $17.5 billion yearly in the early 1990s.

†One way to enforce this rule would be to apply the sliding scale tax to *all* cash benefits received by every high-income family *after* it has collected everything it has earned. Perhaps a more palatable way would be to apply it to *a portion* of cash benefits received by every high-income family *throughout* its retirement—where the portion is determined by the ratio of total benefits earned to total benefits expected. Either way, no family would be affected if its income for a given year should fall beneath the high-income definition.

(3) Benefit Reduction. The Primary Insurance Amount (PIA) formula used to calculate initial Social Security awards is designed to be "progressive"; in other words, it translates a greater percentage of wages into benefits for low-income earners than for middle- or high-income earners. Under current law, for instance, single workers retiring at sixty-five in 1988 receive an initial benefit check equivalent to 90 percent of their first $321 in "average indexed monthly earnings" (AIME), plus 32 percent of their AIME between $321 and $1,934, plus 15 percent of their AIME over $1,934 (up to the taxable maximum). Lowering the second and third replacement rates would both reinforce the progressive welfare dimension of Social Security and realize substantial savings. Another way to achieve the same goals would be to freeze the second two "bend points" in the PIA formula for a number of years (these are currently raised annually in accordance with the growth in a wage index). Either reform measure would better target Social Security benefits at those retirees who need them most, while reducing the universal subsidy to middle-and upper-income Americans.

(4) Retirement Age. No reform is more vital to the long-term future of Social Security than a significant increase in the "normal" retirement age. As we have already noted, the terms of the 1983 Social Security act already provide for this age to be raised to sixty-seven for those individuals retiring after 2022; the measure would thus apply to workers in their mid-twenties today. Given increased longevity and a smaller future work force, however, this modest reform is entirely inadequate to meet the changing needs of our aging society. Consider the following numbers: if Americans retired at seventy-two today, they would on the average live as long in retirement as Americans who left the work force at sixty-five in 1940; by the year 2020, the equivalent retirement age would be just shy of seventy-five. In other words, even if the "normal" retirement age were raised all the way to seventy, the typical American would still enjoy more years of Social Security benefits than his or her parents and grandparents.

The long-term savings that could be achieved through raising the retirement age are of course enormous, since they would be directly proportional to the reduction in the number of years the average retiree receives benefits. If the retirement age were raised to seventy, for instance, Social Security outlays would be reduced by approximately one-quarter, while payroll-tax revenue would rise due to longer average working lives. (However much we choose to raise the retirement age over the next generation, a subsequent and more durable solution might be to "index" the retirement age to further increases in longevity.) But even more important, the division between the productive and nonproductive populations would be set at a more realistic age, and the "young elderly" would be encouraged to contribute their skills and wisdom to tomorrow's shrinking and hard-pressed work force.

(5) Counterbalancing Reforms. If the reforms we have suggested were accompanied by a series of counterbalancing measures, Social Security would not only be made workable once again; it could become part of an entitlements system that better serves a useful social function. In the first place, some of the savings achieved through Social Security reform should be directly reallocated to programs designed to meet the needs of the elderly poor. It is generally estimated that raising the average SSI benefit from its current level to 100 percent of the poverty line (both for the elderly poor *and* for nonelderly disabled persons) would require about $5 billion annually in additional revenues.* Compare this figure with the $15 to $20 billion that would be saved annually if 85 percent of Social Security benefits were taxed; or with the $65 billion in annual outlays that would be saved by the year 2000 if Social Security were indexed to the "CPI minus 2" formula.

Not only should resources be reallocated toward poverty relief, but cost-saving reforms should be accompanied by the elimination of measures that systematically discourage the participation of the elderly in the work force. Under current law, any Social Security beneficiary under age seventy with annual earned income over about

---

*There are currently about 4 million SSI beneficiaries (half elderly and half nonelderly disabled). Since the current income threshold for eligibility in most states is set at roughly 80 percent of the official poverty line, most remain poor after receiving benefits. The CBO estimates that raising the benefit level to 90 percent would cost an additional $3 billion in 1986. The Urban Institute estimates that raising it to 100 percent would cost $5 billion (plus $0.7 billion in state funding) and add an extra one million (mostly elderly) SSI beneficiaries. Although this reform would offer unprecedented poverty protection for the elderly, it would not "eliminate" elderly poverty since many (especially those near the poverty line) would still choose to avoid the stigma and complexity of applying for "unearned" means-tested benefits. We have, of course, eliminated any stigma or complexity from our much-larger flow of unearned non-means-tested benefits.

$8,000 loses 50 cents of his or her benefit for each dollar of additional income.* The "earnings test" is unpopular among the elderly—and with good reason, since its ultimate effect is to deter them from contributing their skills to the market economy. If it were eliminated, Social Security would lose about $1.5 billion in annual revenues in the near term, but the long-term benefits that would ensue from encouraging a greater proportion of the elderly to remain productive are incalculable.†

Our intention in these last few pages has not been to present a definitive agenda for reform, but rather to suggest what types of measures will yield the most fruitful results. If Social Security reform is approached along the lines we have described, major budgetary savings could be achieved by the turn of the century. Some of this huge dividend could be used to eradicate poverty among the elderly. Another part could be redirected toward achieving other public goals (such as educating our children and rebuilding our infrastructure). The rest could help us reduce the drain of the federal budget deficit on our net national savings—a project that will certainly challenge us in future years. At the same time, older Americans could be brought back into the mainstream of economic and public life. As Social Security exists today, it is not only bad for the economy and a burden on future generations; it is bad for the elderly themselves. Viewed properly, the aging of America can be seen as an opportunity to forge a new, dynamic vision of old age—one that would replace the nonproductive dependency into which our current entitlements system forces many of the elderly.

---

*The exact earnings threshold ($8,400 in 1988) is now indexed to the yearly change in average wages. Beginning in 1990, the 1983 act will change the "earnings tax" from 50 to 33 percent for everyone under age seventy. What we need, however, is the complete elimination of this counterproductive tax—for all ages.

†Eliminating the earnings test strengthens the equity argument for greatly expanding the taxability of benefits. Otherwise, the result would be unconscionable: most married CEOs working through their late sixties with six-figure incomes, for instance, could collect $1,500 monthly in unreduced and largely tax-exempt Social Security checks.

8

The Federal
Pension Bonanza

"It's a scandal! It's an outrage!"
—*Office of Management and Budget Director
David Stockman to a congressional committee
on the subject of military pensions, February 1984*

B Y ALMOST ANY STANDARD, our two major federal employee retirement programs are far and away the most
generous pension plans in the nation. In fiscal year 1986, civil
service and military retirement together disbursed $42 billion to some
3.5 million beneficiaries. These pension systems cover only about 6
million employees and soldiers, yet the benefits they pay out are
approximately equal to all benefit payments from all private pension
plans for the entire U.S. labor force—approximately 75 million full-
time workers.

The sheer size of these programs—they now account for 17
percent of all federal spending on cash benefits—would demand that
they be scrutinized in any agenda for entitlements reform. Yet even
more than the broad stream of federal dollars they consume, it is the
fundamental inequity of their benefit provisions that calls their
legitimacy into question. During the early and mid-1980s, the federal
deficit explosion—accompanied by wholesale chopping at poverty
benefits—sparked a brief but irate public reaction against the cost and
generosity of federal pensions that ultimately made possible the pas-

sage of reform legislation through Congress. Now that the dust has settled, however, it is clear that these attempts at reform were entirely insufficient. Our civil service and military retirement systems remain a huge bonanza for all current beneficiaries as well as the vast majority of currently employed civil servants and career servicemen, while placing an unjustifiable and unaffordable burden on the nation's future budgetary resources.

Civil Service Retirees: An Elite Among Pensioners

Of all our major cash entitlement programs, which has grown the fastest over the last fifteen years? Which provides the highest benefit levels? And which bears the least conceivable relationship to the financial need of the beneficiary? There is just one answer to all three questions: the Civil Service Retirement System (CSRS), the pension plan that covers the vast majority of federal employees, including Congress and its permanent staff. Not so long ago, civil service pensions occupied such a tiny corner of the federal budget that they hardly seemed worthy of notice. No longer. In fiscal year 1986, their total cost was $24 billion—about what the federal government spent that year on Medicaid, our primary health-care program for 22 million poor Americans.

A further comparison will help to put the magnitude of this figure into perspective. The federal government now spends more in benefits for 2 million civil service pensioners than it allocates in Food Stamps and Aid to Families with Dependent Children to roughly 20 million adults and children in or near poverty. Poverty, incidentally, is just about unheard of among CSRS pensioners. In the census tables, the entry showing the poverty rate for civil service retirement beneficiaries is always the same—an asterisk signifying "statistically insignificant."

From 1970 to 1986, the cost of the CSRS grew nearly tenfold, while as a share of the federal budget it approximately doubled in size—from 1.3 percent to 2.6 percent of all federal spending. As with so many nonpoverty entitlements, most of this explosive growth reflects higher benefit levels per recipient. Ample annuity formulas, escalating salaries, and runaway indexing all conspired to push up the average civil service retirement benefit more than 50 percent faster than inflation over the course of the 1970s. During the same decade that witnessed a virtual stagnation in constant-dollar personal income per American family, the typical CSRS benefit grew at a real rate of 4.3 percent per year.

True enough, the rapid growth of overall federal pension costs was also due to a sizable increase in the number of retired beneficiaries (and their surviving dependents), from 962,000 in 1970 to 2,065,000 in 1988. Much of this increase was nothing more than a long-delayed retirement liability finally coming due. When the federal government hired armies of new, permanent employees back in the 1940s and 1950s, it was inevitable that they would someday retire; over the last fifteen years, the inevitable has finally been happening.

On the other hand, many Americans may have difficulty interpreting this tidal wave of "retirement" as retirement in any ordinary sense of the word. So early can a civil service employee quit work with full benefits that 49 percent of them do so before they reach sixty. (This is almost unheard-of outside the magic circle of civil service and military retirement; very few private-sector pension plans—not to mention Social Security—allow retirement with full benefits before sixty.) As a group, CSRS pensioners are thus relatively young. About 23 percent—almost all of whom enjoy full benefits—are sixty-two years of age or younger, whereas only 16 percent of all private pensioners—almost all of whom have had their benefits reduced for early retirement—are that age. Furthermore, so easily can a civil servant be deemed "disabled" that 27 percent of all former federal employees receiving pensions have qualified under the CSRS disability provisions. In contrast, workers with disability pensions under the Social Security system comprise only 11 percent of the total.

How do federal pensions stack up against private pensions? The typical private pension income (an average of $4,700 per year in 1984) is less than half of the typical pension income received by a CSRS beneficiary (more than $11,000 per year, averaged over all ages and categories). Many CSRS pensioners of course do far better than this: as of fiscal year 1985, new awards averaged more than $13,000 per year, while new awards for employees with at least thirty years of service averaged more than $17,000 per year.

How much CSRS beneficiaries receive would perhaps be none of our business if they financed their own pension plan. The truth, however, is that they do not. Although civil service employees are subject to a 7 percent payroll tax, this contribution covers less than one-quarter of the total CSRS annual benefit cost even on a pay-as-you-go basis. The matching contribution of their employing agencies—

namely, the various departments of the federal government—covers about another quarter. The remaining half is paid for directly out of general federal revenues.

Although the CSRS does have a trust-fund account at the Department of the Treasury that serves (at least on paper) as a repository for payroll taxes and other revenues, like Social Security, civil service retirement is actually a pay-as-you-go rather than a fully funded pension plan—which brings us to the most extravagant part of our story. About $563 billion worth of future CSRS benefits are currently unfunded. This is the sum that would have to be set aside today in order to bridge the gap between, on the one hand, all of the future payroll tax contributions of current workers (including their agencies' matching contributions, plus interest) and, on the other, all scheduled benefit payments to current workers and current retirees.* It is nearly one-third the size of our "official," publicly held national debt; like that official debt, it represents a future promise for which no one has yet assumed responsibility.

The best way to highlight the inappropriate generosity of civil service retirement benefits is to compare the CSRS with typical private pension plans. By whatever objective standard we adopt, it is clear that civil servants are an elite among pensioners.

Initial Benefit Level. A yardstick commonly used to evaluate the adequacy of a pension is the "replacement ratio," that is, the pensioner's first monthly benefit expressed as a percentage of his or her monthly salary before retirement. For those workers in the private sector lucky enough to receive pensions, the average replacement ratio after thirty years of employment is about 30 percent. For CSRS pensioners, the typical replacement ratio is 56 percent—nearly twice as high. Only about 15 percent of all private-sector retirees, even when both their pension and Social Security benefits are counted, enjoy replacement ratios that exceed this CSRS figure. The maximum ratio for civil service retirees is 80 percent earned after forty-two years of service; virtually no private-sector employee can ever attain this

---

*This $563 billion is the total unfunded liability at the end of fiscal year 1986 for future CSRS benefits as calculated by GAO and Treasury accountants. Their standard accounting practice is *not* to subtract from it the current "assets" in the Civil Service Retirement and Disability Trust Fund (about $173 billion), since this is merely a number that Treasury "owes" the trust fund. It does not represent any prior decision to save rather than consume, and therefore does not reduce the eventual burden to taxpayers of paying for promised CSRS benefits. If we did subtract this amount, we would have to add an equal number to the publicly held national (i.e., Treasury) debt.

ratio, no matter how many years he or she has worked.

Like any other "defined-benefit" plan, the CSRS calculates a pensioner's initial annuity with a formula that takes into account both the employee's salary and the length of his service. The primary reason CSRS replacement ratios are so high is that the benefit formula adds a larger percentage of the employee's salary to his pension for each additional year of service (1.87 percent for the CSRS versus 1.00 percent for the typical private plan). But there is another reason. It is clearly to the employee's advantage if the benefit formula is calculated with as high a salary level as possible. Nearly 40 percent of all private plans use the employee's career-average salary; almost all the rest use the employee's salary over the last five years of employment. In contrast, the CSRS uses the three highest consecutive years (the "hi-3" method). Under the CSRS, furthermore, unused sick leave is added to years of actual service—a feature, once again, that is unheard-of in the private sector.

Indexing. In Chapter 6 we discussed the 100 percent of CPI indexing by which the federal government adjusts nearly all of its cash entitlements for inflation. No major private employer uses it; and indeed, less than half of all private pensions enjoy any regular COLA at all. Consequently, not only is the CSRS pension more generous than a private pension to begin with, but its relative advantage increases with each passing year over the lifetime of the pensioner. Incredible as it may seem, CSRS pensioners for many years (from 1969 to 1976) were given an extra 1 percent yearly "kicker" over and above the yearly growth in the CPI. The rationale was that beneficiaries should not be penalized for the inevitable "lag" that occurred between inflation and the yearly indexation of their benefits (though logically this should only have entitled each pensioner to a one-shot "kicker," rather than to a new boost every year). Not even Congress could abide this frill for long, however, and the "kicker" was repealed in 1976.* Even so, the effects of the 1 percent "kicker," which are now locked into the CSRS system, are estimated still to be costing an additional $30 or $40 billion over the lifetimes of the retirees who benefited from this windfall.

---

*Eager to demonstrate that it was not slighting the retiring civil servant, however, Congress replaced the "kicker" with a "twice-a-year" CPI adjustment—a COLA unique among all federal programs. Not until the Omnibus Budget Reconciliation Act of 1981 did Congress agree to put the CSRS on the same annual footing as other indexed programs: along with military retirement, the CSRS was given an annual COLA in March based on total CPI growth between the previous two Decembers.

Over the years, CSRS overindexing has had some unusual consequences. Between 1969 and 1976, the effects of indexing alone pushed up CSRS pension benefits about 22 percent faster than the CPI (which, as we have seen, was itself an exaggerated measure of inflation). Not surprisingly, within several years after retirement, CSRS pensioners frequently make more from their federal pension than their colleagues earn in active service. The retired Speaker of the House, John McCormack, for instance, is reputed to have enjoyed a pension of $92,000 while his successor in office was earning $79,000. And last year, former Senator Albert Gore, Sr. drew $78,055 while his son, Senator Albert Gore, Jr., was being paid $77,400. Nor are these isolated examples. In 1985 it was estimated that 100,000 federal retirees received pensions larger than the *current* salaries of their former jobs, while roughly 325,000 received pensions larger than their former salaries upon retirement. It hardly needs to be noted that both of these situations are unheard-of among pensioners in the private sector.

Retirement Age. As it happens, the high yearly cost of benefits per retiree is only one of the reasons the CSRS is the nation's most expensive pension program. Because so many civil service employees retire at an early age, the typical federal pensioner also draws benefits for many more years than the private pensioner. In the private sector, sixty-five is of course considered the "normal" retirement age. Only 8 percent of all private pension plans allow an employee to retire earlier than age sixty-five with full benefits; and there are only a handful of corporate plans (such as those at a few publicly regulated utilities) that allow retirement before sixty-two with full benefits. To be sure, many private-sector employees do retire earlier than the "normal" retirement age, but in these cases the private plan reduces the initial pension by 3.5 percent to 4.0 percent for each year in order to compensate for the beneficiary's longer expected retirement.

Not so with civil service retirement. After thirty years of service, a federal civil servant can retire with full benefits at fifty-five; after twenty years, with full benefits at sixty; and after five years, with full benefits at sixty-two. (This last provision calls to mind another special CSRS advantage: employees are fully "vested" with pension rights after only five years; the standard vesting requirement in the private sector is ten years.) Furthermore, should a federal worker decide to retire before being vested with full benefits, the actuarial reduction in his benefits (only 2 percent per year) is less than the reduction imposed by the typical private plan.

Given these incentives, it is hardly surprising that civil service employees respond by retiring at an unusually early age. The average retirement age for a civil servant is about fifty-eight, compared with sixty-three in the private sector. One in 6 retires before fifty-five, while only 1 out of 100 private-sector workers retires that early. Moreover, a large share of CSRS pensioners are busy with second careers (32 percent of those under sixty-five). This is an attractive option for many federal retirees because, unlike Social Security, the CSRS imposes no "earnings test" penalty on beneficiaries who decide to continue working.

Disability. Those accustomed to private-sector employment rarely confuse "disability" with "retirement." Outside the federal government, disability is strictly defined. It usually means "total" disability, that is, the inability to perform "any gainful employment." Once again, the rules of the game are very different in the U. S. Civil Service. The CSRS allows an employee to collect disability insurance for a "partial" disability, which may entail nothing more than the inability to perform any single part of his current job description. A civil servant thus disabled is not required to take another position whose responsibilities he could still meet, and no distinction is made between total and partial disability when the pension award is made. Furthermore, unlike Social Security and most private plans, the CSRS generally allows disabled civil servants to retain their pensions if they later secure employment elsewhere. Although the pension is technically forfeit if their new job pays more than 80 percent of their former salary, this provision is rarely enforced.

Disability is therefore regarded by many federal employees as just another route to retirement. Approximately 95 percent of all CSRS disability applications are approved. In the CSRS we can count one disabled pensioner for every three retired pensioners; in Social Security, on the other hand, we can count only one DI beneficiary for every ten retired workers.* One irony of the CSRS's disability policy is that it mocks the recent federal effort to hire the handicapped.

*And recall that the rapid growth of Social Security's DI program—greatly exceeding all projections—suggests that this share itself reflects more than the actual disability rate among all covered workers. As economist Michael Boskin has written of DI, "one need only examine the benefits and enrollments in disability in most Western European societies to realize that *some* disability is publicly financed early retirement." (*Too Many Promises: The Uncertain Future of Social Security* by Michael Boskin; Dow Jones Irwin, 1986.)

Donald Devine, former director of the U.S. Office of Personnel Management (OPM), has observed: "We allow some employees to retire on disability who have much less severe handicaps than many of those we encourage the agencies to hire."

Integration with Social Security. Apologists for the CSRS often argue that it is disingenuous to compare federal pensions with private pensions alone, since almost all recipients of private pensions also enjoy Social Security benefits, whereas CSRS beneficiaries are not covered by Social Security on the basis of their prior federal employment. Two responses are in order. First, the CSRS pensioner (as we noted above) typically enjoys a higher level of benefits than even those private-sector retirees who are lucky enough to receive both Social Security and a generous private pension. Second, the lack of Social Security coverage for CSRS beneficiaries is largely academic, since most civil servants have at some point in their lives worked outside the public sector in "covered" occupations long enough to qualify for OASDI cash benefits. In fact, 73 percent of all CSRS pensioners over sixty-two also receive OASI. In order to qualify for OASI, a worker must have contributed payroll taxes for a certain minimum qualifying period (generally, forty quarters of "covered" employment). Many CSRS pensioners meet this requirement through private-sector employment before or after their stint with the federal government, while an estimated 50 percent qualify for Social Security by working part-time in covered employment while they are still working full-time as civil servants.

Although part-time employment over the minimum qualifying period ensures only a modest benefit level, even this level is heavily subsidized by means of Social Security's "minimum benefit" and its progressive PIA formula. Until these provisions were altered in 1981 and 1983, Social Security could not distinguish between a low-income worker with no other retirement benefit and a high-income civil servant who had worked sporadically in "covered" employment. By guaranteeing the former a high payback rate, Social Security bestowed an extravagant windfall on the latter.* The best deal for CSRS

---

*In fact, the current civil service retiree who qualified for OASI through part-time work gets a much better payback rate than even the lowest-income full-time worker. Consider: the "minimum benefit" or the 90 percent bottom bracket of the PIA formula (whichever is higher) is used to set his initial benefit level as a share of prior covered wages. The lowest-income worker does no better than this. But in addition, since a worker's prior Average Monthly Wages (AMW or AIME), on which his PIA is based, need only "count" his highest-earning years, where the number of selectable years equals the number of years that have elapsed since 1955 or age

pensioners has thus been to contribute no more than a small amount in payroll taxes, but to do so long enough to qualify for the "minimum" retired-worker benefit. In the private sector, only about 14 percent of all retired workers currently receive the "minimum" OASI benefit. Most of them are poor, and many also receive means-tested Supplemental Security Income. Among civil service pensioners, fully 28 percent receive this subsidy.

In 1980 the Department of Health and Human Services (HHS) estimated that "double-dipping" by federal pensioners—a colorful term signifying the simultaneous receipt of both CSRS and Social Security benefits—added 6.4 percent to the total cost of Social Security cash benefits. When justifying their generous pensions, federal employees routinely point out that they cannot rely on Social Security for their retirement security. But when former Secretary Richard S. Schweiker proposed his cost-saving reforms for Social Security (among them the repeal of the "minimum benefit" for those with other substantial sources of income), there was no group that offered such determined resistance to his proposals as the civil service lobby. In pension politics, as in everything else, actions speak louder than words.

Despite the defeat of the Schweiker proposal, Congress did succeed in cutting back somewhat on the abuses of double-dipping by federal employees. In 1981 it eliminated the regular "minimum benefit," and in 1983 it reduced the PIA formula for CSRS pensioners who qualify for OASI cash benefits (the standard 90 percent rate before the first PIA "bend point" has been replaced by a 40 percent rate).† Yet neither change affects those who were already eligible for

twenty-six (whichever is higher), the civil service retiree enjoys a considerable advantage. A worker reaching age sixty-two in 1980, for instance, is required to "count" only his highest twenty-five years of wages. Therefore, the civil servant can simply ignore many of his "zero" years when he was not paying any FICA taxes. The low-income private-sector worker with the same birth year, on the other hand, gets absolutely no additional benefit for all of the extra years in which he may have been paying FICA taxes. If he started work in a "covered" job at age twenty, for instance, this means that *sixteen* of his "covered" years are essentially wasted.

To be sure, the advantage for the civil servant is declining over time; every worker reaching age sixty-two in 1991 or later will have to "count" thirty-five years in averaging his prior covered wages. (This is just one more instance in which Social Security discriminates against later generations.) But even in the long run, this "countable years" rule will still remain unfair to lower-income workers (who typically begin work at a younger age and are more likely to have more than thirty-five years of covered earnings).

†All told, giving future CSRS retirees a 40 percent PIA replacement rate seems very generous considering that, if the CSRS were integrated with Social Security, their initial benefit would be calculated with the 15 percent PIA replacement rate. (This is the rate now applicable at the margin for all preretirement pay between about $1,900 per month and the taxable maximum.)

OASI early retirement benefits in 1982. And still in place are substantial future windfalls that current federal employees—most of those who will be retiring over the next couple decades—will enjoy from Social Security double-dipping well into the next century. Gradual reform is one thing; wholesale "grandfathering" of all current workers, no matter how young, is quite another.

It is important to point out that the 1983 Social Security act mandated that all federal employees hired after December 31, 1983 be automatically covered by Social Security. Together with this requirement, a separate system for all new federal workers, known as the Federal Employees' Retirement System (FERS), was instituted in 1986. In the FERS, a somewhat smaller pension system analogous to the CSRS (together with a thrift plan) is explicitly integrated with Social Security benefits. We will return briefly to the FERS later. For now, it is enough to observe that eventually—when the last CSRS beneficiaries pass away, perhaps in the late 2040s—the FERS will spell the final end of this peculiar abuse called double-dipping.

From "Comparability" to "Model Employer"

Whenever the issue of compensation arises, the civil service lobby has a single rallying cry: "comparability." Public workers, it is argued, should receive compensation on a par with workers in "comparable" private-sector jobs. But the argument is used very selectively. It appears whenever wages are discussed—and vanishes instantly whenever pensions (or other fringe benefits) reach the bargaining table. Indeed, with pensions we are greeted by an entirely different line of reasoning. Here, it is asserted, the federal government should act as a "model employer," presumably in order to "shame" the private sector into offering all workers in the national economy pensions comparable to those received by CSRS beneficiaries.

The "model employer" argument resembles the sort of justification used by contractors who install marble bathrooms in congressional office buildings: Wouldn't it be nice, of course, if everyone had them? We have not yet come across a study that quantitatively describes an America in which everyone enjoys civil service pension coverage, but the idea is worth pursuing. Let us assume that all Americans retired at the same age and became disabled at the same rate as federal workers. How much would it then cost to ensure every retiree and disabled worker the same average benefit level as federal

314

pensioners? According to our calculations, the cost in 1984 would have run to about $550 billion. A federal program that guaranteed this level of benefits to all retirees by supplementing current private, state, and local pension plans could easily consume nine-tenths of all federal domestic spending.*

As an extension of the "comparability" argument, it is sometimes maintained that the relative generosity of federal pensions is a legitimate trade-off with other substandard features of a federal worker's total compensation package. Is there any validity to this claim? Let us first look at fringe benefits. In 1975 the elder of this book's authors served as chairman of President Ford's Quadrennial Commission on Executive, Legislative, and Judicial Pay, charged with reviewing the appropriateness of civil service compensation. Although its members were interested in examining all aspects of compensation (wages, pensions, and other fringe benefits), they were repeatedly informed by expert federal witnesses that there was simply no ready means of measuring the relative value of total civil service and private-sector compensation packages. In the end, it was resolved to solicit an informal review from the personnel officers of several major corporations. The results indicated that according to most significant measures of compensation, federal civil servants enjoyed far more favorable terms of employment than "comparably" situated private-sector workers.[†]

This conclusion, moreover, was later confirmed by President Reagan's 1983 Private Sector Survey on Cost Control, better known as the Grace Commission. Table 8-1, which is based on its findings, compares the value of measurable nonsalary benefits provided by the federal sector with average equivalents provided by large (and therefore generous) private employers. For convenience, all benefit costs have been expressed as a percentage of payroll.

To be sure, the single most conspicuous civil service advantage is in pensions: 87.1 percent versus 14.0 percent of payroll, if we assume that both employers are required to amortize their unfunded pension liability according to the standards of the 1974 Employee Retirement

---

*Along with the CSRS, military retirement, and administrative costs, this would just about perfectly fill the domestic budget. The federal government would then be able to afford only three types of spending: defense, checks to bondholders, and checks to pensioners.

[†] *The Report of the Quadrennial Commission on Executive, Congressional, and Judicial Pay* (U.S. Government, 1975).

Table 8-1	Fringe Benefit Cost as a Percent of Payroll	
	Large Private-Sector Employer	Federal Civil Service
Pension	14.0%	87.1%
Health Benefits	5.8	6.8
Vacation Pay	4.5	7.1
Sick Pay	2.1	3.4
Total	**26.4%**	**104.4%**

Employer cost only; including cost of Social Security for private employer.
Source: *The President's 1983 Private Sector Survey on Cost Control*

Income Security Act (ERISA).* But in addition, the federal sector also came out the clear winner in every other fringe-benefit category. In the case of vacations, for example, a comparison of every length of service, from 6 months to 30 years or more, reveals that federal policy is 15 percent to nearly 100 percent more generous, depending on the service category. Moreover, federal workers have a shorter minimum service requirement (3 months) before qualifying for vacations and can carry over far more unused vacation time from year to year (up to 30 days) than is typical in private-sector employment. Federal sick-leave policy reveals similar advantages in terms of employees covered (all), waiting period (none), and maximum accumulation (unlimited).

But what about federal wages? If civil service jobs were underpaid relative to private-sector jobs, this fact might still provide some roundabout justification for much more generous CSRS pensions. As far as simple averages are concerned, it can be said unequivocally that the typical federal worker is paid 30 percent more than the typical nonagricultural, private-sector worker. Looking at average salaries alone, however, fails to take the "comparability" issue into account. Civil service representatives argue that federal workers' higher aver-

*These estimates vary according to assumptions about future real interest rates. Using different assumptions, a 1984 study by the Hay/Huggins Company concluded that the federal advantage in pensions is somewhat less marked than the Grace Commission figures indicate. *Study of Total Compensation in the Federal, State and Private Sectors,* prepared by Hay/Huggins Company and Hay Management Consultants for the Committee on Post Office and Civil Service, House of Representatives (Washington, 1984).

age salaries are only natural, since the typical public-sector job requires superior skills and entails greater responsibilities than the typical private-sector job. The real question, then, is what the relative compensation levels are for "comparable" positions in the public and private sectors. According to the 1984 Hay/Huggins study cited above, federal pay rates are indeed 10 percent lower on the average than pay rates for "comparably" defined jobs in the private sector. At first glance, this statistic might seem to settle the question in favor of the civil service lobby.

The matter, however, actually turns out to be considerably more complicated than it would appear. In the first place, it is often impossible to find public- and private-sector positions that have equivalent job descriptions and occupational titles, the standard "comparability" measures. In the second place, the rampant problem of title inflation in the public sector ensures that federal "administrative assistants" (who may actually be untrained secretaries) will have their salaries compared with those of true administrative assistants in the private sector.* As an illustration of this point, consider the conclusions of the 1975 Quadrennial Commission: of those federal jobs examined, almost half were misclassified, and among these, fully 85 percent were thereby pushed into a higher salary category. These findings are not isolated. In 1982 the Office of Personnel Management (OPM) undertook a comparison of civil service and private-sector jobs that corrected for title inflation—and concluded that on the average federal workers are better paid by 11 percent.

Leaving aside these methodological difficulties, most experts would agree that there is a more accurate means of comparing remuneration in the public and private sectors: rather than examine the relative pay level for "comparable" jobs, it makes sense to look at the relative pay level for individuals with equivalent characteristics, such as educational attainment and work experience. Studies conducted on this basis invariably suggest that when "human-capital" characteristics and other determinants (sex, age, race, and residence) are statistically controlled, federal workers are paid more than they would be able to earn in the private sector. To cite one example, a 1981 study by the National Bureau of Economic Research concluded that on the average federal employees receive salaries fully 20 percent

---

*As Leonard Reed put it, "Anybody who has ever worked in a government agency knows that job descriptions will endow a file clerk with responsibilities before which a graduate of the Harvard Business School quails." Cited by Timothy Noah in "Federal Pension Scandal," *The Washington Monthly* (May 1984).

higher than those they could hope to command outside the civil service. The only exception to this rule is at the very highest levels of the executive branch, where many jobholders freely admit that power and prestige more than compensate for their relatively lower salaries.*

Another approach to the whole "comparability" issue might be called the "market" test. Economists agree that a job is probably overpaid whenever there are many more qualified applicants than there are positions to be filled. Similarly, it is a strong indication that a job is underpaid when the pool of applicants is small and the turnover or "quit" rate is high. If we apply these "market" criteria to the issue at hand, there can be little doubt that federal jobs are overpaid relative to private-sector jobs. In 1981, for instance, the private-sector "quit" rate was 13 percent for manufacturing jobs and 18 percent for nonmanufacturing jobs; among civil servants, however, the "quit" rate was less than 5 percent. In the end, the argument that generous CSRS pensions are a legitimate form of delayed compensation for an underpaid federal work force thus turns out to be unsustainable.

Old Soldiers Never Die: They're Too Busy Collecting

As a congressional committee witness in February 1984, David Stockman, then Director of the Office of Management and Budget, unleashed a scathing assault on our military retirement system. In Stockman's words, our military leaders are "more concerned about protecting their retirement benefits than they are about protecting the security of the American people." Far from being an isolated outburst, Stockman's comments simply echoed (though in more biting terms) what many policy experts had been arguing throughout the 1970s and early 1980s. Indeed, over the past decade and a half, military retirement has been the subject of half a dozen major studies, all of which have reached the same general conclusions: the benefit provisions are far too generous, the distribution of benefits is grossly inequitable, and the overall benefit structure serves no manpower

---

*This is true for most appointed officials, but less true for many senior career civil servants whose regular salaries cannot exceed certain dollar "caps" determined by the Executive Pay Schedule. Currently, the highest salary for the Senior Executive Service is capped at $77,500; for the General Service employee, it is capped at $72,500 (although performance and presidential awards may push both totals higher). In these cases, large pensions may substitute for below-market salaries—but with great waste, since a smaller, more "front-end" compensation package could easily suffice.

recruitment function that could not be served otherwise with better results and at far less cost.

Before examining the merits of this indictment, let us first put the problem into perspective by looking at some overall numbers. Yearly cash outlays for military pensions have grown more than sixfold over the past fifteen years, from $2.8 billion in 1970 to $17.6 billion in 1986. In terms of numbers of pensioners (1.5 million today) and benefit growth per pensioner (an average real rate of 4.7 percent per year since 1970), military retirement has become a fiscal problem roughly on a par with civil service retirement. Military pension benefits now account for about 8 percent of all defense spending, more than the total yearly procurement cost of new ships for the Navy or new aircraft for the Air Force. Moreover, these figures actually understate the growth in benefit expenditures, since they fail to take into account the generous noncash fringe benefits that military retirees continue to receive.

What are the rules that govern these benefits? The most important is that the serviceman who quits the military before he has served at least twenty years is not eligible for any pension. At twenty years, however, he becomes eligible for a generous annuity for the rest of his life. For any serviceman who entered the military before July 31, 1986, the annuity is equal to 50 percent of his base preretirement pay (the figure is the sum of 2.5 percent increments for each of his twenty years of service). If retirement is postponed, his benefit level then continues to increase by 2.5 percent for every additional year of service, until after thirty years in the military he reaches a maximum benefit level of 75 percent of preretirement pay. Until 1980 the initial benefit was calculated on the basis of the last month of preretirement pay; today, just as with federal employees, it is calculated by averaging the highest three consecutive years. Each year thereafter, the pension receives a cost-of-living adjustment (COLA) equal to 100 percent of the CPI.

For all servicemen who enter the military after July 31, 1986, the 1986 Military Retirement Reform Act has cheapened the deal slightly. The system's essential feature—twenty years of service as the minimum for vesting—was retained, but the benefit's replacement ratios and COLAs underwent a complicated modification. Under the new system, pension benefits for retirees under age sixty-two will be computed at the rate of 2.0 percent of preretirement pay for their first twenty years of service (resulting in a 40 percent replacement ratio for those who retire as soon as they are vested). For service beyond twenty years, the rate is increased to 3.5 percent for each additional year until the maximum benefit level (unchanged at 75 percent) is reached at thirty years. As for yearly COLAs, these will now be equal to the change in the CPI minus one percentage point. This may seem to be a sizable benefit reduction—except for one catch: no matter how young a pensioner is when he receives his initial benefit, his benefit is recalculated at age sixty-two *with the original pre-1986 benefit formula and as though the benefit had always been indexed to 100 percent of the CPI.* From age sixty-two on, the yearly COLA is again set at the change in the CPI minus one percentage point.

These small changes in benefit provisions, the main thrust of the 1986 act, represent just about everything the military lobby has yet conceded to the reformers.* Like the CSRS, military retirement emerged from the torrent of popular criticism during the early 1980s with its generosity relatively unscathed. Indeed, now that the furor is over, one would have to say that it made out even better than the CSRS: the 1986 act affects no military pensioner at all until the year 2006; even then, the future pensioner who is aged sixty-two or over, or who has served thirty years, will experience no reduction in initial benefit.

It is sometimes argued that replacement ratios of between 50 and 75 percent for military pensioners are not as generous as they might appear, since the extensive in-kind income (including food, housing, and medical care) of the serviceman on active duty is not included in the "cash-income" formula on which pension awards are based. What this argument neglects to point out, however, is that military pensioners continue to receive much of this in-kind income even after they retire. In fact, retired servicemen and their families are entitled to take out subsidized housing loans and insurance policies, shop at commissaries, and avail themselves of free health-care services (at either military or Veterans Administration facilities). If this continued stream of in-kind income were taken into account, the typical pensioner's replacement ratio would no doubt appear more generous than the cash-income formula alone suggests.

---

*Everyone close to the military was "grandfathered." Exempt from these changes as of July 31, 1986 were not only those currently in the service, but also those who had ever previously served, enlistees on Delayed Entry Programs, and all service academy or ROTC cadets and midshipmen. Similarly, initial benefit levels for disability, survivor, and Reserve Component benefits (mostly for officers aged 60 and over) remain unchanged.

Taken together, these liberal benefit provisions allow most military pensioners to retire at an unusually young age. The median retirement age for career servicemen is now forty-three. Those who join the services in their late teens can retire in their late thirties. In fact, 49 percent of all current pensioners are fifty-five or younger; 77 percent are under sixty-five. There can be no question that the pattern of early retirement is a direct result of the pension provisions. Very few members of the armed forces (about 5 percent) retire after fifteen but before twenty years of service (the point at which vesting occurs); on the other hand, of those who stay on for twenty years, 75 percent of all officers and over 90 percent of all enlistees retire before completing twenty-five years of service. In the military, serving more than twenty years is disparagingly known as "working for half pay."

The ordinary meaning of the word "retirement" is thus even less appropriate for military pensioners than for civil service pensioners. The typical military pensioner, in fact, spends much more time collecting benefits (thirty-two years) than he spends earning them (twenty-three years). Nor does it make much sense to single out "double-dipping" as a special abuse, since, as of 1957, servicemen have been covered by Social Security. (Military pensions are not offset against Social Security; the retired serviceman receives full benefits under both programs.) Fully 70 percent of military pensioners now over sixty-five receive both a pension and a Social Security benefit.* Many of them, indeed, are "triple-dippers," since most retirees have plenty of time to qualify for private pensions during the course of second careers.† In fact, an incredible 86 percent of military pensioners under fifty-five actively pursue second careers. Yet the basic inequity of this system is that servicemen who retire before completing twenty years in the military receive no pension benefits at all. As it turns out, it is these losers who comprise the majority. Of all the

---

*Until 1956 the SSA granted all servicemen free "wage credits" for time spent in the military; after 1956 all servicemen became OASDI "covered workers." For military pensioners, such coverage is usually irrelevant since most can easily become eligible for Social Security later on. In the future, however, it will serve to exempt them from the reduced PIA formula applicable to CSRS pensioners.

†Or for another federal pension. There are currently about 150,000 employees on the federal payroll who are also receiving a public pension. Some (such as Ronald Reagan, who picks up a $29,000 California pension while earning his $200,000 presidential salary) combine different levels of government. But most are twenty-year military retirees who eventually switch from a federal income of a paycheck plus a pension to a federal income of two pensions. Furthermore, any former serviceman not eligible for a military pension can (incredibly) switch his years of service over to a CSRS pension if he joins the federal civilian work force.

enlistees and officers who ever serve in the armed forces, over 85 percent quit before becoming "entitled" to a share in the retirement bonanza.

The fact that so few servicemen ever receive pension benefits undermines the most common argument made in defense of the current military retirement system. "Fat" pensions, it is claimed, are a necessary incentive if skilled personnel are to be persuaded to make a career out of the armed services. This may be true, but the incentive is unnecessarily expensive and has produced indifferent results. Alternatively, this argument is sometimes turned around. "Fat" pensions, we hear, are needed to encourage the military's "old men" to clear out and leave room for younger bodies and quicker minds. The dangers and rigors we associate with military service might seem to lend this second claim a certain plausibility. Upon closer examination, however, the "push the old men out the door" argument turns out to be less than convincing. The most obvious problem is its premise that at thirty-nine years of age (the average retirement age of a twenty-year pensioner) most men are functionally senescent. Even if this were true for physically demanding tasks, such tasks characterize a small fraction of all military labor. According to the General Accounting Office (GAO), only 8 percent of all service jobs—including infantry, armored, artillery, and naval specialties—require exceptional physical stamina. Moreover, of this 8 percent most are filled by short-term servicemen. Fully 80 percent of all enlisted retirees have *never* served in capacities classified by the GAO as physically arduous. According to Admiral Hyman Rickover (an authority, since he himself retired in his eighties), "there are today few jobs in the military that cannot be performed by persons up to fifty-five years of age or even older."

Far from helping the military, a retirement system that practically pushes people out the door after they complete twenty years of service clearly leads to an extraordinary waste of talent. At precisely the time when a careerist could be making his most important technical and leadership contributions, during his forties and fifties, he is instead handed back to the private sector. In his place, a new recruit must be trained at a total cost in 1983 of $15,000 (for an enlistee) or $50,000 (for an officer). As military operations come to depend increasingly on sophisticated new technologies, this waste of existing talent becomes more flagrant. According to a Brookings Institution study, "the U.S. military's emphasis on youth and vigor has yielded armed forces too inexperienced to operate today's sophisticated weapons systems."* Perhaps one number sums up the point better than any other: only one of every six persons in the armed forces today is thirty-five years of age or older.

Here we must once more return briefly to the Military Retirement Reform Act of 1986. Among the act's explicit purposes was to encourage retention of manpower beyond the minimum twenty years required for pension vesting. The idea was that if pension levels for twenty-year retirees were reduced while those for thirty-year retirees remained unchanged, many more people would be induced to prolong their careers. According to the Department of Defense's own forecasting models, however, the 1986 act will have a negligible effect on overall manpower retention, and may actually encourage certain categories of careerists to retire earlier. The reform does achieve minor long-term budget savings, but in the end represents a woefully ineffective approach to retaining skilled personnel.

Another argument made in defense of the military retirement system's generous pensions is that they are justified compensation for the manifest dangers that members of the armed forces face in the course of their careers. Ever since Roman times—so the argument goes—soldiers have been granted generous early pensions (often in the form of land grants) to compensate for the mortal risks they run in order to guarantee the safety of the rest of us. Does the argument make sense for today's military? A GAO study recently concluded that more than three-quarters of all retiring enlisted men served for twenty years without seeing any combat experience; and less than 10 percent of their total service time was spent on "hazardous duty" (for which soldiers, in any case, already receive a special bonus). A related issue that might be raised is that millions of short-term enlistees have indeed seen combat in America's wars without receiving a pension. Were their risks any less real than those of the careerists? Another major war could of course quickly raise the percentage of our armed forces who have served under fire. But then again, in an era of "mutual assured destruction," many urban civilians may well wonder whether their own risks are significantly less than the dangers faced by those in uniform.

But even if we accept the "danger" argument for the moment, we still might want to ask: How do military pensions compare with retire-

*Martin Binkin and Irene Kyriakopoulos, *Use or Experience? Manning the Modern Military* (The Brookings Institution, 1979).

ment plans for workers in other hazardous jobs, such as police and fire fighters? The answer is that police and fire-fighter benefits, though quite generous relative to the private-sector norm, for the most part don't even come close to military benefits. Very few plans for police and fire fighters allow such early retirement with an immediate annuity; all require more than thirty years to reach the maximum benefit level; most require an employee wage contribution (servicemen contribute nothing in payroll taxes toward their pension plans); and only a couple of plans (New York City's, for example) feature 100-percent-of-CPI indexing.

Still another defense of the military retirement system is based on the widespread misapprehension that members of the armed services are underpaid. Lobbyists for the military have played this one to the hilt, arguing—just like civil service lobbyists—that generous pensions are simply delayed compensation for meager salaries. Most independent studies, however, have concluded that military salaries (when correctly measured to include in-kind income) have become increasingly competitive in the national labor market. Over the last decade, investigations made by the RAND Corporation, the Conference Board, the Senate Armed Services Committee, and the General Accounting Office have all determined that service pay is at least equal to private-sector pay for workers with equivalent qualifications. If pensions are included in the calculation, there isn't even a contest. The RAND Corporation, for instance, estimated that total compensation in the military is 30 to 50 percent higher for enlistees and 70 to 100 percent higher for officers than it is for workers with equivalent qualifications in the private sector.

The gains in military pay over the past fifteen years have been the direct result of the transition from a conscript to a volunteer army. Back in the 1950s and 1960s, the military simply did not have to worry whether jobs filled primarily by conscripts were competitive in pay. To that extent, it may then have been true that lucrative pensions "compensated" for low average pay levels (at least for those few who actually stayed on for twenty years). The introduction of a voluntary personnel policy, however, was accompanied by a deliberate effort to make all types of military work an attractive alternative to private-sector employment on the basis of pay alone. Since 1970 average military pay has increased at a faster pace than average private-sector pay; meanwhile, the traditional generosity of military pensions has remained unchanged.

Ironically, by encouraging career personnel to retire early, the military's "fat" pension policy has been instrumental in forcing the Department of Defense to push wage levels still higher in order to attract enough new recruits. This situation is almost certain to get worse over the foreseeable future, since the Baby Boom has already passed enlistment age and the pool of potential new recruits is no longer expanding. Reform of the military retirement system may therefore be advisable for personnel reasons alone. The 1986 reform act made modest cuts in benefit provisions for newly enlisted members of the armed forces, but left the twenty-year vesting rule untouched. Mature men and women with talents to contribute to the military should be given some incentive to stay where they are. Likewise, the "deadwood" who have already served ten years should not be forced to serve another ten just so that they can pick up their munificent lifetime annuity.

A Final Look at Comparability

Before outlining a few simple reform measures, let us take a final look at the key question in any discussion of civil service and military pensions: comparability with the private sector. The left-hand bars in Figure 8-1 compare the average monthly pension benefit received by five groups of households in 1984: first, households receiving Social Security only, and then (regardless of whether they also got Social Security) households receiving income from private pensions, state or local employee pensions, federal employee pensions, and military retirement pensions. Figure 8-1 reveals at a glance that the benefit levels for civil service and military pensioners tower above those for private-sector pensioners—by 140 percent and 157 percent, respectively.

It might be argued that this comparison is misleading, since nearly all retired persons with private pensions are also receiving OASI benefits from Social Security. But don't forget: most civil service and nearly all military retirees have qualified for Social Security as well during the course of second careers. The right-hand bars in Figure 8–1 reveal that the Social Security benefits of private-sector retirees by no means bridge the gap. In 1984 households receiving civil service or military pension benefits reported a total average income of $31,720 and $42,660, respectively. Households receiving private-pension income reported $23,460. And remember, a minority (one-third) of all private-sector retirees receive any private pension at all; average total household income for the other two-thirds, including

FIGURE 8-1   **Average Monthly Pension Income and Total Household Income for All Households Receiving Pensions in 1984**

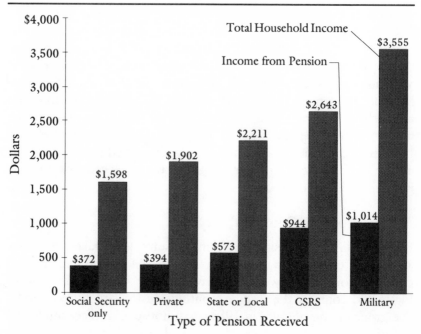

Self-reported cash income, including all categories of benefits (retired, disabled, dependent, survivor).

Source: Current Population Reports (Series P-70, Census)

Social Security, was $19,180.

Many of the CSRS and military pensioners, of course, are still earning salaries and are not yet eligible for Social Security. What about those who are retired and receive both a federal pension and Social Security? Census data again confirm that these combined benefits beat the private sector by a wide margin. Consider the average income received solely from the following pension combinations in 1984: Social Security with CSRS ($12,672), with military retirement ($17,796), and with a private pension ($9,912).

This dramatic pension gap is due to both the higher initial benefit levels of federal pensioners and the 100 percent of CPI indexing by which these levels are subsequently maintained. In one crucial respect, however, these numbers understate the total disparity between

FIGURE 8-2   **Distribution of Pension Recipients by Age for Different Types of Pension in 1984**

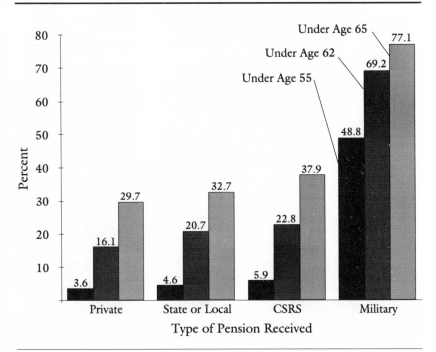

Includes all categories of benefits (retired, disabled, dependent, survivor).

Source: Current Population Reports (Series P-70, Census)

federal and private-sector pensions because they fail to take into account that retirement lasts much longer for a federal retiree. For example, an age breakdown of beneficiaries for four types of pensions (see Figure 8-2) shows that the share of all CSRS pensioners under age fifty-five (5.9 percent) is about two-thirds larger than the share for all private pensioners (3.6 percent); the share of all military pensioners under age fifty-five (48.8 percent) is nearly fourteen times larger. Higher benefit levels together with longer retirements generate a huge overall advantage. The General Accounting Office has found that civil service retirement offers its pensioners more than twice as much lifetime income as a private plan; military retirement typically offers its pensioners between eight and nineteen times as much.

There is yet another (and more accurate) method of measuring these differences in pension costs. "Normal cost," to use actuarial

FIGURE 8-3   **Federal Civil Service and Military Retirement: Funded and Unfunded Actuarial Cost as a Percent of Payroll in Fiscal Year 1980**

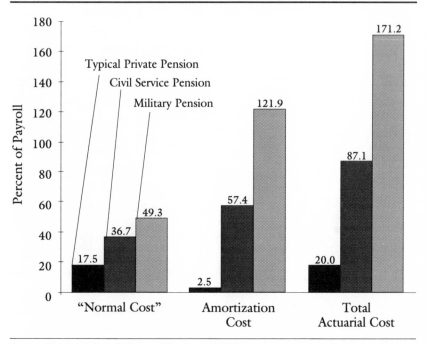

Source: Employee Benefit Research Institute (1983)

terminology, is the fraction of an average worker's payroll that would have to be set aside in an interest-earning trust fund, throughout his working years, in order to pay for his expected pension. For the private sector, Figure 8-3 assumes a relatively generous retirement benefit package with a normal cost of 17.5 percent of payroll (including employer and employee OASDI taxes). The 1980 estimated normal cost for federal pensions is much higher: 36.7 percent of payroll for the CSRS and 49.3 percent of payroll for military retirement. These latter figures assume no Social Security coverage for federal workers.

A discussion of normal cost leads naturally to a discussion of pension liabilities. Until very recently, civil service and military retirement operated, both formally and practically, as pay-as-you-go systems. For civil service retirement, employees and agencies traditionally paid a combined 14 percent of total payroll into a federal trust fund—less than half of what would be required to fully fund future benefits. For military retirement, there was no trust fund at all; pensions were simply paid out of the defense budget as the need arose.

Very little, therefore, has ever been "saved" for the purpose of future benefit payments, and the result—as we have already mentioned in Chapter 2—is a total unfunded liability for these two programs of more than $1 trillion. When a private plan finds itself in a similar situation, it is legally required not only to *calculate* the sum total of these unfunded obligations, but to *amortize* them (that is, charge them to its current cost) over a thirty-year period. The two right-hand bars at the center of Figure 8-3 show what the federal government would be charged if it were required to follow its own law. For the civil service, the amortization cost alone would amount to 57 percent of payroll, yielding a total pension cost (amortizing past incurred liabilities plus funding new liabilities) of 87 percent of payroll. The figures for military retirement are even more daunting: 122 percent of payroll in amortization, and an incredible 171 percent in total pension cost.

In the early 1980s, the formal accounting for these two programs was partially "reformed." Unfortunately, these were merely paper reforms—and are likely to remain so indefinitely until we carry out a wholesale reconstruction of our federal budgetary practices. For civilian workers, the reform accompanied the new FERS system that covers all new employees hired after 1983. Under the FERS, workers and agencies make trust-fund contributions equal to the normal cost of future benefits (though the past and future costs of the ongoing CSRS program will remain as underfunded as ever). For military servicemen, legislation passed in 1983 requires the defense department to begin paying the full normal cost for future retirement benefits into a newly created "Military Retirement Fund" (though again, past underfunding is simply treated as water under the bridge).*

Why are these "reforms" without substance? Quite simply, for the same reason the paper surpluses of Social Security are without effect:

---

*Technically, it can be said that the CSRS trust fund is being reimbursed for some of the rise in unfunded liabilities that it has incurred since 1970. Likewise, the Military Retirement Fund was reimbursed for prior unfunded liabilities in 1984. But since these "payments" were made directly by the Treasury (not through the budgets of the employing agencies), they are paper transactions of the purest variety. Through a similar transaction, for instance, the Treasury could "absolve" Social Security of its total unfunded liabilities with one effortless stroke of the pen. All the trust funds would then be "funded" and the U.S. Treasury would be trillions more in the red.

these "trust funds" merely represent sums that the federal government owes itself. The current balances of these trust funds are entirely internalized within the federal budget and as such have no influence on either federal spending or federal borrowing. To prefund military retirement, for instance, the Treasury simply "credits" an extra yearly sum to the Defense budget that is called a "surplus." As years go by, these accumulated surpluses are called trust-fund "assets"—which are numbers in a computer representing what Treasury "owes" the Defense Department. Meanwhile, we can behave in practice as though these numbers did not exist. On paper, it may be correct to observe (as the CBO has projected) that by 1993 the CSRS and military trust funds will have a combined surplus of $43 billion. But the federal budget is already counting on spending this "income" and calculates its current and projected budget deficits after already earmarking it as revenue.

Stated differently, the federal government will never achieve a truly balanced budget until its revenues match its expenditures *exclusive* of all of its Social Security and pension trust-fund accounts. Until then, truth-in-borrowing ought to require that the Treasury introduce a new species of debt classification: along with T-bills we should count what the Treasury is borrowing from its trust funds as part of the publicly held national debt. Perhaps we could call them twenty- and thirty-year "R" bills—"R" for retirement.

Options for Reform

There are several reasons why reform of civil service and military retirement should remain high on our entitlements agenda. The first reason is equity. We have already documented the generosity of the federal pension systems by describing their lopsided advantages over pensions in the private sector. If the beneficiaries of these programs paid fully for their own benefits, the generosity would be legitimate. But of course these beneficiaries do not. If the programs helped to alleviate poverty or serve some other public interest, the generosity might be justified. But again, these programs do not. It is unfair— indeed disingenuous—for us to promise such generous future retirements to our federal work force when we know that we may have difficulty delivering a much lower level of benefits through Social Security to the rest of our work force.

The second reason is efficiency and morale. Years of nonaccrual (or "cash") accounting has encouraged Congress to cut current costs by limiting increases in the take-home pay of federal workers while allowing future pension liabilities to keep rising. Since 1967, for instance, civil-service pay schedules have been raised by 181 percent, while the average CSRS pension has risen by 276 percent. When we overcompensate our federal employees by granting them huge future pensions, moreover, we make it difficult for cost-conscious federal agencies to hire new workers or (in the case of the military) keep experienced workers. Instead we encourage a variety of wasteful alternatives—from understaffing and poor customer service to "temps" and outside contractors. The inevitable result has been the rise of a "three-caste" hierarchy: the retiree, who does best of all; the active civil servant, whose pay is often topped by the pensions of those who formerly held his job; and the outside (and younger) contracted help, who frequently work without any benefits or pension coverage at all. Such "tiering" creates widespread dissatisfaction within our federal work force; ironically, it also mirrors the same profound age-based inequities that permeate the entitlements that this work force hands out to the public at large.

The final reason is cost. Over the last fifteen years, the budgetary outlays for these two programs have risen nearly as rapidly as our entirely open-ended health-care programs. *Taken together, CSRS and military retirement now spend as much as all federal means-tested programs (except Medicaid) combined.* Their present size does not reflect a public consensus on federal spending priorities. Instead, by fulfilling unaffordable and formulaic entitlements promises, these programs simply crowd higher priorities out of the budget. Although the growing cost of federal civilian and military pensions is projected to decelerate over the next several decades, it still may exceed the growth rate of our economy. In the best case, it locks in a permanent 17 percent drain on the share of total federal outlays we now devote to cash benefits. Even if the best case occurs, moreover, this relative stability in cost will be due almost entirely to a fall in the relative number of new retirees—not to any sizable decline in benefit levels enacted by recent reforms.

This last point deserves special emphasis. For civilian workers, the primary effect (and purpose) of the new FERS plan introduced in 1986 is to switch part of our future benefit liability from the CSRS to Social Security. It will accomplish this by adding the effective normal cost of OASDI (11.8 percent of payroll) to the benefit package and subtracting a roughly equivalent normal cost (11.0 percent of payroll) from civil service pensions. The FERS does not, therefore, reduce total federal outlays to future pensioners—and remember, the FERS does not *begin* to pay out full benefits until well into the Baby Boom's retirement.* As for military servicemen, the 1986 act generates such minor long-term savings that one needs a telescope to find them. The act saves virtually nothing before the year 2010; in constant 1986 dollars, it saves $1 billion yearly by the year 2017 and about $3 billion yearly by the year 2040. Altogether, we are looking at a 7 percent improvement relative to pre-1986 law after fifty-four years.

A reform program should not only seek to reduce the cost of these entitlements; it should also insist on comparability for *total* compensation packages (pensions and fringes as well as pay) both between the public and private sectors and within the public sector itself. Many different avenues for reform remain open. They include COLA cuts, postponed retirement age, and reductions in initial benefit levels.

COLA Cuts. The first target of reform should be cost-of-living adjustments. As with Social Security, it might make sense to alter indexing formulas to either 60 percent of the Consumer Price Index or to the "CPI minus 2." Either of these changes would still leave federal pensioners with a more generous indexing scheme than the vast majority of private pensioners enjoy. They would, in addition, protect federal pensioners from the capricious and unpredictable "one-shot" COLA freezes that Congress will inevitably resort to in the absence of reform.† In the case of the CSRS, one proposal that

---

*The fact that the entry-age "normal cost" of the FERS is equal to that of the CSRS means that they will eventually cost the same in future federal outlays. To be sure, some of the specific provisions of the FERS are less generous (such as various COLA reductions), but these are compensated by other, more generous features (such as even-higher replacement rates). Pension experts thus conclude that the FERS is actually a better deal than the CSRS for 40 percent of all current employees. If very few "old-law" civil servants (less than 2 percent) are exercising their option to switch over from the CSRS to the FERS, it is not because the FERS looks bad on paper. Rather, it is because they count on the future untouchability of the CSRS; they do not have the same faith in the FERS or Social Security.

†Although it has refused to enact permanent COLA changes, Congress has repeatedly flip-flopped over temporary COLA cuts in recent years—creating the least possible budget savings and the most possible uncertainty for pensioners. In 1981 Congress fixed the federal pension COLA to an annual 100 percent of CPI adjustment, payable in March. In 1982 it changed its mind: thereafter, the payable date would be delayed one month each year until 1985 and the COLA would be capped for military retirees under age 62. But in 1983, it shifted the payable date all at once to December and in 1984 it got rid of the COLA cap. One year later, a provision in the newly enacted Gramm-Rudman law eliminated the December 1985 pension COLA altogether. It would have done so in future years as well (so long as the Gramm-Rudman deficit targets were not met), but Congress repealed this provision in 1986 after a lobbying blitzkrieg by federal pension interest groups.

seems appealing on an equity basis is to exclude from current pensioners' benefits the portion that is directly attributable to the 1 percent CPI "kicker" they enjoyed from 1969 to 1976. As we already pointed out, it is estimated that this "kicker" will cost the federal government between $30 and $40 billion over the lifetimes of the retirees who benefited from this windfall.

Alternatively, as the National Committee on Public Employee Pension Systems (PEPS) has proposed, CPI indexing could be limited to the first $10,000 of total federal retirement income (whether it comes from the CSRS, Social Security, a military pension, or some combination of the three).* Such a reform would both maintain a floor of protection and achieve huge savings. In 1985 PEPS estimated that a $10,000 COLA cap would save as much as *$400 billion* (in nondiscounted dollars) over the remaining lifetimes of retirees and currently vested federal employees.†

Retirement Age. Early retirement options must be curtailed gradually but surely. Federal pensioners already retire many years earlier than private-sector retirees who have worked at similar jobs. In light of recent legislation outlawing mandatory retirement at seventy and the scheduled delay in full Social Security retirement until sixty-seven, this discrepancy between federal and private retirement ages is especially perverse and should not be allowed to grow even wider. Curtailing early retirement will also work powerful and positive changes in the long-term financial balance of federal pensions. Not only is total spending reduced by cutting the number of years that a federal pensioner receives benefits, but trust-fund income is raised proportionately by increasing the number of years that payroll contributions are made by and on behalf of each federal employee.

Under current law, civil service workers can retire with full benefits at fifty-five with thirty years of service, at sixty with twenty years of service, or at sixty-two with five years of service. A modest delay to

---

*Letter from the National Committee on Public Employee Pension Systems to Congress (June 21, 1985). Former Congressman Hastings Keith, cochairman of PEPS, points to himself as a prime example of undeserved bounty: in 1988, he is receiving $1,452 *per week* in combined Civil Service, military, congressional, and Social Security benefits. Amazingly, a full 57 percent of this amount is due to COLA raises since he first started receiving benefits.

†Massachusetts, for example, now uses a COLA only on the first $9,000 in annual benefits per state pensioner. To grasp intuitively the savings possible at the federal level, consider that one-quarter of the cost of the annual CSRS COLA now goes to beneficiaries receiving *at least $30,000 annually from their CSRS pensions alone—not including their other Social Security and military pension income.*

sixty, sixty-two, and sixty-five would still leave the civil service more generous in its retirement-age provisions than practically any private employer. An alternative approach to retirement age suggested by the PEPS committee would be to peg the "normal" retirement age for the civil service at sixty-five, just as with Social Security, with an eventual increase to sixty-seven, as mandated by the reform legislation of 1983. At the same time, a steeper actuarial reduction in benefits for those who opt for early retirement would bring the civil service system closer into line with pension plans in the private sector. This would take us one step closer toward our goal of item-by-item comparability between federal and private retirement compensation packages.

The military retirement system allows, for men and women who joined the military before 1986, pensions at 50 percent of pay after twenty years of service and 75 percent of pay after thirty years of service. Although the 1986 Military Retirement Reform Act reduces the percentage before thirty years of service (at least until age sixty-two), it fails to encourage longer terms of service. We should go much further. Beginning now, we should gradually increase the qualifying number of years for all *current* as well as future members of the armed services to twenty-five years and forty years (for reduced and full pensions, respectively), and use part of the resulting savings to offer some pension to those who only serve between ten and twenty-five years. This last reform would eliminate the huge and unfair discontinuity that currently occurs at the twenty-year mark. Some critics have argued that lengthening the military career would deter good officers from staying with the armed forces. Others have argued—more convincingly—that this sort of reform would enable the military to keep for a longer time the talent that has already been discovered and trained. Longer military careers might therefore be a good idea regardless of the budget-savings issue.

Initial Benefit Levels. The computation of retirement benefits for both the civil service and the military pension systems is based on the highest three consecutive years of salary. At the very least, an average based on the final five years, such as is commonly used in the private sector, should be adopted. In addition, the "factor multiplier" used for current civil service workers to compute benefit levels could be reduced from 1.87 percent to 1.0 percent for years of coverage up to thirty years, and to 0.5 percent for each additional year of coverage. This would bring benefit computation for the CSRS much closer into line with the norms that govern private pensions. Finally, qualification for disability under the CSRS should be made to conform to the more stringent guidelines that are set for both Social Security's Disability Insurance and for private pension plans.

Some combination of these measures would both achieve considerable budget savings and make our federal pension systems more equitable. Neither the creation of the FERS nor the 1986 Military Retirement Reform Act affects current retirees or the vast majority of currently employed civil servants and soldiers—and neither is likely to achieve significant long-term savings. As things stand, federal pensions remain an unparalleled bonanza for their privileged beneficiaries while making a disproportionate claim on our limited national resources for decades to come.

9

Health-Care Policy:
Facing the Painful
Trade-Offs

> "What impresses me is that in comparison with the U.K. it
> seems very seldom that the U.S. physician ever states that
> there is no surgery that would help, no drug that is advanta-
> geous, and no further investigation that is required. There
> seems to be an irresistible impulse to *do something*. . . ."
> — *British internist, cited in* The Painful
> Prescription: Rationing Hospital Care,
> *by Henry J. Aaron and William B. Schwartz*

THE ATTITUDE OF Washington policymakers toward the
crisis in U.S. health-care spending can only be described as
schizophrenic. On the one hand, there is the purely rhetorical
consensus: before national audiences, every politician intones
gravely—and correctly—that something "must" be done soon to
control runaway costs. On the other hand, there is the political reality:
before all the insider groups, from health trade associations and
insurers to senior lobbies and physicians, every politician boasts of
what he has done to make health care bigger, better, and more freely
accessible to all who are persuaded they have a right to it.

We have already surveyed the dimensions of our national health-
care cost crisis in Chapter 5. Here let us simply review the bottom line.
By engineering an open-ended system of benefits, tax subsidies, regulations, and law in which most of us are largely insulated from the real
cost of our health-care purchases, public policy has transformed the
United States into far and away the most profligate health consumer
in history. Compared with other industrial countries, we spend about
3.5 percent more of GNP on health care. This *extra* spending is 40

percent larger than our total net fixed investment in business plant and equipment. Since our per capita GNP is larger, the difference in terms of per capita *dollars* is even more dramatic. Indeed, in absolute per capita dollars our *extra* spending would be enough to double our net fixed business investment, our total corporate spending on R&D, our total net additions to public infrastructure, our total federal and state cash benefits for the poor, and our total federal aid to child nutrition and education. With its extravagant bias toward specialized and acute care, moreover, our system of health care gives us no better health. Instead, it wastefully piles on layer after layer of subsidized coverage for those whose public claim is least legitimate (especially wealthier and older Americans) while denying it for those whose public claim is most legitimate (especially poorer and younger Americans).

The growing generational inequity of our health-care policy, in truth, bears every sign of attrition warfare against our own future. Outside the fortress of our public generosity subsist a large and growing number—30 to 40 million—of Americans under age sixty-five who are entirely uninsured. They include nearly a million poor working families dropped from Medicaid eligibility in the early 1980s; several million poor children dropped as well from child nutrition programs; most of the growing share of all children no longer vaccinated against "conquered" diseases; about one million young women each year who get no care before childbirth; and nearly all of the estimated one million families who need treatment for a serious illness each year but do not seek it. About one-third of these uncovered Americans are officially in poverty. Half are under age twenty-five; most of the rest work full-time for poverty or near-poverty compensation—on which they make 15 percent payroll "contributions" to those (within the fortress) who have generous coverage. And an additional 30 million young and primarily low-income Americans receive little or no public help in paying for policies that lack even a major medical indemnity.

What about those within the fortress? Here we find working Americans who are older, better paid, and more likely to have jobs with large corporate or public-sector employers. They get the lion's share of our giant employer tax subsidy. And here we find our retired elderly, whose outsized consumption of health care continues to far outpace the growth of our economy. Americans over age sixty-five comprise 12 percent of our population; today they receive 73 percent of all federal health benefits and well over 50 percent of all health benefits from every level of government. The per capita dollar value of such benefit outlays is *twice* as large as what the "socialized" health-care systems of the other major industrial countries spend on the elderly. In comparison, the amount we spend publicly per child is barely *half* as large as what these other countries spend on children.*

As we have already seen, spending on health care is currently the most intractable force behind the growth in our overall entitlement budget—and will remain so over the next generation. Those of us who benefit from it like to think we are paying our own way, but of course we are not. To make possible our spending, we are accumulating those multitrillion-dollar liability mountains that no one likes to talk about: in our public-sector Medicare system, in private-sector retiree benefit plans, and in the IOUs we are signing over with such furious abandon to the savings accounts of foreigners (whose eyes are quite clearly fixed on their own demographic future). A few optimists may expect that younger Americans will someday be able and willing to pay off our bills. The rest of us may be hoping for something else: realistic and affordable reform that will substantially reduce the total cost of our health-care system while improving on its equity between age-groups and income brackets.

Now let us turn our attention to Washington. Large-scale reforms of our federal health-care policy are indeed a major focus of debate by our 100th Congress. One, "catastrophic" coverage for Medicare beneficiaries, has already been passed and signed into law.† Others that

---

*Based on IMF data on public spending by age-group for 1980 and applying it to OECD national health-cost data for 1984 with purchasing-power parity exchange rates. The 1984 result for the United States is $3,079 in public-sector health spending per elderly person (aged sixty-five and over) and $210 per child (aged fourteen and under). The 1984 average per capita result for the other "Big Seven" nations (Japan, Canada, United Kingdom, France, Italy, and West Germany) is $1,556 per elderly person and $372 per child. Relative to the others, the U.S. average benefit level thus stands at 198 percent for the elderly and 56 percent for children. Due to IMF and OECD estimates for some countries, as well as to differences in years, these figures are of course approximate.

†The "catastrophic cost" amendment to Medicare (originally the "Stark-Gradison" bill, H.R. 2470, and the "Bentsen" bill, S.R. 1127) was passed by Congress in June and signed by President Reagan on July 1, 1988. It leaves current Medicare benefits unchanged, but adds to them new benefits that would (1) eliminate any beneficiary cost-sharing for HI beyond a single yearly deductible ($564 in 1989); (2) eliminate any beneficiary cost-sharing for SMI over a modest yearly cap ($1,370 in 1989); (3) pay for most prescription drug expenses (80 percent after 1992) over a modest yearly cap ($600 in 1989); and (4) somewhat widen Medicare reimbursement for assorted other services, including skilled nursing care, home care, and "respite care." For most of the elderly, this law simply relieves them (or their former employers) of the expense and bother of medigap insurance. The law currently provides that beneficiaries will pay for these benefits themselves through a combination of flat-rate and progressive premiums, but most of the gray lobby is still fighting this provision. Projected federal cost: between $10 and $20 billion annually by 1993.

create vast new health-care entitlements—mostly for those already receiving public benefits—are still being hotly debated and will continue to preoccupy Congress for the next several years.*

Schizophrenic may be a harsh word, but it is difficult to find any other way to characterize the discussion over these bills. Are supporters aware of the runaway cost of the policies already in place? "Yes," they typically answer, "Horrible. Don't bother with the numbers—I already know—it's absolutely unsustainable. But don't worry, we've already done a lot of cost control and we'll do more soon." And is it fair to add yet another layer of insurance for elderly at all income levels while millions of poor children have no coverage at all? "Poverty among American children is shameful. Unacceptable. But don't worry, we'll get around to that soon too."

The point is not that the issues addressed by these proposals—catastrophic costs, long-term care, and uncovered workers—are undeserving of legislative attention. They are. The point rather is that

---

*Four examples:

1. *Home-Care Benefits for Medicare* ("Pepper" bill, H.R. 3436). This proposal would leave current Medicare benefits unchanged, but would add a new benefit that would pay for a wide range of medical, nursing, social-work, and homemaker services at the homes of chronically ill elderly and disabled persons. Eligibility, services, and credentials of caregivers would be authorized in practice by "home-care management agencies." There would be no means test, no deductible, and no cost-sharing. Cost per person would initially be limited to about $10,000 to $15,000 per year. Every beneficiary would receive a "home-care bill of rights." Projected federal cost: unknown (the CBO estimates $6 billion by 1990, but it admits the cost would be much higher if it did not project that the additional demand for home-care would rapidly exhaust the limited supply of credentialed home-care professionals).

2. *Long-Term Care Benefits for Medicare* ("Mitchell" bill, S.R. 2305). This proposal would leave current Medicare benefits unchanged, but would add (1) a home-care benefit, including paid "homemaker and chore-aid" assistance after a $500 yearly deductible and with a 20 percent copayment; (2) a "respite-care" benefit, which would pay 50 percent of the cost of hiring professional help (up to $2,000 yearly) to relieve unpaid caregivers such as family members; and (3) a nursing-home benefit, which would pay 70 percent of nursing-home costs starting two years after admission. Projected federal cost: $16 to $18 billion annually.

3. *Comprehensive Long-Term, Chronic, and Preventative Benefits for Medicare* ("Pepper" bill, H.R. 65). This proposal would leave current Medicare benefits unchanged, but would add a series of new benefits under the rubric Medicare "Part C": physical exams, eye care, dental care, hearing care, prescription drugs, and long-term (at-home and nursing-home) care. Fixed monthly premiums might pay for part of the cost, but there would be no deductibles, cost-sharing, means test, or waiting periods. Any patient grievances would be resolved by appeals boards, at least half of each comprised of beneficiaries. Projected federal cost: $60 billion annually.

4. *Mandated Benefits by Employers* ("Kennedy-Waxman" bill, S.R. 1265). This proposal would require all employers in firms with more than five workers to purchase health insurance for all employees. "Minimum" coverage requirements would be generous (they include mental-health and diagnostic benefits) and could be raised by states to include further mandated benefits. Employees would be required to pay for 80 to 100 percent of the cost of coverage. Projected employer cost for 23 million persons: $27 billion annually.

the proposals are selective, open-ended, and vastly overpriced solutions that only add—never subtract—from our collective generosity. To the extent they are enacted, they will feed even faster our insatiable demand for health-care consumption. To the extent they are not, it will be because we cannot afford them. We cannot afford them because we cannot afford the system we already have. And we cannot touch what we already have because that would involve painful and unthinkable choices. The inequity of our current system, therefore, goes hand in hand with its excessive cost. Change has become doubly unaffordable, genuine reform never happens, and any alleviation of the inequity as well as the cost of our system must ever remain something that someday we will "get around to." As we have already seen in Chapter 5, the result is an all-or-nothing entitlement and "feast or famine" coverage.

Let us emphasize that the perverse outcome of this health-policy gridlock is not limited merely to inequity between the young and the old. The elderly themselves suffer from it. An important case in point is already becoming a hotly debated issue in America: home care. As yet, the vast majority of the chronically ill elderly receive no Medicare coverage for home care; instead, they must first go broke, at which time they become eligible to enter a Medicaid-funded nursing home. Given home care's manifold advantages—efficiency, equity, and humanity—Medicare's refusal seems illogical. So why do we have nothing but Medicaid funding for nursing homes? Precisely because nursing homes are inherently unattractive to most of the elderly, and because Medicaid's means test makes them doubly so. The result is that the public cost tends to control itself. Universal home-care, on the other hand, is not self-selecting. Offered on the same terms as other services covered by Medicare—that is, on a fee-for-service basis to all with little cost-sharing and no limit on quality or quantity—it would be instantly and prohibitively expensive. Indeed, for many of the services needed by the chronically disabled (such as help with cooking, cleaning, and eating), such an open-ended benefit would be virtually indistinguishable from general cash grants. What would be both affordable and desirable, on the other hand, is an integrated Medicaid-Medicare program offering home care, along with other chronic- and acute-care coverage, in a way that maintained cost-saving incentives and that distinguished between beneficiaries according to need and health status. But such a program would be alien to our notion of entitlement, and no one in Washington even dares suggest it.

Ironically, then, our refusal to face painful trade-offs is itself a trade-off. Where we gain is the luxury of not having to make difficult ethical choices. Where we lose is public coverage that is either uncontrollably expensive or entirely unavailable. In the case of chronic-illness home-care, we have decided for the time being to keep it unavailable—to pretend that this humane and efficient option does not exist. Trying to avoid pain, in short, we end up with all-or-nothing coverage that needlessly generates pain.

A favorite hope nowadays is that more effective federal intervention into the allocation of health care can squeeze "all the waste" out of the system and give us more health care at much lower total cost. For a few this intervention would take the form of mandatory national health insurance and even direct federal supervision of providers. For most it would be more modest: the same system we have now, but with comprehensive regulation of the price and quantity of all health-care services provided within it. Implicit in all such arguments is the comforting idea that there is a magic solution that can painlessly solve our problem for us. All we need do is wait until the politicians "get around" to it.

Unfortunately, this is mistaken: we cannot finesse the fundamental trade-offs. Advocates of regulation point out quite correctly that the U.S. private-sector system—in which health-care services are supplied by independent and profit-making agents—has had very little success in bringing market discipline to total national health-care spending. In Chapter 5 we have seen why: our system simply subsidizes the effective purchasing power of the favored patient until all the parties selling or buying services get what they want. But the advocates of regulation do not recognize that our experience with regulation has been much the same. In complexity and breadth, the "cost-control" rules that we have instituted in the United States between patient and provider—on top of all the rest of our health-care regulation—have no equal in any other nation. In the end, however, we always give both parties sufficient leeway to buy and sell whatever they want. In short, even if we "socialized" U.S. medicine we would only end up with an extremely expensive and inequitable system of socialized health care.

It is not for lack of effort that regulation has failed to control costs. It is for lack of wisdom. So long as our message to the majority of American health-care consumers is that no cost will be spared, it is senseless to expect that we can spare costs through silent regulatory add-ons. Or to put it differently, if Americans have decided politically that they will not let the market deny them, they are hardly likely to let regulators deny them either. The difficult truth is that a cost-effective and equitable health-care system does not await the right regulatory solution. It awaits a solid public consensus that favored patients and favored providers must be forced to change their everyday behavior in the face of tougher choices—about prevention, testing, treatment, and care. In the absence of such a consensus, we will make little progress.

Here we briefly review the history of cost-containment regulation—a history that is not an encouraging testimonial for those who remain optimistic about this avenue of policy. We then spell out a few basic principles that could take cost control beyond a mere rhetorical consensus and explain what changes they would imply for current federal policy. Finally, we turn to the tangible, real-life trade-offs that any effective reform must ultimately face up to.

The Failure of Cost-Containment Regulation

Supply Control. Back in the early 1970s, the federal government initiated its first cost-containment policy, supply control. The logic behind it was simple: to the extent that there is less to sell—especially if what is sold is "wasteful"—there is also less to buy, and total spending as a consequence must decline. But the means used to carry out this strategy were far from simple. A multitude of federally sponsored groups (with acronyms like HSA, SHPDA, HSP, and PSRO) were called upon to regulate virtually every aspect of the health-care industry's business: whom it could employ, where it could build, and what treatment it could provide.

Significantly, supply control was not the original or primary purpose of any of these groups when they were first founded. The 200 or so regional "comprehensive health planning agencies" (or CHPAs, which were also known by many other funny-sounding names) were originally established in the late 1960s to facilitate broader public access to specialists and hospitals in all geographic regions. Similarly, "professional standards review organizations" (PSROs, or simply PROs since the early 1980s) were groups of physicians set up by Congress in early 1972 to assure that all Medicare and Medicaid beneficiaries receive "quality care." As the 1970s wore on, however, mounting concern about excessive national health-care spending persuaded these groups to "do something" about cost control. In 1974 Congress directed the CHPAs to limit the equipment and institutional capacity available to regional providers and asked PSROs to start reviewing "excessive" treatment utilization by physicians. At the same time, federal and state benefits administrators began to "disallow" reimbursement for types of treatment that they did not consider cost-effective.

In practice, this strategy has created a growing regulatory web of mind-numbing complexity. The CHPAs, for example, have tried to enforce regional ceilings on everything from the size of new hospitals to the number of new nursing-home beds to the quantity of specific new technologies (such as computerized axial tomography, or CAT scanners) that health-care providers can purchase. CHPA limits are enforced through "certificates of need" (CONs) issued by these agencies. PROs, meanwhile, must employ hundreds of doctors and nurses in each state to conduct "utilization reviews" of their peers designed to detect cost-raising practices, from Medicare reimbursement fraud to excessive rates of surgery or hospitalization. The U.S. Department of Health and Human Services, after studying these reviews, can order the PRO to reduce the number of specific types of treatment in its region. The penalty for ignoring the CONs or disobeying the PROs is the threat that doctors and hospitals might be prohibited from receiving reimbursements from federal programs.

Health-care experts have devoted considerable attention to the effectiveness of CON and PRO regulation. They have looked at the correlation between supply controls and total health-care spending by state, by region, and by type of treatment. Their conclusion has been nearly unanimous: neither effort has had any appreciable success, and in some instances may have actually accelerated the climb in spending. Certainly it has been difficult to see much success at the national level. Between 1965 and 1973, the years when our major medical benefit programs were founded and when we might expect spending growth to be fastest, total U.S. health-care costs climbed from 6.1 to 7.8 percent of GNP, or by about 0.2 percentage points per year. Between 1973 and 1983, when the full impact of implementing supply controls should have been felt, total U.S. health-care costs rose to 10.5 percent of GNP, or by about 0.3 percentage points per year.

The fundamental problem with supply-control regulation is its underlying theory. It presupposes that more supply generates its own demand and thus raises total cost.* This may be true in certain cases, such as new technologies whose very availability raises the price of "accepted" treatment, but in general this theory directly contradicts elementary economics (that greater supply reduces the price and thus lowers total cost). To be successful, we would have to be quite certain in each case that supply control is making things better and not worse. But the CHPAs and PROs cannot provide that kind of certainty; each regional health-care market is simply too complex, encompassing thousands of patients, providers, and third-party payers—as well as countless health-care services, every one of which can be performed at different prices and with different combinations of technology and labor. No one can possibly know in advance how demand and prices will respond to a limit on one supply "input."

For example, if CAT scans have become the "norm" in medical treatment, a limit on CAT scanners may not reduce the price and the quantity of services rendered. Instead, it may raise the price for the same number of CAT scans, or force physicians to use more costly methods of reaching the same certainty of diagnosis. Such ambiguity naturally gives rise to policies running at cross-purposes. At about the same time that the supply-control vogue caught on, for example, Congress was also trying to bid down health-care prices by encouraging the creation of new and innovative HMOs. Yet supply-control regulation had just the opposite effect: it typically limited the plant and equipment any new HMO could buy, suppressed the supply of young physicians new HMOs could hire, and vetoed any new or irregular treatment patterns HMOs might try. Such an approach might well be characterized as simultaneous pressure on the gas and on the brakes.

A further problem with supply regulation is that the regulators have never been certain whether cost containment is more or less important than "best possible" treatment in every case. Unfortunately, the best opportunities for genuine savings through supply control inevitably involve a direct conflict between these two objectives. Many health experts believe that the most effective supply control measures are those that tend to prevent a new and expensive procedure from becoming standard practice. But such measures put administrators in the painful position of categorically denying an effective (or even life-

---

*The notion that health-care supply creates its own demand goes by many names: "Roemer's Law," for instance, says that hospital use is determined by the number of available hospital beds; the "target-income" hypothesis says that each doctor will create whatever services he needs in order to earn the income he expects.

saving) treatment to everyone regardless of the circumstances. For years Medicare tried to discourage heart transplants by refusing reimbursement for them. In 1986, after thousands of patients had received heart transplants with private money, Medicare relented and began to pay for them.* When applied to existing "standard" procedures, categorical supply rules are often circumvented; when applied to new procedures, they are often (and perhaps rightly) regarded as arbitrary and politically intolerable.

The most insidious failure of supply control, however, is that it can be so easily twisted to serve the interests of providers rather than the public. All too often it has suppressed competition and preserved high-priced inefficiency—precisely the opposite of its policy intent. CON regulations, for example, have at times been selectively applied so that new low-cost providers such as outpatient community health centers and nonhospital "surgicenters" are denied the possibility of expanding their facilities. It is revealing that the Justice Department has been warning health-care providers since 1980 that regional agreements between hospitals to "close down" existing capacity (with or without the direction of a local health-planning agency) might constitute an antitrust violation.

Since the late 1970s, enthusiasm over a uniform and comprehensive strategy of supply control has waned. Few experts any longer try to defend its poor track record, and fewer still believe that industry-wide rules can be kept up to date with the rapid changes in today's health-care marketplace. In the early 1980s, Congress in essence killed CON regulation as a federal strategy by agreeing with the administration's request to cut drastically federal funding for local CHPAs. Today, as a result, CON regulation thrives in some states (such as New York, which still has *both* the longest average hospital stay per patient in the nation *and* the worst shortage in hospital beds), but is practically moribund in other states (such as California, which has always had one of the shortest stays per patient). But we have been reluctant to do away with supply control altogether. Many of the other main avenues of supply control—such as PROs, reimbursement review for new treatments, and federal pressure to reduce the doctor "glut"—remain alive and well.

---

*Due to treatment advances (most notably immunosuppressant drugs such as cyclosporin), heart transplants in the United States have risen from 62 in 1981 to 1,368 in 1986. Fortunately for HHS, the total cost need not be explicitly controlled since the number of operations is limited by the number of available donors. In practice, administrators are rationing the procedure by giving the youngest and (otherwise) healthiest patients first priority.

Price Controls. The origin of health-care price controls dates back once again to the early 1970s. Not long after the establishment of Medicaid and Medicare it was recognized that open-ended "fee-for-service" reimbursement without patient cost-sharing could generate practically unlimited costs. After all, if public funds were picking up the full tab, what would prevent individual providers from setting the fee as high as they wished? For Medicare, the initial federal response was an ad hoc refusal to allow full reimbursement on bills that seemed excessive. But then in 1972, Medicare moved to a more formal "CPR" system of screening reimbursements. For Medicaid, state administrators soon followed suit and moved to CPR or similar systems for screening bills.

The CPR system is a real number cruncher. To begin with, it assigns a single code number to each of thousands of services a physician or hospital might render to a patient. Then it keeps track of every bill submitted by every provider in every region. Finally, it reimburses each provider by whichever amount is lower: (1) the bill actually submitted, (2) the median price the provider has charged all patients for that particular service during that year, or (3) the seventy-fifth percentile of all prices charged for the service by all providers in the region during the year.* The resulting reimbursement is called the "customary, prevailing, and reasonable" (or CPR) price. By checking each bill against all of these averages, the CPR system has been fairly good at preventing unusual or fraudulent pricing by *individual* Medicare providers. However, because the averages change along with the prices charged by *all* providers for *all* patients the CPR system cannot possibly be effective as a strategy for overall price control.

This became painfully evident during the late 1970s and early 1980s as health-care spending kept climbing and providers kept billing Medicare and Medicaid for ever-higher prices that looked perfectly "reasonable" according to CPR. Policymakers in the Ford and Carter administrations complained long and loud about the failure of CPR to keep costs down. But for the most part, they refrained from advocating a stricter strategy of price control; instead, they put their faith in ever-vaster supply-control schemes.

---

*Since 1974 this last "prevailing" barrier has been further limited by using the lesser of (3) or the 75th percentile in the previous year multiplied by a national medical-price index (the "Medical Economic Index," or "MEI"). When Congress "freezes" the CPR rates, it typically limits the percentage growth in the "prevailing" barrier and rebases the MEI accordingly.

The one exception was hospital fees, the dominant item in public-benefit budgets and the one whose per diem price was rising faster than any other component of health-care treatment. At the federal level, special hospital price-control measures were proposed by both Presidents Ford and Carter, but nothing came of them.* At the state level, there was more action. From the mid-1970s on, a growing number of states initiated various types of "per diem" or "total-revenue" cost-control programs on all hospital care; by 1980 eight states had such programs. In retrospect, none of them appear to have been very successful. The best we can say is that hospital costs in states such as Massachusetts and New York have risen somewhat less rapidly (relative to the national norm) after price controls than before. On the other hand, hospital costs in most of these states were quite a bit higher than the national average before price controls, and remain higher today.

During the early 1980s, as hope for supply regulation faded, Congress and the administration were at last forced to agree upon a more determined approach to price control for Medicare. This strategy had two parts. For the HI side of Medicare, Congress decided in 1983 to phase out entirely the old cost-plus system of reimbursing hospitals and to replace it, over a three-year period, with a new "DRG" prospective- payment scheme. For the SMI side, Congress in 1984 decided simply to freeze the existing "prevailing" price in the CPR system at its 1983 level. This SMI freeze originally was to last only one year, but Congress has subsequently extended it off and on ever since. For most physicians, the SMI freeze remains in effect today.

The DRG reform of HI reimbursement is a radical departure from fee-for-service pricing. Since 1984 hospitals can no longer bill HI for each service they render. Instead, they receive only one predetermined (or "prospective") payment for each patient they admit; the size of this payment depends upon the condition of the patient (there are about 470 "diagnosis-related groups") at the time of his or her admission. The DRG system, therefore, has a distinct cost advantage over any (frozen or unfrozen) fee-for-service system: the provider cannot "pass through" its service volume. The hospital no longer gets more by doing more; instead, it gets more by doing less. Before, the hospital

---

*In 1977 President Ford proposed reviving Nixon's "Phase II" price controls on hospital fees (which had expired on April 30, 1974). But President Carter killed the Ford proposal after coming to office. Carter later drew up his own cost-containment scheme that called for total revenue limits for every acute-care hospital. Congress in turn killed the Carter proposal in 1979.

needed to be supervised to make sure patients really needed everything they were being given. Now the hospital needs to be supervised to make sure patients are really being given everything they need.

As we have already seen in Chapter 5, however, DRGs have failed to provide effective cost containment for Medicare. The reason is that DRGs cover only one often discretionary service (hospitalization) and therefore do not cover all care for all beneficiaries. Once a patient is admitted to a hospital, DRGs do indeed act like true prospective payment—which is why their most visible success has been to cut down on hospital use. In 1984, the first year DRGs were effective, the average length of stay for Medicare hospital patients dropped by over 20 percent (from 9.6 days to 7.4 days); at the same time, nationwide occupancy rates for hospital beds dropped to their lowest level since the early 1960s.

Before and after hospitalization, however, DRGs openly invite providers to game the system. The DRG system—unlike fee-for-service reimbursement—promises hospitals huge profits on patients who are healthier (and need less care) than the average patient in his or her "diagnostic-related group"; similarly, it promises huge losses on patients who are sicker. This gives every hospital two incentives: first, to admit patients who are healthier rather than sicker (given the same DRG), and second, to classify admissions in the most expensive DRG possible. The first tactic is less feasible for deathly ill admissions, but quite feasible for milder conditions that could be treated outside as well as inside a hospital. The anomalous result is that physicians are now complaining that they must give ambulatory or home-care treatment to many Medicare patients who should be (but are not) hospitalized, while over 10 percent of Medicare hospitalizations remain (according to HHS) "unnecessary." The second tactic, known as DRG "bracket creep," is common to all price-control schemes (among CPR-reimbursed physicians it is known as "code creep"). All it takes is for the admissions staff to use a bit of creative discretion in interpreting the various DRGs.*

---

*A careful review of sampled hospital admissions by HHS (released in February 1988) found evidence of both strategies. It reported that about one-fifth of all Medicare hospital admissions are being placed in the wrong DRG category—with most misclassifications in the hospitals' favor. It also reported that about 10 percent of hospital admissions were medically unnecessary and that most of these were for unusually profitable DRGs (such as cataracts) or for DRGs encompassing a wide range of possible needs (such as prostate problems, dizziness, bone disease, mental retardation, digestive disorders, and back pain). Such admissions, the study estimated, added $2 billion to the cost of HI in fiscal year 1985.

FIGURE 9-1   **Total Medicare Benefit Outlays in 1986 Dollars**

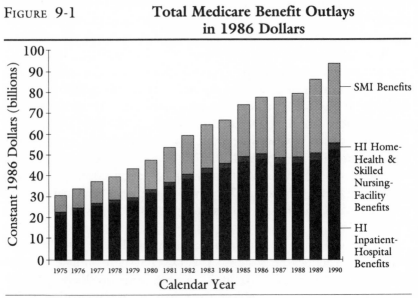

Values for years 1988–90 are II-B projections by HCFA.

Source: HCFA

But the biggest problem with DRGs is that even after a hospital lets in a Medicare patient, the hospital is compelled to limit its care to a minimum and to push as many services as possible to fee-for-service outpatient settings—regardless of the total expense. Increasingly, for instance, physicians and labs are redundantly purchasing their own testing equipment so that Medicare patients can receive all of their tests before admission. Similarly, patients are now discharged "quicker and sicker" from hospitals so that they can recover in expensive ambulatory, home-care, or skilled nursing-home environments that are still reimbursed according to services rendered.

Has all of this hurt quality of care? Not demonstrably. What it has done, though, is to offset much of the savings from HI's inpatient budget through rapid growth in all other components of Medicare— HI's home-health and skilled nursing programs, and, most of all, SMI's reimbursements to physicians (see Figure 9-1). HI spending, which had grown at an annual real rate of 8.4 percent from 1980 to 1984, slowed to only 1.3 percent from 1984 to 1987. Real SMI spending, meanwhile, accelerated from 10.3 percent to a blistering

12.5 percent. Since the introduction of DRGs, the share of physician charges attributable to outpatient services has climbed from two-fifths to more than one-half.

It may seem odd that SMI costs could race upward at such an unprecedented pace at a time when physician fees were "frozen." Yet this is simply testimony to the superiority of DRGs over simple price freezes, and the unwillingness, once again, of Medicare administrators to deny patients and physicians the services they want. If they cannot get them inside the hospital, they will get them outside the hospital. In practice, most physicians can use any number of ploys to get around technically "frozen" CPR prices: redefining a service as a more expensive service ("code creep"); deliberately multiplying the number of services rendered for the same condition ("second visits"); "unbundling" an old service into several, more profitable smaller services; and introducing new services altogether. Ironically, most of these ploys can be performed far more easily by the specialist (whom our system already favors) than by the generalist (the primary physician or pediatrician, whom our system already penalizes).* The effort to tighten up SMI through price freezes is therefore tilting the relative rewards in precisely the direction where it will cost the most for the least benefit.

Cost Shifting. The example of HI and SMI ought to make us cautious about evaluating regulatory solutions. Quite often, in instances where they appear effective, what has actually happened is that costs have been "shifted" to another payer. In the case of DRGs, shifting costs from HI to SMI may seem rather pointless—they are, after all, two parts of the same Medicare program. But remember that the federal government is obligated to publish long-term projections of the costs of HI (as a payroll-tax funded program); it is not obligated even to estimate the long-term costs of SMI. Quite apart from the desirability of cutting down on wasteful hospitalization, in other words, cost-shifting in this case has political advantages that may not be obvious at first glance.

*Perhaps the single most important reason why the CPR system is kind to specialists is that the cost of new procedures tends to fall sharply after they are first introduced, giving the specialist a large and growing margin over time between the original "customary" rate and the later cost. Examples: heart bypass surgery, cataract surgery, pacemaker implants, and x-rays. In each case, the time, equipment cost, assistance, and complication rate for each patient has been plummeting. A specialist in such procedures can thus earn far more, working half time, than a general practitioner or pediatrician working round the clock.

Far more obvious are the political rewards of shifting costs entirely out of the federal budget—especially when it does not seem to take anything away from anyone. Indeed, this strategy of pseudo-cost containment has become so popular with Congress and the Reagan administration in recent years that it is remarkable how fast federal health-care benefits have soared in spite of it. Where can federal costs be shifted? One easy target is state and local budgets. Our federal policymakers tightened Medicaid eligibility and cut back on health-care block grants in the early 1980s; state administrators have had to spend more to make up the difference. Another target is private payers. Since 1982 Congress has saved billions in federal outlays by making Medicare a secondary payer for employed beneficiaries who also have private health plans.* It has also saved money by "mandating" that large employers continue to offer health insurance to laid-off work-ers.† Whether or not these initiatives were good policy, one thing is clear: whatever the federal budget saved, the private sector ended up paying.

Aside from cost shifting through legislative fiat, the federal government can also engage in indirect cost shifting through use of its market power. Consider the case of Medicare. Although Medicare's reimbursement rate to physicians and hospitals has historically climbed at about the same speed as payments from private patients and insurers, it is generally assumed that the federal government has always gotten a bargain—perhaps 10 to 20 percent off the "private" price. How Medicare gets this bargain is no secret: as the single largest national purchaser of health care, accounting for about 30 percent of all hospital income and 20 percent of all physician income, Medicare can demand a sizable volume discount. Quite simply, most providers would rather accept narrower margins on Medicare patients than lose Medicare's business altogether. Providers, of course, must make up these narrower margins by charging higher rates to private purchasers.

The market power of the federal government as a benefits purchaser raises several fundamental questions. To begin with, who are

---

*The Tax Equity and Fiscal Responsibility Act of 1982 (TEFRA) makes Medicare the secondary payer for active employees aged 65 to 69 (and their spouses) who are covered by an employer-sponsored health plan. In 1985 Congress expanded this rule to include employees over age 69 as well.

†The Consolidated Omnibus Reconciliation Act of 1985 (COBRA) requires any employer with a health plan covering twenty or more workers to offer continued coverage to all former workers and their dependents (at the worker's expense) for at least eighteen months after job loss.

the winners and losers from market cost shifting? The answer to this question is straightforward: taxpayers are the winners (through lower levels of federal spending) and privately insured persons are the losers (through higher insurance premiums). Since most of us are both, most of us are both winners and losers, which means that all of us are paying more—through a lump-sum "regulatory tax" levied on rich and poor alike—than federal outlay numbers alone would indicate. So how can we tell when a benefit program really saves everyone money and when it merely pushes the costs to another purchaser? The key is behavior: benefit programs save everyone money when they succeed in changing the behavior of patients and providers so that fewer or less expensive services are rendered, regardless of what money appears to change hands. If behavior remains unchanged, we can assume instead that costs are being shifted and that for every winner there is a loser.

A case in point is the recent DRG reform that since 1984 (even after the cost shifting from HI to SMI) has succeeded in moderating somewhat the very fast growth in total Medicare outlays. Genuine savings from changes in hospital operating behavior, however, seem to have taken place almost entirely during the first two years (1984 and 1985) after the DRGs were implemented. Since then, federal "clamping down" on the annual increases in DRG and CPR levels has not changed the overall behavior of providers. Instead, they have pushed a rising share of Medicare's costs onto private payers. Consider that from 1980 through 1984, Medicare grew at $5.2 billion per year (in real 1986 dollars); and that from 1984 through 1987, this growth declined to $4.4 billion per year. Meanwhile, however, the real yearly growth in privately funded health care jumped from $10.8 to $12.9 billion per year. At a time when private insurers have been fighting hard to control costs, it is hard to believe that such an inversion in growth trends is mere coincidence.

Clearly, cost shifting is not a strategy that can be pushed indefinitely. At some point providers will quit trying to shift costs and simply refuse to serve publicly funded patients. For many means-tested beneficiaries, this point has already been reached. In some states, budget austerity programs have frozen reimbursement rates for so long that most doctors categorically turn away any business from Medicaid patients. For Medicare beneficiaries, we may be nearing this point. Since 1984, for instance, most hospitals and many physicians have seen their profit margin from Medicare plummet; in 1987 one-third of all hospitals reported actually losing money on Medicare admissions.

What will happen? Most likely, the federal government will soon ease its policy and allow Medicare reimbursement again to rise at least as fast as private prices (a trend that HCFA is already projecting after 1987). One reason is that Medicare beneficiaries are politically powerful and will fight any de facto limit on the availability of hospitals and doctors. But a more important reason is that an extension of our current DRG and CPR freezes is a needlessly painful and arbitrary way to contain health-care costs. Some regions and hospitals will remain eager to serve Medicare enrollees when the allowed price happens to be generous; other regions and hospitals will shut them out when the allowed price is unattractive. Some physicians (especially specialists) will still know how to turn a profit off the right "code"; others (especially primary physicians) will deem any contact with Medicare a net loss. It is difficult enough politically to contain costs in an equitable and efficient manner. It is unthinkable to believe we can do it through regulatory strangleholds that leave the underlying "have it all" incentives intact.

Toward New Principles

Our experience with federal cost-containment regulation has now come full circle. In the mid-1970s we had great hopes for comprehensive supply controls on the entire health-care industry; when these fell through in the early 1980s, we turned toward price controls. Here our expectations were more modest: they might not solve the national problem, we felt, but they would at least limit health-care benefit spending out of the federal budget; and some may have hoped that they would serve as a salutary example for the private sector as well. Unfortunately, the results of price controls have also been disappointing. With the single and quite limited exception of the DRG reform, they have failed to meet the most important criterion for genuine cost containment: changing the behavior of providers and patients. And to the extent that they have achieved any budget savings, they have done so primarily by shifting costs to other payers, so that—far from helping the private sector—they have merely burdened it with an extra regulatory tax. Today we have reached the point where further cost shifting away from the public sector is unfeasible. So once again the health-cost juggernaut rises in all sectors, public and private, as fast (or even faster) than it ever did. Once again, as in the early 1970s, we sense the need for an entirely new and comprehensive alternative.

Let us suggest a few basic principles upon which we might experiment and build an alternative, all of them in keeping with our underlying approach toward entitlements reform. The fundamental prerequisite, as we have emphasized both here and in Chapter 5, is the development of a political consensus. We must agree that our current policies are unaffordable as well as inequitable. We must also agree that limiting and reallocating our consumption of health care will require us to change old habits, make new choices, and face up to painful trade-offs both in our public and private lives. With this consensus, we could act on the following principles with a fair opportunity for success.

First, to the extent that we finance health care with public funds, *we must move gradually but surely toward prospective budgeting.* The United States is the only country in the world that places no boundaries on how much it will pay publicly for health care.* Instead, our implicit message is "spend whatever you feel you have to and send us the bill." Politically, a prospective budget—including targets for future years—would focus our attention on how much as a nation we want to spend on health care and force us to confront the macro trade-offs. If we want to spend more, where will we find the resources? If less, where else should we invest them? Procedurally, a prospective budget that encompassed tax subsidies as well as direct outlays could force everyone, from the program administrators down to the health-care providers and patients, to think in terms of doing their best within finite spending boundaries. In time, prospective budgeting at the federal level would be the natural counterpart to prospective "capitation" at the individual level.

Second, *the most important goal of program reform must be to reshape patient and provider incentives.* If our past attempts at regulatory cost containment have failed, the most important reason is that they relied on mechanical formulas or sleight of hand while consistently ignoring incentives. But the incentives facing the patient and provider should not come last; they should come first. On the one

---

*Virtually every other government outside the United States actually "budgets" a more or less fixed amount yearly for total public health-care spending. How this fixed amount later flows down to individual providers differs, of course, from country to country (sometimes the state owns the hospitals and pays the doctors directly; more often, the state bargains and contracts with insurers, hospitals, and local governments). But whoever gets the money is responsible for staying within the budgeted cost boundaries. As Brian Abel-Smith wryly notes, "Europeans do not see how a 'budget' can be anything but prospective." ("Containing Costs of Health Care in Western Europe," *Milbank Memorial Fund Quarterly,* Winter 1985).

hand, letting the patient bear some responsibility for his choices enhances individual dignity and is just common sense. The patient is ultimately the best judge of what "good health" means and how important it is relative to other ends in life. On the other hand, letting the provider also bear financial risks is the only way to ensure that the services rendered are worth the cost. The provider knows better than anyone else how "good health" can best be achieved. The provider is also the one who gets paid. We should make sure that the knowledge is linked with the incentive whenever possible.

Third, *our universal age-based health-care programs must begin to adjust benefit levels according to financial need.* One of the gross injustices of our current system of health-care benefits is that it "entitles" many of our richest citizens while depriving many of our poorest. Thousands of retired American millionaires can walk into a hospital and get a free lens implant for a cataract while millions of impoverished American youngsters cannot afford to see a doctor no matter how serious the illness or injury. As we have stressed already, these two circumstances are directly and causally related: the latter has been allowed to happen because the former has grown unaffordable. There is no way we can both contain total health spending and make more health care available to those in need, while at the same time subsidizing the health-care consumption of those who do not deserve, do not need, and have not earned the subsidy.

Fourth, *for those in financial need, we must improve and equalize the access to means-tested health care.* There are currently at least sixty million Americans who are either not covered by any health insurance or whose private coverage is so poor that they could easily be bankrupted by a serious medical emergency. Obviously, we must work to fill in these gaping holes, starting with minimal coverage for the greatest number of those in most financial need. As we begin, we must also recognize that the coverage offered by our current means-tested program (Medicaid) is very unequal, even for the destitute. The elderly poor receive the best (though still spotty) coverage; the single-parent poor receive second-best coverage. All others, especially the younger working poor in intact families, are almost categorically ineligible for help. Equal treatment—if not a public interest in the health of younger Americans—implies that we start first with the least-covered groups.

Finally, *we must shift the emphasis of our public health spending away from acute care and toward preventative care.* Many experts estimate that a large share—perhaps most—of all illnesses and injuries are linked with preventable individual behavior (from tobacco and diet to auto accidents and hypertension). Over 95 percent of our federal health-care dollars, however, pay for the acute-care treatment of illnesses and injuries after they occur, and most of the rest pays for research on even more expensive methods of acute-care treatment. Similarly, those who teach us preventative health at a young age are among the least-trained and lowest-paid of all professionals (with typical salaries at $20,000 to $30,000), while those who give us specialized acute care at an advanced age are among the best-trained and best-paid of all professionals (with typical incomes of $200,000 to $300,000). It is time we reverse this illogical order of priorities. We must insist that our public spending reflect our genuine public interests and not merely chase after "quasi-entitled" consumer demand.

Reforming Acute Care for the Elderly and Disabled

There is little doubt that Medicare reform should be the single most important item on our national entitlements agenda. Of all public health-care programs, it is by far the largest and most rapidly growing (accounting for nearly half of all public-sector health benefits); its benefits and eligibility standards have the least connection (in fact, no connection) to financial need; and its front-end benefit coverage is the worst-suited to the back-end insurance needs of most of those who receive it. Just as important, as it is currently structured, Medicare will almost certainly become unaffordable sometime early in the next century. We have already described in earlier chapters how the combined forces of demography and medical technology will push total Medicare spending to between 5.8 percent and 11.0 percent of GNP by the year 2040, up from 1.8 percent today. These projections *include* the anticipated savings from economizing reforms already enacted, but of course *do not include* the future costs of further benefit expansions that Congress may still choose to enact. (Nor do they include the cost of one recently enacted expansion, the "catastrophic cost" amendment.)

Medicare: Near-Term Options. Over the next several years, the smaller SMI program must be the focus of Medicare reform. The most obvious reason is that SMI is now growing much faster than HI. Since 1980, in fact, the cost of SMI benefits has nearly tripled (from $10.6

billion to $30.8 billion), and at its current soaring growth rate SMI may hit $50 billion by 1990. Yet a more important reason is that HI already has a prospective payment system (DRGs) that, though inherently inadequate in the long term, is not even working in the near term mostly due to SMI's manifest inability to control its own spending growth. As we have seen, the biggest problem with DRGs is that they allow massive cost shifting to SMI, forcing HI administrators to choose between going easy on reimbursements or watching surgery leave bankrupt hospitals for doctors' offices. Better control over SMI, therefore, will in and of itself help HI cost control.

What to do? First, we should trim the generosity of SMI's front-end coverage—generosity that encourages unnecessary second visits to physicians and has no place in a non-means-tested system anyway. The best place to begin would be to raise SMI's $75 annual deductible. Incredibly, this deductible (first set at $50 in 1966) has not only fallen far behind the rise in medical prices over the years, it has not even kept pace with the general price level. Indeed, if it had been indexed since 1966 to average SMI spending per enrollee, the SMI deductible would today be about $500. Let us be moderate and raise it to at least $200 (on par with the current deductible in many employer plans), and index it thereafter to SMI spending per enrollee.* Its cost would be fairly and widely borne, and as a modest incentive to prudent consumption it would reduce total SMI costs by as much as 5 percent, according to the CBO. Even discounting any change in patient behavior, the deductible income alone would net us about $2 billion yearly by 1990.

Second, we might consider raising SMI patient copayments slightly—from 20 percent to 25 or 30 percent—up to an annual "stop-loss" ceiling. Furthermore, in order to take some of the burden off DRGs as a means of limiting hospitalization, we might also consider a modest copayment (say, 10 percent) for the first five days of any hospital stay. The rationale for front-end increases in deductibles and copayments is not merely that they reduce federal spending on services already provided. Just as important, they encourage all Medicare patients to make more informed choices about where and how they obtain treatment, and thus allow us to afford more generous protection for catastrophic and chronic-care costs. At the same time, they would further our goal of shifting patient incentives away from

---

*In order to discourage needless recourse to physician services, it has also been suggested that special deductibles be applied to each doctor visit.

excessive reliance on acute care and toward an active interest in vastly more cost-effective pursuits, such as prevention and health-maintenance.

Third, we should raise the SMI insurance premium so that a greater share of SMI's cost is borne by those who benefit from it. When SMI was founded, the original legislation provided that the premium fee should be changed yearly so that premiums would always finance about 50 percent of total SMI outlays. In 1972—that year of historic generosity—Congress repealed this provision. Thereafter, the premium (like the deductible) has risen nowhere near as fast as the program's cost. By 1986 SMI premium revenue was only covering 21 percent of SMI's cost. Since 1986 Congress and the administration have been trying to get SMI back to 25 percent premium financing, but even this halting gesture has aroused the fury of practically every senior lobby. The history of the SMI premium would in fact make an illuminating chapter in any general discussion of the "generational contract." More often than not, those who most vigorously invoke this "contract" neither know nor care about its actual historical terms.

We should go much further than 25 percent. We should gradually increase the premium so that it covers somewhere between 30 and 50 percent of total SMI benefit outlays, and thereafter index it to future growth in SMI spending per enrollee. (In 1989, moving to 50 percent would mean raising the monthly premium from about $25 to $50.) By fiscal year 1990, assuming no change in SMI spending trends, raising the premium to cover 30 percent of benefits would save $2.5 billion yearly; raising it to cover 50 percent of benefits would save $11.1 billion yearly. Unlike the higher deductible, the higher premium would not provide a *cost-sharing* incentive to reduce health-care utilization. It would instead provide a *political* incentive for the elderly to take a more active interest in the exploding growth of real per capita SMI spending—a growth that since 1972 has been paid for almost entirely (96 percent) out of the general taxpayer's pocket.* Yet like the higher deductible, the higher premium would be a cost fairly borne by all beneficiaries. Those who cannot afford it could (or should) have the bill paid by Medicaid.

Fourth, we should scrap SMI's CPR reimbursement mechanism right away. Our ultimate goal should be to move toward a combined

*From 1972 to 1986 (year ending June 30), the real value of annual SMI premiums per enrollee (in 1986 dollars) rose by $20, from $166 to $186; the real value of general revenue subsidies per enrollee rose by $508, from $282 to $790.

HI-SMI capitation system (see "long-term options" below). But so long as we are stuck with price controls, let us at least use price controls that make sense. The CPR mechanism is complex and costly to administer. It does not allow doctors and patients to know the price of a service when it is rendered. And most seriously, its formulaic price structure invites gaming and adjusts far too slowly to innovation and changes in medical practice. When "frozen," CPR prices often end up starving the generalist while feeding windfalls to the specialist. A feasible near-term option would be to collapse the number of treatment codes and fix prices to a "relative value scale" (RVS) that could be altered by periodic surveys of actual treatment *costs*. An additional cost-control device (allowing flexibility and reinforcing physician incentives) would be a sliding-scale reduction in reimbursements to physicians with a high service volume per Medicare patient.*

Taxation of Medigap Premiums. In Chapter 5, we pointed out that only about 20 percent of the elderly actually pay for Medicare copayments out of their own pockets, primarily because so many of them are privately insured for these expenses. By eliminating Medicare's cost-sharing incentive structure, medigap policies are implicitly subsidizing a higher use of covered services. Economists who have studied this problem suggest that a 30 percent tax on medigap premiums would neutralize their implicit federal subsidy.† Such a tax would not only generate federal revenue, it would also force insurance companies to offer policies that retain some of Medicare's cost-sharing incentives. As a matter of policy, taxation of medigap premiums should be carried out in conjunction with increases in copayments and deductibles.

Integration with Social Security and Benefit Taxation. Medicare reforms should be coordinated with parallel reforms in Social

---

*Annually negotiated fee-for-service scales, combined with a rate adjustment for high volume and a cap on total income for each physician, is a widely used system abroad. Critics claim that such scales (as well as prospective budgets) make health-care financing subject to nonstop political infighting among groups of providers and between providers and patients. But of course that is precisely their virtue: they get the interests out in the open where voters can examine and judge them.

†This estimate is corroborated by the findings of Charles R. Link et al. (in "Cost Sharing, Supplementary Insurance, and Health Care Services Utilization Among the Medicare Elderly," *Health Care Financing Review*, Fall 1981). Controlling for other variables, they concluded that medigap insurance induced a 33 percent rise in hospital days and a 40 percent rise in doctor visits among Medicare beneficiaries.

Security cash benefits. For example, if the eligibility age for receiving full OASI retirement benefits is raised to sixty-seven early in the next century (as provided by current law), the same adjustment should be made to Medicare. Another important parallel reform would be to tax the average *insurance value* of Medicare benefits not paid for by the contributions of program participants. For SMI this percentage share is obvious—about 75 percent of benefits (or 50 percent if the premiums were raised to 50 percent of SMI spending). For HI most proposals assume (incorrectly) that only 50 percent of the insurance value of benefits should be considered taxable income. (The theory here is of course that as employees beneficiaries have already been taxed on their half of the HI payroll contribution.)

According to the CBO, taxing 50 percent of Medicare's insurance value would generate new revenues of $6.4 billion by 1990. We could get even more savings if we implemented the same tax reform that we suggested for Social Security cash benefits: use a sliding-scale rate of up to 100 percent *to tax away the insurance value of unearned Medicare benefits above relatively high income levels.* Taxation of Medicare benefits is an attractive option for at least two reasons: the share of the program's total costs financed through intergenerational transfers would be reduced, and most low-income beneficiaries (since they are in effect not subject to taxation) would be exempt. In no case will this implicit means test rob retirees of what they have "paid into" Medicare. Only HI is partially funded through prior payroll taxes; remember too that the typical elderly person retiring in the mid-1980s will be entitled to health benefits worth more than twenty times his or her personal HI payroll-tax contributions plus interest. The equity argument for partial taxation of Medicare benefits is thus even stronger than for partial taxation of Social Security cash benefits.

Medicare: Long-Term Options. The measures discussed so far either create more cost-conscious consumers and providers or increase the share of Medicare financed by beneficiaries themselves. In the long term, however, a more fundamental restructuring of Medicare will be necessary if we want to move toward truly predictable and controllable health-care spending. The problem is to make our health-care benefits budget truly prospective. The best solution is to design a flexible "voucher" system based on the principle of prospective capitation payment. In such a system, each beneficiary would be issued a voucher (worth a fixed dollar amount) that could be used to buy coverage in any qualified insurance or health plan. The potential advantages of a voucher system—simplicity, variety, equity, and efficiency—make it an attractive alternative to the complicated rules and backward incentives that accompany even the best-designed regime of regulated cost control.

Senior lobbies often argue that vouchers would constitute a radical and unconscionable assault on quality care for the elderly. But in fact Medicare already offers a voucher system. In 1982 the Tax Equity and Fiscal Responsibility Act (TEFRA) stipulated that HMOs be encouraged to enroll Medicare beneficiaries on an "at-risk" basis. In return for taking on a beneficiary, a qualified HMO receives a fixed capitation payment equal to 95 percent of the average per-person cost of Medicare (both HI and SMI) in the fee-for-service market. To the extent the new subscriber costs the HMO less than this fixed rate, the HMO may make a profit. In this case the money saved is shared by Medicare and the HMO, not by the beneficiary himself, but the basic idea is similar to a voucher. By the end of 1986, nearly one million Medicare beneficiaries had been enrolled in HMOs operating under TEFRA guidelines. According to HCFA findings, the benefits offered under these plans are (as we might expect) far more comprehensive than under standard Medicare rules, catastrophic coverage is automatic, and hospital use rates are well below the national average for Medicare beneficiaries—and all of this is at a lower cost and without any adverse impact on quality of care.

We need to encourage this development, and we could do so in a way that allows some freedom for Medicare beneficiaries in choosing physicians. Besides HMOs, for example, we could have voucher holders choose among qualified "managed-care" or conventional insurance plans. The idea is simply that the provider would be at risk for covering costs and that beneficiaries would have to pay out of their own pockets (through less generous front-end coverage or higher supplemental premiums) for the more expensive or "convenient" options. The provider therefore has an incentive to give the best care for the least cost, while the beneficiary has an incentive to select, among provider options, the mix of services, efficiency, and convenience he or she most prefers. On both counts, the overall demand pressure on U.S. health-care spending would be lessened, which would benefit all consumers.

Catastrophic Insurance. Ever since Medicare was founded, one of the most frequent complaints has been its perverse failure to provide back-end coverage for the low-probability risk of catastrophic out-of-pocket costs—which, after all, is the most basic function of insurance. Until the end of 1988, SMI copayments will continue to have no cap and HI coverage will continue to decline from 100 percent to 75 percent after 60 hospital days, and then cease altogether after ninety days (and upon the exhaustion of the "lifetime reserve").

Many low-cost solutions might have been possible. One strategy would have been to enact a complete "stop-loss" limit for all beneficiaries and fund this coverage out of part of the savings generated by reductions in front-end coverage. Another, even lower-cost strategy would have been to means test this new benefit to the poverty line; any nonpoor Medicare beneficiary would then be required to maintain or purchase a minimal private medigap policy, or else would be assigned to a local-area HMO under Medicare's new TEFRA guidelines. (HMOs as a rule cover all catastrophic costs.) Senior lobbies protest the idea of any elderly person being "forced" into an HMO. But such protests are shameless. Many companies (such as Lockheed and Rockwell International) are now making HMOs mandatory for newly hired employees—the very workers whose payroll taxes make Medicare possible.

The newly enacted "catastrophic-cost" amendment to Medicare makes talk about such sensible, low-cost solutions—at least for now—irrelevant. But the basic principles of need and equity cannot be suppressed indefinitely. We can of course postpone their emergence, but we do so at growing cost and economic peril.

Reforming Long-Term Care for the Elderly

The financing of long-term care for the disabled elderly is rapidly becoming the focus of heated policy debate in America, and for good reason: though only a minority of the elderly ever need lengthy long-term care, the cost (with nursing homes averaging about $22,000 yearly per patient) can obviously be devastating when the need arises. Given our extensive front-end coverage of acute care, one might naturally suppose that we would offer at least some protection against this risk. Unfortunately, with the single exception of Medicaid, neither public benefits nor private insurance will have anything to do with it. Of all persons currently in a nursing home, only 3 percent are funded through Medicare and only 1 percent through a private health plan. Funding for the other 96 percent is split about evenly between Medicaid and personal sources. This makes long-term care far and away the greatest catastrophic-cost risk facing the elderly; on average, every elderly household spending over $2,000 out-of-pocket annually for health-care services spends 80 percent of it on long-term care.

Medicaid, to be sure, provides ultimate relief to households driven into poverty by these costs. But even here the system seems awry. Bedfast elderly who are "spending down" to Medicaid wonder why Medicare cannot afford to give them even a weekly nursing visit while it can afford to give their friends tests from multimillion-dollar NMR machines free of charge. What's the use of "insurance" when it doesn't pay you a cent until you don't have a cent left? Health-care economists shake their heads and wonder why the government cannot give the disabled elderly care at home before forcing them into an institution at twice the cost. Despite these potential efficiencies, institutions remain our preference: in 1986 we spent $38 billion on nursing-home care (half of it out of public budgets) and less than $10 billion on at-home care (two-thirds of it out of public budgets).

Meanwhile, worried state Medicaid administrators wonder how they can serve the basic goal of their program—ordinary acute care to their state's younger, poverty-stricken residents—when nursing-home costs are devouring their budgets. In 1984 nursing homes accounted for 7 percent of all Medicaid beneficiaries and 43 percent of all Medicaid spending. In 1982 twenty-six states spent over 50 percent of their Medicaid budgets on nursing homes. Fiscal austerity measures have turned these state Medicaid budgets into yet one more arena for a silent but ghastly generational conflict that the young are once again losing. Let's face it: the cost of Medicaid nursing-home care is practically irreducible; the poor elderly cannot of course be ejected, nor can the per capita cost of their stay be cut without driving nursing homes out of business, inhumane treatment, or both. Apparently, however, the cost of serving the younger poor can be reduced. Young families can be cut from Medicaid eligibility, doctors can be price-controlled out of serving Medicaid patients, and prevention and community programs can be slashed.

So what accounts for the illogic of our long-term care policy? As we suggested earlier, the explanation is straightforward: it is the only policy that is both affordable (at least for now) and allows us to avoid painful and politically sensitive trade-offs.

Quite simply, the long-term care that we now pay for publicly is just the tip of a cost iceberg, and we know of no easy way to improve public coverage without the entire mountain appearing in public budgets. The numbers speak for themselves. Just to pay publicly the full bill for those *already* in a nursing home would double public outlays. Then consider that for every elderly person in a nursing home *there are two living in the community who require a similar level of care* and currently receive it from family and friends. Universal nursing-home coverage, assuming that only half of the potential population now in the community would use it, would therefore quadruple the public expense. A public home-care benefit might economize somewhat on per capita spending, but we would then face an even vaster multiplication of the eligible population. Currently, about 2 percent of the elderly receive nursing-home care at public expense—but about 18 percent of the elderly are sufficiently disabled to benefit from at least some regular program of paid assistance.* That is a 9-to-1 ratio of potential to current beneficiaries.

These figures are only static computations. A dynamic analysis taking into account induced demand might show even greater potential costs. It is generally believed, for instance, that "free" care tends to create its own demand by encouraging dependence among those who use it. It is also probable that it would discourage families from preparing to meet such costs on their own, through saving or living together. Finally, but most emphatically, we must remember that whatever costs we face today will be multiplied even further early in the next century as our population ages and as the elderly themselves age (see Chapter 4). Over the next fifty years, we can expect the number of disabled elderly to grow between four- and sixfold.† Moreover, they

---

*For the number of elderly persons living in the community requiring nursing-home levels of care, see Pamela Doty et al. in "An Overview of Long-Term Care," *Health Care Financing Review* (Spring 1985). According to the 1982 National Long-Term Care Survey, 18 percent of the elderly population had some limitations in "activities of daily living"—the standard definition of disability.

†The scenario II-B estimates in Figure 4-3 show nearly a fourfold (273 percent) increase in total elderly nursing-home residents from 1980 to 2040. Not surprisingly, this is quite close to the II-B growth in the number of elderly over age eighty. Although we lack nursing-home estimates for scenario III, the growth in the number of elderly over age eighty between 1980 and 2040 under this scenario—over 500 percent—serves as a reasonable proxy.

will be older, they will have fewer children to help them, and these children will be more likely to be working or to be elderly themselves.*

Clearly, our current policy of dealing with our crisis in long-term care (or rather of hiding the problem by cutting back on Medicaid eligibility or by using CON regulations to cut down on nursing home beds) is a nonsolution. Yet it is equally clear that any "universal" fee-for-service entitlement for long-term care has not the least prayer of affordability. A responsible policy must make extremely painful trade-offs while doing its best to protect and encourage family responsibility. We suggest a three-pronged strategy: first, a very high (but absolute) Medicare "stop-loss" on the total cost of long-term care incurred by any elderly household; second, a modest Medicare home-care voucher with strict eligibility requirements; and third, extensive experimentation with new forms of long-term-care treatment and financing.

The "stop-loss" would simply be a universal and non-means-tested agreement by Medicare to pay for all long-term care after a high ceiling of private payment (perhaps a time ceiling of three years, or a cash ceiling of $75,000). This would serve the proper insurance function of Medicare.† It would prevent the large number of short-term nursing-home admissions from becoming a public charge (only 25 percent of nursing-home admissions stay longer than one year; only 17 percent stay longer than three years).‡ It would accelerate the marketing of private long-term insurance policies by greatly reducing their premiums. And it would encourage families to save and insure themselves against out-of-pocket costs beneath the ceiling by offering them some expectation that they might weather the storm financially

---

*Already in 1982, survey data indicate that the average age of caregivers for the impaired elderly was fifty-seven years; more than one-third were over age sixty-five. Clearly, this average age will increase in the future. Meanwhile, the number of elderly who tend to have the fewest family caregivers—the never-married, divorced, widowed, childless, or those whose children are working full-time or divorced—will grow much faster than the total elderly population. (See *Changes in the Living Arrangements of the Elderly: 1960-2030*, Congressional Budget Office; March 1988.)

†The advantages of a global Medicare "stop-loss" provision—which might include all forms of acute and long-term care—have been articulately described by health economist Jack Meyer (in testimony before the House Ways and Means Subcommittee on Health; March 31, 1987). A "stop-loss" provision is also a promising design feature of the Mitchell bill (S.R. 2305) currently before Congress. To keep it affordable, however, the ceiling must be set high. Its purpose is to eliminate the risk of "tail-end" losses for the family or insurer, not to bear a major share of the long-term-care cost burden.

‡According to Marc Cohen et al., "The Lifetime Risks and Costs of Nursing Home Use among the Elderly," *Medical Care* (December 1986).

even if the nursing-home stay is indefinite. Currently, most families suspect that private insurance will just end up saving money for Medicaid by delaying the inevitable. As one health-care expert acerbicly observes, "to put their hopes on the private insurance mechanism, public officials have to hope that their constituents will be dumb enough to make an irrational investment to reduce their potential consumption of tax dollars."*

A Medicare home-health benefit for chronic disability is also desirable, but only if its cost is strictly controlled.† We can make no attempt to provide publicly all the care that we would like to see every disabled person receive. The benefit should only be received by those whose demonstrated disabilities could just as easily (absent paid or informal assistance at home) make them a nursing-home resident. It must be modest in cost and free from nonmedical "credential" regulations. And the cash value of the benefit must be taxable. Perhaps (as with our earlier suggestion for HI and SMI) we should tax away the full value of the benefit above a certain income level.

Finally, experimentation with new forms of long-term care treatment and financing must be a high federal priority. One possibility may be prospective payment for at-home and nursing-home care, a strategy now being tested by new "Continuing Care Retirement Communities" (CCRCs) and "Social HMO" (S/HMO) demonstrations. Unlike fee-for-service long-term care, which rewards indefinite dependency, prospective payment gives the provider an incentive to use every means to make the patient as healthy and as self-sufficient as possible. An effective financing device may be tax-favored Individual Medical Accounts (IMAs), which would enable younger Americans to save against the risk of future long-term care just as they now save for retirement through pensions and IRAs. Because we still have so much to learn, we must start now to probe, to examine, and to test. It is hard to imagine a more cost-effective means to prepare ourselves for the next century. The very solvency of our economy may one day rest on its success.

---

*Bruce C. Vladeck, "The Static Dynamics of Long-Term Care Policy," in Marion Ein Lewin (ed.), *The Health Care Policy Agenda* (American Enterprise Institute, 1985).

†It is sometimes argued optimistically that a home-care benefit will save money by keeping the elderly out of nursing homes. Just about every pilot program carried out thus far, however, indicates that such "substitution" savings are negligible in practice—which is what we might expect given the vast number of partially disabled elderly living in the community. A chronic-illness home-care benefit will not "fund itself," but it could provide limited assistance to those who are most in need and who would otherwise receive nothing.

Reforming Benefits for the Poor

Our public efforts to extend health-care coverage to low-income Americans are in such disarray that they can hardly be called a policy at all. Medicaid, the federal-state program offering means-tested benefits to the poor, does nothing for the majority of poor Americans; the minority it does help has shrunk in percentage terms over the last decade; its criteria for selective eligibility among the poor make little sense; and the money it spends on them is not cost-effective. As for our only other income-related health benefit program—tax deductions for employer-paid health care—this policy is entirely counterproductive. It gives to those who already have the most health care, and takes from those (through higher income taxes and higher medical prices) who have the least health care.

Let us begin with Medicaid. It is quite obvious that we cannot hope to achieve budgetary "savings" on Medicaid. The cost of Medicaid will grow. Indeed, it must grow if we wish to ensure that all poor Americans have access to at least a minimal level of medical attention, and to avoid having our health-care system likened to those of Third World countries. We should reconcile ourselves to this at the outset, and should recognize that it will make it all the more urgent that we cut outlays in the rest of our health-care budget.

Several steps are needed. First, we should "decouple" Medicaid eligibility from AFDC and SSI eligibility. A national choice not to pay cash benefits to many poor American families should not affect the very different national choice—or rather, imperative—to prefer to see that these families are healthy rather than sick. Second, we should require that all states raise the income level of Medicaid eligibility to about the poverty line (leaving to them the option they already have of raising it further). Finally, and most generally, we cannot allow Medicaid to define itself primarily as a private affair between the poor patient and his or her physician. Instead, we should begin to think of Medicaid as a public investment in a public good, so that even if we are not impelled to act on humanitarian grounds we can act out of prudent concern for the future physical and mental health of disadvantaged Americans.

This last point has many implications. It may mean, for example, that we should insist that states spending federal Medicaid money attach their highest priority to preventative care (such as vaccinations, checkups, and drug-abuse programs) in every possible school or community setting. It may also mean that we insist that the best quality care always be available for poor young families and their children. Such priorities may seem to be little more than common sense. Today, unfortunately, we see the opposite in many states. Since personal acute care has a direct and potent consumer orientation, preventative care is often the first item to be scrapped. And since poor young families are as a rule politically invisible, it is tempting for any government agency to regard them as "out of sight, out of mind."

To say that we must spend more on Medicaid does not, of course, mean that we cannot spend it efficiently. The question of exploding nursing-home costs aside, most experts agree that there are two major problems that compromise Medicaid's ability to deliver cost-effective health care: restricted access to price-controlled primary physicians and (partly as a consequence) inappropriate use of acute-care hospital facilities. One solution would be to ease the limits on doctor fees and instead implement a fairer cost-saving measure: nominal deductibles for each doctor visit. Such deductibles (say $5 per visit) could be afforded by everyone who needs treatment and have proved effective in reducing unnecessary visits.

A superior long-term solution would be, again, to move more state Medicaid programs toward prospective capitation. We already know that prospective "managed care" does a good job in delivering nonepisodic, cost-effective care to a large number of Medicaid beneficiaries. Ever since the 1981 Omnibus Budget Reconciliation Act (OBRA), many states have requested and received waivers that exempt them from Medicaid's rigid fee-for-service guidelines and allow them to substitute systems of HMOs or "primary care case management" (PCCM). Under PCCMs, Medicaid patients are required to select (or, alternatively, are assigned) a case manager from an approved list; in return for a capitation payment, this provider (whether a physician, a clinic, or an HMO) agrees to "manage" the beneficiary's health care. In some cases, "case management" means providing primary care and authorizing other treatment; in others, it means furnishing the beneficiary with all necessary medical services.

As of mid-1986, some 850,000 Medicaid beneficiaries in twenty-five states were enrolled in HMOs, PCCMs, and other forms of prepaid group practice. In Arizona and Wisconsin, where Medicaid reform has been vigorously pursued, HMO enrollment is mandatory. Preliminary indications are that capitated payment in Medicaid—just as in most other settings—can yield considerable cost savings (HCFA studies have shown these to be in the range of 5 to 10 percent) without compromising (and often improving) the quality of care. The cost savings may increase in future years. Clearly we need to encourage this promising approach.

And what about nonpoor (but generally low-income) American families that lack any health insurance coverage? Clearly this problem needs a swift answer: as health-care providers become more competitive, it is becoming increasingly difficult for them to shift the cost of their charity care or bad debts onto other purchasers. Many solutions have been proposed, but perhaps the best is one that would take advantage of the fact that the vast majority of these families are headed by adults who work at least part time. We could require, as a condition of employment, that all employees enroll in an HMO or subscribe to minimal major medical coverage.* Such a requirement could be enforced annually through the employer's tax filings, and it could be left up to the employers and employees how they want to split the cost. Although many legislators have proposed similar schemes, most are flawed by their insistence on expensive coverage that includes full compliance with state-mandated benefits. Apparently, they want everyone to emulate their own pattern of health consumption. But the typical uncovered minimum-wage employee does not want or need to pay for the extra cost of psychiatric coverage or low deductibles, and it is inequitable to force him to help bear the cost of those who do.

Finally, we come to our poverty policy-in-reverse: the tax deduction for employer-paid health benefits. Here there is little question that we should repeal it entirely or, failing that, "cap" the allowable deduction at the lowest possible level. One benefit of repeal is that we would stop subsidizing the health-care purchases of those who are best off and consuming the most. Another benefit, of course, is that it would broaden the tax base and automatically raise about $40 billion annually for the federal budget by 1989. We could dearly use this to lower the deficit. Alternatively—just to illustrate the magnitude involved—*we could use it to pay for all of the above-suggested expansions in means-tested (acute-care, nursing-home, and preventative) benefits.*

---

*After all, states currently use the same approach for all automobile drivers. Leaving type of coverage and means of payment up to the employers and employees avoids the difficult issue of episodic or part-time workers, dual jobholders, and workers covered by other family members; many employers will clearly find it profitable to provide group coverage on their own. Persons who have no group coverage and cannot find individual policies should be helped through expanded state-run "risk-pools."

An extra $40 billion, for example, would be enough to *more than double* what the federal budget currently spends on Medicaid.

Reforming Military and Veterans Benefits

Military Health Care. As we have already seen in our examination of military pensions, our defense budget is by no means exempt from the growth in "entitled" consumption. Yet consider also the cost of military health care: from 1979 to 1987, it has risen from $4.1 billion to $11.1 billion—a 170 percent explosion in only eight years. If our spending on military health care had risen no faster than general inflation since 1979, we would now be saving over $5 billion annually. That is enough to fund the current annual cost of our Strategic Defense Initiative, or purchase one new nuclear-powered aircraft carrier (complete with aircraft) each year.

Why is the cost of military health care such a problem? One obvious reason is the steep rise in the number of nonactive beneficiaries. Less than a quarter of those who receive military health care are active-duty personnel; about half are now military retirees and their dependents. But a more serious reason is that the system essentially offers fee-for-service care without cost-sharing, a combination which feeds uncontrollable increases in the cost per person served. On the one hand, beneficiaries can ordinarily receive treatment at military facilities with negligible deductibles and no copayments. On the other hand, the military facilities themselves are budgeted on a cost-plus "caseload" basis and always retain the option of rerouting their most expensive or least convenient cases to an auxiliary civilian program (CHAMPUS). Even at CHAMPUS, all active-duty families and most retired families can avoid significant cost-sharing.

The inevitable result is that military beneficiaries, despite their younger age and better health, consume far more health care than the average civilian. They visit doctors 40 percent more often than the norm for *all* civilians (including the elderly); they spend nearly twice as many days in the hospital as civilians of the same age. And because the military has so few incentives to use personnel or equipment efficiently, the cost per doctor visit or per hospital day is also higher.

To be sure, we should never expect to pay for military health care at bargain-basement prices. We certainly want active military personnel to be in excellent health, and we acknowledge that military health facilities must bear unique costs (such as maintaining a large unused capacity in preparation for wartime emergencies). But there can be no excuse for day-to-day incentives that all point toward waste. A fundamental reform would be to erect a strict barrier between civilian and military providers.* We could, for example, require all retirees and their dependents to choose between a civilian HMO or conventional civilian insurance with standard deductibles and copayments. The defense budget chiefs could organize and subsidize these plans, pending a more complete review of the *total* retiree benefit package.† Active-duty families, meanwhile, could be limited entirely to military facilities. The efficiency of this care could best be improved by budgeting each facility through prospective capitation and allowing each facility the freedom to make its own administrative and treatment decisions. If military bureaucracy makes this (HMO) model unfeasible, the second-best solution would be to institute modest cost-sharing for all patients.

Veterans Health Care. When the first Veterans Administration hospitals were constructed after World War I, their purpose was to provide health care to veterans with service-related injuries. Soon after World War II, however, the VA began using its excess capacity to offer care to veterans with health problems unrelated to military service. As the demand for care from this secondary beneficiary group expanded, so too did the VA's facilities. Today the VA operates 172 hospitals, 228 outpatient clinics, and 119 nursing homes; it employs a staff of about 200,000 to serve a veteran population of 27.7 million (plus dependents); and each year it treats 1.5 million inpatients and handles 18 million outpatient visits. The annual cost of the program is $9.9 billion. These benefits are entirely free for most veterans, yet only 30

---

*The Reagan administration has recently proposed cutting the cost of civilian care through a "CHAMPUS Reform Initiative" (CRI). CRI directs the military to contract out all civilian care to at-risk regional systems on a per-service basis; these systems will in turn try to reduce their own costs by enrolling beneficiaries in "preferred-provider" programs. The problem with CRI, however, is that it leaves all options open to beneficiaries: between the military system and private plans (obtained by other working members of military families); between military facilities and CHAMPUS; and between traditional CHAMPUS and the new PPOs ("CHAMPUS Prime"). Cost projection thus remains difficult and full capitation remains impossible.

†They could also examine the egregious cost of the health-care entitlements they are passing out to the employees of major weapons builders. A recent GAO survey of the ten largest contractors found that the defense budget reimburses their health insurance plans (most of which offer, for instance, negligible deductibles and free dental care) at *twice* the per-worker cost the federal government pays on behalf of its own employees. The federal cost due to insurance premiums in these ten companies alone currently amounts to over $1 billion yearly.

372

percent of VA patients currently have service-related disabilities, and only 16 percent are actually being treated for those disabilities.

Society clearly has an obligation to provide health care (as well as income support) to poor veterans who suffer from service-related disabilities. Beyond this obvious welfare function, it is difficult to justify entitling veterans to free health care simply because they obeyed the call of duty during wartime. Moreover, the cost of this entitlement will increase sharply as the veteran population continues to age. The 10 million surviving veterans of World War II will cause the number of all veterans aged sixty-five and over to rise rapidly during the 1990s. But even after their number peaks in 1999, the aging of our 4 million Korean War veterans and 8 million Vietnam War veterans will prevent that number from falling back to today's level until the year 2030. According to the projections we developed in Chapter 3, the cost of all non-means-tested veterans benefits (including disability compensation) will grow much faster than our economy over the next fifty years.

Congress and the administration have recently been moving in the right direction by limiting benefit eligibility for upper-income veterans with nonservice-related disabilities. In 1986 they ruled that this group (defined, for example, as veterans with one dependent having yearly incomes over $25,325) *may* be denied care or *may* be required to pay for *some* portion of its cost.* Clearly, however, such reforms fall far short of what is equitable. Besides differentiating between "service" and "nonservice" disabilities, we need to distinguish between those who are in need and those who are not. A $25,000 "poverty" threshold for disabilities having nothing to do with service is patently inequitable so long as nonveterans with half that income are not eligible for any means-tested assistance in any state. The proper solution would be to make health care available to veterans without service-related disabilities on terms that are no more preferential than those enjoyed by Americans at large.

---

*The 1986 legislation essentially divides all veterans into three groups, of which the first two get highest-priority care without charge. The first group, Category A, comprises all veterans with service-related disabilities (incurred on or off duty), "poor" veterans with no such disabilities (income under $15,195 for a vet without dependents), and various other blanketed-in definitions (all pre-World War II vets, all former POWs, all agent-orange and radiation-exposed soldiers, etc.). The second group, Category B, comprises veterans with nonservice-related disabilities whose income (again, for a beneficiary with no dependents) is below $20,260. Category C is made up of higher-income vets without service-related disabilities. How much— or whether—this last group should pay for VA care is now the focus of a debate between the administration and Congress.

Reforming Regulation and Law

Regulatory Reform. Effective incentives presuppose a reasonably open market where consumers enjoy alternative choices and providers must compete for their dollars. As we saw in Chapter 5, however, our health-care market is currently choked by multiple layers of restrictive regulation, much of which defends not the individual interests of patients but rather the collective interests of health-care professionals and providers. The fundamental goal of regulatory reform should be to defend the former, not the latter. We can no longer afford to accept the health-care industry's bribe that in return for allowing their professionals to cartelize their business as they wish, they will ensure us quality health care. That was the same argument used by the airline industry—until the late 1970s—to defend the "price and entry" rules of the Civil Aeronautics Board. Notwithstanding such protests, we abolished the CAB and relegated safety regulation to a body (the Federal Aviation Agency) specifically designed for that purpose. And whatever we may think of the FAA's current performance, no one today proposes that the CAB be resurrected. We did not buy that argument then, nor should we buy it now.

In practice, market-oriented reform should work to complete the dismantling of the ineffective supply-control systems—Health Planning Boards, Certificate of Need regulations, and the like—that the federal government created or expanded during the 1970s. At the same time, we must encourage the states to overhaul the labyrinth of certification boards, utilization-review groups, and scope-of-practice and quality-control regulations that serve mainly to protect professional specialties and suppress cost-saving innovation. Just as important, all parties must have open access to market information if they are to make rational decisions. To this end, the remaining advertising restrictions on health-care providers should be lifted and the federal government should be encouraged to step up its current effort to make comparative quality-of-care data on hospitals, HMOs, and nursing homes freely available to consumer groups, insurers, and providers.

Reform must also move to the market for private health insurance. In recent years, the Federal Trade Commission has brought antitrust suits against provider-controlled insurance plans that enjoy regional monopolies (chiefly the state Blue Cross and Blue Shields). This watchfulness should be extended to situations in which medical professional associations negotiate "acceptable" price schedules with large insurers. Also, if we want HMOs to continue their recent expansion, the federal government must relieve them of excessive regulation and protect them against unfair practices by those physicians and hospitals who do not wish them well.

Malpractice Law. Liability suits remain a major inflator of health-care costs. As we noted in Chapter 5, it is not just that premiums for physician malpractice insurance have been climbing rapidly (between 20 and 30 percent yearly throughout the 1980s); even more important, the threat of lawsuits has led to the costly practice of "defensive" medicine. According to a 1983 survey conducted by the American Medical Association, 40.8 percent of responding physicians reported that they prescribe additional tests because of their concern about lawsuits,* and 27.2 percent indicated that they provide additional treatments for the same reason.

It is hardly surprising that doctors and hospitals are alarmed at the growth in malpractice suits. More striking is that no one else is satisfied with the system either. Insurers don't like it because its costs are lumpy and unpredictable. Patients don't like it because it raises their medical bills. Judges don't like it because it clogs their courts. Not even plaintiffs like it: they undergo trauma, they often must wait years for a settlement, and the rulings go against them in three out of four cases. Among those plaintiffs who receive compensation a mere 2 percent account for two-thirds of the dollar value of total awards. Lawyers may indeed be the only group that likes our present malpractice system, since their contingency fees (which are generally set at between 30 and 50 percent) give them lottery-like windfalls.

Many reforms of malpractice law have been proposed, and some have been adopted in a number of states. One approach is to limit the contingency fees that lawyers can collect in large settlements and to penalize them for filing frivolous suits. Another is to place a fixed "cap" on noneconomic and punitive damages, or to require that awards be paid in installments rather than in huge lump sums. A more radical approach is to take most malpractice claims out of the courts altogether. This could be accomplished by setting up voluntary arbitration boards or statewide review panels (consisting of doctors, lawyers, and laymen) that would screen suits and, in some proposals, settle cases

---

*Note that the cost of every variety of testing—as opposed to the cost of actual acute-care procedures, of rehabilitation, and of chronic care—comprises an estimated 20 percent of our national health-care bill.

before they ever get to court.

As we consider the options for malpractice reform, however, it would be wise to recall the biblical admonition: "Physician, heal thyself." Gross incompetence is rare and malpractice is often committed by doctors with long records of questionable conduct. State licensing boards, however, are slow to bar even these doctors from practice. Indeed, despite the jungle of regulation surrounding the health-care professions, it is almost unheard-of for a physician to lose his license—and even when it comes to this, he is often able to resume practice undetected in another state. There is no clearer demonstration of the dangers of granting any group absolute regulatory control over its own professional standards.

Facing the Trade-Offs

Can we bring health-care costs under control without bearing real sacrifices? Up until a few years ago, the answer of many health-policy experts was a qualified yes. Get rid of the pure waste in the system, they said, and we can have much cheaper care with no loss at all in the best available technology and comfort. It was in this spirit that government and business initiated policy reforms in the early 1980s. After all, if the Reagan administration was about to succeed in curbing the growth in federal budget outlays by painlessly deleting "waste, fraud, and abuse," then there was no reason health administrators could not do the same.

More recently, however, the expert consensus has been shifting in a negative direction, in no small part due to the disappointing results of the efficiency reforms we have so far enacted. The problem, it seems, is that "waste" is nearly always mixed with some measure of benefit. What one observer regards as "wasteful" another may regard as "necessary"—and even for procedures that everyone finds wasteful we often cannot find substitutes that cost much less.

It is instructive to look at one area where, it was once hoped, vast savings could be achieved through eliminating pure waste: hospitalization. For years, experts had called attention to the huge difference in the *average* cost of treating patients in institutional settings versus treating them as outpatients or at home. By the late 1970s and early 1980s, policymakers listened and began to encourage patients to make more efficient choices. In one sense, this policy shift can be judged a success: hospital admissions and bed-days have experienced a sharp per capita decline. But in the most important sense—keeping down total cost—it must be judged a failure. The problem, we discovered, was that the patients who changed procedures were generally the *least expensive* of all institutional consumers and the *most expensive* of all outpatient or at-home consumers. The shift has indeed triggered a depression in the inpatient hospital industry (and sparked a raging boom among outpatient clinics and home-care companies), but it also raised the average cost of treatment in both settings, negating the vast overall savings we once expected.*

The same lesson may have varied applications to many of the efficiency acronyms we so often hear about, from DRGs and PPOs to URPs and RVSs. Although we can easily shift costs from one provider or form of treatment to another, at some point we must face the fact that effective cost containment means confronting patients and providers with the basic choices they will always evade so long as cost-free options remain open to them. The problem is not so much economic as political, for it requires us to distribute pain—a Herculean task for a political system such as our own that is much more used to distributing pleasure. Successful reform, in short, will involve a solid public consensus about what, ideally, we would like our health-care system to achieve, as well as a clearheaded assessment of what it can realistically accomplish. At that point, we will have to make the difficult ethical trade-offs.

What sort of trade-offs? Let us start with the distinction between "cure" and "care." Most of us, if we are honest with ourselves, understand that much of what we want from health-care providers is not just "cure"—the sort of thing that shows up in our national vital statistics—but "care." Consider that well over three-quarters of all visits to doctors are by patients with "self-limiting" conditions, that is, complaints or ailments that will go away, or at least not become life-threatening, even if no treatment is given. Some self-limiting conditions, such as the flu or a sprained ankle, are relatively trivial and rarely involve much expense. Others seem trivial to everyone but the patient and may involve considerable expense. Take, for example, cosmetic surgery for a socialite, knee arthroscopy for a serious jogger, or psychiatric sessions for a demoted employee. Which if any of these treatments deserves public subsidy? Should we—and could we afford—to

---

*According to most health economists, the original expectation that outpatient costs would average 40 to 50 percent of inpatient costs has been betrayed by subsequent experience. A recent survey of four common medical procedures by Corporate Health Strategies, for instance, reports that they have ranged from 85 to 95 percent of inpatient costs.

make the subsidy available on equal terms to every American? Alternatively, are there other public goals which we should meet first?

Self-limiting conditions, of course, can be much more serious. There is the infant with a deformed foot, the adult suffering from crippling arthritis, or the infirm elderly widow who can no longer manage her household. In these cases, the difficult question is not so much whether the public should be disposed to help, but rather who should be helped (how do we define need?), to what extent should we help (up to $5,000, $500,000, without limit?), and how long should we help (chronic care for life?). There is no limit to the amount of care that can be usefully provided for such conditions, and we would be hard-pressed to define easy boundaries between "deserving" and "nondeserving" persons or conditions.

Consider this example. One reason why per capita health-care spending is so much lower in Britain than in the United States is that about 500,000 British patients must "queue up" before receiving elective surgery. An elderly American with an arthritic hip can have hip replacement surgery performed almost on demand (three-quarters of all such operations are paid for by Medicare). An elderly Briton, on the other hand, must wait an average of two years before the National Health Service will even consider an operation. This policy does not affect British life expectancy, yet few would deny that it affects the quality of life of those concerned.

Let us now turn to "cure." At first glance, this is an activity that allows clear definition, but in practice it too encounters trade-offs that are just as difficult as those surrounding "care." As any doctor will tell you, "cure" is always a question of probabilities. No matter what the disease or injury, there is no such thing as an absolutely certain cure; and, more to the point, there exist few diseases or injuries for which one additional dollar spent (even if no dollar is wasted) would not in some degree increase the probability of success.

Often we face such trade-offs in high-probability cures with small risk. Nonetheless, the costs involved can be quite large. One typical question is when (and for how long) to place a post-operative patient in intensive care, at a cost of $1,000 to $2,000 per day. Placing every patient in intensive care (even after routine surgery) would undoubtedly save lives, since frequent blood tests, electronic monitoring, and round-the-clock personal surveillance would occasionally detect emergencies that no physician could have foretold. Such a practice, on the other hand, would entail extra outlays of several billion dollars yearly in overall hospital spending. Other typical questions involve expensive testing, such as biopsies, X-rays, or CAT scans. In many cases, where we test thousands of patients at a cost of millions of dollars for each serious condition detected, the difference between "wasted" and "conservative" treatment rests on nothing more than the subjective opinion of the doctor in charge. Here too there are instructive U.S.-British comparisons: Americans, per capita, spend over three times as much on total parenteral nutrition; take four times as many X-rays; use six times as many CAT scanners; and have five to ten times as many intensive-care beds.*

Then there is the different set of trade-offs surrounding low-probability cures—situations in which patients are unlikely to survive in any case. Sometimes we confront them when dealing with the very young. The cost of keeping alive a three-months premature infant (who has doubtful chances of survival) can easily run over $20,000 per week. More often we confront them when dealing with the elderly. Medicare records tell us that nearly one-third of all hospital spending on behalf of the elderly is for patients in their last year of life. Heroic technology, when used to support the life of the elderly, frequently has little to do with "cure." Instead, it involves that supremely difficult issue of medical ethics: the right to live and the right to die, and what role the patient, family, provider, courts, and public should play in resolving the matter. Many experts believe that much of this expense could be avoided by prior agreements between all parties on what care should be given. Our cost-plus, third-party tradition of financing acute care, however, works against any direct incentive to exercise such foresight.

It is often remarked that many of our health dollars are spent "prolonging death" rather than "prolonging life." Here again we might consider the British example. Any American suffering from total kidney failure is eligible for Medicare-financed dialysis treatment (at a cost of about $30,000 per year per patient) no matter what the odds of long-term survival. The British National Health Service will also pay for dialysis treatment; but not only does it stress at-home dialysis, it generally refuses treatment for those too unhealthy or too old to withstand the chronic traumas associated with the procedure. Patients over age fifty-five are rarely accepted. Britain, as a result, spends less than a quarter of what we spend per capita on dialysis.

*See Henry J. Aaron and William B. Schwartz, *The Painful Prescription: Rationing Hospital Care* (Brookings Institution, 1984).

With our need to contain health costs pushing one way and technological discoveries pushing the other, there is no way America—alone among medically advanced nations—can forever evade these ethical dilemmas. They are already breaking over the horizon. Oregon's Medicaid program, facing a budgetary squeeze, decided early in 1988 to refuse to pay for certain high-risk organ transplants on the grounds that their exploding cost—at $150,000 to $250,000 per operation—did not justify a success rate of under 50 percent. The state argued that many private plans did not cover such transplants and that the same amount of money could save many more lives if spent on preventative and neonatal care. Predictably, the debate in Oregon surrounding this decision has been heated. As state Medicaid chief administrator Freddye Webb-Petett put it: "There are limits we have to face. In the past nobody accepted that. So we have spent billions on health care without judging its value. We can no longer afford that way of life." Let Webb-Petett's decision be an omen. Willingly or not, the American public will soon have to "set limits" and "judge" both the economics and ethics of medical miracles.

If costly technology must sooner or later be rationed, how will we make difficult treatment decisions? How will we weigh the cost, the success rate, the age of the patient, and the long-term quality of the life saved? Even more importantly, how will we assess potential health benefits against alternative claims on our resources, such as education or business investment? How many of these alternative claims must first be met in order to create the economic growth that makes possible still further medical discoveries?

In his recent and controversial book, *Setting Limits: Medical Goals in an Aging Society,* Daniel Callahan suggests that we must make a collective decision to stop devoting resources to the discovery and use of medical technologies whose primary purpose is to prolong life beyond its "natural" span.* He believes, moreover, that once individuals have reached the limits of a "natural" life span, all acute care should be rationed. Continued heroic medical interventions on behalf of the aged constitute an unaffordable and unjustifiable claim on society's resources, he argues; the elderly, after all, have already accomplished and enjoyed most, if not all, of what they can reasonably expect in life. At the same time, Callahan proposes, increased resources should be devoted to improving the general health and quality of life

*Simon & Schuster, 1987.

380

of all age-groups. As far as the elderly are concerned, this would entail redoubled efforts to make advances in the effective delivery of chronic and long-term care.

We must be cautious about the premises of Callahan's argument. We still have no idea, for example, where the "natural" life span ends. Nor can we easily identify which technologies benefit the old as opposed to the young; quite often the same technology has some benefit for all age-groups. Even the assumption that "heroic technology" is a major cause of rising health-care spending has been questioned by many health experts. Far more costly than artificial organs for the elderly, say these critics, is the proliferation of "little-ticket" items—such as extra diagnostic tests—for patients at all ages. Yet whatever the merits of Callahan's answers, the great virtue of his book is that it asks the right sort of questions and sparks the right sort of debate. If there is one American trait that startles health-care providers in all other countries, it is the American illusion that every malady is curable, that every cure is affordable, and perhaps that death itself is forever avoidable. Needless to say, it an illusion that could bankrupt us.

Thus far we have been grappling with different "care" and "cure" treatment options. But behind these is the still broader trade-off: the choice between all forms of treatment on the one hand, and prevention on the other. It has often been said that the United States spends too much money on doctors and too little money on health. There is a more precise way of formulating this observation: our public health programs and private insurance plans overwhelmingly favor treating conditions (at great cost) rather than preventing them (at small cost).

One important piece of evidence that this bias exists—and that it may be a major reason we pay so much in return for so little—is the incredibly skewed distribution of our spending. It is frequently estimated that the most expensive 1 percent of our population (in every age-group) accounts for 25 percent of our total national health-care costs; that the most expensive 5 percent accounts for 50 percent of all costs; and that the most expensive 10 percent accounts for 75 percent of all costs. Considerable asymmetry is perhaps inevitable; some of us get very sick and need expensive treatment while others of us remain perfectly healthy and need nothing. But it is difficult to argue that an imbalance of this magnitude reflects a judicious allocation of our health-care resources. More probably, it reflects how our public policies—from benefits through regulation—practically force the delivery of our health care into a highly formal (and usually institutional) acute-care treatment package. Avoiding illness by keeping people well gets relatively little encouragement; what we spend publicly on prevention, in fact, amounts to no more than about one penny out of every dollar in federal health-care outlays.

It is well known, for instance, that billions of dollars in eventual health-care costs could be saved if we treated the millions of undetected cases of hypertension and diabetes. Hypertension screening and treatment programs cost as little as $2,000 per life-year saved. Dealing with the eventual complications of hypertension through organ transplants and dialysis, on the other hand, costs between $50,000 and $150,000 per life-year saved. As we move from the issue of medical to "personal" prevention, of course, we run across statistics that many of us already know, but whose cost implications we are unwilling to confront: fully one-third of all deaths from cancer and respiratory illness are directly attributable to tobacco, and the vast majority of crippling injuries from motor vehicle accidents could be easily prevented if everyone used seat belts and motorcycle helmets and there were half as many drunken drivers on the roads. Prevention in these two areas alone could alleviate great suffering and save over $30 billion annually in national health-care costs.

So why don't we have more prevention? Once again, the reason is more political than economic, and more cultural than medical. Acute care can be administered by others on demand; prevention must be practiced by oneself in advance—or it must be forced on people in a manner that does violence to our national instinct for personal liberty. Acute care, moreover, ministers to actual and highly visible needs; prevention only ministers to potential and invisible needs. The resource trade-off is therefore rigged against prevention at the outset. The price of our collective choice shows up in the expensive acute-care treatment of persons who lead self-destructive lives between hospital visits, or in the chronic-care treatment of persons who played the tobacco or seat belt lottery—and lost. A generation ago, many of these patients and victims did not survive long or could not be treated. Now they do. Today there are huge clinics that specialize in chronic care for emphysema patients or in life-support systems for brain-dead accident victims. Almost all of these patients sooner or later end up having their medical bills paid out of public budgets.

In instances such as these, we have to face unavoidable ethical questions. Isn't there, perhaps, some point at which self-preservation must be construed as a public duty? Cannot some forms of prevention be behavior for which individuals bear direct responsibility? Because most forms of prevention require time to pass between the act and the reward, our ambivalence about prevention shows striking similarities to our ambivalence about saving and investing. And in many cases—with unfunded liabilities for Medicare benefits now in the trillions of dollars—we may soon have to recognize that the two issues raise precisely the same questions. If staying healthy must be construed as a private act having public benefits, can we look much differently on the personal decision to save income or otherwise insure oneself against expenses of chronic care in old age? Yet both attempts at self-sacrifice run against the strong current of our consumption ethos, which says, in effect, do anything you want; we'll take care of the consequences later.

Nowhere are these questions more pressing and salient than in the current policy debate surrounding long-term care for the disabled elderly. The fundamental issue here is the extent to which we should make publicly funded care a replaceable substitute for privately funded or family care. To the extent we do not, we risk creating a "two-tiered" system. But to the extent we do, we devalue one of the primary rewards of saving household income, of raising a family, or of caring personally for one's elderly relatives. This is perhaps the most painful macro trade-off Americans will be facing as we enter the next century. It has become fashionable in recent years to worry about the "moral hazard" of means-tested welfare and about its effect on the incentive of the poor to work or to live responsibly.* Yet all of us who are nonpoor so seldom reflect on the awesome changes we may be inducing in our own behavior through universal entitlements. Considering the number of dollars or people involved, the so-called welfare problem is certainly trivial by comparison.

Prevention in the broadest sense of the word should be kept in mind as we redesign our health-care system so that it better reflects our public interest. No matter what policy avenue we emphasize—regulations or incentives—we are up against a politically formidable task. Either way, we will have to practice collective self-denial. But if we have put more emphasis on cost-conscious incentives over regulations in this chapter, it is not simply because they "work better" over

---

*Consider, for instance, the lively debate over the best-seller by Charles Murray, *Losing Ground: American Social Policy, 1950–1980* (Basic Books, 1984).

the short term. It is also because they may be indispensable to our forward progress as a nation over time. Regulatory policies that indulge our uninvolved "third-party" mentality may ultimately require additional regulatory policies to pick up where private savings, personal responsibility, and families leave off. True, Americans might enjoy having a professional cadre of administrators make the painful trade-offs for them. Unfortunately, they may also need someone to do their thinking for them about resource allocation throughout the rest of the economy as well. How well our own form of government—as opposed to governments in other nations—could perform these broader tasks remains a proposition most Americans would probably want to leave untested.

Conclusion

10

The Failure of the Libertarian Welfare State

"When we build, let it be such work as our descendants
will thank us for: And let us think, as we lay stone on
stone, that the time will come when men will say as they
look upon the labor and the substance, 'See! this our
fathers did for us.' "

— *John Ruskin*

I T IS UNPOPULAR in the United States to discuss the possibility of a dim future, perhaps because most Americans are optimistic by nature and dread being associated with the reviled "doom
and gloom" school, which holds that all outcomes are bad and that all
options are hopeless. The picture we have painted in this book is not
always pretty, but we trust we will not be misunderstood and called
pessimists. We are not suggesting that America has a predestined
rendezvous with economic disaster or that Americans as a people lack
the political will to make farsighted choices. Rather, we have written
this book to explain why our entitlements policies reflect an indiscriminate preoccupation with public and private consumption at the
expense of savings and investment, and to underscore that the less-
pleasant consequences of these policies are avoidable only if we *choose*
to change course.

We are convinced that we *must* change course, sooner or later. If
we change course sooner, it will be because Americans will have made
a farsighted choice in favor of future generations, a rising standard of
living, and a more equitable distribution of society's resources. To act

387

sooner will mean that we can regain control over our own destiny. This will require entitlements reforms that entail some sacrifices, but—as we have pointed out in the last three chapters—these sacrifices can be phased in gradually and need not affect anyone near the poverty level. In fact, entitlements reform is a precondition for more substantial and more universal poverty relief than we can currently afford.

If we change course later, it will be because events will have forced our hand after untold years of economic stagnation—years that will undoubtedly be marked by cuts in progressive public spending, a decline in our international influence, and a growing cynicism about our collective historical destiny. Although it is easy to imagine how the events that will drive us toward entitlements reform could include a very serious recession, they need not be especially apocalyptic. They may simply be a series of painful signals, such as higher interest rates, higher tax rates, swifter inflation, and uncompetitive industries, each indicating unmistakably that we are living beyond our means. And for years to come our response may continue to be the one of incremental adjustment that we have already witnessed during the 1980s—enough change to avoid collapse, but not enough to promise us a better future. In the end, however, far-reaching entitlements reform will be un-avoidable.

Since we feel compelled to defend our book's thesis, the reader might suppose that our assumptions are highly controversial. Surpris-ingly, this is not the case. It would be fair to say that a decided majority of today's policy leaders, if forced to respond directly (and if allowed to respond privately), would concede that entitlements will in future years make a progressively larger claim on our economic resources. Yet in the same breath many would object to our "negative" perspective. Since the root cause of our economic problems is our failure to invest in the future, they argue, reform initiatives should concentrate on positive solutions: not on where we have to cut spending, but on where we have to commit new resources. In other words, let's talk about more support to education, to research and development, to capital formation, to health insurance for the young and poor, to AIDS research—but not about reducing entitlements.

There is a fatal flaw in this reasoning. So long as we keep talking about where to spend resources without having any idea where we will find them, our discussion is bound to lose meaning and wander without purpose. Policymakers advocate new programs that Congress does not dare to pass in the face of an endless future of multibillion-dollar budget deficits. Researchers discover breakthrough technologies that corporations cannot afford to fund at high and unpredictable real interest rates. Candidates for political office speak of bold "new ideas" that opponents deflate merely by naming the price tag. The public grows disillusioned and we get no closer to our goal of providing for the future.

There is no question (as we noted in Chapter 1) that the foremost challenge facing America in the years to come is to raise our savings and investment balance on virtually every ledger—foreign, private, and public. Raising the balance with foreigners will mean producing at least $150 billion more for export each year and getting nothing in return for it except the satisfaction of gradually weaning ourselves away from foreign creditors. Raising the balance in our private domestic economy will mean reversing the steep decline in our net investment in housing, plant, and equipment that we have suffered over the last fifteen years. And raising the balance in our public sector will mean reallocating budgetary funds from entitlements to infrastructure—and even more importantly to the provision of technology training, education, and health care to younger and poorer Americans, for these are the individuals on whose productive capacities the future of our country rests.

If we are to set this process in motion, America will at a minimum have to raise its net national savings rate (now 2–3 percent of GNP) to 6–7 percent of GNP over the coming five years (a rate still below our level in the 1970s) and to 10–12 percent of GNP within twenty years (a level far below that of Japan, but just about on par with the average for today's industrial countries). By the first decade of the twenty-first century, in other words, we will have to be rechanneling yearly into investment some $450 billion that we now spend on private and public consumption.

It is easy to nod in agreement until we emphasize this last fact: within the next twenty years, we must gradually choose to cut the share of yearly national income we consume by between 8 and 10 percent. Then it is hard not to take a few gulps. We are a society accustomed to endless discussion of how we can consume and apply resources. But we are not at all accustomed to talking about the trade-offs involved in freeing up resources for new goals by reducing our current levels of consumption in other areas. Why? Because we still think in terms of buoyant economic growth through which "productivity dividends" are continuously making additional resources available. We have yet to come to terms with the unsettling fact that America is no longer enjoying that sort of growth—and that the task of saving that lies ahead of us may require an absolute reduction in real per-worker consumption in many of the years to come.

Underlying our economic problem, then, is both a political and a cultural problem. The American character has always emphasized optimism, unfettered energy, "win-win" choices, and the direct pursuit of dreams. The supply-side, "we can always grow out of it" message is less a school of economic thought than the latest manifestation of an abiding and bipartisan national instinct. Circumstances, however, are finally forcing us to change our behavior in a direction that has no precedent: toward self-denial, collective discipline, and "win-lose" choices. For at least the past few decades, we have fixed our attention on spending and consuming in both our private and public lives. Now we will have to fix it on producing and saving. We can no longer talk only about where we can spend more. To make that possible, we must also talk about where we must spend less.

How We Got Here

The least productive enterprise in which Americans can engage is to try to blame what has happened to our economy over the last couple of decades on one political party or ideology. To be sure, it is easy to find fault with the conservative leadership of the current administration. We can all recall the absurd, "Laffer-Curve" promise of the 1981 across-the-board tax cuts; the pseudosacrificial chopping away at the means-tested and investment corners of the federal budget; the extravagant weapons purchases; the silent approval of the massive increase in nonpoverty entitlements; and the unwillingness to take the ominous deficit issue directly to the public.

The current administration claims to have "fought the good fight" for fiscal austerity against the largess of Congress, even though its proposed budgets have averaged only $8 billion less per year than the spending that Congress has eventually authorized. Protecting the "social safety net" for the poor was supposed to be one of its top priorities. Yet the administration successfully engineered a sizable reduction in the small poverty-program section of the budget, while the President himself passed up a historic opportunity for far greater long-term savings in May 1985 when he decided not to support his own party's willingness to freeze cost-of-living adjustments on non-means-tested entitlements. The unreality of the administration's economic program was nowhere better expressed than in President Reagan's 1984 "Morning in America" campaign—a campaign based on three premises that, taken together, are irreconcilable with healthy economic growth: not touching defense, not touching Social Security, and not touching taxes.

But clearly the liberals and Democrats are equally to blame. Long before Reagan came to office, it was liberal opinion leaders who had persuaded the public to regard the budget and tax code as the means to cost-free national consumption. It was a Democratic Congress that argued in favor of deficit spending for so many years that no one could remember (with only one budget surplus since 1960) the rationale behind fiscal balance. And it was a Democratic president (the reader will recall President Johnson's Medicare "bargain") who pioneered the art of disingenuous forecasts. That this art is still very much alive is attested to by the catastrophic and long-term health-care proposals passed or debated by the 100th Congress: they advertise more benefits than they will deliver, and they will certainly cost more than what is now projected.

It was the very success the Democrats enjoyed in promoting consumption, in fact, that persuaded Reagan's conservative backers to "dish the Whigs" and beat the opposition at their own game. One measure of how completely Reagan has co-opted the substance of Democratic policy—though he has dressed it in very different rhetoric—has been the inarticulate confusion of the Democratic reaction to Reaganomics.

Perhaps, then, the American public is more to blame for our troubles than either political party, for we apparently encourage a consistent direction in economic leadership no matter whom we choose to lead or what the leader says. Back in the 1960s, the Democrats promised Americans a large and dynamic government that would pursue all sorts of farsighted national goals, from the eradication of poverty and all threats to world peace to the institution of permanent prosperity and the rebuilding of our cities and schools. By the end of the 1970s, it seemed to most Americans that this vision had been fundamentally betrayed, not simply because the goals had not been achieved, but because the vast and hypocritical welfare state they now saw before them no longer had any intention of achieving them. Instead of a future-oriented instrument of national progress, we had created a vending-machine government, which, in return for clever lobbying, mindlessly dispensed huge packages of consumption for any and all groups at any and all income levels.

So Americans elected Ronald Reagan, who promised to cart the machine away. But rather than remove the machine, the new administration simply took out the few public-purpose packages left in it and stripped the rest of their misleading public-interest labels. Now Americans could grab the goodies faster than ever while at the same time being told that government was nowhere in sight, that free lunches had vanished, and that a self-reliant private sector was responsible for their comfort.

What Americans must appreciate is that the historic ideologies of the left and right are now irrelevant to the issues at stake. Both sides assert that "entitlements" are fundamentally about transferring income and status from the rich "haves" to the poor "have-nots." The left claims to advocate them for this reason and the right to oppose them for the same reason. But reality belies this supposed ideological conflict. As Mancur Olsen, author of the classic *The Rise and Decline of Nations*, pointedly observes:

> In fact, when we focus on government policies that are designed to aid low-income people, we are looking at only a tiny part of what governments actually do. Most of the redistribution of government is *not* from upper-income and middle-income people to low-income people. Most of the redistribution of income in fact is from middle-income people to other middle-income people, or from the whole society to particular groups of rich people, or from one group to another where the groups are distinguished not by one being poor and the other being rich, but only by the fact that some groups are organized and some are not.*

Olsen describes what many have dubbed the "social-democratic" welfare state, a term that captures the essence of the political economy of so many postwar industrial democracies. Today in America, after the heralded triumph of a conservative vision hostile to big government, we have repudiated the inefficiencies and confused cross-purposes of the social-democratic welfare state. But in its place we now find a purer self-contradiction, a "libertarian" welfare state, explicitly purged of collective goals or stewardship.

---

*"Ideology and Economic Growth" by Mancur Olsen in *The Legacy of Reaganomics: Prospects for Long-Term Growth,* ed. by Charles R. Hulton and Isabel V. Sawhill (Urban Institute, 1984). See also his *The Rise and Decline of Nations: Economic Growth, Stagflation, and Social Rigidities* (Yale, 1982).

Ours is a welfare state because it empowers an elected government to reallocate economic resources in peacetime. Over the past two decades—through hubris, inadvertence, and interest-group lobbying—our own perverse reallocation choice has been to ensure that only a small and declining share of our national income can go anywhere except into private or public consumption. But lately it has become "libertarian" in that its foundation has been shifted to private, contractual arrangements with government. The welfare no longer justifies itself with a public interest nor even pretends to have a public design. Instead, it consists of individual rights to debt-financed consumption held by a vast cross section of the population who feel they have earned them—the elderly, foremost, but also home owners, banks, veterans, health insurers, farmers, hospitals, defense contractors, federal retirees, protected industries, and so on down the long and varied list. We have come to regard all of these rights to consumption as permanent contracts between "entitled" private parties and the state, and as such the new libertarianism finds them acceptable.

The welfare-libertarian contradiction of the 1980s helps to explain an apparent mystery. Why was the growth of social spending in the late 1960s accompanied by so much public optimism, goal setting, and social controversy? And why is the growth still going on today accompanied by a deafening and embarrassed silence (with occasional complaints about austerity and the whir and click of indexing formulas in the background)? The reason, we believe, is that Great Society spending involved decisions to divert private resources to the future achievement of public goals. These kinds of decisions naturally gave rise to passionate debate over contrasting visions of our collective future. Today's spending growth, on the other hand, merely reflects the increased funding required to fulfill a host of "locked-in" quasi-contracts. There is no longer any pretense that public goals are being carried out, and hence no substantive debate—only legalistic protests about whose rights are being infringed.

At the bottom line of this libertarian-welfare ethos are the enormous liabilities that we are passing on to our children as intergenerational transfers: a mountain of debt, domestic and foreign, and of unfunded future entitlements. In 1965 about 33 percent of all federal spending went into non-means-tested retirement and disability benefits plus interest on the national debt. By 1986, despite the huge growth in federal spending relative to the size of our economy, this share had grown to 54 percent. Extending our current policy course into the future holds out still bleaker prospects for today's youngest Americans. Yet this new generation is not only much smaller in numbers than the giant generation preceding it, but is also, for the first time in our history, less well educated and worse off economically at the same age. Are these the future Americans we are banking on to bring new technologies to fruition, to renew our international competitiveness, to pay off our foreign debts, and to generate sufficient wealth to finance the mounting cost of our retirement benefits and health care as we grow older? It would be hard to imagine a greater disproportion between what we have given and what we are asking.

Since so much of current consumption is financed through intergenerational transfers, it would seem fair to ask whether the generations of older Americans who put our entitlements edifice into place should be blamed for our predicament. In particular, consider the role played by the so-called war generation (those born from 1901 to 1924, and who thus came of age in time to see action in World War II). Dominating the White House longer than any other American generation (from 1961 through 1989, and perhaps further if Vice-President George Bush is elected president), the members of this peer group have exercised extraordinary political power throughout their lifetimes. And in so doing, they have overseen virtually every phase of the expansion in our age-based entitlements system, from the design of Medicare, the enactment of the cash-benefit explosion of the early 1970s, and the decision to index non-means-tested programs to the creation and leadership of an enormous "gray lobby" of the elderly that has since resisted all attempts at reform. The completion of this expansion, it turns out, has roughly coincided with the timing of this peer group's own retirement.

In all fairness, however, apportioning blame by generation would be just as mistaken as apportioning it by political party. As we have already seen, much of this expansion was perceived at the time to be affordable in the light of the common economic and demographic assumptions shared by all generations of Americans. Back at the beginning of the 1970s, for example, all Americans expected that birth rates would remain forever near Baby-Boom levels ("overpopulation," in fact, was considered a potential problem) and that the halcyon economic growth of the 1960s would last indefinitely ("affluence," we might recall, was another problem). The economist John Makin of the American Enterprise Institute has estimated that the official economic projections when Medicare was founded in 1965 called for a Gross National Product of some $5 trillion in 1986. That amounts to a GNP 25 percent higher in real dollars than we actually produced in 1986. With an extra trillion dollars of GNP available today, current levels of entitlement spending would clearly not seem so burdensome.

Perhaps the greatest fiscal tragedy of the early 1970s was the timing of automatic indexing and the huge expansion of benefits in 1972, for it occurred only months before a sequence of economic events—an oil import embargo, accelerating inflation, a devastating recession, and a secular downturn in productivity growth—that would certainly have moderated our decision had we waited just a bit longer. The most obvious consequence of this tragedy was economic: the explosion of entitlement spending as a share of our GNP. A less obvious consequence was political. By sheltering our population of retirees from the sinking trend in after-tax family income experienced by most other age-groups over the past decade and a half, we have effectively insulated the most politically active age bracket of voters from the economic reality of post-1973 America.

All this, of course, is hindsight. At the time, with a booming economy and an elderly poverty rate that was still considerably higher than the national average, the decision to expand non-means-tested entitlements seemed not just affordable, but equitable. It was the war generation, after all, whose enormous sacrifices and generational endowments—from Iwo Jima, the Marshall Plan, and interstate highways to the Apollo Missions, the Salk vaccine, and split-level homes—had made postwar prosperity a reality. Now that this group was aging, America was not about to let its members peer into future prosperity like Moses into the Promised Land, unable to enter where they had led. Instead, we would split the future dividends with those who had done so much in the past.

Moreover, from the war generation's own perspective, this choice seemed all the more justifiable after the great battle of values it had just waged with its own Baby-Boom sons and daughters. Not only did the dominant voice of the Baby Boom have precious little respect for the tangible investments of their parents, but the Boomers often castigated the very concept of deferring current consumption for the sake of future benefits—a concept they considered to be a pathology of their parents' "mind-set." In the end, the older generation threw in the towel* and decided that maybe they did need to "let go" a bit. Ironically, the celebrated and idealistic youth culture of the 1960s that grew out of this ideological clash has turned out to be largely ephemeral. The one development of the period that mattered least to younger Americans—the expansion of age-based entitlements—has turned out to be that period's most enduring legacy. As we have seen in earlier chapters, federal spending on these nonpoverty programs, not on the Great Society's social agenda, will determine how we allocate our national resources for decades to come.

There is still another part to this story. We must emphasize that the great expansion of entitlements engineered by the war generation was never really intended to benefit older age-groups at the expense of younger generations. It is not enough to say, as we have already indicated, that Americans of all ages believed such a transfer of wealth to be both affordable and equitable. What is perhaps even more important is that the war generation itself never perceived this entitlements agenda as necessarily "pro-elderly" or "anti-youth," even though the programs paid benefits primarily to older Americans. The reason for this perception lies in their collective coming-of-age experience, the Great Depression of the 1930s, and the solution that the vast majority of them embraced as young voters, President Roosevelt's New Deal.

To be sure, Social Security and the other associated benefit programs that were founded or expanded in the 1930s as part of the New Deal were designed to insure the elderly (as well as the disabled, orphaned, and widowed) against the worst vicissitudes of modern capitalism by offering them a modest pension. To that extent, our original entitlements system favored the old. But the New Deal programs were at the same time explicitly designed to retire the "old and unfit" in order to make room for young men from intact families in an economy that seemed to offer only a limited number of jobs. (Fifty years ago, "to retire" was still a verb with strong negative connotations, something you did to a worn-out machine.) The general idea was to encourage a more "vigorous" economy, oriented

---

*Literally as well as figuratively. The budgetary savings that appeared when we abandoned the Vietnam conflict—which every war-generation president from Kennedy to Nixon (perhaps mistakenly) insisted was being fought for the sake of future generations—were directly transferred over to the 1972 explosion in Social Security outlays. The decline in defense spending during the early 1970s made this phase of the entitlements expansion fiscally and politically painless, except of course to any younger taxpayer who expected to share in these so-called peace dividends.

396

strictly around youthful, male-led nuclear families. To that extent, our original entitlements system favored the young.

When the members of the war generation in turn assumed political power and presided over the great benefit expansion of the 1960s and early 1970s, to some extent they were simply rounding out the New Deal system, the desirability of which had been inculcated in them during their youth. The federal government, they believed, should hoist into place the final capstone in an economy geared to an ever more educated, energetic, and imaginative cadre of youngsters. And to do so it should construct a cocoon in which all other, more vulnerable groups could be sheltered.

In terms of today's entitlement programs (with the possible exception of military retirement), little of this pro-youth rationale is still intelligible, much less defensible. To begin with, New Deal policymakers had assumed a world in which the number of available jobs was inflexible and consumption, not savings, was the only limit to output. They also assumed that the elderly population would remain affordably small relative to the working-age population, that a large share of the elderly in good health would continue to work, that federal benefits themselves would remain modest and unindexed, that private pensions would be generally unavailable, and that intact families would permanently dominate the work force.

Every one of these assumptions, of course, has been exploded by subsequent history. To go back to the original debates over Social Security is to enter a different world. In the late 1930s, $10 per month was thought of as a minimum "floor of protection," a leading senator could argue (plausibly, though incorrectly even then) that 60 percent of all Americans aged sixty would be dead in five years, and administrators could push for a 50 percent unearned "spousal" benefit on the assumption that few women would ever enter the labor force. To appreciate how much our lives have changed, and not just with regard to aging, consider Aid to Families with Dependent Children. AFDC was a component of the original 1935 Social Security Act designed to benefit young widows with dependent children. It was assumed that when the Survivors benefits portion of the Social Security system matured, AFDC would wither away (all young widows, after all, would then be receiving their husbands' Survivors benefits). New Deal policymakers could never have foreseen today's social world, in which young widows make up a negligible fraction of those eligible for AFDC.

As outmoded as the original rationale for entitlements has become, it still helps explain how younger and older generations of Americans can have such different impressions of the equity of our current social insurance programs. Indeed, this generational rift is wide and growing: older Americans remain persuaded that our entitlements system is a fair trade-off between age-groups; a rising number of younger Americans, on the other hand, are convinced that it forces them to shoulder an insupportable burden without guaranteeing them a commensurate future reward. In the end, these younger Americans are closer to the mark. Divorced from its 1930s social and economic environment, our system of federal entitlements has not only become unaffordable, but has lost all rhyme or reason as a means of allocating national resources. Indeed, there remains today only one effective justification: an appeal to the literal meaning of the word "entitlement," implying a desert based on quasi-contracts or "deals" that need no rhyme or reason. You simply buy and sell them in the political marketplace and do as best you can as you go along in life. Since we assume no collective responsibility for ensuring that the sum total of such transactions adds up to anything saved, our economic future is threatened. Since our children can neither vote nor make deals, younger generations end up losers.* And since taxpayers naturally feel little civic enthusiasm about footing the bill for such contracts, federal dissaving becomes a fundamental symbol of our uniquely American problem.

Toward a New Political Culture

Entitlements cannot be a one-way street, with older generations always receiving and younger generations always giving. Sustainable social insurance also requires that our endowments to younger generations be sufficient to allow the system's continued functioning when today's young become tomorrow's older Americans. In other words, social insurance must always have a strong investment component if it is to survive in the long run. Moreover, it must take a realistic view of economic and demographic change in America. It must

---

*As Samuel Preston, president of the American Demographic Association, pointedly remarked in a celebrated address, political altruism is the only reason public policy looks after kids at all: "Children don't vote; and adults don't vote on behalf of their own childhood, which is water over the dam. I daresay that if we passed through life backwards, adults would insist that conditions in childhood be made far more appealing." (Reprinted in *Demography,* November 1984.)

recognize that we are living longer, having fewer children, and generating productivity gains that are far less impressive than they were a couple decades ago. Our entitlements system, as we have seen, was first forged in the very different world of the Great Depression and the New Deal. If it fails to evolve so as to reflect the changing realities of American life, it cannot possibly survive to fulfill its legitimate functions in the next century.

What America needs is to develop a perspective that will emphasize the "big picture" and will allow us to weigh the priorities we attach to all our society's objectives. In the last three chapters, we have discussed policy reforms that could help reshape our entitlements system in ways that would allow it to better meet tomorrow's challenges. Here we simply want to call attention once more to the new cultural and political values that must underlie those policy reforms if they are to be effective.

Above all, America needs to forge a new and positive image of aging, and at the same time to recognize that age alone can no longer be a blanket criterion for entitlement to a public subsidy. Although they are the winners in our current entitlements system, many of today's elderly still feel like second-class citizens—and with reason, since they are often excluded from the mainstream of economic and public life. Our rapidly growing senior population is not homogeneous, but rather an enormously diverse group that includes, alongside those who are disabled and in need of care, many of the potentially most vital contributors to our society. In light of America's demographic transformation alone, we simply cannot afford to continue furloughing these elderly individuals according to some antiquated New Deal view of aging. But just as important, we must realize that this traditional view—as most gerontologists now stress—is bad for the elderly themselves. By reducing them to a functionless (if sometimes affluent) dependence, it undermines their self-image, their self-confidence, and ultimately their health.

Let us be blunt. Forty years from now, America will be one of the oldest societies in the world. Our median age, now about thirty-two, could well rise as high as forty-five in the early twenty-first century, making well over half our adult population eligible for membership in the American Association of Retired Persons. By then, our attitude toward aging will quite literally determine our self-image as a society. Whether we continue to cling to the notion of the elderly as always needy, or whether instead we forge new and positive attitudes toward aging—attitudes emphasizing continuing involvement in public and economic life—is a choice that may well determine our national destiny.

Along with its new image of aging, America needs to develop new cultural attitudes toward health care. This is a topic we have discussed in previous chapters, and there is no need to retrace our arguments here. It is enough to recall that a modern society's potential demand for health-care consumption is limitless. Given ever more spectacular and expensive medical technologies (coupled with the aging of our population), there is no theoretical limit to the share of GNP we could devote to health-care spending. There is, however, some practical limit, for health care must compete with a myriad of other purposes that have an equally legitimate claim on our national resources. At some point, we must face up to the fact that it will be necessary to refrain from consuming potentially available health-care services. What choices we should make is a question still open to debate, but that we will have to make choices is not. Other industrial countries have already crossed this divide and imposed various forms of health-care rationing; if we manage to avoid rigid "top-down" regulation, perhaps we can yet develop a solution that better suits our national character. If we do, it will undoubtedly involve a shift in cultural attitudes that emphasizes preventative care over heroic intervention, that persuades individuals to insure themselves against catastrophic health-care costs, and that once more encourages families to participate actively in the provision of long-term care.

Third, it is important to recall that our economic preconceptions must change as well. If America is to pay off its foreign debts and once again become a strong investor in its future, we must compel ourselves for many years to produce more than we consume. If we do not succeed in this challenge, we cannot hope that America will put an end to its trade deficit without a strangling rise in interest rates; nor hope that today's children will ever experience the American Dream of enjoying a standard of living significantly higher than their parents'; nor hope that America will remain a preeminent world power by the time today's children are retiring. We freely admit that a higher savings rate is not a *sufficient* condition for a future that we can be proud of. But history tells us, without any question, that it is a *necessary* condition; and because saving is so obviously unpleasant, it is the one activity we are most tempted to avoid. The longer we put off the savings challenge, the more the approaching austerity will be harsh, prolonged, and beyond our control. In a very real sense, the future of social insurance in America rests on our decision to save more today. If we shrink from reform in our nonpoverty entitlement programs, it is ultimately the poor and the vulnerable in our society who will bear the brunt of the consequences.

Finally, we must start asking ourselves some hard questions about the long-term effects of the generational bias of our entitlements system on the integrity of the family and on the extent to which we may be undermining our age-old incentives to pass on family endowments to our children. There was once a time when having children, raising them well, and maintaining a stable marriage was the key to security in old age. There was also a time when attention to one's children was believed to bear more fundamental returns to a family over time than attention to one's career. Clearly, this time is passing. We are the first society in history to socialize the costs of old age while leaving the costs of raising children largely private. Every other combination (privatizing everything, socializing everything, or socializing only the raising of kids) has of course been tried many times. Our combination is without precedent, and we search in vain for landmarks reassuring us that the final outcome will be to our liking.

We need to ask: Is this bias in our public interest? Does it serve our collective future? Or rather does it reflect, in our social policy, the same aversion to investment that permeates our fiscal policy? As a nation, we seem to have taken a great deal of pride in getting both parents out of the home and into the work force; in reassuring older Americans that they need never depend on their children; in cleansing the very concept of early and universal retirement from all negative connotation; and in hiring an army of the best-paid professionals in the world to pioneer space-age organ transplants—while allowing one million pregnant women to come to term each year without so much as a single doctor visit. At some point we have to stop and ask ourselves: Is this direction sustainable? Does it give back as much as it takes from our future? Or are we embarked on a course that causes most Americans, at all ages, to feel some deep inner misgivings?

We have already seen that the "crowding out" concept has both a financial meaning (to siphon private savings away from private investment) and a fiscal meaning (to squeeze public-purpose spending out of public-sector budgets). It may also have a long-term social meaning. No one knows what American society might be like once it has fully accepted static living standards as a permanent way of life. But it is easy to imagine that it would be a far less generous, less hopeful, and less liberal society than the one in which we now live—and that it would have far less to spare for any ideal that transcends the business of just getting by in the world. Let us hope, instead, that in the coming years we can redirect ourselves toward the goal we all desire: a future worth preparing for.

Notes

Organization and Program Acronyms

AFDC: Aid to Families with Dependent Children
BEA: Bureau of Economic Analysis, Department of Commerce
BLS: Bureau of Labor Statistics, Department of Labor
CBO: Congressional Budget Office, U.S. Congress
CHAMPUS: Civilian Health and Medical Program of the Uniformed Services, Department of Defense
CRS: Congressional Research Service, U.S. Congress
CSRS: Civil Service Retirement System, Office of Personnel Management
DI: Disability Insurance (Social Security trust fund)
GAO: General Accounting Office, U.S. Congress
HCFA: Health Care Financing Administration, Department of Health and Human Services
HHS: Department of Health and Human Services
HI: Hospital Insurance (Social Security trust fund; "Part A" of Medicare)
IRS: Internal Revenue Service, Department of the Treasury
NCHS: National Center for Health Statistics, Public Health Service, Department of Health and Human Services
NTIS: National Technical Information Service, Department of Commerce
OASI: Old-Age and Survivors Insurance (Social Security trust fund)
OECD: Organization for Economic Cooperation and Development
OMB: Office of Management and Budget, Executive Office of the President
OPM: Office of Personnel Management (independent executive agency)
OTA: Office of Technology Assessment, U.S. Congress
SMI: Supplementary Medical Insurance (Social Security trust fund; "Part B" of Medicare)
SSA: Social Security Administration, Department of Health and Human Services
SSI: Supplemental Security Income program
VA: Veterans Administration (independent executive agency)

Calendar and Fiscal Years

Calendar years refer to years ending December 31. For 1977 and after, federal fiscal years refer to years ending September 30; for 1976 and before, they refer to years ending June 30. In general, federal fiscal years are indicated in the text by explicit reference. Occasionally, such reference is omitted when the dates refer to federal budget catagories and specific federal programs. All other dates indicate calendar years.

Real or Constant-Dollar Values

"Real" or "constant-dollar" values or growth rates refer to current dollars (the actual dollar amount in any given year) that have been deflated with a price index. This allows a comparison of real purchasing power over time. As a rule, when our object is to look at the *consumer* purchasing power of dollars (such as benefit levels), we employ the Personal Consumption Expenditure (or PCE) deflator. When our object is to look at the *economy-wide* purchasing power of dollars, we employ the Gross National Product (or GNP) deflator. Both deflators are calculated and published quarterly by the Bureau of Economic Analysis.

Net Savings and Investment

(Page 47 footnote) Annual domestic investment is usually defined in national income and product accounts as the annual national expenditures on equipment and structures whose useful economic life is greater than one year. For simplicity and consistency in measurement, both the BEA and the OECD omit equipment expenditures for items purchased exclusively for household use (so-called consumer durables, such as washing machines).

Starting with this definition, investment can be measured either "gross" or "net." Gross investment simply equals the dollar value of all final-sale expenditures on investment items. Net investment equals gross investment *minus* the estimated economic depreciation, during that year, on the preexisting national stock of investment items. Net investment, in other words, tells us what has been added to the nation's capital stock during the current year after subtracting the "wearing out" of prior-year purchases.

There is little question that "net" is a conceptually superior measure of investment, since it focuses on what is "left over" when the year is complete (the very criterion by which we differentiate investment from consumption). It also makes national investment compatible as a measure with national savings (which is nearly always measured "net" of depreciation). The "gross" measure is sometimes defended on the grounds that we have no accurate way of measuring the true rate of economic depreciation. (Some economists argue that the standard assumption of linear depreciation is unrealistically high; others—who stress outmoded technologies—that it is unrealistically low.) Although such complaints are fair enough, ignoring depreciation altogether is clearly not the answer. If we made no estimate of depreciation, we could witness anomalies such as a positive "gross" investment performance in the midst of a shrinking and deteriorating capital stock. Alternatively, we could witness an unchanged "gross" investment performance while shifting to ever shorter-lived assets (and thus to much slower growth in the real value of our capital stock).

This latter possibility, in fact, very nearly describes the postwar U.S. experience—and is consistent with higher real interest rates. Our average rate of gross private domestic investment in the 1980s (at 15.9 percent of GNP) is only slightly smaller than it was in the 1950s (16.1 percent of GNP). The composition of this gross investment, however, has shifted dramatically away from slow-depreciating assets (such as industrial plant) and toward fast-depreciating assets (such as office equipment). As a result, our annual depreciation bill has risen as a share of gross investment: in the 1950s, net private domestic investment averaged 7.5 percent of GNP; in the 1980s it has averaged 4.7 percent of GNP—a drop of more than one-third in our net investment level.

Several further considerations, some mentioned in the text, make this drop especially ominous: (1) an even sharper decline has occurred in net U.S. public-sector investment; (2) approximately one-third of our level of investment during the 1980s, as low as it is, would not have been possible without borrowing abroad; (3) we have recently experienced a rapid growth in our labor force—unlike our own experience during the 1950s and 1960s or that of other industrial countries today—which should have required a sizable *increase* in our net investment rate if we had wanted to keep our capital-to-labor ratio growing at the same rate as before; and (4) even in "gross" terms our domestic investment rate in the 1980s has remained 4 to 5 percentage points of GNP beneath that of the rest of the industrial world and 10 percentage points of GNP beneath that of the rapidly growing "newly industrialized countries" (such as Korea, Taiwan, Singapore, and Hong Kong).

Note finally that foreign investment or borrowing is ordinarily measured in gross terms, since it combines financial as well as real assets. "Net" foreign investment (positive or negative) does not refer to an adjustment for depreciation; rather, it simply means all U.S. purchases of foreign assets *minus* all foreign purchases of U.S. assets. Net savings always equals net (domestic) investment plus net foreign investment. Alternatively, "gross" savings always equals gross (domestic) investment plus net foreign investment.

Productivity

(Page 47 footnote and Table 1-1) Any economy-wide index of labor productivity requires (in the numerator) a measure of total real goods and services output and (in the denominator) a measure of total labor input. As a measure of output, we use real net national product (NNP, Gross National Product minus capital consumption) for the reasons mentioned above in "Net Savings and Investment." The choice of net national product (or equivalently, national income) has been favored by such renowned scholars of national productivity as John W. Kendrick and Edward F. Denison. We adjust net national product slightly to include net government interest payments (positive or negative) to foreigners. The BEA counts these as "transfers," although between nations such payments clearly represent nondiscretionary payments for services.

As a measure of input, we use the BEA's annual series "workers engaged in production," which includes all employees (on a "full-time equivalent basis") plus all self-employed workers. To take into account changes in total hours worked per full-time employee per year, we then redefine the "full-time" day as a falling straight-line trend from 1948 (8.25 hours per day) to 1986 (7.56 hours per day). The result is an hourly definition of "full-time" worker that changes continuously over time and does not fluctuate from year to year.

With these measures of input and output, we can then generate the annual labor productivity series referred to in the text and in the top row of Table 1-1. The decade-end values and average annual growth rates are as follows:

Year	1949	1959	1969	1979	1986
Real Net National Product (billions of 1986 $)	1,162	1,708	2,540	3,275	3,756
Workers Engaged in Production (millions)	56.565	64.923	79.819	95.272	104.625
Real NNP per Worker (1986 $)	$20,539	$26,300	$31,816	$34,372	$35,898
Decade Change	—	$5,761	$5,516	$2,555	$1,984
Decade Growth Rate	—	28.1%	21.0%	8.0%	5.8%
Average Annual Change	—	$576	$552	$256	$218
Average Annual Growth Rate	—	2.5%	1.9%	0.8%	0.6%

There is, to be sure, considerable variation within each decade that is not reflected in these figures. Most of the productivity growth that took place during the 1970s, for instance, occurred between 1969 and 1973; from 1973 to 1979, real NNP per worker climbed at a mere 0.2 percent per year. Note also that using the raw "hours" data as calculated by the BEA as a measure of labor input would make all the productivity growth rates somewhat higher; it would not, however, change the descending decade order of the growth rates.

International Productivity Level Comparisons

(Page 63 footnote) Ever since the early 1980s, the Bureau of Labor Statistics (Division of Foreign Labor Statistics, Office of Productivity and Technology) has calculated, though it has not yet published, productivity-level comparisons between nations. The measure it uses for each nation is elementary: gross domestic product per employed person. The trick has been to compare different currency values in a way that reflects their underlying "purchasing power" and not merely their current exchange-rate values. The BLS does this with newly developed "purchasing power parity" exchange rates, calculated jointly by the Organization for Economic Cooperation and Development and the Statistical Office of the European Communities. The results, as of their

most recent 1987 release, reveal some consistent trends over time. The following figures, for example, indicate GDP per worker levels in several other countries relative to the United States (which equals 100 percent each year):

Year	1950	1960	1969	1979	1986
U.S.	100.0%	100.0%	100.0%	100.0%	100.0%
Canada	76.9%	80.1%	82.2%	93.6%	95.0%
France	36.9%	46.1%	58.8%	78.5%	84.3%
West Germany	32.2%	49.2%	58.9%	76.7%	80.9%
United Kingdom	53.8%	54.2%	56.0%	66.2%	70.4%
Japan	15.2%	23.3%	41.8%	60.3%	68.9%
South Korea	—	—	15.8%	25.5%	33.2%

Definition of Entitlements

(Page 79 footnote) Starting with the CBO-defined category "Entitlements and Other Mandatory Spending" ($457.3 billion in fiscal year 1986), we redefine it by: (a) excluding General Revenue Sharing ($5.1 billion), (b) including veteran's health care ($9.9 billion), and (c) including the administrative costs of the OASDI, HI, and SMI programs ($3.9 billion). This last inclusion is the only exception to our practice of excluding administrative costs; we include them here only to make total Social Security outlays consistent with the long-term projections of the Social Security trustees.

Federal Balance Sheet

(Figure 2-5) All asset and liability numbers shown (except the liability for Medicare) are taken directly from the cited Consolidated Financial Statement for the end of fiscal year 1986. "Property and equipment" in the asset column ($269.9 billion) includes all property, plant, and equipment (including defense) valued at cost and net of depreciation. Cost estimates are used for land acquired through donation, exchange, bequest, forfeiture, or judicial process. The liabilities shown do not include any estimate of "contingent liabilities" for federal insurance coverage now in force (such as guaranteed lending, insured bank accounts, and flood and mortgage insurance). The "maximum risk exposure" for such liabilities would be equivalent to about $3.8 trillion.

There is (to our knowledge) no recent estimate of the accrued liabilities of Medicare for current program participants. On the basis of SSA research, former SSA chief actuary A. Haeworth Robertson estimated them at $1.5 trillion for HI and $0.4 trillion for SMI as of January 1, 1979 (*The Coming Revolution in Social Security* by A.

Haeworth Robertson; Security Press, 1981). We repriced these estimates to end of fiscal year 1986 with the medical-care component of the Consumer Price Index and subtracted from them the value of the HI and SMI trust funds at end of fiscal year 1986. The result was an estimate of unfunded Medicare liabilities of approximately $3.4 trillion.

Total Fertility Rate

(Page 133 footnote) The problem with standard "birthrate" measures (such as the number of births per 1,000 population or 1,000 women) is that they give equal weight to women of all ages, including women before or after the ages of childbearing. The "total fertility rate" avoids this difficulty by calculating the birthrate—in a given year—of women at each age; it then generates the number of children each woman would bear if she gave birth to that (fractional) number of children at each corresponding age throughout her life. The total fertility rate thus reflects *age-specific* behavior in any given year—unlike the birthrate, which also reflects shifts in the age composition of the female population.

To illustrate, consider the sizable rise in the U.S. per capita birthrate from the mid-1970s to the present (sometimes referred to as the "Baby Boomlet"). The total fertility rate, over the same period, has hardly risen at all. This tells us that the increase in births has been due almost entirely to the increase in the number of women of childbearing age (the Baby Boom), not to an increased propensity to have children at any given age. If the total fertility rate remains unchanged, in other words, we will necessarily see many fewer births in the 1990s and beyond.

The 1988 Report of the Social Security Trustees

(Page 133 footnote) In this book, the most recent figures for both (II-B and III) SSA scenarios and projections refer to those published in the 1987 report of the OASDI, HI, and SMI boards of trustees.

The results of the published 1988 report show no major changes from the 1987 report—and certainly nothing that would change any of our conclusions or recommendations. Since the SSA decided in 1988 to make several technical changes in its method of calculating seventy-five-year average cost rates, income rates, and balances, the "official" seventy-five-year figures for 1987 and 1988 are not exactly comparable. Calculating the 1988 average long-term deficit for OASDI as a percent of taxable payroll in the same way as it was calculated for 1987, however, reveals a very small difference: from –0.60 percent in 1987 to –0.56 percent in 1988 (a 0.04 percent improvement).

In general, in terms of yearly cost rates and deficits, the 1988 II-B results are slightly better in the near term (before 2025) and slightly worse in the long term (after 2025). The 1988 scenario II-B bankruptcy date for OASDI is now 2048—three years earlier than it was in 1987. The 1988 scenario III bankruptcy date for OASDI is now 2026—one year later than it was in 1987. The II-B and III bankruptcy dates for HI are now 1999 and 2005, respectively, a modest improvement from the dates calculated in 1987

Notes

(1996 and 2002).

Far more interesting than such minor bottom-line changes, however, are the ways in which the 1988 scenario assumptions were modified. Following the release of the 1987 report, complaints from the SSA actuaries that the long-term II-B *fertility* and *real-wage-growth* assumptions were overly "optimistic" at last persuaded the SSA trustees to switch to slightly more "pessimistic" ultimate values. Accordingly, the long-term II-B fertility rate was notched down from 2.0 to 1.9 (as it had been once before in 1979), and the long-term II-B real-wage growth rate was shaved from 1.5 to 1.4 percent yearly. (No parallel changes were made to scenario III.) These adjustments, minor though they were, should have caused a marked deterioration in OASDI's long-term balance—alone, in fact, they would have pushed the "official" II-B projection out of "close actuarial balance." But to prevent such an awkward revelation (after all, it is an election year), the SSA trustees also chose in 1988 to make a compensatory adjustment in future *immigration* assumptions (in all the scenarios) that has a marked positive effect on OASDI's long-term balance. For the II-B scenario, the more "optimistic" immigration assumptions just about cancel out the new fertility and productivity adjustments.

What are these new immigration assumptions? They are a decision by the SSA to include—for the first time in SSA's history—an estimate of "other than legal" immigration into the United States. In the II-B scenario, the SSA is now projecting 200,000 "other than legal" immigrants into the United States each year over the next seventy-five years. (Additional immigrants, because they are generally young, behave actuarially much like a higher fertility rate and thus help the system's long-term balance.) To appreciate the magnitude of this adjustment, consider that the previous long-term assumption ("legal immigration") anticipated 400,000 new immigrants per year; the 1988 adjustment thus represents a 50 percent rise in the assumed inflow.

The meaning of this adjustment is, at best, puzzling. Is the American public to understand that the official "balance" of Social Security now rests upon illegal immigrants? Does the U.S. Immigration and Naturalization Service share this long-term policy objective (or even know about it)? And will the SSA actively encourage sufficient payroll coverage of illegal immigrants to fulfill its assumption? This last question is especially intriguing given the recent major initiative passed by Congress (the Immigration Reform and Control Act of 1986) to curtail illegal immigration precisely by checking employers for proper documentation.

Long-Term Federal Outlay Projections

(Page 141 et seq. and Table 3-2) All budget totals for fiscal year 1986 are taken from the CBO, with revisions in "Entitlements" as explained in "Federal Balance Sheet."

Future annual values (fiscal years 1987–2040) for GNP and inflation (the GNP deflator) are taken directly from the 1987 Annual Report of the OASDI trustees and the Social Security Administration's Office of the Actuary. For the interest rate on the federal debt, we start with its actual value in fiscal year 1986 (8.22 percent over all maturities), take it linearly to 6.0 percent for scenario II-B and 7.0 percent for scenario III, and thereafter hold it constant at those levels. Since the II-B inflation rate is 4.0 percent for 1992 and after, and the III inflation rate is 5.0 percent for 1991 and after, this implies a real 2.0 percent interest rate in both scenarios.

The sources and mechanics of our projections are as follows:

OASDI and HI. We use the official II-B and III projections as published in the 1987 Annual Report of the OASDI and HI Trustees.

Military, Civil Service, and Other Retirement. Future values are derived from the following formula: yearly cost equals cost of prior year times the percentage growth in the GNP price deflator times 1.0185. The methodology behind this "inflation plus 1.85 percent" rule was developed by former federal budget analyst James Capra (currently Senior Vice President at Shearson, Lehman, Hutton, Inc.) as an approximate guide to future CSRS and military pension costs.

Veterans Health Care. Here we adopt the same basic rule used for military, civil service, and other retirement. We then further adjust the cost proportionally until the year 2030 for changes in the number of veterans over age sixty-five, as projected by the Veterans Administration (1983 unpublished data, calculated by the VA Office of Reports and Statistics).

Other Non-Means-Tested Programs. Held constant at the same share of GNP as in fiscal year 1986 (0.1 percent of GNP).

Other Means-Tested Programs. Held constant at the same share of GNP as in fiscal year 1986 (1.1 percent of GNP).

National Defense. For scenario III, held constant at the same share of GNP as in fiscal year 1986 (6.5 percent of GNP). For scenario II-B, we assume an "optimistic" reduction in the level of defense spending more in accord with the current CBO projections through 1992: 6.4 percent in 1987, 6.3 percent in 1988, 6.2 percent in 1989, 6.1 percent in 1990, and 6.0 percent in 1991 and in every year thereafter.

Nondefense Discretionary. Held constant at the same share of GNP as in fiscal year 1986 (3.9 percent of GNP).

Offsetting Receipts. Held constant at the same share of GNP as in fiscal year 1986 (negative 1.1 percent of GNP).

Net Interest. For each year from 1987 on, it equals the interest rate times the average of the prior-year (publicly held) federal debt plus the current-year debt.

Total Federal Revenues. For scenario III, we assume they climb to 19.3 percent of GNP in 1987 and then recede to 19.0 percent of GNP for all future years. For scenario II-B, we assume they change more in accord with the near-term projection of the CBO: 19.3 percent in 1987, 19.0 percent in 1988, 19.1 percent in 1989, 19.2 percent in 1990, 19.3 percent in 1991, and 19.4 percent in 1992 and every year thereafter.

SMI and Medicaid. These projections are based on the overall HCFA forecasting model for U.S. national health-care spending (as published in the *Health Care Financing Review;* Summer 1987). Our II-B values for SMI and Medicaid through the year 2000 come directly from the published results of the model. HCFA actuaries do not publish any III values, or any II-B values for years later than 2000. For the years

410

after 2000, however, they do calculate the national health-care cost effects of demographic change alone and the share of each major component of national health-care costs (physicians, hospitals, and nursing homes) that will be paid for by current federal programs. Using these linkages, we were able to compute the future HI, SMI, and Medicaid outlays that would result from any given assumptions about future trends (past 2000) in overall health-care spending per capita. We then solved for the future "utilization" and "factor-intensity" assumptions that generate the HI outlay figures published in the 1987 HI Annual Report for both scenarios II-B and III. We used these same assumptions to generate matching outlay figures for SMI and Medicaid.

Federal Benefits to the Elderly and to Children

(Figure 4-2) The federal outlay figures on benefits for the elderly are calculated by OMB and are apparently published only in the *Statistical Abstract of the United States* (Table No. 580). We estimate the federal outlay figures on benefits for children from various sources, including the 1987 Statistical Supplement to the *Social Security Bulletin,* the *1987 Budget of the United States Government,* and three reports prepared for the House Committee on Ways and Means: *Children in Poverty* (May 22, 1985), *Retirement Income for an Aging Population* (August 25, 1987), and *Background Material and Data on Programs Within the Jurisdiction of the Committee on Ways and Means* (March 6, 1987).

The fiscal year 1986 population of the elderly is estimated at 29.5 million; the fiscal year 1986 population of children is estimated at 64.9 million. The benefit totals used for fiscal year 1986 can be summarized as follows:

Federal Benefits to the Elderly	Amount in Billions of $
Total	269.5
Cash Benefits	180.8
OASDI	146.2
Federal Civilian Pensions	14.2
Federal Military Pensions	4.3
Total Veterans Pensions and Compensation	6.1
Railroad Retirement	5.0
SSI	3.7
Coal Miners Benefits	1.3
In-Kind Benefits	79.3
Medicare	64.4
Medicaid	8.9
Housing Subsidies	5.4
Other	0.6
Social Services	9.4

Federal Benefits to Children	Amount in Billions of $
Total	52.6
Cash Benefits	26.1
OASDI	9.5
Other Pension Survivor and Disability	4.4
AFDC	9.3
SSI	2.9
In-Kind Benefits	16.8
Medicaid and Medicare	2.4
Food and Nutrition	11.1
Housing Subsidies	3.3
Education and Social Services	9.7

Index